THE HISTORY OF MEAT TRADING

GW00644983

Cover: Master Butcher circa 1800

The History of Meat Trading

D Rixson

NOTTINGHAM
University Press

Nottingham University Press
Manor Farm, Main Street, Thrumpton
Nottingham, NG11 0AX, United Kingdom

NOTTINGHAM

First published 2000
© D Rixson 2000

British Library Cataloguing in Publication Data
The History of Meat Trading:
Rixson, D.

ISBN 1-897676-31X

Typeset by Nottingham University Press, Nottingham
Printed and bound by Hobbs the Printers, Hampshire, UK

Acknowledgements

Thanks to:

Len Dutton for providing large amounts of data he had collected on the history and technology of corned beef, canning and curing.

Miriam Parker for information on the foundation of the Humane Slaughter Association.

Professor Ralston Lawrie for his encouragement which was a great help in my completion of the book.

Fred Mallion for supplying material in the course of my research.

Jennie Bowles for assisting in typing the text.

Not forgetting my wife Lea for meticulously and painstakingly reading and correcting all the draft material.

In Memory of Barbara Alice Noddle

In memory of Barbara Alice Noddle MA, MSc, VetMB, MRCVS who died on 19th November 1998. It was Barbara who introduced me to Zooarchaeology which led onto my researches into the history of meat trading and the compilation of the data for this book.

My first contact with Barbara was by replying to a request placed in the 'Meat Industry' in 1969 for anyone in the meat trade who would be interested in the interpretation of butchery evidence on bone assemblages from archaeological sites. I owe a great deal to Barbara for her encouragement and guidance as a true mentor in my involvement in zooarchaeology and my work on this book.

Zooarchaeology owes a great deal to Barbara for the volume of specialist papers and other publications she produced. She was totally dedicated to the furtherance of zooarchaeology.

Contents

Part III. 1550–1750. Paving the Way for Improvements in Livestock Production, Technology and the Commercial Expansion of the 19th Century.

Introduction

Having started to collect the data and to write the history of the meat trade it soon became obvious how much the development of the meat trade through history was dependent on and interrelated with the social, commercial and economic development of the community at large. The butchery trade has throughout history been an integral part of any community. The butcher slaughtered animals not only to supply meat to the people but also to provide a wide range of important raw materials to many of the other craftsmen working to support the community. Of the craft guilds of the Middle Ages, many of them were based on working with animal products (Table 1).

Table 1. Medieval crafts wholly or partly dependent on non-food animal products.

Hides and Skins
  Skinners
  Fellmongers (Separated hair or wool from
    pelts)
  Tanners
  Curriers (Shaved, stretched and greased leather
    after tanning)
  White tawyers (Tawed the leather to make it
    white using alum)
  Cordwainers (Shoemakers)
  Malemakers (Leather travelling cases)
  Pouchmakers and Pursers (Leather pouches and
    purses)
  Botellers (Leather bottles, bombards, gispins,
    black jacks, pitchers)
  Glovers
  Pointmakers (Leather straps)
  Parchment Makers
  Girdlers (Girdles, belts, garters and leather
    covered cases for gunpowder)
  Saddlers
  Coffermakers (Trunks)
  Leathersellers

Wool
  Woolmen (Packing and winding)
  Spinners
  Weavers
  Fullers

Wool (contd)
  Shearmen
  Dyers
  Drapers
  Tailors
  Feltmakers (Hats)

Bone, Horn and Antler
  Horners
  Comb Makers
  Cutlers
  Button Makers
  Dice Makers

Fat (Tallow)
  Tallow Chandlers (Candle makers)
  Soap Boilers
  Apothecaries

Miscellaneous

  Gut String Makers

*Medieval crafts wholly or partly dependent on
mammalian food products*
  Butchers
  Cooks
  Bakers
  Inn and Tavern Keepers

To appreciate the reasons and background to many of the activities of the butchers through history and to understand the butchery indications from archaeological data, it is helpful to be conversant with some of the aspects of meat technology and practical butchery activities. The following is a summary of the more pertinent elements of meat technology and the craft of butchery, particularly where they have some relevance to certain aspects of the activities of butchers and meat trading in the past.

WHAT IS A BUTCHER?

The term butcher has through time been given to any person engaged in any of the activities from the slaughter and dressing (i.e. skinning and evisceration) to selling a pennyworth of meat to an urban housewife. Other trades were divided into a series of distinct crafts from early times as can be seen from Table 1. Today the slaughterman or, more correctly slaughterperson, has this designation and there are the gut scrapers, cutters, boners, etc. Where the title butcher was used in the past it did not immediately indicate the individual's activities. In the early days the key activity of a butcher was that of a slaughterman but as the towns and cities developed the different types of butcher emerged.

Through the course of the development of meat marketing some urban butchers were buying carcases rather than live animals. Some butchers from the villages supplied carcases to the town butcher and by the 16th century the carcase butchers or wholesalers were selling carcases to the retail butchers. A master butcher was a butcher owning his own business and essentially, in most towns, he was a freeman of the butchers' guild or company. The butcher employed by the master butcher was a journeyman butcher who, in most cases, had to be properly qualified by apprenticeship.

The butchers through the ages would have gained their skills and knowledge empirically. They would have learned from their predecessors by oral instruction, the demonstration of skills and then through life, building on these acquired skills and knowledge with experience.

UNDERSTANDING THE TECHNOLOGY AND ACTIVITIES OF THE MEAT TRADE IN THE PAST

Some knowledge of the biological and chemical nature of meat and other animal products and the gross anatomy of the meat animals can be helpful in understanding the activities of the butchers in the past and the way in which the trade developed. In some cases it is a matter of appreciating the perspectives that people at different ages and in various societies would have had with respect to meat, animal products, domestic animals, animal diseases and comparative values.

With the range of products produced today by the chemical industry, which have replaced so many of the animal products, it is difficult to envisage a situation of being totally dependent on natural products. It is evident that once the Palaeolithic people become meat eaters, the progressive utilisation of the rest of the animal followed. Hides, skins, wool, hair, sinews, gut, visceral fat, bones, horn and antler were converted into a wide range of products that became essential to the way of life through the ages, indeed essential to the way of progress. The trade in the animal products other than meat has, through history, been a major part of the meat trade as a whole and has been a vital part of economy of the trade. In latter times, animal products other than carcase meat were referred to as the fifth quarter, the carcase consisting of the first four quarters.

YIELDS FROM SLAUGHTERED ANIMALS

The yield from a slaughtered animal will consist of the edible and the inedible parts. The edible is predominantly the carcase meat, i.e. the musculature and its associated fat, intramuscular, intermuscular and much of the subcutaneous fat. Additionally there are the edible offals. The strictly inedible parts are listed below but there is much of the offal that can be used for food which also has a non-food use and in some cases is more valuable than its use for food. Examples of offals with this dual use are visceral fat, kidney knob and channel fat, intestines (for gut string - catgut), feet and various glands and fat that have a pharmaceutical use.
Test on a 30-month Hereford steer (Gerrard, 1956).

Carcase	62.1%
Edible offals	10.9%
Inedible offals	13.7%
Intestinal contents	13.3%

WHAT IS MEAT?

Meat is generally regarded as all the edible parts of an animal's body. The modern convention is that the edible parts are divided into the carcase and edible offals. The carcase will consist of all or a major part of the skeleton, the skeletal muscles and the fat, tendons, ligaments, blood vessels, nerves, etc., associated with the skeletal muscles. Variations in the dressed carcase are that the head and feet may be removed as is usual with beef and mutton carcases. Kidneys and perirenal fat (kidney knob) are sometimes left as part of the carcase. Pig carcases normally include the head, trotters (feet) and tail, all of which are removed when sides are prepared in the Wiltshire style for bacon; this was very similar to what was referred to as a flitch of bacon in the past, although in most cases it was without the leg (ham) (Experienced Butcher, 1816); the modern term for a side of bacon with the leg removed is a 'spencer'. The offals consist of all those parts removed during the dressing of the carcase which consist of those offals which are edible and those which are inedible (Table 2). The edible offals are not all destined for food as many are important for their non-food uses. Indeed in the past some offals had a much greater value for their non-food use than as food, e.g. fat.

The carcase of an adult bovine is generally between 53% - 58% of the liveweight but can range from 48% - 62% depending on the type and condition of the animal. The edible offals range between 14% - 20% and the inedible offals between 26% - 33%. The carcase consists of the inedible bone, tendons and ligaments (gristles) and the edible muscle and fat. The natural physical development of the locomotor system controls the distribution of muscle (i.e. meat) throughout the carcase. The thickest muscles are the large muscles of the buttocks which power the hind legs for the forward propulsion of the animal. The muscles of the shoulder or fore limb are less thick not having the need for such concentrated power. The lower limb muscles, because of their function do not develop to the same extent, so there is far less meat around the tibia (leg of beef) and ulna and radius (shin of beef).

Table 2. Offals.

The edible offals:
- Liver
- Heart
- Spleen (melt)
- Stomach (paunch and honey comb tripes, omasum or prayer book, abomasum or rennet bag, pigs maw)
- Oesophagus (weasand)
- Intestines (casings or skins for sausages, chitterlings)
- Lungs (lights or lites – low nutritional value due to high elastin content)
- Testicles
- Uterus
- Udder
- Diaphragmatic muscles (body skirt)
- Thymus gland (sweet bread, throat bread, heart bread)

- Pancreas (gut bread)
- Blood (highly nutritious – used in blood sausage, black pudding)
- Tongue lips and masseter muscles (cheek meat, pork chaps)
- Kidney
- Visceral fat (omental or caul fat, mesenteric or gut fat): In a well-fed animal there is a large quantity of visceral fat which can amount to 5% of live weight but is generally between 3% - 4%.

The inedible offals:
- Hide or skin (sheep's skin with wool is a sheep's fell)
- Hair or wool
- Horns and hooves

The distribution of the muscles and their relationship with the skeleton has always been important to the butcher when cutting the carcase for retail sale or in preparation for cooking. The diagram in Fig 0.1 showing the cuts of a beef carcase are not universal but would not vary in a substantial way as most cutting is based on the musculo-skeletal configuration when the carcase goes into rigor mortis hanging by its Achilles tendon. Fig 0.1 also shows the relationship of the skeleton to the cuts and cutting lines. The distribution of the meat throughout the carcase is shown in Fig 0 2. Aitch bone hanging has been introduced in the 20th century which entails suspending the carcase by a hook inserted in the obdurator foramen allowing the hind limb to be at right angles to the torso (Fig 0.3). This results in a significant change in the musculo-skeletal configuration of the hindquarter. The reason for aitch bone hanging is that the buttock and rump muscle fibres are extended when rigor mortis occurs resulting in those muscles being more tender as meat. A slaughtered animal left lying on the ground during the onset of rigor mortis would have the same musculo-skeletal configuration as with aitch bone hanging. The musculo-skeletal configuration of carcases would have been an important factor in the development of butchering carcases, especially for those butchers operating as meat retailers. There is much evidence for splitting beef carcases into sides by chopping down the centre of the spinal column from the 16th century and later, both from archaeological bone assemblages and contemporary illustrations. It was probably in the 16th century when the practice became widespread as archaeological evidence from the earlier periods indicates an inconsistency in the way bovine vertebrae were chopped and in some cases the vertebrae were found whole or nearly whole.

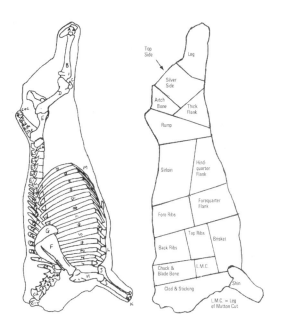

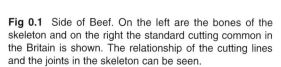

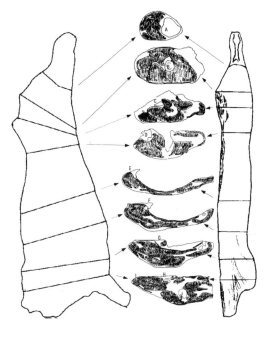

Fig 0.1 Side of Beef. On the left are the bones of the skeleton and on the right the standard cutting common in the Britain is shown. The relationship of the cutting lines and the joints in the skeleton can be seen.

Key to bones:
(A) Tarsals; (B) Tibia; (C) Patella; (D) Femur; (E) Os Coxae (Pelvis); (F) Scapula; (G) Cartilage of Scapula; (H) Humerus; (I) Radius; (J) Ulna; (K) Carpals; (L) Sternum; (M) Costal Cartilages

Ribs - 1 to 13
C1 to C7 Cervical Vertebrae
T1 to T13 Thoracic Vertebrae
L1 to L6 Lumber Vertebrae
S1 to S5 Sacral Vertebrae
Coc Coccygeal Vertebrae.

Fig 0.2 The lateral (outside) aspect of a hanging side of beef. The lines show the cross sections relating to the drawings of the cut surfaces in the centre.

Drawings of the cut surfaces of cross sections of a side of beef.

The medial aspect ⬆

The lateral aspect ⬇

The dorsal aspect ⬅

The ventral aspect ➡

The dorsal aspect of a hanging side of beef showing the same cross section lines.
Key: (A) Distal end of Femur (B) Shaft of Femur (C) Shaft of Ilium (pelvis) (D) 6th Lumber Vertebra (E) 10th Thoracic Vertebra (F) 6th Thoracic Vertebra (G) 3rd Thoracic Vertebra (H) 6th Cervical Vertebra (I) Ligamentum Nuchae (J) Head of Humerus.

The enjoyment of eating meat beyond the need for sustaining life is supported in evidence from earliest times. Meat was usually the main component of a banquet or feast or indeed the centre-point of a feast. Animal bones were found around the entrance to Neolithic tombs in Britain, indicating feasting as part of the burial rituals (Hodder, 1990). The lower classes in ancient Egypt had their main indulgence of meat eating at feast times. Feasting and the sacrifice of animals seemed to go 'hand in hand' (Strouhal, 1992). Feasting and animal sacrifice for the feast were part of religious ritual throughout history. Differences in quality of meat have been appreciated through history from antiquity as evident from the biblical "killing the fatted calf". The upper echelons of

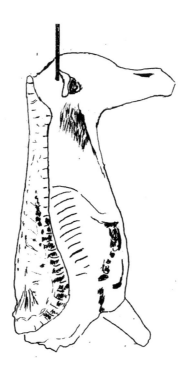

Fig 0.3 The method of aitch bone hanging to improve the tenderness of the hindquarter. This significantly changes the musculo-skeletal configuration of the hindquarter so that the normal method for a butcher to cut the hindquarter cannot be followed.

Egyptian society had a preference for feasting on great quantities of beef and goose flesh which the poorer people could not afford (*Ibid*). Homer, in Book XIV of *The Odyssey*, relates how the swineherd calls to his men to bring the best hog to be slaughtered for a feast to entertain his guest and when the meat is cooked the swineherd offers his guest the choice meat from the chine. The Romans had a preference for the flesh of young animals and deemed wild boar pork superior to pork from domestic pigs (Wilkins, Harvey and Dobson, 1995). During the reign of Henry VIII (1509-47) there were sumptuary laws which specified the quality of food that persons could have according to their rank, as this was a mark of status. The quality of meat served to each guest at a banquet was a matter of strict protocol (Sim, 1997). The largest muscles in a carcase have long been appreciated as the best quality muscles, being the most tender, and from which the carver could produce good slices or steaks (collops). The reason that these muscles are more tender is that the muscle bundles within the muscle are much larger than in small muscles, therefore the connective tissue mesh binding them is spread wider, so the ratio of collagen is lower. As collagen is one of the main factors in toughness, muscles with a lower collagen content are more tender (see skeletal muscle Fig 0.4, page 9). It is the large muscles that are the main constituents of the top side (*M. semimembranosus*), silverside (*M. gluteobiceps* and *M. semitendinosus*), rump (*M. gluteus medius* and *gluteus profundus*) and sirloin (*M. longissimus dorsi*).

THE SLAUGHTERING OF ANIMALS

In the act of slaughtering an animal in the UK and most Western countries, it is required by law to stun animals prior to bleeding. Where the captive bolt is used to stun, it penetrates the brain and is therefore fatal. The high voltage electrical stunning and the 'head to back' electrical stunning is also likely to be fatal. Low voltage electrical stunning will only render the animal unconscious and it is required that bleeding takes place immediately so that the animal dies without regaining consciousness. The purpose of these laws is to obtain the humane slaughtering of the animals but the act of stunning is also to immobilise the animal to make it easier and safer for the slaughterer to carry out the bleeding of the animal.

Ritual slaughter is allowed to be practised in the UK by Moslems (Halal) and Jews (Shechitah) which involves killing the animal by bleeding without stunning.

POST-MORTEM CHANGES OR THE CONVERSION OF LIVING TISSUE TO MEAT

Life is a dynamic state existing in all the cells and groups of tissues in an animal's body as well as the co-ordination of all the body functions. When the animal is slaughtered there is a rapid loss of the co-ordination and the brain cells quickly degenerate and the animal is regarded as dead but a large proportion of the cells remain alive for some hours. The cessation of blood circulation results in the cells losing their supply of nutrients and oxygen and being no longer able to dispose of by-products of metabolism will therefore die. Skeletal muscle is a tissue which can take several hours for the post-mortem processes to run their course and for the death of the cells to be complete. The muscle fibres maintain their dynamic living status by an anaerobic process of breaking down glycogen to provide energy that is necessary to prevent the muscle components (the filaments) from bonding and becoming inextensible in a state known as rigor mortis. This process, anaerobic glycolysis, apart from providing energy, also produces lactic acid so that by the time the process ends and rigor mortis sets in the pH of the muscle of a normal carcase will have fallen from about 7.2 (just above neutral) to about 5.5 (mildly acid). The limbs of a freshly slaughtered animal will be easily moveable but after rigor mortis they become fixed. Before rigor mortis the flesh of the animal is more tender than after rigor mortis. If the pH of the meat is high (close to 7) it will adversely affect the quality of the meat and how well it keeps (Lawrie, 1998).

The main factor affecting post-mortem glycolysis leading to a high pH is the lack of glycogen in the muscles at the time of slaughter. One of the main reasons for this is stress, causing a release of adrenalin which mobilises the muscle glycogen. This would be the case of the hunted animal or animals subjected to stressful conditions just prior to slaughter. A fevered animal would also lack muscle glycogen (Lister, Gregory and Warris, 1981).

MUSCLE

Muscle is divided into three types:

- Smooth or visceral muscle
- Skeletal muscle which is striated
- Heart muscle which is also striated

Smooth muscle is an extensive part of the walls of the alimentary tract and acts to churn up the food in the stomach and the peristaltic action to move the food through the system. It is the smooth muscle that is the main nutritional component of tripe, pigs maw (stomach), chitterlings and other food products using intestines. Smooth muscle is part of the walls of the blood vessels and smooth muscle cells are in the skin to raise the hairs. Smooth muscle is part of various tissues where limited involuntary movement is required.

Skeletal muscle is the muscle that effects the movement of the animal. The usual arrangement of a skeletal muscle is the attachment to a bone at its origin and its insertion is the attachment to another bone, directly or by way of a tendon. By contraction a muscle, or a number of muscles working in unison, can draw two bones towards each other reducing the angle between the bones or flexing the limb. As muscles can only contract it requires another set of counteracting muscles to extend the limb increasing the angle between the bones. Hence the flexor and extensor muscles (Dyce, Sack and Wensing, 1987).

Extensively used muscles develop and enlarge and the bones and joints associated with the powerful muscles will need to be strong. The tuberosities of the bones are prominent where there are large muscle attachments and become more pronounced with muscular activity e.g. the deltoid tuberosity of the humerus, the trochanters of the femur. Where muscles for some reason become significantly underused, they will atrophy (i.e. become reduced in size). Underuse of a muscle may occur due to arthritis restricting the movement of a joint (Smith, Jones and Hunt, 1972).

Skeletal muscle consists of large numbers of muscle fibres arranged in bundles in the muscle running from the muscle's attachment to its insertion. These bundles of muscle fibres can be seen in a piece of meat as the grain of the meat. The muscle fibres are giant cells with multiple nuclei situated peripherally just below the cell wall or sarcolemma. The elements for contraction are the myofibrils which are arranged longitudinally within the muscle fibres. The muscle fibres are covered by a connective tissue mesh of fine reticulin and collagen fibres, the endomysium. Muscle bundles are surrounded and held together by a meshwork of collagen fibres, the perimysium. The whole muscle is enclosed in a meshwork of collagen fibres, the epimysium. Collagen is the main element of connective tissue in the body. These meshworks of connective tissue are inter-connected throughout the muscle and form its attachment to the bone at its origin and extend beyond the muscle to become a tendon for the attachment to the bone at its insertion (Fig 0.4). The perimysium and the epimysium lattice meshworks become stronger as the animal matures by the formation of cross-links between the collagen fibres which is the major factor relating to increased toughness in meat from older animals (Swatland, 1994).

Muscle fibres consist of three types, red, white and intermediate. The red fibres contain large amounts of myoglobin which give the muscle its red colour. The energy for contraction is primarily obtained aerobically, the oxygen coming direct from the blood or the myoglobin. White muscle fibres have a low level of myoglobin because their energy is obtained predominantly by anaerobic glycolysis. While the red muscle fibres are slower to respond than white muscle fibres, the white fibres will fatigue more quickly than the red. This is why the ranging and migrating animals' main

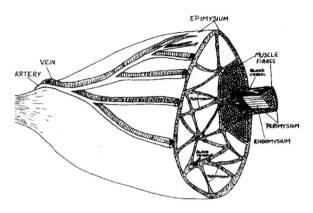

Fig 0.4 A diagram of the structure of a muscle showing the muscle fibres surrounded by the mesh of connective tissue.

muscles are predominantly red, e.g. cattle, horses, geese, ducks. The animals that need a rapid acceleration to escape predators need their main muscle to be mainly white muscle fibres, e.g. pigs, chickens, pheasants, quail. Where the function of a muscle requires a constant action and where fatigue would be dangerous, such muscles in all animals are predominantly red, e.g. diaphragmatic muscles, intercostal muscles (*Ibid*).

Heart or Cardiac Muscle is similar to the skeletal red muscle fibres, as it is essential for its function that the action of the cells is constant without fatigue.

FAT

Fat or adipose tissue is a major tissue distributed throughout the animal's body. The composition of fat varies according to species and its anatomical situation. Some fat depots in the body have a high level of connective tissue such as the intermuscular fat compared with the perirenal fat. The high level of connective tissue reduces the yield of clarified fat. There is also a difference in the fatty acid composition.

Neutral fat is a triglyceride consisting of three fatty acids bonded to a glycerol. The main fatty acids are the saturated palmitic and stearic fatty acids and the unsaturated oleic and linoleic fatty acids. The longer the fatty acid chain the higher the melting point; therefore the harder the fat at ambient temperature. Unsaturated fatty acids have a lower melting point and the fat is soft or liquid at ambient temperature. The fatty acid combinations in the triglyceride affect the nature of the adipose tissue. If the fatty acids are predominantly long chain and saturated (e.g. stearic or palmitic) the fat will be firm; if there is a high ratio of unsaturated fatty acids (e.g. oleic or linoleic) the fat will be soft. For this reason the fat in pigs and horses is softer and greasier whereas the fat in sheep and cattle is firmer and less greasy (Table 3). Apart from genetic differences the animal's diet can have a significant influence on fat.

Table 3. The relative fatty acid composition of the fat of cattle, sheep and pigs.

Fatty Acid	Formula	Melting Point (Lehninger, 1975)	Cattle (Lawrie, 1998)	Sheep (Lawrie, 1998)	Pigs (Lawrie, 1998)
Saturated					
Lauric	$C_{11}H_{23}COOH$	44.2°C	0.1%	0.3%	0.1%
Myristic	$C_{13}H_{27}COOH$	53.9°C	2.7%	3.3%	1.3%
Palmitic	$C_{15}H_{31}COOH$	63.1°C	25%	22.2%	32.2%
Stearic	$C_{17}H_{35}COOH$	69.6°C	13.4%	18.1%	12.2
Unsaturated					
Hexadecenoic	$C_{15}H_{29}COOH$		4.5%	2.2%	2.7%
Oleic	$C_{17}H_{33}COOH$	13.4°C	36.1%	32.5%	32.8%
Linoleic	$C_{17}H_{31}COOH$	-5°C	2.4%	2.7%	14.2%
Linolenic	$C_{17}H_{29}COOH$	-11°C	0.7%	1.4%	1.0%
Arachidonic	$C_{19}H_{31}COOH$	-49.5°C	0.6%	0.6%	2.2%

In life the fat will absorb fat-soluble flavours contained in the animal's diet such as the strong flavours from fishmeal and flavours from herbs. Fat will also absorb fat-soluble pigments such as carotenoids which give the fat a yellowish colour. Fat is the body tissue subject to the greatest variation both in its nature and quantity compared with other body tissues.

Fat Depots in an Animal's Body

Beef carcases in the past included the kidney knob (the perirenal and retroperitoneal fat). Today, in the UK and many other countries, most beef carcases are dressed ex KKCF (i.e. the removal of the Kidney Knob & Channel Fat). The following figures are for cattle of two years or older.

- Visceral Fat   2.5% - 5%
- KKCF   1.9% - 3%
- Intermuscular Fat   5.5% - 10.5%
- Intramuscular Fat   0.01% - 0.1%
- Subcutaneous Fat   2.1% - 8.4%
- Bone Marrow Fat   1.5% - 2.5%

Visceral fat

This consists of the omental, mesenteric, and abomasal fat plus fat from the thoracic cavity. Omental or caul fat is the fat deposited in a fold of the visceral peritoneum that is attached to and covers most of the stomach. The omentum resembles lace in appearance until the streaks of fat coalesce, as is common in well-fed cattle. Mesenteric or crown fat is the fat deposited between the folds of the peritoneum that supports the intestines. Abomasal or reed fat is the fat surrounding the abomasum of ruminants. Fat from the thoracic cavity consists of the mediastinal fat that is deposited between the mediastinal folds of the pleura between the right and left lungs and the fat that builds up around the pericardial sac.

KKCF

Kidney knob and channel fat, is the suet in beef carcases. The kidney knob is the perirenal fat (fat surrounding the kidney) and the channel fat is retroperitoneal fat which extends into the pelvic cavity.

Intermuscular fat

Fat between the muscles can be very large fat deposits, such as between the muscles in the buttocks (in the silver side), between the muscles of the shoulder cranial to the humerus (in the clod and sticking) and the fat between the pectoral muscles (in the brisket).

Intramuscular fat

Fat within the muscle between the muscle bundles, (the marbling fat).

Subcutaneous fat

The fat under the animal's skin which covers the outside of the carcase and includes the scrotal fat (cod fat, plentiful in castrates) and mammary fat (dug fat, largely replaced by lactating tissue during the initial pregnancy).

Bone Marrow Fat

The marrow fat is the fat that replaces much of the red bone marrow as an animal reaches maturity. The fat is mainly in the marrow cavity and in the spongy bone tissue. The total amount of bone marrow is approximately 4.5% of total body weight (Leeson & Leeson, 1970). When an animal reaches maturity more than half of the red bone marrow will have been replaced by fat. Most of the remaining red bone marrow in the adult animal will be in the vertebrae, sternum, ribs and skull with most of the limb bone marrow having converted to fat.

PRESERVATION OF MEAT

The decomposition of meat would have presented a challenging problem to man from his earliest days of becoming a meat eater. Decomposition does not always constitute spoilage as the process of hanging or ageing meat results in a decomposition process that is most desirable. Certain natural enzymes of the muscles (cathepsins) are released post mortem and during ageing these enzymes break down some of the muscle structures resulting in improved tenderness of the meat; there is also an improvement in the flavour. Ageing is an autolytic process whereby tissues are broken down by the body's own enzymes and in the same way autolysis can result in spoilage of meat but from a practical point of view this takes so long that before such spoilage becomes significant meat would have undergone major spoilage due to other factors.

Oxidation is a spoilage problem principally in two respects; oxidation of fat and oxidation of myoglobin. The unpleasant odour and taste of rancid fat is the result of the oxidation of unsaturated fat molecules. Fats with higher levels of unsaturated fatty acids (e.g. pork fat) are more vulnerable to oxidation or rancidity than fats with lower levels of unsaturated fatty acids (e.g. mutton fat). Mutton will therefore remain palatable for longer after slaughter than pork, especially in warmer weather. Myoglobin is the colour pigment of red meat muscle and when the meat is first cut into exposing the cut surface to the atmosphere the myoglobin absorbs oxygen resulting in the cut surface becoming bright red. If the meat is left it will progressively undergo oxidation of the myoglobin, changing from bright red through shades of reddish brown to brown, until finally it will become dark brown or black. Although the colour changes do not in themselves affect the eating quality they are invariably accompanied by bacterial spoilage. Modern consumers regard meat as not fresh and undesirable if the colour has deteriorated and it is reasonable to suppose there was the same attitude in the past.

The major spoilage problem has always been microbial decomposition or putrefaction. When healthy animals are slaughtered it is unlikely that there will be any organisms within the tissues of the carcase (Ingram & Simonsen, 1980). This means that the contamination of meat with micro-organisms occurs when the carcase is cut, exposing meat surfaces to the ever present micro-organisms, causing putrefaction with an unpleasant odour and slime. It is a long standing empirical knowledge of the butcher that the meat keeps better and longer if carcases are left whole and only cut as required. A reasonable covering of subcutaneous fat on the outside of the carcase protects the muscle underneath against bacterial contamination and also acts as a barrier against atmospheric oxygen diffusing into the myoglobin. An important factor necessary for the growth of the putrefactive bacteria is the surface moisture of the meat or the 'water activity (a_w)' (Lawrie, 1998). Drying the surface of the meat, thereby lowering the water activity, will retard the growth of the putrefactive bacteria slowing up the rate of spoilage. Evidence from most periods of history indicate the practice of hanging carcases and joints of meat to allow air circulation which would tend to dry the surface of the meat and avoid pockets of air where the relative humidity would rise. A model of an Egyptian slaughterhouse from the 11th dynasty tomb of Meket-Rē' (Winlock, 1955) shows the cut joints of meat hanging in a well-ventilated area above the slaughtering area. These practices would have only improved keeping meat for short periods (a few days), whereas thorough dehydration of thin strips of meat which were usually air dried would extend the period that this meat could be kept to several months. Examples of dehydrated meat are: biltong of South Africa, pemmican of the North American Indians and charqui of South America (Lawrie, 1998). While these products were useful for people on long journeys their palatability was no challenge to fresh meat, or indeed cured products.

For longer term storage of meat salting or curing was the chief method available until the advent of canning and refrigeration in the 19th century. The effect of salt is to enhance the osmotic pressure of the meat which inhibits the growth of micro-organisms and therefore the putrefactive spoilage of the uncured meat. There are some bacteria that are salt tolerant (*halophilic*) but their rate of spoilage is much less (*Ibid*). One of the disadvantages of preserving by curing is that the salt concentration has to be high as lower concentrations do not sufficiently inhibit the growth of the bacteria and the meat would quickly deteriorate. Very high salt concentrations render the meat less palatable. Curing was either the dry cure whereby salt was spread over the surface of the meat and left for a period for the salt to diffuse into the tissues or the wet cure with the meat being immersed into a brine. One way of storing the cured meat was to keep it immersed in brine until required. The alternative was to hang the cured meat for the surface to dry and the combination of salting and drying significantly improved its preservation. In some areas the climate was ideal for drying the cured meat but in the temperate areas hanging the cured meat from the rafters in the kitchens resulted in the meat drying in the rising warm air from the fire. By using a fire to dry cured meat it was soon discovered that smoking the meat could be an advantage by producing an alternative flavour. Smoke contains numerous ingredients that kill bacteria and it reduces the rate of fat oxidation so adding to the preserving effect. The inclusion of nitrates or nitrites into the curing salts increases the preserving effect and in particular inhibits certain pathogenic bacteria but the main purpose for its inclusion is that nitrite combines with myoglobin to give the bacon, hams and salt beef that attractive pink colour (*Ibid*). Without the nitrite all cured meat would have an unappetising grey colour. While nitrite is the active form it is as nitrate that it is more readily available as nitre or saltpetre; the forms of saltpetre are potassium nitrate (KNO_3), sodium nitrate ($NaNO_3$) or Chile saltpetre and calcium nitrate ($Ca(NO_3)_2$)or lime saltpetre or wall saltpetre. These nitrates are reduced to nitrite during the curing process or in the curing brine.

The use of salt for curing dates back to the early civilisations of the Near East and China as early as 3000 BC and there have been numerous references to salting meat from most periods. What is not clear from the evidence is the use of nitrates as part of the curing salts, although in many cases the salt used would have been contaminated with nitrate and in some cases water used to make brines would have contained nitrite. Saltpetre was gathered in ancient China and India and lime saltpetre obtained from the walls of caves was used by the ancients to cure meat (Jensen, 1954). The effect of nitrite on the colour of meat must have been appreciated from early in the history of curing but it was not until the late Roman period there was any reference to the fact.

THE NON-FOOD VALUE OF ANIMAL PRODUCTS

In the archaeological analysis of the domestic animals grouped together as food animals, the economic analysis is often biased towards their meat value. The non-food value of these animals as suppliers of a wide range of very important raw materials should receive adequate consideration in respect of the economies of the past. There is also the need to bring into the economic equation the value of these animals in life; the beasts of burden, providers of wool, milk, cheese and not least their dung to fertilise the crops. In the 18th and 19th centuries sheep flocks were kept by arable farmers essentially for their manure value when folded on arable fields. The *Annals of Agriculture* gave the returns per ewe in a South Down flock as 12s-10d; 10s for the lamb, 1s-4d for the wool and 1s-6d for folding (Culley, 1807). It was probably due more to these multipurpose attributes that the main 'food animals' proliferated to such an extent, becoming a major part of the economies through history.

The list in Table 1 is some indication of the importance of non-food animal products to medieval industrial and commercial activities and indeed to the medieval economy. From the time of the Palaeolithic hunter-gatherers and the Neolithic farmers through to the industrial revolution the non-food animal products have played such an important part in the industries and economies of the periods that they would have often been of greater value than the meat.

NON-FOOD PROPERTIES OF FAT

The essential non-food properties of animal fat that give it such a wide range of uses are:

- Lighting
- Thermal Insulation
- Capacity as a Water Repellent
- Therapeutic Properties
- Lubrication
- Soap

Lighting

Upper Palaeolithic people occupied caves in Europe in which they produced the cave paintings such as at Lascaux. These caves extended considerable distances from the openings and were therefore in complete darkness. There is evidence that the cave occupants used lamps burning animal fat for illumination (Bahn & Vertut, 1997).

Candles and Tapers constituted an important part of everyday life in most periods of history. Tallow was the most used constituent of candles resulting in a high demand and therefore a high price for tallow. The consequence was constant efforts to control the supply and price of tallow.

Laws placing restrictions on the sale of fat and tallow were a feature of the medieval period due to its importance for candles and other industrial use. An ordinance of London in the reign of Edward III (1327-77) prohibited the "sale of suet, tallow or lard by butchers or their wives for the purpose of being taken beyond the sea". A later Statute of the 15th century forbade the export of tallow from the city for fear of causing a rise in the price of candles. Many ordinances of the towns contained a clause forbidding the sale of tallow by butchers except to tallow chandlers or candle makers (Pearce 1929).

Edinburgh Magistrates in the 16th century issued an order to the effect that Fleshers were required to sell their tallow to the "candlemakers and neighbours, and no others, and their houses and booths where tallow users are to be made patent for buying" (The Scotsman 1902, Edinburgh).

Autumn preparation for the winter, according to the household accounts of the Dowager Countess of Pembroke at Goodrich Castle, show that animals were slaughtered followed by the salting and other activities including candles being made from tallow (Pullar, 1970).

The wax chandlers supplied the luxury end of the market with their non-smelly wax candles which were comparatively expensive.

Thermal Insulation

Butchers working with cold meat in a cold shop on a winter's day have their hands protected from the cold by fat from the meat (personal experience).

A practice in the past for winter protection against the cold was to smear fat over the chest, especially of children.

For the first attempt to ship frozen meat from Australia in the sailing ship *Northam* the holds were insulated with 15 inches (38 centimetres) of tallow; tallow being in plentiful supply in Australia at the time (Hammett & Nevell, 1929).

Capacity as a Water Repellent

During the First World War soldiers in the trenches were required to cover their feet with fat or oil, often whale oil, to guard against 'trench foot'. The object was to protect the feet when soldiers were standing in water for many hours without waterproof foot wear. The powder of cartridges for guns in the 19th century were sealed in with melted fat. The East India Company issued new Enfield rifles to the Indian sepoys which required them to bite off the fat sealant of the cartridges to load the rifles. Rumour had it that the seal contained pig's fat and the fat of cows, resulting in both Muslims and Hindus refusing to use the rifles, culminating in the Indian Mutiny (Microsoft Encarta 98).

In the recent past tallow was a regular material for use by plumbers as an aid for waterproofing joints. The plumber's bag of tools and materials always contained some lumps of tallow.

Animal fat was used to waterproof leather (*see leather dressing*).

Therapeutic Properties

Animal fat has long been appreciated for its therapeutic value in respect of the skin. A long-standing empirical treatment for burns is to treat the affected part with fat. Animal fat is a good protection against chilblains and chafed or cracked skin and is very effective in keeping the skin soft. Today the pharmaceutical and cosmetics industries are second only to the soap manufacturers as major users of animal fats and oils (Grantley-Smith, 1998).

In Ancient Egypt oils and fats were perfumed for various cosmetic purposes including cones of perfumed fat placed on the heads of highborn ladies at banquets so that the fat would slowly melt into the hair. A treatment for greying hair was the blood of a black cow boiled in oil. The Egyptians used unguents made from fat or oil to rub into the skin to keep it soft and supple. Animal products such as blood, milk, bile, urine and fat were used in a number of medical preparations and fat was often the main ingredient for ointments. The Egyptian language distinguished animal fat as *adj* and vegetable fat as *merhet* (Strouhal, 1992).

Some of the early books on recipes and general guidance for running a household also contained recipes for medicines. In the 17th century Lady Goring recommended that "hoggs' fat clarified and beaten into egg white till it become an ointment, should be kept ready to put on burns and scalds, annoynting the sore twice a day". Also from the 17th century:

"an oynment for the pocks when they begin to change at top and prevent holes. Clarify bacon fat and then mix it with red rose water. Put in a Gallypot and when you use it, melt it and with a feather anoynt the face day and night, once in a quarter of an hour, till the scabs clean off" (Isitt, 1987).

'*The Compleat Houswife*' by Eliza Smith (1758) has a recipe for 'Green Ointment' which is based on four pounds of butter and three pounds of boars-grease melted together with a large variety of herbs. There is another recipe for a poultice for a sore breast, leg or arm, made up of boiled wheat flour and boars grease, to be applied hot.

Hogs fat or lard was the base ingredient in a number of recipes for veterinary ointments in Francis Clater's 18th century '*Every Man His Own Farrier and Cattle Doctor*' and William Taplin's '*Farriery*' (1796).

Lubrication

The nature of animal fat with its range of textures and melting points makes it ideal for industrial lubrication. The following are examples:

- Greasing the axles of vehicles.
- Greasing bolts, locks, hinges.
- Moving metal parts.
- Tallow on the runners of drawers.
- Neat's-foot oil for lubricating fine mechanical instruments.
- Leather dressing.

After the tanner had tanned a hide it was the job of the currier to smooth the leather by shaving it with special knives and then applying animal oil and grease to the leather and the process of stretching it incorporated the oil and grease into the corium or inner layer of the skin. The result was to waterproof leather (Mayer, 1968). Neat's-foot oil obtained from the feet of cattle was used and apart from dressing leather it was also used on textiles (Encyclopaedia Britannica 99). Archaeological bone reports sometimes include evidence of cattle hides being obtained by the tanner from the butcher with the feet attached. While the feet would have had little value to the butcher they provided useful handles to the hide especially for the butcher in the course of flaying the animal. It is possible that the tanner wanted the feet to obtain the neat's-foot oil for dressing leather. The same type of oil was obtained from the feet of sheep but the only true neat's-foot oil was from the feet of neat cattle.

Strouhal describes what is frequently portrayed as the act of two tannery workers pulling the tanned hide taught across a trestle (Strouhal, 1992). This description fits the currier's action to incorporate the applied grease into the fibres of the leather for its protection and waterproofing. There is similarly a passage in Homer's *Iliad* when he describes men pulling at the body of Patrocoles as "like a party of men who have to stretch an ox hide soaking with grease and pulling away standing in a ring till the natural moisture runs out and the grease runs in – the hide is well stretched with all those men pulling" (Rouse).

Soap

Soap is produced by the saponification of fat. It results from the separation of the fatty acids from the glycerol molecule and these free fatty acids combining with sodium or potassium. Glycerine is a by-product of soap production. Early soap making was achieved by using animal fat and wood ashes which provided the alkali in the form of potash. Pliny the Elder describes the Phoenicians making soap from goat's tallow and wood ashes *c*. 2300 years ago. Soap was widely known in the Roman Empire and the Greek physician Galen refers to soap as a medicament and as a means of cleansing the body (Encyclopaedia Britannica).

Early soap making was achieved by using the ash from beech wood which provided the alkali in the form of potash. Seaweed burning was another good source of potash. Soap was made in Italy and Spain as early as the 8th century. The soap industry was introduced into France from Italy by the 13th century (Microsoft Encarta). The introduction of soap into Britain was by the importation of soap from the Continent and from 1500 the production of soap in England began to grow into a significant industry competing against the tallow chandlers for the butcher's fat (Fig 0.5).

Fig 0.5 Drawings of a soap boiler and a button maker from a 1647 set of illustrations of occupations.

RELATIVE VALUE OF FAT HISTORICALLY

The very high value of tallow relative to meat in the past underlines the importance of the non-food use of fat. The incentive for butchers would have been to sell less fat with the meat and make more money selling it as tallow. Where there is evidence of long bones having been split to obtain marrow fat, the question is - what use was to be made of the fat? The relative value of fat declined in the 19th and 20th centuries and today the value is negligible compared with the value of the carcase.

1373:	(London) Tallow chandlers ordered by the Lord Mayor not to sell candles more than 2d lb. and butchers not to sell rough tallow at more than 18s per wey. And melted tallow at 22s per wey. (Jones, 1976)
1371 – 1380:	Average price per head of oxen – 15s 10d. (Rogers, 1866)
1568:	"The price of a waie of tallow was this yere rated by the Lorde Mayor at 30s." (Pearce, 1929)

By contrast, according to Stow (1598), it was enacted in 1533 that butchers should sell their beef not above a halfpenny the pound and mutton a halfpenny half-farthing. A feast given to the Duke of Norfolk in 1561 included 8 stone of beef (14lb = one stone) at 5s. 4d. which is 57d. per lb (Ainsworth-Davis, 1931); (waie or wey = 168lb (76kg) (Jones, 1976); waie = 196lb (89kg) (Pearce, 1929).

A carcase analysis of a 5-year old ox in 1798 valued the tallow at 4 shilling per stone compared with the hindquarters at 5 shillings and the forequarters at 4 shillings. The tallow total, 16 stone, was valued more than the hide (Culley, 1807).

A costing given by Thomas Horne to equate the deadweight value to liveweight value puts the value of the quarters at 3 pence per lb, the tallow or extra fat at 4 pence per lb and the hide at 3 pence per lb (Horne, 1810).

In 1995, for the 210,000 tonnes of tallow produced in the year values ranged from £180-320/tonne (8p – 14.5p per lb). Sides of beef averaged 100p per lb.

BONE, ANTLER, HORN AND HOOF

From the time of the earliest human ancestors eating meat they started using bones as tools. As a raw material for making artefacts bone has a number of advantages. Fresh bone consists of one third organic (mainly collagen) and two thirds mineral. Compact bone is heavy having a specific gravity of 1.9 and is very hard with a compressive strength of about 20,000 lb per square inch and its tensile strength averages 15,000 lb per square inch (Sisson & Grossman,1953).

As bone is hard and strong, implements such as needles, tools for making holes in leather, combs, etc., will stand up to constant use. A major advantage was that the various shapes of bones required little working to convert them into useful implements, e.g. a scapula for use as a shovel or spade, a bovine metatarsal as a handle for a knife, an ulna for use as an awl for making holes in leather etc. Another advantage with bone is that it can be cut, carved and shaped, which along with its durability, makes it suitable for the manufacture of many things including ornaments, buttons, jewellery, needles and dice (Fig 0.5).

Excavations in the Southern European caves which were occupied by people in the late Palaeolithic period, yielded various artefacts manufactured from bone including heads of harpoons, spear throwers and needles. The technology of warfare produced the composite bow in China more than 3,000 years ago and this type of bow was also used by the archers of the Roman armies. Composite bows included bone or horn as well as wood (Hodges, 1970). Small compact bones such as the astragali of sheep, referred to as knucklebones, were used by children from earlier times for games such as jacks (fivestones). Picks fashioned from red deer antlers were used in the Neolithic flint mines. It was estimated that 50,000 antler picks were produced for mining the flint during the working lifetime of Grimes Graves flint mines in Norfolk (Encyclopaedia Britannica, 1999).

Excavations at the Romano-British site at Verulamium yielded a variety of bone products including knife handles, spoons, needles, pins, hinges, plates for tablet weaving of braids and a number of decorative items (Frere, 1972). There is widespread archaeological evidence for bone working industries in the Anglo-Saxon period producing a wide variety of bone tools and decorative items including the manufacture of bone and antler combs (Riddler, 1990). Excavations at Beverly, Humberside, yielded a range of bone and antler artefacts from the late Anglo-Saxon period to the 14th century. These included pin-beaters or weaving tools, bobbins, needle cases, styluses for writing, toggles for fastening clothes, bone casket mounts, a variety of pins and the remains of ice skates made from horse metapodials (Forman, 1992). Apart from finding the bone artefacts the recovery of the residue of bone working is an indication of where the bone working industries were situated and some of the techniques involved in the original working (Greep, 1987). The archaeological reports that include finds of bone and antler tools, decorative items, etc. and bone working residues are so numerous, testifying to the extensive use of animal bone as an industrial raw material in all ages.

Horn is not part of the skeleton but is a keratinous sheath of the horn that is continuous with the skin covering the horn core, as distinct from antler which is a bony outgrowth from the skull. The horn core is the centre of the horn and is a bone growth from the skull and contains a hollow sinus that is continuous with the frontal sinus. Horn, once removed from the horn core, was easily converted into drinking vessels or containers for powders or granular materials such as gunpowder to recharge a pistol or musket. The shape of most horns predispose for easy conversion into a musical instrument which was utilised in the early civilisations of Mesopotamia, Egypt, Israel (the shofar), Greece and Rome. The shofar or ram's horn is still used in Jewish rituals for Rosh Hashana and Yom Kippur. The Roman trumpet or *buccina* was originally developed from cattle horns. Cattle horns were used to make hunting horns in medieval Europe (Encyclopaedia Britannica, 1999).

Horn can be heated and moulded like plastic to produce medallions bearing the head of a dignitary or moulded into a snuffbox or similar objects. Using hot metal dies, horn can be decorated by embossing and separate pieces of horn can be fused together using heat and pressure. By heating powdered horn it can be fused and moulded into different shapes. Because the nature of horn is a laminated structure, layers can be separated to produce thin translucent sheets (O'Connor, 1987).

Those medieval craftsmen making dice found a ready demand by those seeking amusements, although gambling was often illegal.

GUT STRING, LIGAMENTS AND TENDONS

The gut string makers produced catgut from the animal's intestines consisting of the submucosa which is almost entirely collagen. The result is a strong cord that does not stretch used for stringing musical instruments, longbows, tennis rackets, etc.

Ligaments and tendons were useful as cords because they do not stretch except the ligamentum nuchae consisting of elastin fibres which relies on its elasticity for its function in supporting the weight of the head.

SKINS AND HIDES

The skin of a sheep or the hide of an ox could have been worth almost as much as the carcase in the medieval period. Leather had a high value due to its importance in the manufacture of so many essential products e.g. foot wear, clothing, harnesses, straps, belts, bottles, cases, trunks, etc.

There was also the hair of the cattle hides and the wool from the sheep's skins. Calfskin was valuable for the pages of books or documents (vellum) and later for binding books.

Coney skins (rabbit skins) were in demand as furs.

Fallen livestock or animals that had 'died of themselves' (died of natural causes) would almost certainly have been skinned because of the high value of the skin or hide. The fat from these animals may not have been of much value for tallow as the conditions leading to death often depleted the animal's fat, and what remained was often gelatinous.

PRIMARY PRODUCT OR BY-PRODUCT

In the modern trading situation the carcase of the slaughtered animal is substantially the primary product and all the rest, the edible offals and the non-food products, are the by-products. It is important in assessing the developments of meat trading through history to consider the much greater economic aspect of the non-food animal products. During earlier periods the non-food slaughter products of cattle or sheep could have been the primary products with the carcase constituting the by-product. In any case the non-food products would have represented a major part of the animal's value. With regard to pigs their carcases would always have been the primary product because the yield of non-food products would have been lower in value. Pigskin leather, of course, has a high value and there were good uses for pigs' bristles.

Another part of the economic equation was that the primary product of the dairy cow was milk and the cull cow's carcase and offals at slaughter were the by-products of the dairy industry. For the wool producing flocks of sheep the primary product was wool. For the oxen, their primary value was as a draught or plough animal. Another significant value for livestock was to produce manure for the arable land. Some sheep flocks were kept by arable farmers essentially for their manure value when folded on arable fields.

MARKET FORCES

Through the whole history of meat trading developments the expansion of the trade has been due to some form of stimulus. The principal inducement for any entrepreneur to seize opportunities is the potential acquisition of wealth.

For most trade developments the stimuli has been the increase in demand. The reasons for increases in demand for meat will have been due to either increase in population, expansion of some social groups or increased affluence. The increase in urbanisation resulted in the need for the town's people to be supplied with their meat. The establishment of the first towns and cities in ancient times gave rise to the earliest meat traders in the context that the term would be defined today.

In the early middle ages the growth in towns and the decline in feudalism or seigniorage paved the way for the expansion of trade. The early trading was mainly conducted by individual craftsmen or merchants selling their wares and therefore their businesses were vulnerable to being undermined by outside traders. The guild system was developed for the protection of the burgesses trading in the town. In the course of time commercial activity increased and the monopoly of the guild system was seen as a barrier to competition and expansion of trade. This led to the attitude advocated by the maxim in the 1702 House of Commons journals, "Trade ought to be free and not restrained" and the further rise in support for the free market embodied in *"An Inquiry into the Nature and Causes of the Wealth of Nations"* by Adam Smith in 1776.

To deliver the changing requirements of the market the butcher has needed to acquire new skills and, in some cases, developments in technology were necessary e.g. refrigeration.

CONCLUSION

Meat and the other animal products have been an intrinsic part in the ascent of man. The contribution was much wider than the value of meat as a form of sustenance. The development of social organisation and technology was an essential part of the growing success of the hunter-gatherer societies. The domestication of the meat-producing animals was a fundamental feature of the rise of farming in the Neolithic era which paved the way for the early civilisations.

All through history the domestic meat-producing animals have played an important part in the wealth of nations. Indeed there were many instances where wealth was measured by the size of herds and flocks of animals and rates of exchange and currency values were based on cattle (e.g. Pecuniary – of money from the Latin *pecudes* = cattle). Meat-producing animals and their non-food products have been a major impetus for the establishment and growth of national and international trade through time.

Part I

**The Ancient Origins of the Meat Industry
from the Palaeolithic to the Roman Empire**

Chapter 1

The Palaeolithic Origins of Butchery

INTRODUCTION

To understand how and why meat trading evolved as it did it is necessary to appreciate the social, commercial and technological developments that either influenced the growth and direction of meat trading or made possible changes in the nature of meat trading. The meat trade is one of the craft trades that requires more than the acquisition of a commodity which is then traded. There is the need for the butcher to use his skills to process the live animal into a product of a size and condition to suit the consumer. The very beginning of meat trading began when our distant ancestors developed the meat eating habit and the subsequent skills of butchery. It was the social organisation that evolved among the prehistoric hunter gatherer groups, in particular food sharing, that in all probability paved the way for the trading patterns that became an important part of the first civilisations. Throughout history where there has been a need or an opportunity, it has brought to the fore individuals with entrepreneurial tendencies to fulfil those needs or exploit the opportunities.

THE BEGINNING OF THE HUMAN SPECIES

The earliest of the primates to walk upright were a group of hominids called *Australopithecines* who changed from the tree-living habitat of their ancestors to a life on the plains of Africa some five million years ago. Discoveries in the 1990s of fossilised hominid bones at Kanapoi, Kenya, were dated at about 4 million years old and given the name *Australopithecus anamensis*. This hominid is considered to be the ancestor of the later *A. robustus* and *A. afarensis*. The well-publicised fossil remains of Lucy, a female *A. afarensis* were found at Hadar, Ethiopia, and according to radiometric dating she lived between 3.6 and 2.9 million years ago (Leakey & Walker, 1997). These hominids may have eaten small animals, birds' eggs and insects but archaeological evidence indicates that they had a predominately vegetarian diet. They used sticks and stones as a primitive form of tool but there is no evidence to point to them making stone tools. Groups of chimpanzees can be observed today using sticks and stones to a level of success that was probably achieved by the *Australopithecines* (Leaky & Lewin, 1992).

There is consensus among palaeontologists that the ancestors of modern man originated in Africa but there are differences of opinion on how development progressed to the ultimate *Homo sapiens*. There is one view that the early ancestor was *Homo erectus* who later migrated to Asia and Europe and *Homo sapiens* evolved in all these areas to which *Homo erectus* had migrated. The other theory is that another species, *Homo ergaster* was ancestor to *Homo erectus* and another species, *Homo heidelbergensis* and it was the latter that was the direct ancestor to modern man, with *Homo erectus* becoming extinct.

Fossil evidence discovered at a number of sites in East Africa shows the existence of the earliest *Homo species* living about two million years ago. A major find was the fossil remains of the "Turkana boy" in Turkana, Kenya in 1984 which was the major part of the skeleton of a *Homo species* youth who lived about 1.6 million years ago and who would have had an appearance very close to that of a modern human (Leaky & Lewin, 1992).

THE USE OF STONE TOOLS AND THE ORIGINS OF BUTCHERY

The earliest stone tools were found in East Africa and are about 2.5 million years old. There were no human fossil remains found with these stone tools but at later sites, dated at some 2 million years ago, there were stone tools, human fossil remains and butchered animal bones. These sites were at the Olduvai Gorge, Tanzania and East Turkana, Kenya (Tattersall, 1997).

The evidence indicates that the diet of early *Homo species* consisted of a higher proportion of meat than that of *Australopithecines*. Apart from small animals, the flesh of larger animals was also forming part of their diet. The remains of these larger animals were almost certainly the prey of carnivores, such as lions or the large sabre toothed cats, or they may have been animals that had died naturally or by drowning. As the teeth and jaws of this human ancestor were, as with modern humans, totally unsuitable for tearing the flesh from a carcase or indeed getting through the hide or skin of an animal, it was necessary to use the sharp edges of stone tools for removing the flesh or cutting through the hide. Appropriate stone tools have been found along with the fossil remains of hominids at Omo Valley and Hadar in Ethiopia and Laetoli in Tanzania (Leakey, 1981). The stone tools found at these early sites would have been very effective for butchering carcases; in fact some archaeologists have carried out experiments to show that they are quite efficient for butchering even an elephant carcase (Tattersall, 1997).

This was the very ancient origin of the craft of butchery (Fig 1.1).

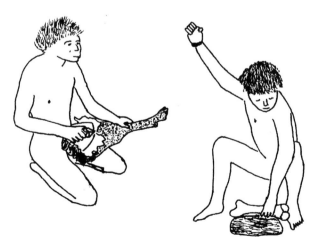

Fig 1.1 Use of a hand-axe to skin the leg of an animal (left) and the use of a hammer-stone to break a marrow bone to obtain the marrow fat (right). There is much archaeological evidence from Palaeolithic sites for this activity having taken place.

The first stone tools that were used would have been pieces of stone picked up and found useful for different purpose. The next part of the process was for early human ancestors to discover ways of fashioning stone into something more suitable for use as a tool. These would be the first generation of tool makers living about 1.5 to 2.5 million years ago and marked the beginning of stone tool technology which was a fundamental factor in the progress of human development, and indeed the early development of the butcher's craft. The tools that were made were more appropriate for their intended use, such as stone hand-axes, stone cleavers and the flakes of stone with sharp edges for cutting. There were highly standardised types of stone tools made during different periods such as *Abbevillian* and *Acheulian* stone tools (Fig 1.2).

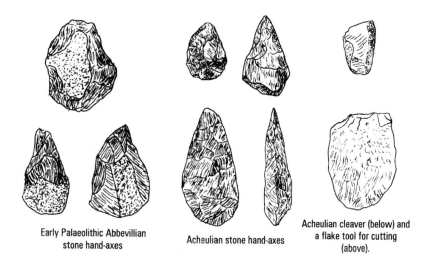

Early Palaeolithic Abbevillian stone hand-axes

Acheulian stone hand-axes

Acheulian cleaver (below) and a flake tool for cutting (above).

Fig 1.2 Early Palaeolithic Abbevillian and Acheulian stone hand-axes

Although it has been generally hypothesised that the early human ancestors principally hunted for their meat, some palaeontologists are now considering the likelihood of these hominids obtaining much of their meat by scavenging (Davis, 1987).

HUNTING OR SCAVENGING FOR MEAT

The scavenging hypothesis was considered in detail in an article by R. J. Blumenschine and J. A. Cavallo in the *Scientific American* (October 1992). One argument that supports this theory is that for these small stature hominids (males about 45Kg.) to hunt and kill large animal prey was improbable, yet the bones of such large animals were found associated with the fossil remains of early humans. These animal bones had cuts and scratches that could only have been made by the sharp edge of a stone tool. Evidence from some of the archaeological sites in East Africa is of limb bones broken open to obtain the marrow and skulls smashed for the removal of the brain. Hyenas and hominids were the only scavengers capable of breaking open these bones; hominids using large stones for this purpose. There is also the lack of evidence from these early Palaeolithic sites of the weapons that would have been needed for hunting large prey. The early human would have been the best adapted scavenger to exploit a leopard's kill left hanging in the branches of a tree. Studies of humans living in primitive conditions indicate a tendency for opportunism; therefore it is reasonable to conclude that the early human ancestors would have used scavenging as a means of changing from a vegetarian to an omnivorous diet. The palaeontologists R. J. Blumenschine and J. A. Cavallo studied the habits of predators and scavengers in East Africa around one of the noted archaeological sites at Olduvai Gorge. They related their findings to the hominid and animal remains and the stone tools from the various archaeological sites of East Africa, to form the basis of the scavenging hypothesis. Their studies indicated that at certain times of the year, particularly the dry season, carcases from the kills of the predators would be more abundant, whereas the vegetable side of the hominids diet (fruits and roots) would be scarce, therefore increasing the need for the meat diet of the hominid.

FOOD SHARING

The development of behaviour patterns and social organisation during the early period of the ancestors of modern humans was an important process in human evolution. Glynn Isaac in an article in the *Scientific American* (April 1978) elaborated on the hypothesis that food sharing within the social group or community was fundamental to organisational and technological developments. The behaviour patterns within the social groups of chimpanzees allow the scrounging of food from each other, which does not amount to organised sharing. This was probably the type of behaviour pattern inherited by the first *Homo species.* For the food sharing pattern of behaviour it was necessary for the members of the food collecting group to obtain food in large enough quantities for the whole community. It was suggested by Glynn Isaac that the male members of the group obtained the meat, whether by hunting or scavenging and the females collected the fruits, nuts, tubers, insects, etc., constituting a division of labour; a fundamental feature of social organisation.

Even scavenging was a job for the bigger and stronger male as it would often mean leaving the relative safety of the wooded areas to reach the carcases left in the open country by lions or sabre toothed cats. Archaeological evidence points to the fact that the hominids dismembered parts of the carcase and carried them back to their home base where they could, in relative safety, remove the flesh and break open the bones to obtain the marrow. Dismemberment of carcases of large animals required suitable stone tools and skill in their use; therefore the development of tool technology and improvement of butchery skills must have been a concurrent process. In all probability these hominids developed artefacts that were used for carrying meat, fruits, tubers, etc., as the carrying of food back to the home base was an essential part of food sharing. Such artefacts would have been made of materials that have long since disintegrated. Evidence from some archaeological sites such as that of Kay Behrensmeyer indicates that the stone for making tools was carried to the site.

To succeed with this food sharing social structure hominids needed to develop certain characteristics to a much higher level than was demonstrated by their predecessors. These characteristics were:

1. Dexterity of hands and fingers to be able to manufacture stone tools and other artefacts and then the ability to use the tools effectively in the dismembering of carcasses, skinning animals, etc.
2. Organisational ability to carry out tasks by groups on behalf of the whole community.
3. Higher levels of communication with the probable development of early forms of language.
4. Exploiting the upright posture in order to carry things more easily.

For this it was necessary, as archaeological evidence shows, for *Homo species* to have a larger, more developed brain than its predecessors. Natural selection for all these characteristics, including the larger brain, may have been an important factor.

The development of tool making by the *Homo species* more than a million years ago, which was largely for the purpose of butchery, was the beginning of technology. Food sharing behaviour of these early communities required the procurement of meat, whether by hunting or scavenging, carrying the meat back to the home base and distributing it to the members of the community.

This was the beginning of the 'meat trade'.

THE HUNTER GATHERER SOCIETIES

The advance in tool making produced the necessary instruments for hunting and killing prey. There was a progressive improvement of the tool making technology from the older type known as *Abbevillian* to a more advanced type of technology called *Acheulian*. The stone tools they produced enabled wood, bone, horn, antler and leather tools and equipment to be fashioned, providing a wider and more flexible range of implements for use. This would have aided the progress and advancement of these early societies. The stone toolmakers also discovered that they could sharpen the edge of a stone tool by rubbing it on an abrasive stone, such as a piece of sandstone. The *Acheulian* hand-axes and cleavers were not only used in a chopping action, their sharp edges enabled them to be used as knives for skinning prey and cutting flesh from the carcasses. A blow from a hand-axe to the head of an animal of medium size would have quickly resulted in unconsciousness and death. The stone tool users were also the stone toolmakers and as they developed skill in the use of the tools they would have become aware of the innovations that could improve tools for their intended use, of which butchery was an important part. In this way stone tool technology advanced and for early man to become an effective hunter the development of stone tool technology was essential.

MAN THE HUNTER

At an East African Palaeolithic site discovered by Louis and Mary Leakey dated between 700,000 and 400,000 years ago, *Acheulian* stone tools were found and bones of animals that had been butchered. Many of the bones were from a large extinct type of baboon, *Theropithecus oswaldi* which weighed about 65kg. The baboon bones represented some 90 individuals of which a high proportion were young animals, according to the evidence of their teeth. This indicates that these animals had been hunted, and the fact that there was evidence of butchery by hominids led to the conclusion that hominids were the hunters. This conclusion was further supported in that all parts of the animals' bodies were represented by the bone residues (Davis, 1987).

Richard Klien studying animal bones from late Stone Age sites (40,000 - 20,000 years ago) in South Africa found that there were greater numbers of bones from very dangerous species such as the ferocious wart hog or bush pig compared with the earlier Palaeolithic sites, concluding that the late stone age people had developed a greater capability for hunting. Their improved technology in producing spears and bows and arrows enabled the hunters to kill or disable their quarry at a distance, reducing the danger to the hunter. There would also have been the necessity for a higher level of organisation and skill within the hunting group (Davis, 1987). The need for hunting would have provided an impetus for higher levels of technology in producing hunting weapons.

The evidence points to numbers of *Homo erectus* migrating to Europe and Asia. They were living in the Indonesian Island of Java 700,000 years ago (Java Man). At Choukoutien there was Peking man (Collins, 1976) estimated to have lived 400,000 years ago. It has more recently been considered that the date of the first migrations into Asia should be revised to more than one million or even nearer two million years ago (Tattersall, 1997). Further migrations took place much later through the Indonesian islands and Borneo with the first ancestors of the Australian aborigines arriving in Australia about 50,000 years ago. It is generally believed that the first migration of *Homo sapiens* into the Americas was about 12,000 years ago. They travelled from Asia across a bridge of land called Beringia. Beringia was a stretch of land that connected Siberia with Alaska when the oceanic waters were very low during the last Ice Age. Some palaeontologists believe that evidence from some excavations indicates the presence of humans in the Americas as long ago as 30,000 years.

The earliest evidence of humans in Europe was the discovery of human fossil bones along with some simple stone tools in the Gran Dolina caves in Northern Spain which were dated to 780,000 years ago. These human remains were attributed to *Homo heidelbergensis,* considered the immediate ancestor of modern man *Homo sapiens*. At a nearby site a large number of fossil human bones were found dated about 300,000 years ago. These bones could be from predecessors of the Neanderthals (Tattersall, 1997).

The earliest record of human remains in Britain was the discovery in Boxgrove, Sussex, in 1994 of a piece of a femur estimated to be half a million years old. Prior to this there was the discovery of some fragments of a human skull at Swanscombe, Kent, estimated to be between 200,000 and 300,000 years old. This skull has similarities with the skull found at Steinheim, near Stuttgart, which was from the same period (Collins, 1976). In the Swanscombe gravels, along with the Swanscombe skull, a number of stone tools were discovered. There is much wider evidence for human presence in Britain with the many discoveries of flint tools. Some of the stone tools found were in levels dated to about 500,000 years ago. Many flint tools have been found at numerous sites spread throughout Southern England, relating to the Hoxnian period, from about 350,000 years ago and includes the time of the Swanscombe occupation. At a site near King's Cross, London, a hand-axe was found in 1690 and the find was reported in 1715 becoming the first published report of Palaeolithic stone tools (Wymer, 1991). *Acheulian* tools were found at a number of the later Palaeolithic sites in the South and East of England. These flint tools would have been used for butchering the animals from which these early inhabitants obtained their meat.

The Neanderthal people, *Homo neanderthalensis,* were prominent in Europe from about 100,000 years ago and were using a form of tool technology. With the spread through Europe of modern man, *Homo sapiens,* (sometimes referred to as the Cro-Magnon people) about 40,000 years ago the whole process of human development gathered pace. These late Palaeolithic people developed tools and weapons, including spear throwers and the bow and arrow, which improved their effectiveness as hunters considerably. They also developed art in the form of bone carving, clay modelling and cave paintings. There is much evidence to suggest that these people had a well organised social structure. It is postulated by many archaeologists that presence of *Homo sapiens* competing in the same environment caused the extinction of the Neanderthals.

The greater prowess at hunting by the late Palaeolithic hunters is sited as a major factor in the extinction of many species of animal throughout the world. Many species of large mammal became extinct in America between 11,000 and 9,000 years ago, including species of horse, North American camels, mammoths, mastodons and peccaries. These extinctions are considered to be largely the result of over hunting by the Palaeoindians. There is evidence from a number of archaeological sites in America that the Palaeoindians carried out mass killings of bison in the Autumn and in the Spring. They would create a pound or enclosure using the natural contours of the land and fencing made up of tree branches and shrubs. They would then drive a herd of bison into the enclosure and when the bison were trapped, the Palaeoindians would kill them using stone tipped arrows or spears. The result was often many more animals being killed than were needed for meat. In some cases these mass kills were effected by driving a herd of bison over the edge of a cliff. A considerable number of Palaeoindians were necessary to carry out these mass killings of bison and they would have had to be well organised with a good knowledge of the nature of the bison.

THE ICE AGE

About 450,000 years ago the temperature of the earth dropped by an average of 5°C and the northern ice cap began to build up with more snow adding to its thickness in the winter than could melt away in the summer. The result was that the glaciers of this great ice sheet extended south to cover much of Europe and the British Isles, reaching as far south as the present northern outskirts of London. At the same time the level of the sea dropped, with large areas such as the continental shelf, at present covered by sea, becoming dry land and producing a land bridge between Britain and mainland Europe. There were periods of warmer weather, the interglacial periods, when the ice sheet receded but this was followed by further glacial periods until the final glacial period that ended about 10,000 years ago. During the glacial periods most of the animals and humans would have been forced to migrate from Britain although the south of England would have been a tundra type of environment supporting some animals. The interglacial periods would have resulted in the animals and humans recolonising Britain (Merriman, 1990).

The early human populations of Europe would have had to withstand very cold conditions, especially to survive on the edge of the ice sheet during the successive glacial periods. The use of the skins of their prey for clothing and construction of shelters would have contributed to their survival. Another factor would have been their increased reliance on meat as their main diet, perhaps up to 80% or 90%. This fact similarly applied to the Eskimos and Laps in more recent times. Animal fat would have been a very important component of the diet, its contribution being its high and sustaining energy value. The early Europeans would probably have appreciated the value of animal fat and grease for its heat insulating properties. Rubbing fat into the hands and face would have been good protection against harsh winds and weather, keeping the hands and fingers more comfortable to perform tasks. Fat rubbed on the body and particularly the feet would have added to the heat insulation of the clothing, a practice known to have been carried out in the past and with a number of cultures in parts of the world. Fat has the added advantage of its water-resistant properties, protecting the skin from the damaging effect of prolonged soaking. Porous fabric can be made waterproof with animal fat. The therapeutic value of animal fat was probably appreciated for treating burns or chafed or cracked skin from exposure to severe weather.

The range of animals hunted and butchered for meat in Palaeolithic Britain varied considerably. During the warmer interglacial periods straight tusked elephants and hippopotami were hunted and during the cooler periods Palaeolithic man hunted mammoths and woolly rhinoceros. There were also deer, reindeer, aurochs (ancestor of modern cattle), horse, wild boar, bear, and duck. This variety of animals would have been a challenge to the skills of the Palaeolithic butchers. The excavation of a site at Uxbridge, London, revealed a scatter of bones of reindeer and wild horse along with the flint tools used to butcher them (Merriman, 1990). At another site at Crayford, Kent, flint tools were found with the bones of butchered animals, mainly woolly rhinoceros (Wymer, 1991).

THE PALAEOLITHIC CAVE PAINTINGS

Apart from the technological advances in tool making and their increasing ability to hunt large animals, the late Palaeolithic *Homo sapiens* developed a high standard of art demonstrated by the cave wall paintings and their ornate carvings in bone, antler and ivory. The period of the cave paintings was from about 32,000 to 10,000 years ago, coinciding with the last period of glaciation. Caves in which these paintings were discovered are in areas covering Southern Europe with a concentration in Southern France and Northern Spain. Most of the cave pictures were of animals which could have represented the animals that the artists hunted and would certainly have been the animals seen in the area around them. The difficulty in interpreting these paintings is to distinguish between factual representation of the animals and the activities of the hunters and the degree of elaboration by the artist (Fig 1.3).

The horse was one of the animals most frequently represented and it could be assumed was commonly hunted. Bison and aurochs (the ancestor to modern cattle) were also frequently depicted in the paintings and it is fairly certain that they would have contributed a major part of the Palaeolithic communities' diet. There were paintings of mammoths in caves across Europe to support other evidence that they were widespread during the late Palaeolithic period. Many of the paintings are of red deer and reindeer along with the ibex, although some of these may have been the mouflon.

These caves extended considerable distances from the openings and were therefore in complete darkness. The evidence points to the cave occupants using lamps burning animal fat. The earliest known discovery of a Palaeolithic lamp was 1854 but acceptance of the authenticity of lamps did not occur until 1902 after the discovery of a lamp made of sandstone in 1899 by Emile Riviere in the La Mouthe cave in the Dordogne. Analysis of some of these lamps indicated that fatty acids of animal origin had been present. Animal fat would have been placed in the lamps using some form of fibrous material as a wick. Experiments have shown that 500 grams of fat would keep a lamp burning for 24 hours (Bahn & Vertut, 1997).

To hunt successfully and then skin and butcher this range of animals would have required a considerable knowledge and craftsmanship. The stone-age people of the late Palaeolithic period were by no means primitive in their level of achievement (Fig 1.4).

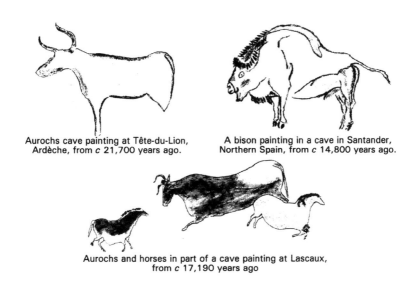

Aurochs cave painting at Tête-du-Lion, Ardèche, from *c* 21,700 years ago.

A bison painting in a cave in Santander, Northern Spain, from *c* 14,800 years ago.

Aurochs and horses in part of a cave painting at Lascaux, from *c* 17,190 years ago

Fig 1.3 Drawings of some of the paintings on the walls of caves in Europe occupied by Palaeolithic people during the last Ice Age.

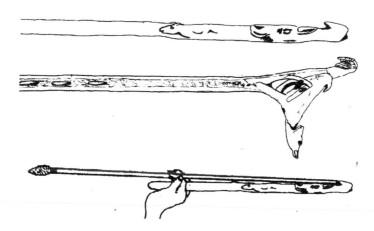

Fig 1.4 Above; two Upper Palaeolithic antler spear throwers with carvings of animals. They are from the Magdalerian period (*c* 15,000 - 10,000 BC). Below is an example of how spear throwers were used.

Chapter 2

From Hunter-Gatherers to Farmers

DEVELOPMENT OF MEAT TRADING IN THE NEOLITHIC PERIOD

The end of the last ice age *c.* 12,000 years ago heralded a steady transition from the hunter-gatherer way of life to farming for many communities across the world. The primary centres for the domestication of plants and animals and the beginning of agriculture were the Middle East (10,000 years ago), China (8,500 years ago), North America, Central America and South America (all 4,500 years ago) and Sub-Saharan Africa (4,000 years ago).

It is generally accepted that after the development of Neolithic farming in the Middle East it spread along the northern Mediterranean coast and then north through the rest of Europe.

The debate continues on what combination of factors induced the hunter-gatherer communities emerging from the ice age to change their way of life to that of farming communities. Apart from the cultivation of crops and the herding of animals these communities turned to a sedentary way of life with their permanent settlements and there was a significant growth in the population. In the areas where the first Neolithic settlements occurred, the combination of soil, climatic conditions and availability of water was a significant factor in the domestication of plants and animals, leading to the first farming (Smith, 1994). A change to sedentary communities in the early settlements resulted in a major increase of population estimated to be greater than twentyfold (Collins, 1975). The reason for this increase was the rise in the proportion of live births mainly due to the change from a nomadic existence and the greater reliability of food supply.

The immediate period after the last ice age, from *c.* 12,000 to 10,000 years ago was termed the Mesolithic period that was largely the transition period from the Palaeolithic hunter-gatherers to the Neolithic farmers. The Mesolithic period continued until 7,000 to 6,000 years ago through most of Europe. In the Levant (an area consisting of the present day Syria, Lebanon, Israel and Jordan) there was a Mesolithic people, the Natufians, whose main subsistence relied on hunter-gathering but they were also herders and produced stone sickles for harvesting the wild cereals and stone slabs for grinding the seeds (Fig 2.1). The Mesolithic people were in possession of a well advanced stone tool technology developed during the late Palaeolithic period along with weaving, basketry and woodworking skills and the ability to create artistic carvings and paintings, along with other crafts, that was a foundation for the evolvement of the Neolithic cultures. Evidence points to the Natufians being the first people in the Levant to construct circular dwellings and live in collective settlements or villages (Davis, 1987).

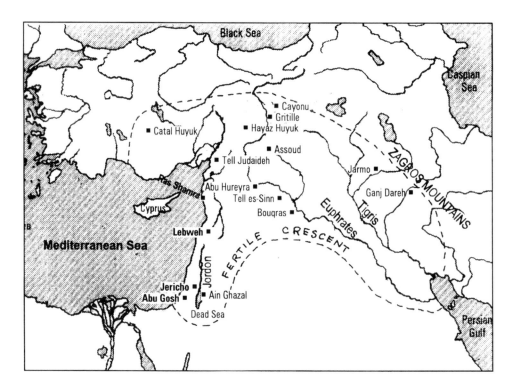

Fig 2.1 Map of the Near East showing the sites where evidence was found of the earliest domestication of cattle, sheep, pigs and goats.

THE FIRST FARMERS

The first farming communities of the Middle East are identified by the remains of settlements together with evidence of domesticated animals and plants. The main criteria for distinguishing between bone assemblages (collection of bone remains) of domesticated animals and their wild predecessors are; (a) the age and sex profile of the animals represented in the assemblage, (b) skeletal changes that occur with domestication, (c) change in dimorphism (i.e. the difference in the size of males to females), (d) reduction in the size of domesticates and (e) introduction of species into areas. The sex profile changes in that the number of females to males increase in a managed domestic herd and the age profile reflects selective slaughtering in contrast to the random effect of hunting. There was also evidence of some animals surviving to a greater age due to the protection of the herdsman. There were a number of skeletal changes due to domestication, as with sheep the number of domesticated ewes being hornless, whereas all wild ewes had horns. Horns were notably smaller for all horned species. The third molar of the domestic pig was smaller than that of the wild boar. The difference in size between males and females was less and the overall size of domesticates was reduced compared with their wild predecessors. There is much evidence of domesticated species being introduced into an area where the wild species had not previously existed (Davis, 1987).

The earliest farming villages so far identified were in the Levant. Excavations at Jericho have produced evidence of a farming village in occupation *c.* 10,000 years ago. These earliest agricultural communities farmed cereals and would appear to have obtained their meat, animal skins etc., by hunting.

The first herdsmen were hunters turned herders. The skill of a hunter was to build up an intimate knowledge of the animals he hunted, their herding instincts, patterns of movement and migrations. The huntsman needed to develop the technique of manoeuvring or driving his prey. These skills of the hunter were just the skills necessary to begin herding and domesticating animals and for the continuity of successful pastoral farming. These skills were also important for them to protect their flocks from predators. Many of the first farmers were pastoralists often leading a nomadic existence, moving with their herds or flocks seeking new pastures.

THE FIRST DOMESTIC ANIMALS

The wild animals that were domesticated had certain characteristics that made them suitable for domestication such as breeding freely in the captive herd state, herding instincts (living in interacting social groups), being susceptible to human manipulation and above all, having an economic value (Clutton-Brock, 1981). In assessing the economic value of animals the meat value was only one aspect; the non-food products derived from animals were the raw materials of many crafts and industries; i.e. wool, skins, hides, bones, horns, fat, catgut, tendons and ligaments.

It was essential for the potential domesticates to have the genetic capacity for adaptation to the different environmental conditions imposed by domestication. The nature and flexibility of domesticates in respect of their growth and development and in particular their reproductive biology (oestrus, conception, gestation, lactation) enabled them to adapt to the conditions for domestic animal production. Barbara Noddle in *"Flesh on the Bones"* (1989) covers concisely the wide range of metabolic processes that have an important effect on the performance of domestic animals and the extent of their tolerance to changed diet and environmental conditions. Climatic tolerance was established in the wild predecessors of cattle and pigs as they had a wide geographic range but the wild predecessors of sheep and goats had a much more limited geographic range. Nevertheless domestic sheep and goats were able to adapt to a wide range of climatic conditions. The same applied to chickens and turkeys.

The major adaptations necessary for all domestic animals was the differences in the type, quantity and continuity of diets. The early domestic herbivores had to support themselves entirely by their own foraging but in the course of time it became apparent to the Neolithic herdsmen of the need for conserved fodder. This was necessary to sustain the animals when there was inadequate herbage for foraging, such as during the winter in northern Europe (Noddle, 1989).

The evidence for the first domestication of animals was found at the sites where the farming of these animals was established. The first attempts at herding the wild antecedents of these animals would have begun much earlier. There is very little chance of finding evidence of the preliminary attempts at herding wild animals.

It is most remarkable that these Mesolithic hunter-gatherers cum Neolithic farmers domesticated goats, sheep, pigs, cattle, chicken, geese and ducks, which are still the core of the meat producing industry today. There is no evidence from the sites in the Middle East of any attempts to domesticate the other species that were hunted in the area such as gazelles, oryx and ibex.

The area in the Middle East where the first farming and domestication of animals took place is referred to as the 'Fertile Crescent'. It includes the Levant, parts of Turkey and Syria and the area along the Tigris and Euphrates rivers.

DOMESTICATION OF GOATS

Goats appear to be the first of the herd animals domesticated. The Middle Eastern bezoar goat (*Capra aegagrus*) has been identified as the wild ancestors of the domestic goat (*Capra hircus*) (Fig 2.2). There was evidence at Ganj Dareh (a site in Iran) for the earliest domestication of goats *c.* 9,000 years ago and further evidence at Jarmo for domestication 8,700 years ago, these sites being in the Zagros mountains, the habitat of the wild bezoar goats. There were a number of other sites for the presence of domestic goats at Jerico, Abu Gosh, Ain Ghazal, Assoud, and Ras Shamra between 8,700 and 8,200 years ago, these sites stretching around the Fertile Crescent (Smith, 1994).

Fig 2.2 A line drawing of a bezoar goat (*Capra aegagrus*)

DOMESTICATION OF SHEEP

The wild ancestor of domestic sheep (*Ovis aries*) was the Asiatic mouflon or red sheep (*Ovis orientalis*) which has been determined by the comparison of bones and by genetic studies. Evidence for the earliest domestication indicates a period between 8,700 to 8,200 years ago in an area where the habitat was suited to the Asiatic mouflon and consequently their domesticated descendants (Fig 2.3). This area was in the central part of the Fertile Crescent, an area covering much of present day Syria. The sites yielding much of the evidence for the earliest domestication of sheep were Tell es-Sinn, Abu Hureyra, Çayönü, Hayaz Hüyük and Bouqras (Smith, 1994).

Fig 2.3 A Soay Ram. Soays are very close in size and type to the early domesticated sheep

DOMESTICATION OF PIGS

The wild ancestor of the domestic pig is the wild boar (*Sus scrofa*) and the Latin name *Sus scrofa* is used for both as they are regarded as the same species. The natural habitat for wild pigs is marsh and woodland where the vegetation is rich. This was the type of habitat in the northern part of the Levant covering present day Lebanon and the western part of Syria where there was evidence for the earliest domestication of pigs. Çayönü was the site for the earliest domestication *c.* 8,500 years ago. At other sites in the same area at Gritille, Assoud, Tell Judaideh, Ras Shamra and Labweh there were domestic pigs *c.* 8,000 years ago. There was probably the separate domestication of pigs in China about the same time as in the Fertile Crescent. These would have been domesticated from the wild pigs of China at that time (Smith, 1994). The Chinese domestic pigs, either due to their origins or their domesticated development, were shorter snouted and were better meat animals than their British counterparts in the 18th century, hence the importation of Chinese pigs in the latter part of the 1700s to improve the British stock.

DOMESTICATION OF CATTLE

Modern cattle (*Bos taurus*) were domesticated from the wild ox, the aurochs (*Bos primigenius*) (Fig 2.4). The evidence for the earliest date for domestication was *c.* 8,000 years ago at Çatal Hüyük in Anatolia (Turkey). At a number of other sites in the Fertile Crescent there was evidence for the presence of domestic cattle between 8,000 to 7,000 years ago. The domestication of the aurochs was later than the other animals, possibly because of the size of the aurochs bulls which measured 1.5 to 2 metres at the shoulder plus having long formidable horns (Smith, 1994).

Fig 2.4 A line drawing of an impression of an auroch bull (*Bos primigenius*) which could be up to 2 metres (6.5 feet) at the shoulder.

DOMESTICATION OF POULTRY

The domestication of poultry probably began *c.* 8,000 years ago with the earliest evidence being the domesticated chickens (*Gallus gallus domesticus*) in China 7,400 years ago. They were domesticated from the red jungle fowl (*Gallus gallus*) (Smith, 1994). There is evidence for the domestication of ducks in China from the wild mallard. The Latin name *Anas platyrhynchos* refers to both the wild mallard and the domestic duck. The modern domestic goose was domesticated from the greylag goose, the Latin name *Anser anser* is for both. The ancient Egyptians reared domestically three or four species of duck and goose. The turkey was domesticated from the wild bronze turkey (*Meleagris gallopavo*) in Mexico long before Columbus discovered America. The Latin name for the domestic turkey is *Meleagris gallopavo gallopavo* (Larousse Encyclopaedia of Animal Life, 1974).

The *Galliformes* (chickens, turkeys, pheasants) and *Anseriformes* (ducks, geese, swans) have in their nature factors that made them conducive to domestication. They do not feed their chicks like most other species of bird but brood them i.e. the mother ushers them around to feed themselves which makes it relatively easy for humans to rear chicks, ducklings or goslings. To brood their offspring it is necessary for them to all hatch at the same time so the mother will not start sitting on the eggs until she has laid a large enough clutch. If eggs are removed before the clutch is large enough the bird will continue to lay more eggs; hence the potential existed to convert these birds into providers of eggs for human consumption.

ARCHAEOLOGICAL METHOD OF DETERMINING DOMESTIC ANIMALS FROM WILD ANIMALS

The presence of domestic animals as distinct from their wild predecessors in the bone assemblages is determined by:

(a)   The reduction in the size of the animals which is a factor of domestication.

(b)   The change in the age profile of the animals, indicating slaughter of herded animals as opposed to hunted animals.

(c)   A higher ratio of females to males.

(d)   Many of the female sheep were polled (hornless) which is not the case with wild sheep.

(e)   The head of domestic pigs was relatively shorter and there was a noticeable reduction in the length of the third molars.

SPREAD OF NEOLITHIC FARMING

The practice of farming and herding livestock spread from the Middle East to most parts of Europe during the Neolithic period reaching Britain *c.* 5000 years ago. The first movement of domestic animals from the Middle East was probably to the Northern Mediterranean countries. There is evidence that some of the hunter gatherer communities in Greece, Italy and Southern France started herding sheep and goats from *c.* 8000 years ago. These animals would have been brought from the Middle East as there is no evidence of their wild predecessors existing outside the Middle East. Wild cattle (aurochs) and wild boar were distributed throughout Europe in the post glacial period which raises the possibility for cattle and pigs to have been domesticated in various parts of Europe or brought to Europe from the Middle East (Smith, 1994).

From *c.* 7000 years ago the transition to the Neolithic agricultural systems was well under way in the fertile areas around the Mediterranean. By 6000 years ago the farming culture was spreading across Central and Northern Europe.

THE NEOLITHIC BRITAIN

Evidence for the early presence of domestic animals in Britain is for sheep *c.* 5400 years ago at Lambourn, Berkshire and goats *c.* 4600 years ago at Windmill Hill, Wiltshire. Cattle were probably the most prevalent livestock in the Neolithic period. During the Early Neolithic period wild cattle (aurochs) were still present in Britain and may have interbred with the domestic cattle. The aurochs had probably become extinct in Britain by 3000 years ago (Clutton-Brock, 1989). From the archaeological evidence it would appear that domestic pigs were less important in the Neolithic period than in later periods. Wild boar was widespread in Neolithic Britain and hunting them provided extra meat.

After the end of the last ice age and the consequent rise in temperature the British Isles became heavily forested; the boreal period. This existed during the early Neolithic period which was more conducive to herding cattle and pigs and providing a reservoir of wild cattle, wild boar, deer and other game. In the later Neolithic period the level of forestation declined, the Sub-boreal period resulting in large areas of grassland or open land (Evans, 1975).

One of the best preserved Neolithic village sites in northern Europe is Skara Brae in the Orkney Islands. This village was continuously occupied from *c.* 5100 to 4500 years ago. The inhabitants grew cereals and kept cattle and pigs. Due to the lack of suitable flint for stone tools bone was the principal material for making tools.

Extensive excavations of the burial mounds or barrows have revealed the ritual inclusion of cattle skulls and other cattle bones in the burial chamber which indicates the esteem with which cattle were regarded. In front of the barrows quantities of bones were found, predominantly from pigs, which indicates feasting forming part of the rituals (Hodder, 1990).

FROM NEOLITHIC HAMLETS TO SIZEABLE TOWNS

The domestication of plants and their successful cultivation along with the domestication of animals led to the production of surpluses by the early Neolithic farming communities beyond their subsistence needs. This gave scope for the development of manufactured goods and manufacturing to be carried out by part of the community. The beginning of pottery manufacture dates back to *c.* 8500 years ago, one of the earliest sites being Çatal Hüyük in Anatolia. Pottery became important not only for cooking food but also for its storage (Maisels, 1993). Querns were produced for grinding corn and there was the manufacture of many articles from the non-food animal products such as hides, bones, fat, etc. Weaving cloth from wool and linen from flax was much in evidence. In all, this was a basis for a division of labour and the establishment of craft skills. The skills of the butcher will have come to the fore as the slaughter of domestic animals is quite different from killing an animal in the course of the hunt. The skill of skinning the animal will have become paramount as skins and hides were of considerable value and poor skinning would result in damage. The skills in handling and preparation of the meat and non-food animal products will have gained in importance.

There was evidence from the late Palaeolithic period of rituals in burials which continued through to the Neolithic period, with the establishment of shrines, which in some cases indicated a veneration of cattle, as in a shrine at Çatal Hüyük decorated with many horn cores (Clutton-Brock, 1981). The institution of priests and a religious structure was a natural development which would have included paying homage and the provision of sacrifices by the community. This religious element, along with the payment of tribute to the chiefs or lords, resulted in an infrastructure which the primary food producers had to support. As the towns became larger with populations reaching a thousand and more such as in Jericho in the Jordan Valley and Hacilar and Çatal Hüyük in Anatolia, their infrastructure became more widely spread and they were progressing towards the type of system that would support the cities of the early civilisations. While rearing domesticated animals was a significant feature of these communities, hunting still played an important part in the provision of meat for the inhabitants. Indications of the animal bone remains from a number of these sites are that gazelles were a major source of meat. Other hunted animals were aurochs, wild boar, fallow deer, hare and birds such as quail, partridge and rock dove.

The domestication of animals suitable for draught purposes or as pack animals giving rise to transportation (i.e. cattle, asses, horses and camels) was another essential first step towards the early civilisations with their urban communities. Means of transportation has always been an essential factor for any civilised society. Pack animals played an important part in transportation overland before the advent of roads suitable for wheeled vehicles. Pack animals were used extensively by armies on the march. Although records of the use of cattle as pack animals is scant, it would have been just as practical to use them for this purpose as for pulling carts or ploughs.

The developments of the Neolithic period created the environment for the early trading with the surpluses of food and other products, the growth in manufactures, regional access to raw materials and the availability of animal transport. The ability to trade added to the desire to acquire attractive products and the need for raw materials were the ingredients to initiate trading. There is much evidence for trading in the early days of the Neolithic settlements. There was considerable trade in such materials as obsidian and seashells in Çatal Hüyük

The domestication of livestock, the institution of trading and the creation of urban populations requiring a supply of food were the fundamentals necessary for the establishment of meat trading.

It is apparent that the division of labour was an intrinsic part of the evolution of the Neolithic communities and was an essential aspect of the economies of the succeeding societies through history. The economic importance of the division of labour was specified by Adam Smith in *An Inquiry into the Nature and Causes of the Wealth of Nations* published in 1776.

Chapter 3

The Earliest Civilisations

THE PRELUDE TO CIVILISATION

The advances of the Neolithic communities paved the way for the emergence of the first civilisations. The Neolithic settlements or villages existed before 7000 BC in the Middle East. The village farming cultures of Hassuna and Samarra in Mesopotamia that date from at least 6000 BC had a well developed social organisation and an advanced standard of pottery. The very large Neolithic settlements or towns, such as Jericho in the Jordan Valley and Çatal Hüyük and Hacilar in Anatolia with their supporting farms, were approaching the nature of the first cities. Estimates put the population of Çatal Hüyük at 5000 inhabitants. In these early neolithic towns the inhabitants, many of whom would have been employed in urban industries e.g. as potters, weavers, etc., needed to barter with the local farmers to obtain their food. Archaeologists excavating ancient sites have found evidence of areas which were used as markets for the sale of produce (Maisels, 1993).

The village farming cultures of Hassuna and Samarra were the forerunners of the Ubaidian culture about 4000 BC which led to the earliest civilisations in Mesopotamia at Sumer about 3500 BC. Then came the civilisations of Egypt, and the Indus Valley, these cultures moving into the Bronze Age (Fig 3.1). These were followed by a progression of civilisations leading to the great civilisations of Greece and Rome. The establishment of urban communities, by necessity, resulted in a much more elaborate social structure than existed in the Neolithic farming communities. There was the emergence of the different tiers or levels of society and in the earliest stages of these urban societies there developed an autocratic structure with a king supported by the ruling classes or families. Priests were also in leading positions in the hierarchy. At the bottom of the social structure were the labourers and slaves with a range of administrators, artisans, etc. in the middle ranks.

Between 6000 and 3000 BC there was the invention and development of much of the technology that was basic to the emerging civilisations. The eminent prehistorian, V. G. Childe, wrote "Between 6000 and 3000 BC man has learnt to harness the force of oxen and of the winds, he invents the plough, the wheeled cart and the sailing boat, he discovers the chemical processes involved in smelting copper ores and the physical properties of metals and he begins to work out an accurate solar calendar. He has thereby equipped himself for urban life, and prepares the way for a civilisation ...".

THE FIRST MESOPOTAMIAN CITIES

The build up of urban communities from about 6000 BC resulted in the creation of a trading

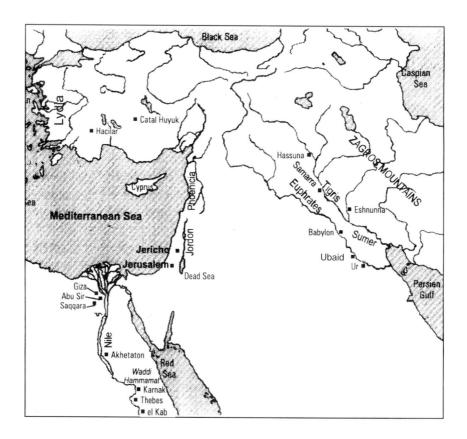

Fig 3.1 The Anatolian, Mesopotamian and Egyptian sites referred to in Chapter 3.

infrastructure and this included a system for selling meat to the people; hence the specialist butcher and meat trader. In the early cities, there grew up separate quarters for different trades and butchers established themselves in one part of the city for trading (Saggs, 1989). The same arrangement was common in the Roman Empire, as in Pompeii, with streets named after the trades carried on there; e.g. Vicus Sandaliarius, Street of Cobblers, Vicus Bubularius, Street of Cattle Dealers (Brion, 1976). Butchers' Row is a medieval street name still to be found in many towns in Britain, but alas there are few butchers in those streets today.

Evidence indicates that sheep and goats were the most common meat animals of these Mesopotamian ancient city states, including the pig in some areas. The wool from the sheep was an important commodity as in most other times (Whitehouse, 1977). Cattle, though fewer in number, were greatly esteemed as is apparent from the statuary, paintings and reliefs. Geese were also commonly reared and used for food along with other water fowl. Although the hunter gatherer and Neolithic farming communities ate the meat of the horse, ass, camel, and dog, these were not generally used for meat throughout the early civilisations, which may relate to some of the early dietary laws. A stone inlaid frieze decorating the temple of Ninhursag at Ubaid, one of the earliest Sumer sites, is the scene of a well organised dairy that shows a cow being milked, while its calf is tethered by the cow's head, which was necessary to cause the milk to flow in these early domesticated cows (Canby, 1980). A thriving dairy industry is usually complementary to an active beef industry (Fig 3.2).

Fig 3.2 Line drawing of part of a stone-inlaid frieze from the temple of Ninhursag at Ubaid showing the milking of a cow while the calf is tethered by the cow's head.

During the excavations of Ur the "Standard of Ur" was found in a grave, elaborately made of wood inlaid with shell and lapis lazuli and depicts a series of processions offering tribute to the king, in which cattle, sheep and goats are prominently represented (This was dated to about 2600 BC Fig 3.4) (Whitehouse, 1977). From archaeological findings the lyre would seem to be the most common musical instrument during the Sumer civilisation and most of these lyres had an ox head decoration (Fig 3.3) (Canby, 1980).

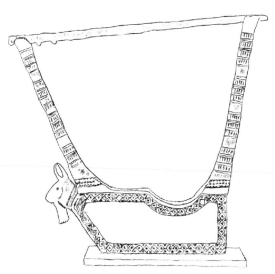

Fig 3.3 Drawing of a restored Sumerian lyre decorated with a bull's head. The original was discovered in the Royal Cemetery at Ur.

Trade between the cities and the various areas of that part of the world known to the people of these first civilisations, developed from the trading practices of the late Neolithic period. Trade was in finished goods such as pottery, ornaments, tools, etc., and raw materials such as precious stones, gold, silver, copper, timber, etc. There was also trade in slaves and livestock. Sea trade was carried out between the early civilisations of Crete (the Minoans), Syria and Egypt (Saggs, 1989). This was followed by the navigational achievements of those renowned sea traders, the Phoenicians, who even reached the British Isles as far back as 450 BC.

Fig 3.4 Line drawing of part of the 'Standard of Ur' which was made of wood inlaid with shell and lapis lazuli. It was from a royal grave at Ur *c* 2600 BC . This part depicts cattle, sheep, goats and fish as tribute or for a feast.

ANCIENT EGYPT

During the Predynastic period of Egypt, *c.* 6000 – 5000 years ago, the rainfall was much higher than in modern Egypt, resulting in the Nile valley having a more lush vegetation and supporting a wide range of animals. This included hippopotami, buffaloes and ostriches, which along with the gazelles, aurochs and a wealth of wild fowl provided the hunters with plenty of game (Fig 3.5). As the rainfall reduced there was a slow encroachment of the desert but the Nile valley remained fertile. The Predynastic period was the time of the Neolithic farmers (Johnson, 1978).

Fig 3.5 Drawing of two wild boars, part of a wild boar hunting scene depicted in a Sassanian rock relief. The Sassanian dynasty ruled Persia from 226 AD.

The beginning of civilisation in Egypt was somewhat later than Mesopotamia which had the Sumerian city states by 5500 years ago. In the case of Egypt it was the development into a nation state from *c*. 5100 years ago as opposed to separate city states (Johnson, 1978). Egypt was basically a totalitarian system, an autocracy with hierarchy of officials, administrators and priests controlling the mass of the population. The system was largely sustained by a strong religious structure based on the Pharaoh as a god-king and a strong conviction of an afterlife that was dependent on compliance with rules and laws of their society.

There seemed to be little scope for meat trading or free trading generally. Most of the craftsmen including the butchers were employed by the estates or temples and the produce from the estate or the estate farms went to fill the silos or store houses of the estate. The status of a craftsman depended on the status of the master of the estate although there was a hierarchy in the work place from apprentices, assistants, up to master craftsman, and supervisors.

Fig 3.6 Drawing of a wall painting from an 18th dynasty (*c*. 1550 - 1307 BC) tomb showing a herdsman bringing cattle for inspection by the owner. The scribe is on the left checking the numbers.

A common theme for the tomb paintings was the bounteous tributes or dues received from the estates (Fig 3.7, Fig 3.8). They show the royal or noble lord of the estate, usually seated, receiving the tributes brought in procession or arrayed around him. Red meat and fowls make up a large proportion of the items presented. Shoulders of an ox or cow are often shown along with the bodies of whole oxen. Beef buttock cuts, calves heads, geese and ducks feature frequently in these paintings. The paintings indicated the concentration of the wealth and produce being in the hands of the ruling classes.

TRAINING AND THE CRAFT OF THE BUTCHER

The butchers, particularly the top craftsmen, would have enjoyed a reasonable status among the Egyptian craftsmen, a factor borne out by their appearance in paintings and wall reliefs (Fig 3.12, Fig 3.13). The butchers of the temples who carried out the ritual slaughtering would have been highly skilled and would have had an important position in the temple.

Fig 3.7 Drawing of part of a section of wall paintings from the tomb of Kemsit (XI Dynasty *c* 2134 - 2010 BC) showing some of the products from the owner's estate. These include shoulders of beef, pieces of meat (probably beef) with the bone in, a calf's head and the head of a goose which probably represents numbers of geese reared on the estate.

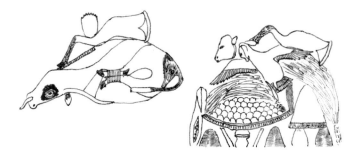

Fig 3.8 Part of the offerings for the posthumous benefit of the Vizir Mereruka which were represented in a line drawing on the wall of his burial chamber at Saqqara. (*c* 2320 BC) On the left is a slaughtered ox with one of its shoulders on top of its body and on the right is a stack of offerings including a calf's head, a shoulder of beef and a goose.

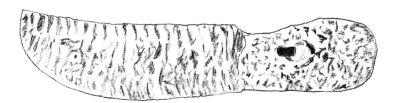

Fig 3.9 A flint knife from the Predynastic period discovered by General Pitt-Rivers at Sheikh Hamada near Sohag. The knife had an ivory handle and a finely serrated cutting edge.

Fig 3.10 An Egyptian metal butcher's knife.

Training had been an evolving process since the early hunter-gatherer groups largely based on the father teaching his son by example and guidance; an essentially hands-on process. This was very much the system in ancient Egypt except that the whole craft and industrial system had become very highly developed and specialisation had separated the artisans' activities within the craft. The butcher slaughtered and skinned the animals and the tanner prepared the skins and a variety of leather workers would convert the skins into a finished product. Part of a craftsman's training would have been the relationship with the associated crafts. There is a picture of a boy assistant handing the butcher a joint of meat. He was probably the butcher's son but there were occasions where the butcher had no sons and he would take on and train a boy from another family under a form of apprenticeship. Formal systems of training in the nature of apprenticeships became part of life in ancient Egypt (Strouhal, 1992).

In the early stages of the development of these civilisations butchers still had to rely on stone tools but these had been much improved, especially with the polishing and sharpening of the cutting edges. A knife found by Pitt-Rivers belonging to the Late Predynastic period had precise serrations along the cutting edge making it an extremely sharp cutting tool and predated the invention of the modern serrated knife by *c.* 5000 years (James, 1988) (Fig 3.9). The benefit of the developing metal technology providing them with metal knives helped them to develop even higher levels of craftsmanship. These knives would have been bronze until about 900 BC when the technology of iron smelting became more widespread. The degree of craftsmanship of the Egyptian butcher is shown in numerous paintings and other illustrations of butchers at work; also illustrations of joints of meat showing the end result of their work (Fig 3.10).

SLAUGHTERING ANIMALS IN ANCIENT EGYPT

A model of a slaughterhouse was found in the tomb of Meket-Rē'at Thebes, a landowner of the 11th dynasty, 2106 – 1963 BC. This is considered to be the model of the slaughterhouse of the Meket-Rē' estate. It consists of a large room with a high ceiling and the upper part of the front wall open for air circulation. The model shows the slaughterhouse at the height of its activity with two cattle being killed and their blood collected in bowls by the slaughterman's assistants. Two men carrying wooden sceptres denoting their status, supervised the activity. Blood was being cooked in two large containers resting on braziers which were attended by two men stoking and fanning the fires in the braziers. Sitting in one corner a man plucks the feathers from a goose or duck. On the balcony above the slaughtering area there are two lines on which cuts of beef were hung (Winlock, 1955). The air circulation around these cuts of meat would have caused some surface drying of the meat that would help it to keep longer in a reasonable condition (Fig 3.11).

It appears from the Meket-Rē' model and a number of wall paintings and reliefs, that the method of killing the cattle was by throwing the animal onto its side and tying its feet together so that it was immobilised. [This was practised in 18th century Britain to shoe oxen (Horne, 1810).] With the animal trussed in this way the head was pulled back and a cut made into the neck, as shown in the model, probably severing the carotid artery and jugular vein. Throwing and trussing the animal enabled the killing by bleeding only, with less danger to the butcher and fewer men needed to hold the animal (Fig 3.12, Fig 3.13). The practical alternative for killing cattle was to fell the beast with a blow to the head with the back of an axe or a poleaxe that instantly immobilised

Fig 3.11 Drawing of the model of an estate slaughterhouse found in the tomb of Meket-Rē'. On the left is a man plucking a goose or a duck and beyond him are two large pots in which the animal's blood is being boiled. The slaughtermen are cutting the throats of the cattle and their assistants are collecting the blood. Two men are supervising the operation. In the raised section at the rear of the slaughterhouse there are cuts of meat hanging up to allow the surface of the meat to dry, which would retard bacterial growth.

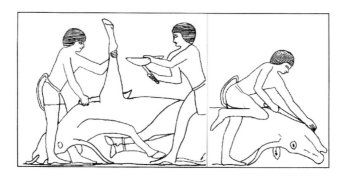

Fig 3.12: Drawing of sections of a wall relief from Sakkara now in the museum in Berlin. On the left is the depiction of a butcher removing the shoulder from an ox and moving towards him is another butcher probably sharpening his knife. On the right is a butcher either killing an ox or opening up the body.

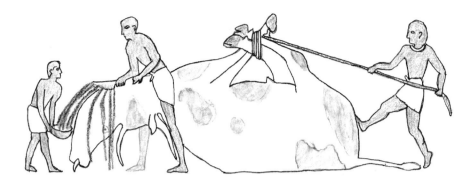

Fig 3.13: Drawing of a wall painting from the chapel of Ity, Geblein dated to the first intermediate period, *c* 2190 - 2010 BC. It shows the animal having been thrown and its feet tied to immobilise it to enable the slaughterman to kill the animal by cutting the major arteries in the neck (carotid arteries) and death ensuing as a result of bleeding.

the animal which was then bled. It would be reasonable to assume that during their time in Egypt the Hebrews would have adopted the Egyptian method of killing cattle; indeed throwing cattle was the way of carrying out ritual slaughter until the introduction of the casting pen in the 20th century. This method avoided a blow to the head; therefore no damage occurred to the skull and was consistent with what was written in the Talmud.

Sheep and goats were slaughtered by the complete severance of the head. The collection of blood at the time of slaughter was common; sometimes a physician was present to check if the blood 'smelled right'. The fresh blood was immediately boiled. After evisceration the entrails were washed and were taken for quick use. After skinning the hides and skins would go direct to the estate tanners and the butchers would cut the carcases into joints of meat (Strouhal, 1992).

An excavation in 1984 by a Czechoslovakian team uncovered a ritual slaughterhouse, the 'House of the Knife', near the temple of Raneferef at Abu Sir. The slaughtering area was in the open air where there were three limestone blocks used for tethering the animals. After the animals were slaughtered, eviscerated and skinned the carcases were taken to a nearby room containing a brick-walled chopping block on which the carcases were cut into joints for roasting at the site or drying for storage. A papyrus fragment from the Raneferef temple archive records 130 bulls being sacrificed in a ten-day period (Strouhal, 1992).

ANCIENT LARGE SCALE MEAT OPERATIONS

Apart from the large numbers of people living in the cities of the old civilisations there were also large armies going out on expeditions and vast numbers of workers employed on great building projects such as the temples and pyramids. This required a well organised structure to feed these people. At a stone quarry at Waddi Hammamat, Egypt, towards the end of the Old Kingdom in the third millennium BC, 100 stone masons, 2,200 labourers and guards were provided with 50 cattle and 200 goats each day for the supply of their meat. A team of butchers would have been employed to kill these animals, dress the carcases and prepare all the meat for cooking (Johnson, 1978).

MEAT CONSUMPTION IN ANCIENT EGYPT

There was considerable variety in the diet of the Egyptians as indicated by the paintings and the food placed in the tombs for the benefit of the dead during their journey to the next world. The food found in the tomb of a minor noble's wife at Saqqara [2nd Dynasty *c.* 2890 – 2686 BC] included cooked quail, two cooked kidneys, a pigeon stew, boiled fish, beef ribs, small loaves of wheat bread, cheese and jugs of beer or wine (Strouhal, 1992).

The upper classes in the early Egyptian society are reputed to have eaten large quantities of beef, which is borne out by the various paintings showing the large numbers of cattle or beef joints as the produce of an estate or in some cases presented as tribute. The priests and the temple officers enjoyed consuming the large quantities of beef from the regular sacrifices according to Herodotus the 4th century BC Greek historian (Wilkins *et al*, 1995). The other much favoured meat was the flesh of water fowls of which many came from the marshes of the Nile and the Nile Delta. These consisted of a large variety of ducks and geese along with pelicans, flamingos, cranes, herons, cormorants and ibises. A popular offering at the temple was a stuffed and roasted waterfowl (Johnson, 1978).

The common people had little meat except at feast times and then usually a sheep or goat slaughtered for a feast among friends. Pork was consumed in quantity in Lower Egypt in the Predynastic period (4000 – 3000BC) but not so in Upper Egypt. Reliefs show the domestic pigs in the early periods as thin, long-legged animals and having long snouts, typical of the Neolithic pig. The opposition to pork consumption in Upper Egypt extended to the people of Lower Egypt after the unification of the country although the embargo seemed not to apply to the working classes. There are records indicating the widespread breeding and rearing of pigs. The relief in a tomb at el-Kab shows the noble Renen inspecting his stock of 4500 pigs. In a workers' village south of Akhetaton the remains of animal enclosures were found with evidence that they were for the large scale breeding and rearing of pigs. There were whitewashed areas presumed to be for the butchering of the pig carcases after slaughter and scalding to remove the bristles. Domestic poultry and wild fowl; i.e. ducks, geese, cranes, quails, were another source of meat for the working class. Herodotus relates how ducks, quail and other small birds were sometimes prepared by pickling and then eaten raw (Fig 3.14). Dovecotes were a feature of Ancient Egypt to provide birds for the table. The birds kept were probably rock doves, the predecessor of the domestic pigeon (Strouhal, 1992).

There were large numbers of animals on many estates but it was mainly cattle that were depicted in the tomb paintings. Much care was taken over inspecting and recording the cattle. This work was carried out on a regular basis (James, 1985).

DIETARY LAWS

A number of the old civilisations of the Middle East had dietary laws that forbade eating the flesh of certain animals. The Egyptian dietary laws forbade the eating of pork and fish. In spite of these laws the working classes continued to eat pork as this was more readily available to them. It was the ruling classes and the priests and temple officials who complied with the dietary laws by not eating pork but enjoying large quantities of beef. Eating pork seemed to have been an element of class distinction.

Fig 3.14 Preparation of geese from a painting in a tomb in West Thebes.

The best known dietary laws of the ancient world are those of the Hebrews as contained in the book of Leviticus which were attributed to Moses who lived in the 13th century BC (approx.). Leviticus (11:v) specifies those animals that were 'clean' and could be eaten. Those animals specified as 'unclean' would render a person eating or even touching their flesh, as 'unclean' until the evening. The flesh of mammals with completely divided hooves and who chewed the cud, was 'clean' and allowed to be eaten. It was forbidden to eat the flesh of pigs as they did not chew the cud and camels because their hooves were not completely divided; likewise the flesh of horses or asses was forbidden as these animals did not have cloven hooves. Also forbidden was the flesh of the hare, the coney (rock rabbits or hyraxes) and fish that did not have scales. It has been suggested that the reason for excluding pigmeat from the diet was due to health hazards in a hot climate but this explanation cannot possibly apply to all the other animals excluded. According to Saggs the pigmeat taboo of the Israelites related to the fact that as nomadic herdsmen they lived by their grazing animals and were extremely antagonistic towards the settled farming Canaanites who relied heavily on the pig as a source of meat (Saggs, 1989). Another reason for the taboo may have been that the Israelites during their period of slavery in Egypt would probably have eaten pork along with their Egyptian counterparts, while their Egyptian masters ate beef. Pork eating may have had a stigmatic relationship to slavery. The eating of pork was forbidden by the Egyptian religious laws but only the ruling classes could afford to comply; they had beef as their main meat leaving pork for the lowest ranks of society.

Leviticus (17:v) forbade the eating of blood:

> "You must not eat the blood of any creature, because the life of every creature is in its blood; anyone who eats it must be cut off."

Deuteronomy (14:v) reiterates the flesh that may and may not be eaten and adds that it was forbidden to eat the flesh of "any thing that dieth of itself". The Hebrew laws (Leviticus 22:v) were more particular with regard to the animals that were offered for sacrifice at the temple in that they were sound in body and with no defects. The flesh of these animals was often consumed by the priests.

It is sometimes considered that these laws were aimed at protecting the health of the people but the probability is that they were more concerned with spiritual pollution than with bodily pollution. The present laws governing Shechita, Jewish ritual slaughter, are based on the Babylonian Talmud.

As well as the dietary laws of the ancient civilisations there were also laws to regulate trading practices. Laws of Ur-Nammu, who founded the Third Dynasty of Ur in about 2100 BC, included the setting up of standards for weights and measures. There were laws controlling the prices of certain goods and services in the Old Babylonian kingdom of Eshnunna (Saggs, 1989). Some Egyptian tomb paintings show types of beam balance scales in use.

THE SIGNIFICANCE OF DOMESTIC ANIMALS

The frequency that domestic animals appear in the paintings and statuary and the way they were represented indicates the appreciation by the people of these early civilisations of the importance of the animals to their society. This is also supported by the various texts that have been deciphered. Domestic animals, especially cattle, featured significantly in their religions. There was an Apis bull which was believed to be the incarnation of the god Ptah and was kept in palatial quarters at Memphis. When an Apis bull died it was given a regal burial at Saqqara and its successor was specially chosen by the priests according to its body marking (James, 1988).

The meat animals played an important part in providing food but in the case of feasting on animals slaughtered as part of a sacrifice or other religious activity, eating the flesh could have been regarded as absorbing spiritual power rather than satisfying the appetite (Strouhal, 1992).

Apart from meat the animals provided the many products that were fundamental to the way of life in these early societies. Wool and skins were used for clothing and soft furnishings. Leather had a multitude of uses in the trades and industries in the form of leather straps, harnesses, plaited leather ropes, armour, containers, pouches and many other manufactures including clothing and footwear. Horn and bone was used for tools, combs, ornaments and jewellery. Animal fat was a basis for cosmetics (as it is still used today). In Ancient Egypt oils and fats were perfumed for various cosmetic purposes including cones of perfumed fat placed on the heads of highborn ladies at banquets so that the fat would slowly melt into the hair. A treatment for greying hair was the blood of a black cow boiled in oil. The Egyptians used unguents made from fat or oil to rub into the skin to keep it soft and supple. Animal products such as blood, milk, bile, urine and fat were used in a number of medical preparations and fat was often the main ingredient for ointments. The Egyptian language distinguished animal fat as *adj* and vegetable fat as *merhet* (*Ibid*). Animal fat was valuable for greasing the wheels of carts and the machines, illumination by way of candles and for dressing leather.

An important contribution by domestic animals to the early civilisation was power; the power for ploughing, transport and numerous industrial activities such as raising water, threshing and milling corn (Hodges, 1970). Peter Reynolds found his Dexter cows were capable of pulling carts or sledges with weights three times their body weight (Noddle, 1989). On this basis a pair of yoked oxen in ancient Egypt would have been capable of pulling weights of over 2000kg on sledges (sledges were a common means of moving heavy loads in ancient Egypt).

THE FIRST COOKERY GUIDE

The earliest known recipes were three cuneiform tablets probably about 1600 BC from Mesopotamia. The first tablet contains 25 recipes of which 21 were meat based. There was a meat bouillon, lamb bouillon and a bouillon of pigeon, all of which were flavoured with garlic, leaks, and a variety of herbs and spices. The second tablet only had seven recipes, all for poultry, each with considerable detail of the preparation and cooking. These tablets support other evidence that these early civilisations had established advanced and sophisticated standards of meal preparation, use of herbs and spices and the optimum way of cooking the dishes. The privileged upper classes were able to enjoy very rich and flavourful meals (Wilkins *et al,* 1995).

FOOD FOR SUSTENANCE OR ENJOYMENT

The basic requirement for food to sustain life was always a fundamental need of the working classes and particularly the slaves. Eating for pleasure among the upper classes was a clear attribute of civilised society. Even as far as sacrifices were concerned the meat was usually of the best, even if it was purely the prerogative of the priests to eat the meat. Banquets were a regular feature of life for the aristocratic rulers and the high officials which may explain the corpulence of many of the top people as depicted in the paintings. Even the lower classes would have their occasional feast, mostly religious feasts.

For the main dishes at a feast there was a preponderance of meat and poultry and poultry dishes with, in some cases, whole animals being roasted. It seems to be part of human nature to eat large quantities of meat when it was available, particularly roasted meat. This fact has always acted as a stimulus to the meat trade and to the status of the butcher.

BRONZE AGE BRITAIN

At the time of these civilisations developing in the Middle and Far East, communities in Britain were still somewhat small and localised with the Neolithic herding and farming systems still in place. A significant change was the arrival of the Beaker People in about 2000 BC who introduced copper working and the use of the alloy of copper and tin or bronze. Bronze is much harder than pure copper therefore producing much more durable tools. Evidence indicates the Beaker People originating in the Iberian Peninsula and migrating to many parts of Europe. They were probably traders throughout Europe (Collins, 1975).

There was a decline in the forests and an increase in the grasslands along with sheep numbers becoming much more predominant in respect of the livestock of the country (Evans, 1975). The Bronze Age is considered a period during which pastoral farming predominated with the herders in many parts of the country droving their animals to the uplands for the summer grazing and returning them to enclosed lowland areas for the winter (Trow-Smith, 1957). It would have been much more practical to graze sheep on the uplands because they have much less need for the regular availability of water than cattle. This is due to the sheep's greater physiological efficiency in conserving water and their adaptability to irregular intakes of water; in fact sheep grazing fresh grass obtain enough moisture from the grass for their needs (Houpt, 1970).

The development of an economy based more on the wider exploitation of animal products is more in evidence for the Bronze Age. Spindle whorls, weaving combs and other indications of utilising wool as cloth were found at the Bronze Age sites at Eldon's Seat, Dorset and Deverel–Rimsbury (Davis, 1987).

Archaeological evidence indicates the presence from the early Bronze Age of a strain of cattle with narrow heads and short horns, referred to as Celtic Shorthorns (similar to Jersey cattle). Animals with skulls of this type were described as *Bos longifrons* by Owen (1846) which although indicating a separate species was in fact a strain of *Bos taurus*, domestic cattle (Clutton-Brock, 1989). The Celtic Shorthorns (*Bos longifrons* also referred to as *Bos brachyceros*) are considered to be the progenitors of the Welsh Blacks and the Kerry cattle of Ireland (Reynolds, 1979).

According to the bones from Bronze Age sites the pigs were rangy and relatively long-limbed which corresponded to an animal with considerable speed and agility (Noddle, 1997). An experimental crossing of the European wild boar with a Tamworth pig at the Butser experimental farm produced offspring that were difficult to contain and had the speed to outrun a dog (Reynolds, 1979).

IRON AGE BRITAIN

The earliest iron technology was used by the Hittites before 1500 BC. The first iron working in Britain was *c.* 650 BC (Cunliffe, 1974). Iron ore was more easily obtainable than copper and tin ore, resulting in iron products being more readily available than bronze products (Merriman, 1990). Iron technology provided improved tools for the farmers and craftsmen including better and more durable knives, choppers and cleavers for the butcher. A good craftsman reaches the peak of proficiency with the right tools.

Metal technology also resulted in better facilities for cooking, such as metal pots and cauldrons which could be placed directly over the flames for stewing the food. The Belgae came to Britain and among a number of iron objects they introduced there were tripods with chains and hooks to suspend the cauldrons above the flames. There were iron firedogs which were placed on the hearth to support logs as they burned (Fig 3.15). These firedogs had uprights at each end with prongs, often in the form of the horns on animal heads, to support the metal spits. Stewing meat became a more common way of cooking meat and for serving, it was taken from the simmering cauldron using a flesh-hook (Fig 3.16) (Wilson, 1973).

There was a marked development in the social structure of the Celtic speaking people across Europe developing *c.* 200 BC with the emergence of a horse riding warrior aristocracy. This gave rise to a distinct social stratification; at the top were the chieftains and their courts which included a whole range of craftsmen; also at a high level were druids, bards and seers. Then came the unfree tenant farmers and at the bottom strata were the slaves who worked on the farmsteads. Many of the slaves were the spoils of war and raiding. With craftsmen being part of the court it was an impetus for the broadening of crafts and an improvement of skills (Merriman, 1990). There was the practice of placing food in the tombs to sustain the dead on their journey to the next world. Victims of the Roman assault on Maiden Castle, AD 47, had legs of mutton interred with them while in the Belgic tombs at Hertfordshire the meat was pork (Wilson, 1973). There is a considerable

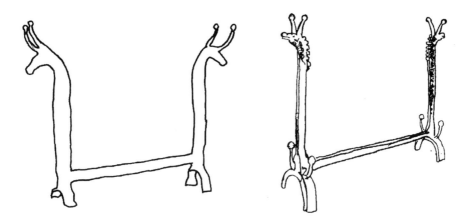

Fig 3.15 Drawing of Iron Age firedogs; the one on the left was found at Lord's Bridge, Cambridgeshire and the more decorated one on the right was from Welwyn, Hertfordshire. Firewood was supported by the cross bar which gave a draught to the burning wood and meat on a spit could be held by the horns of the animal heads decorating the firedogs.

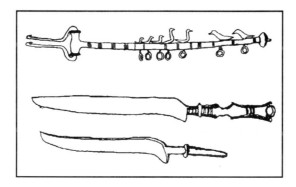

Fig 3.16 The top drawing is of what is considered to be a flesh-hook from the late Bronze Age discovered at Dunaverney, County Antrim. Flesh-hooks, far less elaborate, featured throughout the Medieval period and were used to pull meat out of the boiling stew pot or cauldron. Below are two examples of Bronze Age knives (originals in the British Museum).

body of evidence for the ritual slaughter of animals. In many cases whole animals were killed and buried whole but equally large numbers were slaughtered as part of a ritual and the meat consumed by the people (Noddle, 1989).

Food production increased during the Iron Age partly due to the iron ploughshares which were not only more efficient, ploughing deeper, but also enabled the heavy clay soils to be ploughed. The widespread introduction of cereals was a boost to agricultural productivity and was to pave the way for Britain being a major supplier of corn in the Roman Empire. The general increase in food supplies led to an increase in the population in the later Iron Age.

There was a growth in urbanisation with an expansion of the towns and the establishment of oppida or fortified towns e.g. Camulodium, Hengistbury Head, Calleva (Cunliffe, 1974). These were the centres for trade and served as market towns. The hill forts such as Maiden Castle,

Dorset, and Walbury, Berks, were large fortified towns with an urban population and a market centre. Apart from local trading there was a marked development in trading with Europe, particularly Gaul and the Rhineland (Merriman, 1990).

The movement of goods and chattels was not only through trading but also the result of raiding which occurred frequently between the tribes. Cattle were an obvious target for raiders as they were not only very valuable but were also mobile. Cattle raiding could have been a way of life in the Iron Age as in later years in the Scottish border country.

The first appearance of coinage in Britain was *c.* 200 BC consisting of gold coins which were brought in from Gaul or Belgica so would not indicate a money economy. It was not until after 100 BC that there is evidence for coins being minted in Britain (Merriman, 1990). Apart from gold and silver coins, potin (a form of bronze) coins were also produced which had a lower value. Money would have started to feature in trading although bartering would still have predominated in the day-to-day transactions.

Common among the artefacts from Iron Age sites were loom weights, spindle whorls and bone weaving combs, indicating an active woollen industry which would have been supported by large numbers of sheep. Collective evidence indicates that cattle would have been the main source of meat with significant amounts of mutton and pork also being eaten. The size of domestic animals showed a marked reduction by the Iron Age according to the measurements of bones from Iron Age bone assemblages. The average height at the withers (shoulders) for Iron Age cattle was 1.1m compared with Neolithic cattle 1.25m and the aurochs at 1.57m for bulls and 1.47 for cows. (Davis, 1987). The Neolithic cattle of Orkney were much larger than those of Southern Britain (Noddle, 1989).

Salt was already established as an important adjunct to the meat industry for its use in meat preservation. Sprinkling salt on the meat side of fresh hides and skins is an ancient practice which may have occurred at this time. There is evidence for the existence of salt pans in the coastal areas. These were shallow clay lined depressions that were filled with seawater and natural evaporation left behind the sea salt. There were some Iron Age bowls from Dorset which were used as salt containers (Cunliffe, 1974). Extraction of salt from the brine springs of Cheshire and Worcestershire is considered to have been exploited as a primary source of salt in the Iron Age.

Chapter 4

Ancient Greece and the Roman Empire

NEOLITHIC FARMING IN GREECE AND ITALY

Neolithic farming and the herding of livestock began in Greece and Italy from *c.* 8000 years ago (see chapter 2). The sheep and goats would have been imported from the Middle East as there is no evidence of their wild predecessors existing in Greece and Italy. Wild cattle (aurochs) and wild boar were a different matter as they did exist throughout Europe in the post glacial period so they could have been domesticated locally. There is evidence of farming communities in Italy on the Tavoliere Plain about 7000 years ago and in Greece on the Macedonian and Thessalian plains about 7500 years ago (Fig 4.1). The main livestock for these communities were sheep and goats (Smith, 1994).

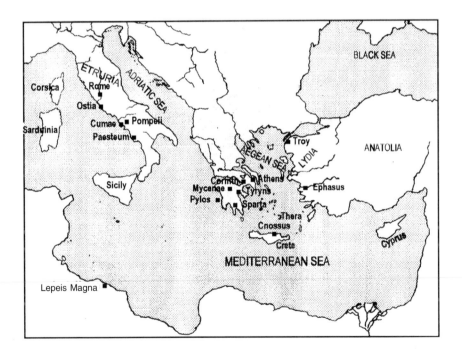

Fig 4.1 A map of the Mediterranean showing the towns and other sites referred to in the text.

THE GREEK CITY STATES

The earliest record of civilisation in Greece was Mycenaean communities from about 3000 BC, which flourished as palace societies, to about 1600 BC at Mycenae, Tyryns, Lerna and Pylos on the mainland and the Minoan culture at Cnossos, Mallia and Phaistos on Crete. The volcanic explosion of the island of Thera, which by latest estimates is put at 1626 BC, buried a Minoan town on the island now known as Santorini and was originally thought to have destroyed the Minoan settlements on Crete but this is now considered to have been the result of a Mycenaean invasion. The Dorians from Northern Greece made a series of incursions from *c.* 1200 BC and destroyed much of the Mycenaean civilisation. After about four centuries of the 'Dark Age' there emerged a society based on the *polis*, a central city ruling over the surrounding countryside. Initially it were dominated by a hereditary aristocracy but from *c.* 500 BC democracy became the system of government giving every man (not women) a vote. The dominant city states emerged as Athens and Sparta. The *polis* gave rise to the market place (Agora) becoming the political arena as well as the place for trade (Stobart, 1964). This dual function of the market place and the centre for meetings and administration was adopted by the Romans as the Forum which was the centre point of the Roman towns and cities.

The Ancient Greeks became highly successful maritime merchants trading with Egypt and the other Near Eastern countries bordering the Mediterranean. They also migrated to many places around the Mediterranean establishing communities in Cyprus, Anatolia and Italy at Paestum and Sicily before the rise of Rome. The Ancient Greeks absorbed much of the art and technology developed in Egypt and the other Near Eastern societies (Saggs, 1989).

THE GREEK MARKETS (AGORA)

The establishment and growth of the urban populations gave rise to the natural development for an area in the town to become the place for trading, hence the market. Farmers from the surrounding countryside brought their produce to the market place to trade with the inhabitants of the town. The original trading was based on bartering but as the volume of trading increased bartering became less and less adequate as a means of trading. Metals, especially gold and silver, were found to be useful as a medium of exchange because of their physical durability as well as their stability of value. In the law codes of Ur-Nammu (2112-2095 BC), the King of Ur prescribed fines of one mina of silver for some offences and half a mina of silver for other offences (*Ibid*). The first use of coinage was attributed to Lydia in Asia Minor in the 7th century BC and was then widely adopted by the Greeks (Wedgwood, 1984). The civilisations of Mesopotamia and Egypt were largely autocratic systems with the kings and lords of the estates or the temples controlling the produce, even the manufactured products, as the estates and temples employed the craft workers, who in many cases were slaves. The same situation pertained for the early Greek palace societies. With the development of the *polis* commercial activities expanded and became more diverse among the different levels of the community, which was facilitated by the introduction of coinage. The expansion of trade stimulated the widespread use of coinage.

The Greek Agora, the centre of the city for administration purposes and for meetings, was a place where proclamations were made and a place for social gatherings as well as a place for trading. The Agora was a major part of ancient Greek cities both in Greece, Asia Minor and other areas of Greek influence (Fig 4.2). The Agora in Athens was probably established in the early days of the city which began in the 9th century BC. There were a number of different facilities from which the commercial activities were conducted. Craft workshops were part of some of the houses in the Agora and there were covered colonnades (stoa) which lined the sides of the Agora (Fig 4.3). There were the rings (kykloi) for the display and sale of meat, fish and a variety of other products; it was also the place where slaves were displayed. The kykloi were defined spaces in the Agora and may have been raised platforms. There were also tables that were used by the bankers (Webster, 1969). Xenophon wrote in about 360 BC "any servant you tell to go and buy something for you in the Agora will have no difficulty: he will certainly know where to go and find such things. The reason is that each is in its appointed place." (*Ibid*) It is clear that traders selling the same type of goods or produce established themselves in the same place. (There were indications from the earlier civilisations of sellers of like goods trading in the same part of the market or town.)

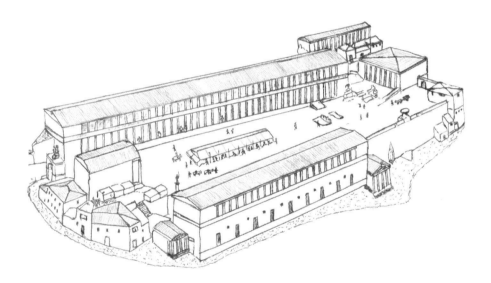

Fig 4.2 A line drawing of an impression of a Greek Agora (market place). The sides are lined with *stoa* (covered colonnaded) shopping areas. To the right is the *bouleuterion* (assembly hall) and to the left is a temple. Traders would also set up stalls and sell their wares in the open area within the agora.

Ten *Metronomoi* were appointed each year for the Athens Agora who were the controllers of the weights and measures. Sets of standard weights and measures have been recovered by archaeologists. There was also the appointment of ten *Agoranomoi* (market officials) who inspected the produce offered for sale to ensure it was up to standard (*Ibid*). The Athens Agora like many others included temples, administration and records offices and was a place where the process of law was carried out and plays and other entertainments were presented; features that became a standard aspect of the marketplaces throughout the medieval period.

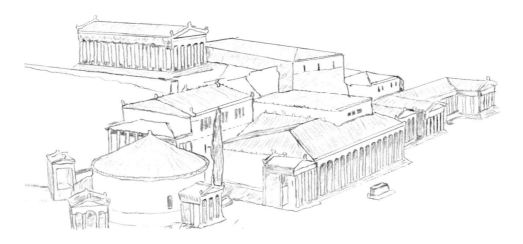

Fig 4.3 Drawing of the reconstruction of the Athens Agora with the temple on the high ground overlooking the agora.

MEAT CONSUMPTION IN ANCIENT GREECE

It is not clear as to the relative level of meat consumption in Ancient Greece and it is probable that there was less meat available to the Greeks than was later consumed by the Romans. What is clear is the high ritual significance associated with eating meat. Domestic animals for slaughter were sacrificed to the gods and the diners would eat the meat in the context of sharing the sacrificial flesh with the gods (Wilkins *et al*, 1995). The sacrificial slaughter of the animals was carried out by the *Mageiroi* who were the butchers cum meat chefs and carvers. The *Mageiroi* would slaughter the animal, butcher it, cook the meat and then carve and serve it to the diners (Wilkins & Hill, 1994).

Apart from religious festivals the holding of banquets for weddings or other celebrations would warrant engaging a *Mageiros* to sacrifice animals for the occasion. The *Mageiroi* were very proud of their skills and often boasted of their prowess as a carver (Webster, 1969). The animals for sacrificial slaughter were domestic animals, cattle, sheep or goats; wild mammals, fish and birds did not come into the category of sacrificial animals (Wilkins *et al*, 1995). All things to do with red meat, the slaughtering, butchering, cooking, serving and even to a certain extent the eating, were the province of men; women were not involved. Dinners and banquets for men only were the rule rather than the exception and the women joined together for their own feasting. As far as the men's banquets were concerned young women entertainers were often present.

From various accounts it would seem that fish played a predominant part in the diet of the Ancient Greeks, not least according to Achestratus, a Sicilian Greek whose poem from *c*. 330 BC related in prose much about Greek dining. Much of the poem consisted of recipes which were predominantly fish dishes with meat represented by one recipe for hare, one for goose and one for sow's womb (uterus) which was an after dinner relish.

THE HOMERIC ACCOUNTS OF FEASTING

The epics, *The Iliad* and *The Odyssey*, were told by Homer in the 8ᵗʰ century BC and are set in the period of the Trojan wars in the 13th century BC. The descriptions of meat preparation and eating probably relate more to the practices in Homer's time than the period of the Trojan wars.

Homer writes in *The Iliad* that when Aias and Odysseus, envoys of King Agamemnon, arrived at a meeting with Achilles and Patroclos (*Iliad* Book IX):

> "Patroclos was busy at once. He set a meat block by the fire and put on it a shoulder of mutton with another of goat, and the chine of a fine fat hog. Automedon held the meat and Achilles carved when it was cut up and spitted. Patroclos made a good fire and when the flame had died down, he scattered the ashes and laid the spits over them on the fire dogs, sprinkling the grill with salt. Soon all was done brown and set on platters; Patroclos handed round baskets of bread, and Achilles served the meat."

A good description of the preparation and method of cooking meat which would seem to be an early form of kebab. From description of the meal it must have been predominantly meat.

Pigs were a major source of meat according to *The Odyssey*; the following are two excerpts from Book XIV:

> "The swineherd broke off, hitched up his tunic in his belt, and went out to the sties where the young porkers were penned in batches. He selected two, and carried them in and slaughtered them both. Next he singed them, chopped them up and skewered the meat. When he had roasted it all, he served it up piping hot on the spits, set it in front of Odysseus and sprinkled it with white barley meal."

The swineherd apologised for the meal being only young porkers, fatted hogs would have been more acceptable. At a later stage in the epic the swineherd called to his men:

> "Bring in the best of your hogs, I want to slaughter it for a guest I have from abroad" (Odysseus)
> "He (the swineherd) then chopped some firewood with his sharp axe, while his men dragged in a fatted five-year-old hog and brought it to the hearth. The swineherd, who was a man of sound principles, did not forget the immortals, but began the ritual by throwing a tuft of hair from the white-tusked victim into the fire and praying to all the gods that the wise Odysseus might come back to his home. Then he drew himself up and struck the animal with a billet of oak which he had left unsplit. The hog fell dead. They slit its throat, singed its bristles, and deftly cut the carcase up. The swineherd took a first cut from all the limbs, laid the raw flesh on the rich fat, cast the whole into the flames and sprinkled barley meal on top. Then they chopped up the rest of the meat, pierced it with skewers, roasted it thoroughly, and after drawing it off the spits heaped it up on platters. And now the swineherd….. distributed to the to the company. But he paid Odysseus the honour of helping him to the tusker's long chine."

In Book III of *The Odyssey*, it relates how Nestor the Gerenian charioteer sacrifices a heifer to Athene in honour of Prince Telemachus:

"A goldsmith was employed to embellish the heifer by covering its horns in gold foil. Next Stratius and Echephron led the heifer forward by the horns, and Aretus came out from the storeroom carrying in his right hand a flowered bowl of lustral water for their use, and in the other a basket with the barleycorns, while the stalwart Thrasymedes, gripping a sharp axe, stood by to cut the victim down, and Perseus held the dish to catch its blood. The old charioteer Nestor now started the ritual with the lustral water and the scattered grain, and offered up his earnest prayers to Athene as he began the sacrifice by throwing a lock from the victim's head on the fire. When they had made their petitions and sprinkled the barleycorns, Nestor's son Thrasymedes stepped up and struck. The axe cut through the tendons of the heifer's neck and she collapsed… The men lifted the heifer's head from the trodden earth and held it up while the captain Peisistratus cut its throat. When the dark blood had gushed out and life had left the heifer's bones, they swiftly dismembered the carcase, cut slices off the thighs in ceremonial fashion, wrapped them in folds of fat and laid the raw meat above them. These pieces the venerable king burnt on the faggots, while he sprinkled red wine on the flames, and the young men gathered round with five pronged forks in their hands. When the thighs were burnt up and they had tasted the inner parts, they carved the rest into small pieces, pierced them with a skewer and held the sharp ends of the spits to the fire until all was roasted."

The collapse of the heifer could be explained by the axe partially cutting through the cervical vertebrae and severing the spinal cord which would paralyse the animal. This was the same effect as produced by a practice in the 18th and early 19th centuries called pithing which entailed passing a thin bladed knife between the occipital bone and the 1st cervical vertebra to sever the spinal cord. The ritual and the slaughter required a number of people, each to carry out a particular function. The cooking and consumption of an animal's flesh immediately after slaughter would mean that it was pre-rigor mortis and therefore more tender.

It was noted in *The Odyssey* that the best parts of the animal which were given to guests of honour were the beef sirloin and the pork chine.

THE ROMAN EMPIRE

Rome began its development on the hills overlooking the river Tiber in the 7th century BC. In the early days it was under the occupation of the Etruscans who brought to Rome some of the techniques for the development of the city, building roads, paving the forum and erecting buildings (Wedgwood, 1984). The Etruscans were defeated by the Greeks at Cumae and withdrew from Rome *c.* 509 BC. After the Etruscans left the Romans continued the development of their city and expanded their boundaries (Stobart, 1964). The Celtic Gauls invaded the Italian Peninsular and sacked Rome in 390 BC from which the Romans recovered and went on to dominate the countries of the Mediterranean and by the 1st century BC established the Roman Empire (Grant, 1978). The success of the Roman army under Julius Caesar in the Gallic wars extended the Roman Empire to the English Channel (Stobart, 1964). Apart from the incursions into Britain by Julius Caesar in 55 and 54 BC it was not until AD 43 that Emperor Claudius ordered the invasion of Britain and the Roman legions commanded by Aulus Plautius landed at Richborough on the Kentish coast (Burke, 1978).

Romanisation of the Empire resulted in the introduction of the villa estates, increased urbanisation and the building of roads to connect the towns throughout the Empire. Although this was essential to support and supply the Roman army it also resulted in an expansion of trade with a trading network throughout the Empire.

VILLA ESTATES

The success of the Roman Empire relied on a thriving economy that would feed and equip its armies, maintain its towns and cities and support its complex infrastructure. The system of Roman villas, which were well organised and managed as profitable entities, formed the basis of the Roman economy (Percival, 1986).

The villa estates were agricultural based estates similar to the mediaeval manorial estates. In addition to the villa buildings on the large estates providing the wealthy owners with luxury living accommodation, the buildings were the management centre for the estate. Villa estates provided the towns with food and a range of other products and were strategically important for the supply of food to the army garrisons. Villas also produced surpluses which were traded with other parts of the Empire. In Britain the villas' main exportable surpluses were grain and wool for which there was a ready demand in the Empire (Burke, 1978).

The large villas had a workforce with their families, amounting to a community of several hundred people. At the other end of the scale the villa consisted of a modest farm run by the farmer and a small number of workers. As the towns were essential for channelling surplus produce and thereby increasing the owner's wealth it was important for the villa to have a good connection by road to the town (*ibid*).

THE ROMAN MARKET PLACE OR FORUM.

The low-lying area close to the River Tiber was drained and became the first market place in Rome; the Forum Boarium (cattle market) (Grant, 1978). Forum is Latin for 'market place' or 'open place' and the Roman Forum was very much in the style of the Greek Agora used not only for trading but also as the meeting place, political centre, administration centre and also the place of law courts and temples. Over time the Forum developed with covered colonnades and shops built along the sides of the open space and with the addition of covered markets (*macella*) (Fig 4.4). As some cities grew, separate Forums (*civilium*) were built for administrative and legal affairs and there was often a number of trading Forums (*venalia*), each dedicated to a different group of commodities (*Ibid*).

The Forum Romanum Magnum of Rome was the most notable but many large and impressive Forums were built throughout the Roman Empire including *Londinium*. There was a large market built at Lepcis Magna in North Africa during the time of Augustus (8 BC). A large Forum has been excavated at Augst in Switzerland (Fig 4.5). When the Romans took over Corinth in Greece and Ephesus in Asia Minor they carried out reconstruction and further building to the very prominent Greek Agoras in those places (Liversidge, 1976).

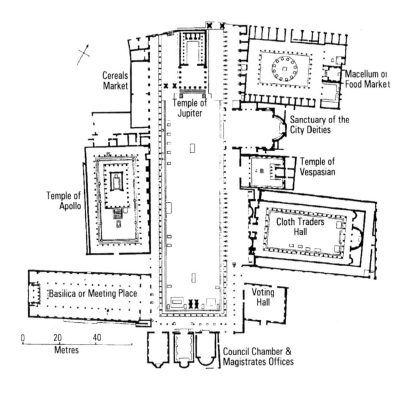

Fig 4.4 Plan of the Forum at Pompeii prior to its destruction by the eruption of Mount Vesuvius in 79AD.

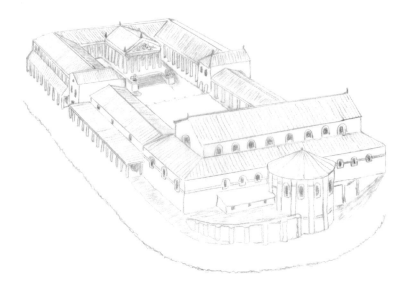

Fig 4.5 A reconstruction of the Forum at Augst, Switzerland.

Many of the Roman towns in Britain owed their original planning to military architects which influenced the type of Forum (Wacher, 1974). The Forum usually occupied a central position in the town which was a large open court with a basilica (town hall) at one side and covered colonnades on the other sides. Opening onto these covered colonnades were a series of rooms used as offices or shops. The Forum was the major concentration of trading for the town and the surrounding area. If the surrounding area was a rich agricultural area or had other thriving industries, the commercial activity of the town would develop and the town expand, becoming prosperous. Towns needed the surrounding agriculture to supply food and other products for their urban population and in return the farming community could obtain manufactured goods from the artisans who had set up workshops in the towns. A major benefit for the farmers was a market for their surplus produce. The town was the centre for the collective protection for the area and the centre for administration as well as being the point of contact with Rome and the rest of the Empire. The towns of the Roman Empire formed a trading network linking all parts of the Empire with Rome at its centre.

The Forum in London in the early Roman period was of moderate size but was replaced by much larger Basilica and Forum as London grew in size and status. The whole complex of Forum and Basilica extended to an estimated 3.2 ha (8 acres) covering an area either side of the present Grace Church Street between Cornhill and Lombard Street. The Bacilica was a very large building, the largest in Romano-Britain, 167 m (548 ft) long and 52.5 m (172 ft) wide and consisted of a large hall and some separate rooms. The Basilica was on the north side of the Forum with three wings on the other sides of the open courtyard of the Forum. The wings on the east and west of the Forum were 85 m (279 ft) and the south wing was 167m (548 ft) with porticoes or colonnades along each side facing into the courtyard and the roads bounding the Forum (Marsden, 1987). These wings contained the shops where the inhabitants of *Londinium* could buy their meat, bread and other food, including a wide variety of other goods. This was an extensive shopping precinct by any standard (Fig 4.6).

Remains of Fora have been found at Caerwent, Chichester, Cirencester, Colchester, Gloucester, Leicester, Silchester, Verulamium (near St Albans), Winchester, Wroxeter and York. A market hall or *macellum* was part of a town's commercial facilities where traders could rent space to display and sell their wares (Wacher, 1974). Remains of *macella* have been found in Verulamium, Cirencester and Leicester.

SHOPS IN THE ROMAN EMPIRE

From an early stage in the development of Rome, shops became a common feature both in Rome and in the towns of the Roman Empire. The Roman shops were in many cases narrow with the front opening onto the street or the portico of the Forum with living accommodation at the back or above. The front of the shop had shutters to close it in at night (*Ibid*). One piece of research catalogued 600 shops in Pompeii (Wallace-Hadrill, 1994).

Some of these shops were butchers' shops, recognisable as such today. An example can be seen in a bas-relief in the Dresden Museum. This shows the butcher chopping a piece of meat on a three-legged block using a chopper that is not dissimilar to the present day choppers. Various cuts and offals, including a pig's head, are shown hanging from hooks or spikes along the top of

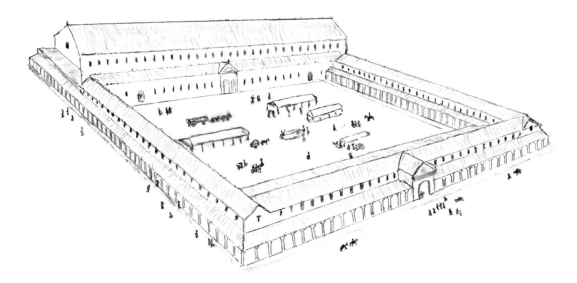

Fig 4.6 Drawing of a reconstruction of the *Londinium Forum* which covered 3.2 hectares (8 acres). The basilica runs along the whole width of the forum in the top part of the drawing and porticoes (covered colonnades) were along the other three sides facing into the forum and backing these were even longer porticoes facing onto the adjacent streets (Marsden, 1987).

the shop. A scale can be seen hanging from the upright at the side of the shop (Fig 4.7). A stone relief from Dijon in France shows a wine shop and part of a butcher's shop next door. There are what appear to be sausages hanging in the shop and meat lying on the counter. There is another relief from a tomb of a butcher showing the butcher chopping a pig's head on a block. Hanging from the hooks or spikes in a cross beam above the butcher's head is another pig's head, half a leg, a pig's (probably a sow's) udder and next to it what could be a pluck (trachea, lungs and liver). Someone has carved "To Marcius always drunk" on the relief which maybe why the butcher in this relief looks more agitated than the one in the Dresden Museum relief (Fig 4.8) (Grant, 1986). The Latin term *laniare* means to cut up meat and it is from this that the term *lanius* for butcher and slaughterer comes. A butcher's shop was a *laniena* and was also the slaughterhouse. *Laniena* used for slaughtering would generally be situated on the outskirts of the town along with the tanneries, where such trades were relegated, enabling the hides and skins to go straight from the slaughterman to the tanner. The retail butcher who traded in the shops in town or in the *macellum* (market) was the *macellarius* (Frayn, 1995). Whether the *macellarius* conveyed the meat from the slaughterhouse as carcases or smaller cuts is not clear but there was probably a mix of cuts and carcases.

The type of scale used for weighing in common use in the Roman Empire was the same design as a steelyard although the name steelyard originates from the 15th/16th century taken from the Hanseatic League's premises in London called the Steel Yard or Stiliard. The term Roman balance was used for the scale in numerous documents reflecting the earlier origins of the scale. The movable weights used for this type of scale were often very elaborate, such as a bronze head. A number of such scales were found during excavations at Pompeii (Brion, 1976) and elsewhere, including Britain. A scale from the Silchester excavations was the combination of a balance and steelyard having one pan for the product to be weighed and another pan for the weight and there

Fig 4.7 Drawing of a carved bas-relief from the tomb of a butcher, which is now in the Dresden Museum.
On the right is a set of Roman balances and cuts of meat are held by the spikes projecting from the cross beam. From the left these cuts would appear to be a pig's head, pluck (trachea, lungs, heart and liver), hand and belly of pork, possibly a knuckle bone, leg of pork and the rib end of a loin of pork. The three-legged block was a very practical design which would remain in use another 1600 - 1700 years.

Fig 4.8 Drawing of another relief from a butcher's tomb showing the butcher chopping a pig's head. The meat cuts hanging from the spikes in the cross beam from the left are a pig's head, leg of pork, sow's udder, what may be half a side of pork including the leg and on the right, a pluck.

was a sliding weight on the beam to gauge the extra weight of the product over the weight in the pan. Another scale from Silchester was the steelyard principle but it had three separate hooks from which to suspend the product, each hook at a different distance from the fulcrum of the scale to give a wider range of the product weights (Quennell, 1959). Similar scales are widely used today in the markets in the East and are operated by meat being placed in the scoop, the scale held up by one hand and the weight moved by the other.

There is evidence of butchers' shops and meat markets having existed in all parts of the Roman Empire. At Aquincum (Budapest) there was a meat market with shops on three sides. The Greek city of Corinth began to be transformed into a Roman city in the 1st century AD resulting in alterations to the Greek Agora (market place) with shops on both sides having rooms behind and above. By the 2nd century AD Corinth had become the administrative capital of Greece and the council and administrative offices were situated with the shops on the south side of the Agora. In the centre of the Agora was a dais where the Governor or other officials addressed the people. Whereas in many parts of the Roman Empire shops were associated with houses, the shops in the Agora in Corinth followed the Greek tradition of being separate and in neat rows. In Ephesus, where the great temple of Artemis stood, the Greeks had built an Agora and under the later Roman occupation the Agora was in a substantial building. Lepcis Magna (Libya) had a large market building in the 1st century consisting of colonnades along each side and two kiosks for the officials in the centre around which traders set up their stalls. Under the Emperor Septimius Severous who was born in Lepcis Magna, there was extensive redevelopment, including a market hall with stone counters, that can still be seen (Liversidge, 1976).

In many towns in the Roman Empire there were large houses with a row of shops along one side of the building. The 2nd century BC House of Sallust in Pompeii had a row of shops facing the road with the entrance to the house between the shops (Fig 4.9) (Brion, 1976). There was even a butcher's shop in the front part of the house of the noble Roman Scipio Africanus (the general who defeated Hannibal and conquered Carthage). Many houses along the important thoroughfare in Rome, the Via Sacra, had shops built into their frontages, a practice that may have begun as early as the 6th century BC (Wallace-Hadrill, 1994). There was a building of this type in the town of Vaison, east of Orange in the South of France. The shops, which formed one side of the building, opened onto a colonnaded street. They appeared to consist of a single room but may have had a loft above the shop. The shops were open fronted and the stone sills across the entrance had grooves in them which were for folding wooden shutters that were drawn across to close the shops at night. In the Roman town of Volubilis (Morocco) there was a large third century house known as the 'House of the Gold Coins' which had a row of shops on the street fronts on two sides of the building. The owner of the house would have enjoyed an income from the rents of these shops. Many of these shops were too small to have living accommodation therefore they were used as lock-up shops, being closed in at night by folding shutters; the shopkeepers living elsewhere in the town (Liversidge, 1976).

The remains of rows of shops have been found during excavations in Britain at Cirencester, Colchester, Leicester, London and Verulamium. There were also *macella* (provision market halls) where traders could rent stalls and these would have included some meat stalls. Itinerant traders could set up temporary stalls on market days. Excavations at Verulamium revealed a number of shops. Associated with one (an early 4th century AD building), bones of old horses were found from which the flesh had been stripped before being discarded. It was considered that the meat was used to make sausages (Wacher, 1974).

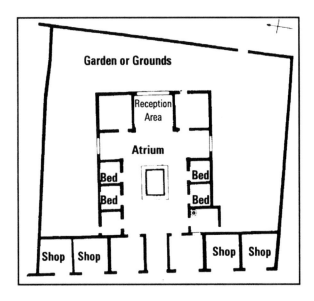

Fig 4.9 Plan of the House of Sallust, Pompeii, 2nd Century BC, with shops along the front of the house facing the street.

At Cirencester, a building was found along side the Forum, which consisted of a row of rooms (roughly 18ft square) that probably served as butchers' shops forming a meat market. Pits filled with animal bones showing evidence of butchery were found below the floors and in front of these shops. Close by was an open courtyard which it is thought had been used as a cattle market and functioned in combination with the meat market. Specialist markets of this type were well known in Rome and the Empire (*Ibid*).

The shops in Roman Britain were generally narrow fronted as in other parts of the Empire to enable the maximum number of shops to be built in one street (frontage on main streets has always been at a premium). The space necessary for the trading activities of the shop was obtained by building farther back and often building onto the back of the shop. Some shops included workshops. Many of the tradesmen lived in accommodation above or behind the shop (living over the shop is an age-old tradition) (*Ibid*).

The development of the urban trade produced a flow of wealth which resulted in an urban elite. These were the property owners with their rows of shops producing a good income and in some cases the buildings included multi-occupation blocks of tenements above the shops like those at Ostia (Fig 4.10). Unlike the medieval urban rich who were generally the successful traders and merchants directly involved in commerce, the Roman property owners simply exacted payment for rent of the shops. This was nevertheless recognition of the growing wealth that urban commerce could produce (Wallace-Hadrill, 1994).

ROMANO-BRITISH SHOPKEEPERS

The creation of Roman style towns in Britain resulted in some changes to the Celtic type of

Fig 4.10 Reconstruction of tenements with shops on the ground floor at Ostia.

Fig 4.11 Map of England and Wales showing the towns included in the text.

society (Fig 4.11). There was the creation of the merchant and shopkeeping classes. This coincided with the establishment of Fora in towns and the development of the commercial significance of towns. As well as the citizens with large town houses taking advantage of their position by building shops to rent on the street side of the house there were other wealthy individuals, such as landowners, who built shops in the towns as a speculation (*Ibid*).

Those working in the shops were either freeborn citizens of the lower classes or slaves. The responsibility of management of shops was often given to slaves. In some cases by freeing a slave and making him a tenant of a shop owned by the master, the master obtained a more profitable return from the man than keeping him as a slave. The masters seem to have appreciated the greater effort put in by a self-employed shopkeeper rather than by a slave, which profited them both. The indications are that the shopkeepers, including butchers, of Roman Britain were the owner of the shop, a free-born manager or tenant, a freedman tenant or a slave working as a manager (*Ibid*).

TRADE GUILDS (*COLLEGIA*)

Collegia or guilds consisted of persons following the same trade or craft in a town. They did not have any influence with regard to the administration of the town or control over the conduct of their trade as did the medieval guilds. This would have been forbidden by the Roman authorities. The similarity existed between the *collegia* and the later guilds where members of the same trade had a common interest and would meet for social reasons, such as having a *collegium* dinner. Slaves engaged in the trade were able to become members of the *collegium* with the permission of their masters (Stobart, 1964). A *collegium* had its patron deity which the members would worship collectively and a number of the *collegia* had their own hall or meeting place. Some *collegia* functioned as burial clubs to ensure their members an adequate funeral and in some cases the association had its own tomb or section of the cemetery. It was common for a *collegium* to have a patron, a prominent citizen who was given the title of 'Father of the *collegium*' and whose generosity was a major source of funds. If a *collegium* did well by their patron they would erect a statue in his honour (Grant, 1978).

A law attributed to Julius Caesar required all *collegia* to be licensed, initially by the Senate in Rome and later by the Emperor or his representative. Under Alexander Severus in about AD 230 the *collegia* were incorporated by charter so that the industries to which they were related became close corporations. The effect was that many trades and crafts tended to become hereditary (*Ibid*).

APPRENTICESHIPS

The system of apprenticeship training was a feature of the ancient civilisations and was integral to the establishment and development of many trades and professions that were an essential part of these civilised societies. Systems of apprenticeship existed in ancient Egypt (see chapter 3). Training would have consisted essentially of oral instruction and demonstration.

Apprenticeships were a common feature in the Roman Empire as a means of training the next generation of skilled craftsmen. Sons or relatives of craftsmen would be trained to continue the family trade but often it was necessary to take on apprentices from outside the family. Formal agreements were entered into between the master craftsman and the trainee covering the general conditions and days off for public holidays. These agreements or contracts had to be officially registered (These contracts were the early equivalent of the apprentice's indentures). The periods of apprenticeship varied from two to three years for a weaver to as long as 10 years for a sculptor. On completion of the training the master would present the apprentice before a panel of three other master craftsmen to be tested and approved as a qualified craftsman (Liversidge, 1976). The *collegia* or trade guilds were not involved with apprenticeships as were the guilds of the medieval and later periods.

MEAT CONSUMPTION IN THE ROMAN EMPIRE

In Italy the meats most commonly eaten were pork, venison and veal, whereas in Roman Britain the preference was for beef and mutton, which may have been due to a fusion of Roman and Celtic customs (Birley, 1964). Animal bone reports from numerous archaeological excavations of Romano-British sites indicate a variation in the pattern of meat consumption. The relatively high level of mutton consumption by the Britons, pre-conquest, continued in the communities of Britons that had not adopted the Roman way of life but in the towns pork and beef consumption was increased with less consumption of mutton. The meat consumption for the Roman soldiers was predominantly beef (King). The Roman soldiers in Britain would have cooked their own food, meat stew being a regular feature of their menu. Salted or cured meat and sausages formed a regular part of the diet during the period of the Roman Empire and different parts of the Empire became noted for particular products e.g. hams from Gaul and Spain (Birley, 1964).

In Augusta Raurica near Basle, Switzerland, one of the Roman buildings contained a room with a semicircular hearth over which was suspended a cauldron. The smoke from this hearth was guided by a flue to a small chamber where hams or sausages may have been dried and smoked. Many animal bones were found on this part of the site. Other finds include a meat hook and grindstones for grinding herbs for use in sausages (*Ibid*).

REGULATION OF MEAT TRADING

Regulatory systems for the control of traders and markets started during early civilisations probably as a responsibility of the local elders. Ancient Athens had its market controllers of weights and measures and officials to see that the produce was genuine and not adulterated (Webster, 1969). In Roman Britain magistrates had the power to intervene if a trader was suspected of fraudulent practices (Fig 4.12). Augustus made a decree which was aimed at weights and measures uniformity throughout the Empire (Wacher, 1974). In accordance with this decree, the duumviri (magistrates) Clodius Flaccus and Arceus Arellianus fixed standards for which the Pompeiian inspectors of weights and measures established tables (Brion, 1976). The *Edict of Prices* issued by Diocletian in AD 301 was a schedule of maximum prices for every commodity of trade and a maximum wage rate for every kind of service (Liversidge, 1976).

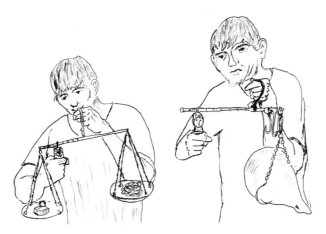

Fig 4.12 Roman balance scales, later called steelyards. On the left is a type found at Silchester, being fundamentally a set of balance scales pivoted at the centre of the beam with the weight in one scoop and the product to be weighed in the other scoop. It has the addition of a moving weight on the beam to produce a finer degree in weighing the product (e.g. a kilogram weight in the scoop and the moving weight recording the extra grammes). On the right is a steelyard type with the product suspended from a hook one side of the pivot (fulcrum) and the moving weight being adjusted on the beam the other side of the pivot to obtain the weight of the product. This particular scale is different from most steelyard types in having three hooks at different distances from the pivot to give a greater weighing range.

Fig 4.13 Drawing of a votive relief from Djemila, a Roman town in North Africa. It is a depiction of religious sacrifices. Top left is a bronze paterna used for pouring libations. The end of the handle is decorated with a ram's head. On the right is a sacrificial knife. In the middle is a flaming alter and next to it a man felling an ox with an axe. Below is a cockerel and a ram. After slaughter, the animals were opened and the viscera examined by a haruspex to ensure they were perfect and free of disease, otherwise the sacrifice would have been unacceptable. If all was well the carcase meat would have been cooked and eaten by the worshippers.

The origins of meat inspection were probably the procedures established for the examination of animals slaughtered for ritual or sacrificial purposes (Fig 4.13). The Hebrew laws of Moses specified various diseases and conditions of animals that would render them unfit as a sacrifice. With sacrifices to the gods in the Roman Empire, the internal organs of the animal were examined for signs of disease and on important occasions an official called a haruspex would examine the liver for abnormalities. A bronze model of a liver found at Piacenza was marked into various areas, which indicates the skill practised by the haruspex in determining whether a sacrifice was acceptable. There were haruspex practising their art in Romano-Britain as indicated by an altar in Bath dedicated to the goddess Sulis by the haruspicis Lusius Memor (*Ibid*).

Part II

The Medieval Period

Chapter 5

Meat Trading in the Anglo-Saxon Period

THE END OF THE ROMANO-BRITISH ERA

The Roman domination of Britain lasted for over three and half centuries. The withdrawal of the Roman troops began in the latter part of the 4th century and the final end of the Roman rule is generally put at AD 410. For a period the Britons, along with some citizens of the Roman Empire who stayed on in Britain, carried on the Roman way of life but after a time the structure of the society declined. Some agricultural lands were abandoned due to their vulnerability to marauding gangs, resulting from the lack of security previously provided by the Roman Army. The trading infrastructure based on the towns could not be sustained without the Roman organisation and the trading links with the Roman Empire (Wacher, 1974).

The entry of the Northern Germanic tribes into Britain (the Angles, Saxons, Jutes and Frisians; collectively known as Anglo-Saxons) began with a number being brought in by the Romans as mercenary soldiers (*Foederati*), some of whom remained after the departure of the Romans (*Ibid*). Armed incursions by the Picts from Caledonia (Scotland) and the Scots from Hibernia (Ireland) increased when the Roman legions were no longer present, which prompted the Britons to invite Saxons into Britain to aid in the defence against these marauders. In return they were given land on which to settle. From these settlements the Saxons in the middle of the 5th century expanded, occupying the lands of Essex, Middlesex and westward to the area that was to become the kingdom of Wessex. The Angles overran the lands of East Anglia extending westwards to form the kingdom of Mercia followed by the Northumbrian kingdoms of Deira and Bernicia. A predominantly Jutish army under the leadership of Hengest and Horsa invaded and conquered Kent, establishing the kingdom of Kent in the second half of the 5th century. In the latter part of the Anglo-Saxon period the Vikings made numerous raids on the coastal regions, invading and settling in the north east with their main centre at York. Their area of influence, referred to as Danelaw, extended as far south as the Thames by the year 900. Edward the Elder (r. 899 - 924), son of Alfred the Great, carried out the reconquest of the Danelaw lands using joint Wessex and Mercian armies (Fisher, 1973).

Written records covering the decline of Romano-Britain and the Anglo-Saxon period are very sparse and not entirely reliable. The main literary records are those of two ecclesiastics; the writings of Gildas in the middle of the 6th century and those of the Venerable Bede in the first part of the 8th century. Additionally there was the Anglo-Saxon Chronicle consisting of several documents written between the 9th and 12th centuries. Historians refer to this period as the Dark Ages; indeed there is very little in the way of illumination of the commercial and trading activities of the period. The more recent archaeological work on Anglo-Saxon sites and the subsequent reports has added to the knowledge of the period (*Ibid*).

TRANSITION FROM THE ROMAN TO THE EARLY MEDIEVAL SOCIAL AND TRADING STRUCTURE

With the breakdown of the Roman administration and the disintegration of the trading infrastructure, most of the inhabitants of the towns moved out, resulting in the markets (fora and macella) and shops having very little business. Many of the markets and shops would have ceased functioning by the time the Anglo-Saxons had become the rulers of much of England. The Romano-British urbanised structure had become almost non-existent by the end of the 5th century (Wacher, 1974). The result was that relatively no urban infrastructure existed as a starting point when the growth of towns around the trading centres (*wics*) and administrative centres (*burhs*) began at the latter part of the Anglo-Saxon period. There was no continuity between the Roman urbanisation and the Anglo-Saxon urban development (Darby, 1976 a). As is evident from early history a structured meat trade relies on urban populations because those populations require the supply of meat to be organised from the surrounding countryside, brought into the town, slaughtered, butchered and presented for purchase by the town's inhabitants. For subsistence or near subsistence farming meat was consumed locally and the butchery function was generally one of the farming activities. It follows that the meat trade that existed during the Roman period became virtually non-existent in the 5th and 6th centuries but was re-established in the latter Anglo-Saxon period to become the meat trade of medieval England. Animal bones from an archaeological excavation at Icklingham and West Stow in East Anglia indicated significant meat markets in the late Roman period but these markets did not continue into the late 5th century (Crabtree, 1994). The environmental evidence for the post Roman era points to a change in the landscape which indicates that much of the arable farming was replaced by pastoral farming (Murphy, 1994).

The Anglo-Saxon period is generally divided into three phases: the early phase, 5th to 7th centuries; middle phase, 7th to 9th centuries; the late phase, 9th century to the Norman conquest. The evidence points to the early Anglo-Saxon settlements being small and largely self-sufficient, indicating very little external trading activity. In the middle phase many of the small settlements joined to form larger population groupings centring on villages and towns (Murphy, 1994). During the late phase many of the towns grew in size, some becoming quite large with York, Lincoln, Norwich and Winchester having populations that probably exceeded 5000 (Miller, & Hatcher, 1995).

MARKET TOWNS AND TRADING

Many *burhs* were established which were administration centres for the collection of taxes or tributes (Carver, 1994). Rents were often paid in the form of agricultural produce (i.e. food rents) although in some cases the debt was discharged by a service such as a number of days ploughing the Lord's fields or other work (Fisher, 1973). Where woodland was leased for pannage (the pasturing of pigs in woodland) the payment was often in pigs (Hagan, 1995). In the terms of a lease in 852 of the land at Sempringham, Wulfred was required to render to Ceolred, abbot of Peterborough, among other things, two cattle for slaughter each year (Swanton, 1996). Æthelwyrd's Will included that Eadric, on succeeding him, was to pay an annual food rent to the community at Christchurch, part of which was a wether sheep, a flitch of bacon, an ox's haunch (hindquarters) and four hens (Robertson, 1956). For the lease of 20 hides of land at Tichborne, Denewulf, Bishop of Winchester paid annual food rents which included two beef carcases, one salted and the other fresh (*hriederu oper sealt oper fersce*), six wethers, four pigs and four flitches of bacon (Robertson, 1956). The laws of Ine (King of Wessex 688 - 726) included a guide by listing the food rent from 10 hides of land as: 10 vats of honey, 300 loaves, 12 'ambers' of Welsh ale, 30 of clear ale, 2 full grown cows or 10 wethers, 10 geese, 20 hens, 10 cheeses, an 'amber' full of butter, 5 salmon, 20 pounds of fodder and 100 eels (Whitelock, 1979). The same system was practised under the Welsh laws with the Welsh Kings receiving animals or carcases as food rent (Hagan, 1995).

This produce collected as taxes or food rents, apart from feeding troops or retinues of dignitaries etc., resulted in surpluses which in turn stimulated trade. Surplus agricultural produce had from earliest times supported craft industries in the towns, which was an indirect way of marketing these surpluses by exporting the craft products. Most of the *burhs* were associated with towns, which as a result of the *burhs* became market towns. Many of these marketing centres had their own mint with the coins carrying the *burh* mark (Carver, 1994).

The major trading centres that developed through the middle and late phases of the Anglo-Saxon period were the *wics*, built up as import/export centres. These *wics* traded with the *burhs* receiving from them manufactured craft goods, wool or other produce and supplied them with imported manufactured goods, wine, spices and other luxury goods. The most practical and economic means of transport of goods was by boat so the *wics* needed to have facilities of a port with good access to the sea routes to the Continent and reasonable access by river to the *burhs* with which they traded. It would be difficult today to imagine a *wic* such as York being a port with thriving trade with the Continent. Two major *wics* were *Hamwic* (*Hamwih*) and *Lundenwic,* (the Saxon name for London). *Hamwic* occupied part of what is now Southampton and was a major south coast port (Vince, 1994). London was well on the way to becoming the major commercial centre of the country while Winchester was still the capital under King Alfred the Great. "London is a market for many people coming by land and sea" so wrote Bede (Darby, 1976 b). The main London wharves were at Ethelred's Hithe (which in the later medieval period became Queenhithe), Dowgate and Billingsgate (Vince, 1990). The main area of Saxon occupation in London was not within the city walls but in the Strand settlement which extended from the west side of the city to Westminster. This was the active trading part of *Lundenwic* (*Ibid*).

The growth of these market towns (*burhs*) and trading centres (*wics*) resulted in the establishment of cattle markets and the butchery trade for supplying the expanding urban populations. An Anglo-Saxon charter of 932 refers to a *hrypera ceap* or cattle market just outside the walls of Canterbury and in 1002 reference was made to *Ryperceap* which suggests a meat market (Fig 5.1) (Hagan, 1995). In London, Cheapside (from *ceap* - market) became a food market with its butchers, bakers and fishmongers and may have originated from the sale of the surplus food rents collected by the Chapter of St Paul's (*Ibid*). A regular cattle market was being held at Smithfield during the latter part of the Anglo-Saxon period, having been well established when Rahere chose it as the place to build the priory of St. Bartholomew the Great (Lipson, 1959). There were Anglo-Saxon droveways from the surrounding areas which converged at Islington and proceeded to Smithfield (Vince, 1990). Winchester had a *Ceap Street* (Market Street) and its Fleshmongers' Street by the 10th century and permanent shops were becoming a more regular feature of the towns (Hagan, 1995). In Anglo-Scandinavian York there were the Shambles (meat market) which survives (in name only) today and is entered in Domesday as a food market. Shambles is derived from *flæsc-scamol*

Fig 5.1 An impression of an Anglo-Saxon Cattle Market held outside the town walls.

which means a stall on which meat is sold. There was also reference to *Ketmangergata* - meat sellers or more precisely horse meat butchers, as *ket* means horse flesh (*Ibid*).

The development of the towns resulted in a greater concentration and more diversity of the industrial craftsmen and the trading craftsmen than was the case in the countryside (Miller & Hatcher, 1995). The growth in those crafts using non-food animal products such as the tanners, shoe makers, harness makers, skinners, weavers, candle makers and many others using hides, skins, wool, tallow etc. will have greatly increased the activities of the butcher. Added to this was the greater demand for the butcher as a retailer of meat in the towns.

Anglo-Saxon coinage began in Canterbury between 775 and 780. Canterbury had strong trade links with the Frankish kingdom and the Frankish silver denarius was adopted as the standard. The denarius became the Anglo-Saxon steorra or sterling with 240 sterlings equalling a pound of silver, hence the pound sterling. As trading developed moneyers became established in the *burhs* licensed by the King to mint coins and the number of moneyers in a *burhs* indicated its level of prosperity. By 1066 London had twenty moneyers, York had ten or more, Lincoln nine, Winchester nine, Chester eight, Canterbury seven and Oxford seven (Darby, 1976a). In the latter part of the Anglo-Saxon period trading and commerce had so developed that there existed what was essentially a money economy when the Normans arrived in 1066 (Fig 5.2, Fig 5.3).

LAWS REGULATING THE TRADE IN LIVESTOCK

There were a series of laws passed by the Anglo-Saxon kings and Welsh laws relating to the trade in livestock. The laws of Ine included codes to protect buyers being sold diseased or unsound animals and safeguards in relation to stolen stock "When anyone accuses a man that he stole cattle or received stolen cattle, he must deny the theft [by an oath of] 60 hides if he is entitled to give an

Fig 5.2 Two sides of a silver penny of the Wessex King Æthelred minted by a Canterbury moneyer, *c* 870.

Fig 5.3 Two sides of a silver penny of the Danish King Halfdan.

oath" – he would have forfeited his right to swear on oath by a previous conviction for crime, especially perjury. Another of the laws states "If anyone buys cattle and then finds any unsoundness in it within 30 days, he shall hand it back to the seller, or the seller is to swear he knew of no fraud when he sold it to him" (Whitelock, 1979).

As a guard against theft, laws were made governing the sale of livestock. An assembly held by Æthelstan at Grately, Hampshire, passed laws, one of which prohibited exchange of livestock without the witness of the reeve (estate manager) or mass priest or lord of the estate or the treasurer or other trustworthy man. If anyone does so, he is to pay 30 shillings as fine and the Lord of the estate is to succeed to the exchanged property (*Ibid*). A later law required that stock was only sold in a market town with the witness of the reeve of the market (superintendent) or other men of credit (Hagan, 1995). Fines were imposed for any contravention. The other point of such laws was the assurance of maintaining the level of income from the market tolls (Lipson, 1959). The Welsh Laws contained similar requirements that only legitimate town markets were allowed for trade (Hagan, 1995).

A law passed by Edgar (r. 959 - 975) laid down that "any man who rides out to make a purchase without having announced it when he set out, he is to announce it when he comes home, and if it is livestock he is to bring it onto the common pasture with the witness of his village. If he does not do so in five days, the villagers are to inform the man in charge of the hundred and he who brought it there is to forfeit the cattle... If the cattle remain on common pasture five days unannounced he is to forfeit the cattle and each herdsman is to be flogged" (Whitelock, 1979). There was a further precaution in the laws of Ethelred (r. 978 - 1016) which states, "where two witnesses are required when stock is killed, the slaughterer is to keep the head and hide of the beast or sheep for three days for production upon any inquiry" (Trow-Smith, 1957).

There were laws of Ine relating to livestock prices "A ewe with her lamb is worth a shilling until 12 days after Easter. A sheep must go with its fleece until midsummer or else the fleece is to be paid for at two pence". And some other price controls, "the horn of an ox is worth ten pence, the horn of a cow is worth two pence, the tail of an ox is worth a shilling and that of a cow five pence" (Whitelock, 1979). The relatively high price of horns is an indication of their value as a raw material.

Laws prohibiting markets or trading on Sundays were a feature of the Anglo-Saxon period. The 10th century laws of Athelstan impose the penalty of thirty shillings fine and the loss of their goods for anyone who trades on Sunday (Lipson, 1959).

MARKET TOLLS

The system of market tolls was well established during the Anglo-Saxon period, the tolls being charged either on the space or stall for selling or a charge for goods or animals sold in the market. These tolls constituted a significant income for the person or institution that held the rights to the market (Hagan, 1995).

Many of the records show that market tolls were due to the king who would often grant part of those tolls to a religious establishment. The foundation of St Peter and St Paul at Winchester was granted the market dues from Taunton. King Edward the Confessor granted a 'third part of the toll on horse loads and market sales' to St Mary's Minster (Worcester Cathedral) in 1062. At Hoxne, Suffolk there was the Bishop's market from which the Bishop received the market tolls (*Ibid*).

Records show the existence of tolls or taxes on salt. There were tolls on cart loads and pack loads of salt at *Saltwic* (Droitwich) and other charters refer to tolls on salt passing through towns or when on sale in the markets (*Ibid*). Salt being an important and valuable commodity has, through the ages, been an attractive source of taxation.

MEAT CONSUMPTION

As with most periods in the past livestock had a more predominantly dual purpose role than is the case with modern western farming. The use of the ox as a plough or draught animal was usually more important than its contribution to meat supplies, so the butcher would get oxen at the end of their working lives. The cow and ewe were expected to provide quantities of milk and cheese before they became meat. Trow-Smith considers that it was the ewe rather than the cow that was the predominant dairy animal. Wool and leather made an important contribution to the Anglo-Saxon economy (Trow-Smith, 1957).

Horse meat was commonly consumed by the early European races and was connected with some pagan rituals. Because of this association Pope Gregory III ordered St Boniface to forbid the consumption of horseflesh by Christians in 732. There is evidence of butchery on horse bones from early Anglo-Saxon archaeological sites but not on horse bones from the later sites except at Anglo-Scandinavian York. The Pope's edict against eating horseflesh seems to have been achieved in Britain. In the Venerable Bede's penitential it states that "He who eats impure flesh, or that of an animal which has died, or one that was torn to pieces by wild beasts, shall do penance for forty days" and Wulfstan's '*Canons of Edgar*' requires that "no Christian man consumes blood". These were in line with the Levitical Laws of the old testament.

Although there were variations in the relative levels of meat consumption of the different species, the major contribution was generally beef but there was a quite significant level of mutton eaten. The archaeological evidence from the animal bones, especially in East Anglia, indicate a high proportion of sheep for the Anglo-Saxon period which is supported by the sheep numbers during the Domesday survey (Crabtree, 1994). Evidence of animal husbandry on the Continent at the time shows that the Saxons predominantly reared cattle with only small numbers of sheep, indicating that keeping sheep was not traditional with the Saxons. Wool was one of the export products developed during the Roman period and although there was a decline in this trade in the post Romano British period the evidence indicates that the trade began reviving in the 9th century. By the time of the conquest the foundations were in place for the flourishing medieval wool industry (Trow-Smith, 1957). The production of wool provided a good supply of meat which was probably the origin of Britain having a tradition of mutton and lamb consumption.

The evidence indicates that the preferences in Roman Britain were for beef and mutton, and pork consumption was low (Birley, 1964). The Anglo-Saxon consumption of pork was much more significant according to the documentary and archaeological evidence. The documentary evidence indicates not only a widespread increase of pig keeping in the country but in some cases the pig herds were very large. A good example is the herds that were included in the Will of Alfred, an Ealdorman (royal official), who died *c*.880 and bequeathed to his wife and daughter a herd of 2000 swine in Surrey and there were further bequests of swine to other kinsman (Whitelock, 1979). This increase in pig keeping compared with the Roman period may be partly due to a decline in arable farming and the increase of pasture and open woodland.

Pigs were reared on pasture and woodland, feeding on the rhizomes of bracken and other roots; in the Autumn pigs were fed and fattened on acorns and beech masts (pannage) (Fig 5.4). Due to this method of feeding and the Anglo-Saxon type of pig, they had a slow growth rate and took about three years to mature. The type of pigs at this time was probably not greatly improved from wild pigs, being long legged, razor backed and with long hair (Trow-Smith, 1957). This would have been largely due to the method of husbandry which was close to the feeding and environment of the wild ancestors of the pigs. A genetically improved modern pig would have been unsuited to this type of husbandry. There were some pigs that were housed but these were very much in the minority on the balance of literary references for woodland and sty reared pigs (*Ibid*). A problem for shepherds and swineherds was the packs of wolves that still roamed the countryside during the Anglo-Saxon period; the long legs of the pigs would have been advantageous in escaping from the wolves.

Terry O'Connor calculated the number of meat animals needed to supply the population of Lincoln in the 11th century (estimated at *c* 4000 people). He concluded that it would require 500 cattle, 700 sheep and 400 pigs to be slaughtered annually to supply the necessary carcase meat (O'Connor, 1983). These animals would have been reared on the farms and estates in the surrounding

Fig 5.4 A line drawing copy of scene from an Anglo-Saxon calendar depicting the month of September, showing a huntsman on the left and a swineherd with his pigs pastured in the woods.

area, producing an income for the farmers and estate owners. This estimated number of animals slaughtered per annum for this town's need helps to put in perspective the sample size of many archaeological bone assemblages.

For a comparison of pigmeat production a genetically modern pig under present husbandry conditions can produce in less than six months, a carcase weighing 55 kg [121 lb] (as for bacon without head, feet, tail, kidneys, kidney fat and flair fat) whereas in two years, an Anglo-Saxon pig would reach a carcase weight of half, or less than half, of that weight.

SALTED MEAT

The importance of salt as the major factor in meat preservation through most of history was equally the case in the Anglo-Saxon period, as well as its value as a condiment. The Anglo-Saxon salter well expounds the value of his craft to society;

"My trade greatly benefits you all. None of you would take any pleasure in your meals or food without my hospitable art. How can anyone appreciate very sweet foods to the full without the savour of salt? Who could fill his cellar or storeroom without my skill? Look, you would even lose your butter and cheese, and you can't even enjoy your vegetables without making use of me." (Hagan, 1992)

According to the Domesday records there were large numbers of salt pans stretching along the east coast and south coast producing salt by the evaporation of seawater. Inland salt production from brine springs was recorded for Cheshire, centred on Northwich, Nantwich and Middlewich and in Worcestershire centred on Droitwich. Salt was transported long distances, often by pack horse along the saltways, according to the records of salt-tolls (Darby, 1976 b).

Salted pork or bacon would seem to have been a significant part of the Anglo-Saxon diet as indicated by some of the records. The inventory of Thorney Abbey includes 43 flitches of bacon and '100 flitches of bacon and all the delicacies that go with them' which were to go to Peterborough (Hagan, 1992). Salted pork or bacon could have become the main reserve of meat in the winter for the poor as it was in the later medieval period.

AGE AND SIZE OF ANIMALS AT SLAUGHTER

Anglo-Saxon domestic animals were much smaller than modern livestock. The average withers height for cattle was 112 - 120cm [36.9 - 39.5 inches] (Hagan, 1995) and an average of 114 – 118cm for four East Anglian sites (Crabtree, 1994). The average wither height for sheep was 58 - 62cm [19.1- 20.4 inches] (Hagan, 1995) and 57 – 63cm (Fig 5.5) (Crabtree, 1994).

Fig 5.5 Comparison of the size of modern farm animals (at the back) with those of the Anglo-Saxon period (in the front).

Of the main meat species, cattle, sheep and pigs, there were a number of animals killed in their first year. These may have been casualty animals or most likely animals surplus to requirements for carrying over the winter to maintain herd and flock numbers. Some animals may have simply exceeded the numbers for which farmers had winter feed. The analysis of the animal bones from the four East Anglian sites indicate the slaughter of a number of lambs (animals in their first year) at two of the sites but overall sheep were slaughtered in their second year or at an older age. These could have been cull animals from wool producing flocks. Sheep in their second year would have been sheared but some animals could have been slaughtered at about a year old with a good fleece providing a heavy fell (skin plus wool) which would have had a high value. The slaughter pattern for cattle was that most were slaughtered as adults, although from one site there was evidence of cattle slaughtered in their first year and some in their second year which may indicate the site being in an area where cattle were produced. The indications for the ages of pigs at slaughter were that most were in their second or third year (Crabtree, 1994).

The animal bones from four sites in *Lundenwic,* in the Strand settlement, indicated that the meat consumption was predominantly beef, followed by pork with mutton being low; this differed from the East Anglian sites where the indications were for a much higher mutton consumption. The main slaughter age for cattle was between two and four years with a number of older animals, which were probably cull animals, draught oxen or dairy cows. There were bones from a number of veal calves (West, 1988).

Chapter 6

The Middle Ages Trading Boom

After the Norman Conquest, although there was a different hierarchy with new Lords and Bishops, rural life and life in the towns remained much the same as it was in the latter Anglo-Saxon period. The commercial and trading activities of the Anglo-Saxons continued to expand during the 12th - 14th centuries which was a period of growing prosperity; in fact it could be considered as a boom period for trade.

As has been emphasised in the previous chapters the development of the meat trade was very much related to the development of trading generally and the expansion of urbanisation. The types of trading can be divided into local, national and international trade. Although the meat trading was essentially local in nature the growth of the trade was considerably influenced by the increase in national and international trade during this period.

INTERNATIONAL TRADE

There were custom records of the export of meat to Europe but it is difficult to determine the extent of meat exports or if there was any regular trade in meat with the Continent. In a document dated 1203 the following were listed as permitted for export; grain, wine, salt, wax, bacon, meat, cheese, butter, honey, herring and salmon. John Cleys and his partners exported 141 bacons from Sandwich in 1299. There was the New Custom in 1303 which was 3d per £. An account of the New Custom on goods exported by aliens from Sandwich (which included the ports of Winchelsea and Faversham) included grain, coal, bacon and beef. Exports from Portsmouth in the early 1300s included bacon, mutton and beef (Gras, 1918). The bacon exported would have survived the journey easily due to the preservation effect of the salt. Whether or not the beef and mutton was salted it is not clear although the short journey across the English Channel would have been reasonable for shipping fresh carcases. The pleural and peritoneal membranes would have protected the inside of the carcase and a reasonable covering of fat would have protected the outside. Crossing the Channel at this time would have been completed in a day, much depending on the wind, of course. William the Conqueror's invasion fleet sailed from the mouth of the River Somme on the night of 27th September 1066 and landed at Pevensey Bay the following day, 28th September. During the 19th and early 20th century it was a common practice to transport beef, unrefrigerated, from Perth to the London market by coastal vessel or by rail (Perren, 1978); a journey that would have taken as long, if not longer, than those shipments across the Channel.

It was much more economic to transport bulk goods by river or sea routes than overland in the medieval period. Some bulk commodities would double or treble their price when carted relatively short distances overland; therefore there were considerable commercial advantages in building towns alongside rivers or near the coast. The lord of an estate could, in many cases, call upon his feudal tenants or villeins to transport produce or drive livestock to the market or fair as part of their feudal service (Miller & Hatcher, 1995).

During the 11th to 14th centuries there was a considerable growth of trade in western Europe and the ambitious merchants spread this trading boom to England (Fig 6.1). The association with Normandy after the conquest aided the trade with France. There was a further strengthening of the connection with the accession of Henry II, the first of the Plantagenet kings, who's Angevin Empire in France extended from the River Somme to the Pyrenees. Scotland also enjoyed an expansion of its overseas trade during this period (Whyte, 1995). International trade had to be two way i.e. something to export to pay for the imports. Trade was generally initiated by merchants seeking the procurement of goods or materials needed in their area. A commodity in great demand in medieval Europe was cloth, or wool to manufacture the cloth. The merchants of Gascony and Flanders descended on Britain seeking wool which was the product of the numerous sheep flocks. In some cases they were coming to buy the finished cloth (Fig 6.2). Wool was by far the major export from medieval Britain. Salt, an important basic commodity, was a significant export probably second in value to wool. Hides, grain and tin featured as important exports in the records of the period. Newcastle was a leading port for the export of hides in the 1200s. The cattle rearing areas of the Cheviots and the slopes of the Pennines were probably a major source of these hides. As a balance against these exports a major import was wine, much of it coming from Gascony. Other imports included cloth, wax, spices, silks, dyes and metals. In the early 1300s England was annually exporting wool valued at £258,000 and importing wine worth £60,000 which in 1300, with the value of wine at £3 per tun, represented a vast quantity of wine (Miller & Hatcher, 1995).

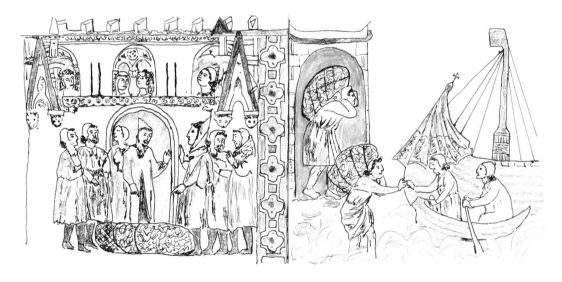

Fig 6.1 Drawings based on two illustrations from the chronicle of the life of Alfonso X (king of Castile, 1252 - 1282) showing, on the left, merchants involved in the sale and purchase of bales of wool and on the right is the transfer of bales of wool to a ship via a rowing boat.

Fig 6.2 A medieval illustration depicting the wool industry. Two of the women are holding sheers and on the left a woman is winding skeins of wool. In the centre wool is being woven into cloth. This illustration demonstrates the development of the industry from just exporting the bales of raw wool to manufacturing into finished cloth.

By this period London had the highest volume of import/export trade but surprisingly Boston was the second port followed by Southampton, Lincoln, King's Lynn, Hull, York and Newcastle in that order. In the early stages the trade was dominated by alien merchants (Italian, Fleming, Gascon and German) many of them having residences in London or other main commercial centres. Towards the end of the 1300s the English merchants were taking over (*Ibid*). (Persons from other countries were referred to as aliens at this time whereas the term foreigner was applied by people in towns to everybody from outside the town.)

The Scottish growth in prosperity through the 12th and 13th centuries reached a high level in the late 13th century during the reign of Alexander III which well matched that occurring in England. This was also largely due to the export of wool, mainly to Flanders. Other exports included hides, skins, herrings and salmon (Whyte, 1995). In 1398 there were new export duties put on salt, meat and suet but there is a lack of records to indicate the extent of the trade in these commodities (Ewan, 1990). A major import was grain from England. There was also the import of wine from Gascony and fine cloth, dyes, iron and spices. Much of the grain was shipped from England along the coast. England was Scotland's main trading partner apart from the disruption due to the Wars of Independence led by Sir William Wallace (1296) and Robert Bruce (1332). Although there was some trade on the west coast of Scotland with Ireland, the bulk of the trade was through the east coast ports (Whyte, 1995). Trading went on between Scotland and the Continent during the wars with England, particularly with Flanders. The main exports were wool, woolfells and hides. Edward III wrote to the Count of Flanders in an attempt to stop this trade (Ewan, 1990).

The importance of the international trade's influence on the meat trade was firstly the increasing prosperity, particularly in the towns where the populations were expanding and more money circulating. The expansion of the wool trade would have had a considerable 'spin off' for the meat trade with the ready availability of sheep culled from the wool flocks for slaughter. The buoyancy for the trade in hides was also advantageous for the meat trade as good prices for hides offset the cost of the carcases. Indeed the hide could have been the most valuable part of the animal in some situations.

The people of the Scottish towns and ports involved with the export of woolfells and hides, such as Aberdeen, Berwick, Montrose and Perth, would have had the benefit of good meat supplies. Archaeological analysis of animal bones indicate that the people of Perth did well for beef, which would relate to the fact that Perth was a major centre for the export of hides (Ewan, 1990).

The trade in livestock from Wales and Scotland to England has a long history. Cattle rearing has been fundamental to the Welsh economy from prehistoric times. Cattle were given great prominence in 900 by King Howell Dda and the value of estates of the Welsh princes was measured by the number of cattle. Welsh cattle were driven into England for sale during the Anglo-Saxon period and probably earlier during Roman times. In 1253 a yearly fair and weekly cattle market was established at Newent, Gloucestershire, which became a regular trading centre for Welsh cattle. An early major cattle drove was the collection of Welsh cattle as supplies for the armies of Henry V when they embarked for France in 1415. When these cattle were gathered together into a large drove they were driven to the Cinque Ports where they 'were to be fed fat' to supply Henry's armies in France (Rankin, 1955).

The earliest evidence of organised droving was a 1359 letter of safe conduct for a year granted to Andrew Moray and Alan Erskyn, two Scottish drovers, with three horsemen and their servants to travel through England for a year with horses, oxen, cows and other goods. Scottish statutes attempting to regulate aspects of the cattle trade in 1369, 1451 and 1480 is confirmation of significant acitivity in the trade (Haldane, 1968).

NATIONAL TRADE

The development of national trade was stimulated by, and often related to, the growth of the international trade. Merchants travelled around the country for the procurement of wool, hides and other commodities for export. Imported goods were moving into the towns and being distributed to the manors and monastic establishments. The development of the money economy facilitated the buying and selling of goods and raw materials.

Salt was a major commodity for inland trading with large amounts of salt being produced from the brine pits in the wiches of Cheshire and Worcestershire. Much salt was also produced in the salterns in the coastal areas. Oxen were used for carting the salt and packhorses laden with salt were driven along the salt ways that connected the salt producing areas with the customers for this commodity in the towns, baronial halls and monastic establishments (Darby, 1976b). Salt was essential for the preservation of meat (curing bacon, salting beef and other meats).

Wool, metals and other raw materials were of growing importance in national trade due to the rise in the craft industries in the towns. The effectiveness of trading would have eased the necessity for local agriculture to supply all the local needs and allowed some specialisation such as pastoral areas producing wool and buying in grain from the arable areas (Lipson, 1959).

Although not strictly national trade, estates were at times required to send supplies, including meat, to their lords when they were in other parts of the country. Livestock was sent from the Earl Marshal's estate at Kennet (Cambridgeshire) to provision his London household in 1278, cattle and rabbits to the Earl's Hanworth (Norfolk) residence for Christmas 1280 and a boar, 10 wethers and 10 ewes in 1297 to London for the Earl while attending parliament. Large numbers of pigs were driven from the estate at Great Shelford to stock the Bishop of Ely's larder at Ely. Agents were sent by the Bishop of Winchester to Lincolnshire in 1208 to buy rams and ewes to supplement his flocks in Wiltshire and Surrey. The Durham Priory bought oxen from Roxburgh, Penrith and Kendal (Miller & Hatcher, 1995).

Sale of the surpluses from the estates was a major element of national trade. The degree of market orientation of the estate managers (or reeves) is apparent from records indicating the number of times that they visited the markets. The reeve of the Cuxham estate travelled frequently to the Henley market in 1290 and the reeve of the Combe estate (Hampshire) made numerous visits to the markets at Andover and Newbury in 1306. The Winchester manors in 1208/9 sold on the market 4,000qtrs of grain, 146 oxen, cows, etc. 1,277 sheep and lambs, 20 goats, 26 horses, 118 hens, 4,135 cheeses, 320 hides, 4,567 sheep and goat skins and 13,496 fleeces. The records of other manors include similar lists of animals and goods sold through the markets, although for most, the quantities are less than those of the very large Winchester estate (*Ibid*).

LOCAL TRADE

The villages still largely relied on self sufficiency in the post conquest period, providing their own food, fuel and material for building etc. The rural areas were predominantly under the feudal system with most of the inhabitants of the villages being villeins i.e. vassals of the lord of the manor or the bishop or abbot where the estate was owned by the church or a monastic establishment. The villeins would be committed to labour service to their lord and also paid rents for their holdings in either produce or money. Apart from money for rents the villagers would also need money to buy items they could not supply for themselves such as implements from the blacksmith, pottery or other craft manufactures. They would also require salt and other merchandise imported into the locality. This meant villagers selling produce or other goods in the local market. There would also be the surpluses from the manor being sold in the local market, which was usually in the nearest town (Lipson, 1959).

Local trade was subject to a marked increase during the 13th and 14th centuries along with the national and international trade. Increased arable agricultural productivity, due to improved methods such as crop rotation and more efficient ploughs, made more produce available for the market. It was also a time of increasing population in England. By 1300 there was an estimated three fold increase of population from the time of Domesday (1086) (population was estimated at between 4 and 6 million in 1300) (Miller & Hatcher, 1995).

In the villages there would have been individuals practising the main crafts but not the wide variety of specialist craftsmen that could be found in the towns where there was a considerable demand for craft products. The craftsmen of the villages, such as blacksmiths, carpenters, potters and butchers would have had a plot of land and grazing rights to supplement their incomes, in most cases to feed themselves and their families. They were in fact craftsmen who were part-time farmers or farmers who were part-time craftsmen. Being less specialised, the village craftsmen

Fig 6.3 From a 12th century manuscript (in Corpus Christi College , Oxford) showing various activities throughout the year. This illustration for February is of a person warming boots over the fire. Note the side of bacon hanging from a beam along with what could be pieces of salted meat stuffed into intestine skins. The effect of the fire drying the surface of the meat was an important factor in its preservation, added to which the penetration of the smoke from the fire into the meat had an additional preserving effect. Meat hanging in the medieval kitchen in February was often part of the November kill.

would have taken on concomitant craft activities. It is likely that the butcher would also have tanned hides.

The modern concept of a butcher is as just a retailer of meat whereas the medieval butcher was primarily a slaughterman. The peasant farmer would often kill a sheep or pig himself but there were always advantages of employing a skilled butcher. As with all craftsmen a butcher had the right tools which he maintained in good order. Unlike today, tools were very valuable in the medieval period and much too expensive for the peasant farmer to obtain for occasional use. The superior end result has always been a persuasive factor for using skilled craftsman. An unskilled slaughterer could cause considerable spoilage of a carcase. An essential skill of the butcher is skinning the animal and if done badly can seriously devalue the skin or hide. The village butcher would almost certainly have had feudal ties to the lord of the manor and probably carried out butchery work for the manor. Where a butcher slaughtered animals for farmers he was likely to receive some part of the slaughtered animal in payment; in fact certain parts of the carcase or offals may have been the slaughterman's due by custom.

The busy time for the butcher was in November when the autumn kill took place (Fig 6.4, Fig 6.5). This tradition of the autumn kill began on Martinmas, the feast of St. Martin on 11th November. The Autumn kill was of those animals surplus to those required for the following year's breeding stock, work oxen, and milch cows. Some households bought in animals in the autumn to fill their stores for the winter meat supplies. The household of Richard de Swinfield obtained 52 cattle

Fig 6.4 An illustration in a medieval book from the latter half of the 14th century showing occupations for the months of the year. The November task was slaughtering cattle. The slaughterman is using the back of the axe head to stun the animal. When the animal had been brought down it would have been an easy matter to cut the major blood vessels in the neck to bleed the animal. The originals are at the Bodleian Library, University of Oxford.

Fig 6.5 A line drawing of pig slaughtering depicted in the December calendar from the Queen Mary Psalter (early 14th century).

Fig 6.6 A drawing of a 15th century stained glass roundel at the Victoria and Albert museum again showing the autumn slaughtering activities. In this case it is the killing of a pig probably destined for bacon.

22 pigs and a number of sheep to slaughter for the winter store. For their work in slaughtering these animals the slaughtermen were paid 2s - 6d. The salt required for salting these carcases was obtained from Worcester (Hammond, 1993). Hugh Spencer (Despenser) the Elder who was condemned by the commonality and banished from the realm in 1321, was recorded as having in his 59 manors: 600 bacons, 80 carcases of Martinmas beef, 600 muttons in larder as well as large numbers of livestock and other goods (Stow, 1598). In the Paston letters (1422 – 1509) was one from the bailiff informing Paston that he had been able to lay in sufficient beef for the Paston houshold to last from late Autumn till Lent. This was salted down and used from time to time when necessary. Sir John Fastolf, a long-standing friend of John Paston, had in his larder 3 great standing tubs, 2 salting tubs, 1 barrel and a butcher's axe which were for use during the Autumn salting of meat (Bennett, 1990). Such equipment was common in the medium and large households in the Middle Ages.

There would be much work to do as the carcases had to be prepared and salted. A considerable quantity of salt would have been bought and stored in the village in preparation for the autumn kill (Fig 6.7). Flitches of bacon were dry-salt cured and hung in the cottages or kitchens for the fire to dry the surface and keep them dry until ready for use. They would also have become somewhat smoked. Some meat was cut into pieces and salted and put into skins (scraped intestines) which were hung up to dry in the same way. Bacon was the main source of meat for the peasant families throughout the winter (Trevelyan, 1949). The bacon was generally very fat and greasy and was often cooked by boiling with dried peas or beans which absorbed some of the salt from the bacon. Peas or beans were grown, in many cases, as part of the crop rotation. Some bacon was saved

Fig 6.7 Slaughter and salting pigs in the autumn to preserve the meat for the winter.

through Lent so that it could be eaten with veal at Easter in celebration of the end of the Lenten fast (Wilson, 1973). When animals were slaughtered the offals were usually the first parts to be consumed as they decompose more rapidly due to the nature of the tissue and the high blood content. This would have resulted in a surfeit of offals during the autumn kill. Another task related to the autumn kill was to make candles from the tallow obtained from the slaughtered animals. These candles would have been essential to provide lighting during the long winter nights

The landowners, lords of the manor etc., had their coney warrens (rabbit warrens) and dovecotes to provide fresh meat in the winter. Royalty and the nobles would have had the benefit of deer from the forests for their winter feasts (Fig 6.8). The Normans are credited with having introduced rabbits into Britain (there is no record or archaeological evidence of rabbits in Britain before the Conquest). There were complaints by the Commons to Parliament in 1389 that "artificers and labourers and servants and grooms keep greyhounds and other dogs, and on holy days, when good Christian people are in church, hearing divine service, they go hunting in the parks, warrens and coneyries of lords and others, to the great destruction of the same". The result was to prohibit the lower orders from keeping sporting nets or dogs (Trevelyan, 1949).

The dovecotes (or columbariums) were often round brick or stone buildings with the inside walls having a series of several hundred nesting places or niches (Fig 6.9). They were stocked with a domesticated blue rock pigeon (*Columba livia*) which are the ancestors of the feral pigeons that inhabit Trafalgar Square and other city centres today. Pigeons only have two chicks in each brood but can have seven or eight broods in a year. The squabs (young pigeons) were considered a delicacy, their flesh being succulent and tender (Hansell, 1988). A dovecote built in 1326 had a diameter of 17 feet (5.2m) and was 16 feet (4.9m) high. The great dovecote at the Grantchester Estate of King's College, Cambridge, provided 2,000 – 3,000 pigeons a year. It was a complaint of the peasants that the lords feasted on the pigeons that had grown fat eating their corn (Trevelyan, 1949). In Scotland the dovecote was called a doocot: doocots were legally the right of the lairds,

Fig 6.8 The same book as in fig. 6.4 shows a rich man's activity in December as feasting.

Fig 6.9 On the right a medieval dovecote in Somerset. On the left is a view of part of the inside walls showing some of the hundreds of nesting places for the birds. The dovecotes (doocot in Scotland) were major sources of fresh meat, especially in the winter. Eggs were available during the spring and summer as well as the plump young fledglings (squabs).

the abbeys or monasteries. The shapes varied; some were square or rectangular and some round. In some cases the upper part of an existing building was converted into a doocot and even church towers were used for this purpose by the minister, much to the discomfort of the congregation below. The doocots were valued for the supply of some fresh meat in the winter in Scotland and squab pie was a noted national dish. Doocots were protected in Scotland by legislation with a law in 1424 against the destroyers of pigeonhouses and in 1503 there was a law that provided for parents of children who broke into a doocot to be fined 13s 4d. In 1567 the penalty for shooting the laird's pigeons was forty days in prison and under James VI the penalty for a third offence was a £40 fine, which if not paid, led to the offender being hanged. Pigeon droppings that built up in the dovecote or doocot made a rich fertilizer which was an added bonus. The droppings were also a good source of nitrate (Buxbaum, 1987).

The major trading outlets for the villages were the towns. Related to the growth of trade and the increase of population there was a considerable urban expansion in the period from 1100 to 1350 (Donkin, 1976). This was not only an increase in the populations of existing towns but also the establishment of vast numbers of new towns (Miller & Hatcher, 1995).

Some of the towns expanded taking in part of the surrounding area and in a number of cases more than doubling the area of the town. Between 1100 and 1250 the enlargement of Bristol took in the old market outside the castle extending across the Avon. Newcastle expanded to encompass the township of Pandon in 1298. Many such urban enlargements were taking place with many towns. Increase of the urban population within existing towns was a more significant factor (*Ibid*). There was much open space within the walls of most towns at the time of the Conquest which became occupied as the populations increased. The burgesses of towns held plots of land in the towns on tenure called a burgage. Parts of these burgages were sublet with houses, shops, workshops, storerooms, stables etc., built on the sites and let for a range of purposes. Many buildings which had workrooms or shops on the ground floor with living accommodation above were very cramped. A number of these in Winchester High Street in the early 1300s had frontages of 8 feet (2.4m), some even as small as 5 feet (1.5m) and the depths were between 7 feet (2.1m) and 21 feet (6.4m) (*Ibid*).

A number of villages grew into towns but many of the new towns were established to provide manors or monastic establishments with the availability of the craft industries of a town, town markets and above all extra income. Kings who were the lords of many boroughs were responsible for founding a number of new towns and many more were established by other landowners. Of the new towns in Gloucestershire, Warwickshire and Worcestershire, 51% were founded by barons, 13% by lessor landowners, 32% by monasteries and 4% by bishops. By 1300 most villages and hamlets in England were within a day's journey of a town and in some cases more than one town. Added to the urban expansion, the monastic establishments were increasing in size and in numbers adding to the demand for produce from the countryside (*Ibid*).

Of the traders in the towns, a quarter to a third were trading in provisions. Some were simply sellers of produce from the land such as vegetables, fruit, etc.; others sold cheese produced by the farmers or villagers. The presentation and sale of this produce often required little space; a temporary stall or space in the market place would often suffice. There was another group who were really merchants such as the pepperers or grocers selling imported spices, sugar, raisins, almonds, etc. and the vintners selling imported wine. This group needed storage accommodation as well as a shop. The third group were the food craftsmen retailers such as the butchers, bakers and brewers who required suitable premises to process or prepare their wares. They also needed tools and equipment and the skills of their trade. The butcher would require a shop in which to prepare meat for sale and facilities to hang meat. A problem for butchers in the towns, which persisted through the ages until the 20th century, was having a place to slaughter and dress the animals where it did not cause a nuisance to other inhabitants. Scalding pigs usually added to the aggravation.

The supplies for the town butchers came from the surrounding area, from the small farmers or the manorial or monastic estates. Often the butchers would have purchased animals in the town

Fig 6.10 Illustration of ploughing with four plough oxen copied from the Lutteral Psalter (1335 - 1340). When the older plough oxen were replaced they went to the butcher for slaughter, forming an important source of beef.

markets or local fairs when they were held. Many of the town butchers had a piece of land on which to hold animals ready for slaughter. Where a village was near a town the village butcher may have slaughtered animals and supplied the town butcher with carcases. There were some village butchers who sold meat in a town or town market. There were also outsiders bringing other goods into towns for sale. This situation caused much concern to the town butchers and the other town traders which led them to take steps to protect their interests.

Chapter 7

The Rise of the Guild Merchant and Craft Guilds

THE STATUS OF THE TOWNS

At the time of the Conquest, London had certain liberties and its own laws granted to it by Edward the Confessor which William I confirmed. The autonomous administration of London progressed with the city having its own mayor by 1200, resulting in the development of London proceeding differently from the rest of the country (Besant, 1906). In many cases towns were part of an estate and subject to the authority of their lord. Many of the older boroughs and cities were under the lordship of the king. The lordship of a town included entitlement to rents and other revenues such as tallages; a medieval form of taxation which the lord could impose upon the inhabitants. Other revenues from a town were tolls on trade and traders, income from the courts and profit from minting coins if the town had a charter for a mint. Administering the monies due to the king was usually the responsibility of the county sheriff (shire-reeve). Certain revenues were often consolidated into a borough 'farm' resulting in a total sum to be paid to the lordship of the town. The administration of this 'farm' was by the sheriff or the local lord's reeve or portreeve (bailiff) who collected the rents, tallages, tolls etc. and paid to the lord or king a fixed sum, making it incumbent on them to ensure the amounts collected covered that fixed amount (Miller & Hatcher, 1995).

THE GUILD MERCHANT

Along with the rapid urban expansion and the marked increase in the commercial activity of the towns during the 1100s, the guild merchant became a prominent feature in most of the towns. Although there was some variation from town to town, the guild merchant was essentially involved in regulating the trading activities in the town. The members of the guild consisted mainly of the burgesses of the town and others of standing. Some of the guild members were not inhabitants of the town but were involved in the trade of the town. It was an important condition of membership that the individual was 'scot and lot' (had paid municipal taxes and shared in the common charges of the community). The head of the guild merchant was the alderman and two to four associates. Merchants were the dominant members of the guild but membership included men of some of the craft trades; butchers, bakers, vintners, tanners, etc., although a number of craft trades were excluded. Many of the charters to the guild merchant were granted by Henry I and Henry II but it is apparent that the guilds had existed for many years before the grant of their charter. These charters gave the guild merchant full municipal powers in their towns. The concept of the guild merchant probably originated from the groups of merchants from the same town who banded together to form a caravan for mutual protection as they journeyed around the markets in Europe. These groups elected a leader and complied with the rules of the group and enjoyed certain privileges in their own town. In the Latin countries they were called *caritas* or *fraternitas* and in Germany they were called *gilde* or *hansa* (Besant, 1906; Lipson, 1959; Miller & Hatcher, 1995).

The advantage for those holding the lordship of a town was that the guild merchant, being able to expand the economy of the town and thereby increase their own members' incomes, was also improving the lord's revenues.

Guild members received benefits in respect of tolls and taxes and the right to trade in the town was restricted to the guildsmen. Foreign merchants (those from other towns) could only sell their merchandise wholesale, not retail, i.e. sell their merchandise to a guildsman who would then sell to the town's people. In fact, the guild merchant sustained the monopoly of trading in the town for its members. The fraternalism of the guild in the 12th century required the support for members who were sick or had fallen on hard times and the guild was involved in the funerals and the funeral rites of members (Lipson, 1959; Miller & Hatcher, 1995).

The control of the commercial activities by the guild extended to ensuring that their members maintained the required standards of the goods they produced or in their conduct of business. Those in default could be fined or excluded from the guild (*Ibid*).

After 1200 the guild merchant declined due to the development of municipal self government and the rise of the craft guilds. The establishment of municipal authorities and the appointment of mayors and other officials gave the burgesses an involvement in their own affairs, for which they had formally relied on the guild merchant; also the craft guilds protected their commercial interests (*Ibid*).

The guild merchant was established in the burghs of Scotland later than England. Perth, Berwick and Roxburgh had guilds by 1200 and by the 1300s at least 13 burghs had a guild merchant. In some burghs craftsmen were included in the membership of the guild merchant but in other burghs they were excluded, especially the crafts regarded as the lower crafts. The Perth guild included craftsmen as well as merchants. In Edinburgh the proportion of craftsmen was low and no craftsmen were members of the Aberdeen guild. The guild merchant continued longer than in England but the craft guilds took over the regulation of their sections of trading in the burghs as they came into prominence (Whyte, 1995).

THE CRAFT GUILDS

The craft guilds (gilds) existed in England before the Norman Conquest. The origin of craft guilds goes back to ancient Greece and Rome. The *collegia* of ancient Rome, which also existed throughout the Roman Empire, were associations of craftsmen or workers employed in the same craft or trade fulfilling most of the social and fraternal functions of the craft guilds. They also had a patron deity as craft guilds had a patron saint. With the fall of the western Roman Empire in the 5th century, the *collegia* were lost to the western European society but continued and flourished in the Byzantine Empire. It is in the opinion of a number of historians that the early development of the medieval craft guilds of Europe were based on the Byzantine *collegia* (Encyclopaedia Britannica CD 1999). The trading and other contacts that the Anglo-Saxons had with the Carolinian Empire resulted in craft guilds being introduced in England in the late Anglo-Saxon period. According to Strype's edition of Stow there was a meeting place for the butchers' guild at Smithfield in 975.

The craft guilds were originally fraternities of individuals following the same craft or mistery (from the medieval Latin *misterium* - craft) sharing social and religious functions, with assistance for members falling sick and on the death of members the assurance of a decent funeral and masses for their souls. The assurance of a properly conducted funeral with the religious rites was of great importance to the people in the middle ages. These fraternities had a patron saint which in the case of the butchers was St. Luke the Evangelist (Fig 7.1). People from the villages moving into the towns would have been accustomed to the support and the close-knit relationship of the rural community; therefore a craft guild would have acted as a substitute. A common feature of the craft guilds was regular gatherings of the guild members to discuss their affairs and to share a meal, which resulted in the need for a meeting place or hall. Craft guilds have been described as the corporate family. The experience of the guild merchant would have prompted a more active involvement in the commercial activities of the craft or trade. The guild system was based on the master craftsman owning the tools and equipment of the craft and having title to premises for the practice of the craft and where trading could take place. Additionally the master would generally need to have the freedom of the craft guild to follow his craft and trade within the town. The craftsmen employed by a master were referred to as journeymen and there was a system of apprentices for those wishing to learn the craft (Lipson, 1959; Miller & Hatcher, 1995).

Fig 7.1 A photograph of a statue of St. Luke the evangelist with his emblem, a winged ox. St. Luke was the patron saint of butchers. His feast day is 18th October. This statue of St.Luke and the other three evangelists are part of the statuary decorating the front of the Duomo in Sienna, Italy. The emblem of the winged ox is the principal feature of the Worshipful Company of Butchers' Coat of Arms.

After the decline of the guild merchant the administration of a town or borough was the municipal authority headed by the mayor, with the craft guilds each responsible for their section of the trade or industry. The craft guilds took a major role in London earlier than the rest of the country due to the continuity of the charter from Edward the Confessor and because there had not been a guild merchant in London. The number of separate craft guilds in each town varied. Some crafts would not be represented in the smaller towns especially the more specialist crafts. In many towns the number of individuals in one craft was so small that they were accommodated by the guild of another craft, which in some cases resulted in a guild representing four or five crafts. The London lay subsidy roll of 1332 indicated inhabitants engaged in over 100 different occupations which corresponded to the number of occupations of the guildsmen of Paris in the late 1200s. York was close to London with just less than 100 different craft guilds, Winchester with about seventy and Norwich with about 60. The more common crafts such as butchers, bakers, carpenters, masons and cordwainers, would have been represented by guilds in all towns. In Scotland there were a smaller number of craft guilds because a number of crafts were combined into one guild, as in the case of the Fleshers' Guild which related to butchers' meat, poultry and fish. The earliest record of a Butchers' Guild in London was in the Pipe Roll, 26 of Henry II (1180). The Guild of Butchers along with at least 18 other craft guilds were fined as being adulterine i.e. being without authorisation. The London Guild of Butchers had ordinances for a limited area in the city in 1331 and obtained their general ordinances in 1423. The London Guild of Poulters had their ordinances approved by the municipal authority in 1368 (Besant, 1906; Lipson, 1959; Miller & Hatcher, 1995).

There was an attempt in 1342 by the 12 misteries in Newcastle, including the Butchers' Guild, to take over control of the municipal authority which met with temporary success but they lost this control in 1345. There was a Butchers' Guild in York by 1349 and in Oxford about the same time (Dodds, 1917; Miller & Hatcher, 1995).

In Edinburgh the Fleshers' Guild was one of 14 guilds incorporated under "The Blue Blanket" which set forth the "powers and prerogatives of the craft thereof". The Fleshers' Guild was incorporated before 1488. There is also documentary evidence for the existence of Fleshers' Guilds in Aberdeen, Dundee, Glasgow and Selkirk (Fig 7.2) (Leighton & Douglas, 1910). There were a large number of fleshers in Aberdeen according to the records, which may relate to a high consumption of meat (Ewan, 1990).

The medieval development of the guild system was occurring simultaneously in Europe. In Germany they were known as *Zünft* or *Innung*, in France as *corporation de métier* and in Italy as *arte* (Microsoft Encarta 98). In Ravenna (Italy) in the 10th century there was a Corporation of Traders and a Corporation of Butchers (Besant, 1906).

LIVERY COMPANIES

The first mention of Guild Liveries was in the 1300s and the term 'company' started to be used in place of 'guild'. Some members of a guild would wear distinctive liveries generally consisting of richly coloured gowns and hats. In 1319 a chronicler of the time wrote "At this time many of the people of the trades of London were arrayed in livery and a good time was about to begin". Many of the guilds were incorporated by the municipality giving them due authority for their mistery

Fig 7.2 A drawing of the banner of the Fleshers' Corporation of Selkirk.

within the town and were therefore referred to as companies. In London in the mid 1300s, the Butchers' Guild, along with other guilds, was summoned to the Guildhall to support the Aldermen in the responsibilities of the City government. On such an occasion the representatives of each guild would have worn their livery (Besant, 1906; Lipson, 1959).

A statute of 1411 permitted the wearing of liveries by the Craft Guilds or Companies which permission was taken up by a number of them to stimulate the feeling of brotherhood but it soon became a mark of status. As the numbers of guildsmen increased the livery became confined to the more substantial members, namely those with a higher standing in the trade (Lipson, 1959). A dispute arose between the butchers of London over the election of wardens, resulting in the Mayor and Aldermen of the City issuing a decree in 1466 that Wardens of the Butchers' Company be elected only by substantial liverymen (Jones, 1976).

Of the City Companies of London in 1502 there were forty-seven with liveries and twenty-three without liveries (Jones, 1976). According to the records of Norwich (1449) all members of a craft guild 'having the means' were ordered to wear the appointed livery (Lipson, 1959).

By the late 1300s the distinction between the different members of the craft guilds was becoming more pronounced with the masters, or more particularly the liverymen, monopolising the government of the guilds. The journeymen and other non livery freemen felt excluded and somewhat marginalized, which led to the formation of yeoman guilds or associations of journeymen.

YEOMEN GUILDS

The constitution of most of the yeomen guilds was based on the model of the craft guilds, the yeomen having their own officials and a common purse. The yeoman guilds varied from craft to craft. Some were formed principally as religious and social associations but in some cases they were formed or became an association of workers (journeymen) to protect themselves from some of the practices of the employers (masters). The formation of a guild for the journeymen of the Cordwainers of Bristol in 1429 was for those "who for their services take wages from their masters". The large number of towns where records show that there were yeomen guilds in the 1400s indicates that they existed in most towns at this time (*Ibid*).

The yeomen guilds are regarded by many historians as the beginning of trade unions. There are a number of accounts of these guilds campaigning for better wages for their journeymen (Microsoft Encarta 98). There were also disputes over the masters taking on numbers of apprentices instead of employing journeymen. Because of these activities some of the yeomen guilds were banned and forbidden to hold meetings although some tried to meet under the pretext that it was only for a religious purpose. In a number of cases the municipal authorities decreed that the contentious yeomen guilds must submit to the rule and government of the masters of their mistery. At Coventry the masters and the civic authority obtained a royal mandate in 1406 to suppress the brotherhood of St. Anne formed by the journeymen; the injunction had to be renewed in 1414. An Act of Parliament in 1548 made it unlawful for journeymen or any workmen to form unions for the purpose of obtaining better wages or the improvement of their working conditions (Lipson, 1959).

A number of the yeomen guilds did not conflict with the livery company of their craft and pursued purely social activities in which they were supported by their masters. By the late 1400s the majority of yeomen guilds had become subordinate associations of the masters' companies and in most cases the masters appointed the executive officers of the yeomen's guild.

CONFLICT BETWEEN CRAFT GUILDS AND MUNICIPALITIES

For most of the country things went smoothly with the craft guilds regulating the trade and industry and the municipal authority administering the law and civic matters generally. Occasionally there was conflict between the municipality and one or more guilds. Norwich was initially opposed to guilds as it was thought they would lead to higher prices in the town. Henry III was persuaded in 1256 to insert a clause in their charter forbidding guilds but the matter was changed in 1286 with craft guilds being recognised. The municipal authority nominated wardens for each guild to report defective wares or fraudulent practices to the town bailiffs. The Norwich guilds were later to appoint their own wardens who had to be sworn before the mayor and were still required to fulfil those previous responsibilities (*Ibid*).

During the latter part of the 1300s a dispute divided the London guilds, with the victualling or provisioning guilds on one hand led by the Fishmongers' Guild and the non-victualling guilds as the opposition. The dispute was an attempt by the victualling guilds to control their affairs with complete independence from the municipal authority and not to submit to the authority in any respect. The basis of the dispute originated from the fishmongers over the control of the sale and price of fish. As the fishmongers had the support of Richard II there was a proclamation in 1391 prohibiting any opinion being passed upon the dispute. With the overthrow of Richard by Henry IV the position changed and the victualling guilds lost the rights and privileges that they had claimed during the dispute (*Ibid*).

All guilds made their ordinances (regulations of the guild) and were required to submit them to the civic authorities for approval. There were from time to time guilds having ordinances which had not been submitted for approval and in some cases these conflicted with the municipal authority control. The Butchers' Guild of London was fined for their ordinances in 1475. The York butchers attempted to keep their shops closed on Sundays but there was such a public outcry that the municipal authorities issued an order for all butchers to remain open on Sundays except during divine service (*Ibid*).

The most common cause of disputes between the victualling guilds and the municipality was the price of food. From time to time there was a scarcity of food, which was quite severe on occasions. To avoid public unrest the municipal authorities often imposed controls over the prices and supply of food without due consideration of the effect on the traders. Conversely there were the occasions when food traders took advantage of the monopoly held by the guild to charge high prices, which was often countered by the municipality breaking the guild's monopoly and allowing foreign traders into the town (i.e. traders from the nearby towns or villages). Country bakers and butchers in the 1400s and 1500s were permitted on certain days of the week to sell bread and meat in Coventry and the town traders were forbidden to interfere with these foreign traders. Records show that foreign bakers and butchers were allowed to sell in Chester on two days of the week in an attempt to "reduce the sale of victuals to a lesser price" (*Ibid*).

There were instances of persons attempting to use a guild to advance their own interest, i.e. to gain advantage of trade or leverage over the journeymen they employed. There were cases where families controlled a guild, as with the Guild of Tanners in Gloucester, where the same family name recurs constantly in the list of Masters of the Guild over a long period. By instituting various means to obstruct newcomers or journeymen becoming masters it limited the competition and kept the journeymen in a condition of economic dependency on the existing masters (*Ibid*). To this end they required the payment of 30 or 40 shillings from an apprentice to enter the guild but a statute of 1531 reduced apprentices fees to two shillings and sixpence (Jones, 1976).

THE GUILD SYSTEM AND THE MEDIEVAL ECONOMY

The post-Conquest economic growth was very closely related to the urban development and the prosperity of the towns. The rural economy relied on the town markets for the sale of produce and as collecting centres for exportable products. The craft guild system was a major factor in the medieval urban economy and therefore the economy of the country as a whole.

The problem with the guild system, as with most mechanisms for regulating commercial and economic activities, was to get the balance right. There was the necessity to restrict the number of traders for each commodity and so enable the individual traders to succeed and prosper. It was the prosperous traders who could expand the commercial activities and facilities of the town and push the economy forward. If there were too many sellers in the market place, including itinerant traders, the market potential was so diluted that it resulted in meagre returns for all. On the other hand, unreasonable exploitation by a guild of its monopoly status, especially with regard to prices and supplies, could lead to economic stagnation and probably unrest among the people.

In Scotland the grant of charters gave the burghs 'liberties' over types and areas of trade, which was in fact a monopoly. The liberty of the burgh pertained to the burgesses and hence to the guilds and in some cases included a monopoly over the buying and selling of particular commodities, not only in the burgh but also in the surrounding area. There were similarities with England in that this monopoly, while protecting the burgesses and enabling them to develop their businesses, stifled free trade and competition. These monopolies enjoyed by the burghs continued well into the late Middle Ages which was much later than in England (Ewan, 1990).

A very important contribution to medieval economic development by the craft guilds was the supervision of craftsmanship and the advancement of the apprenticeship system as a means of ensuring the continuity of that craftsmanship. Many of the craft apprentices were trained in manufacturing products and processing raw materials and there were the apprentices of the merchants who needed to learn about the commodities in which their master traded and the ways of commerce. The apprenticeship system continued through to the 20th century and played a vital part in providing the skills reservoir for the progression of technology and the industrial and commercial expansion through the industrial revolution into the 20th century.

There were various responsibilities placed upon the guilds for the supervision of the markets and shops where their members traded. The manufacturing craft guilds were required to ensure that the level of workmanship was maintained and the victualling guilds had to inspect the food on offer for its quality and fitness.

Other civic responsibilities included maintaining good order among guild members, their workers and servants. There were times when the guilds were called upon for the defence of the town such as supplying men to keep the watch. In 1370 when French galleys were reported lying off the foreland of Thanet the London guilds were required to supply the watch between the Tower and Billingsgate, consisting of 40 men at arms and 60 archers. It was the turn of the butchers along with the fishmongers to supply the watch each Thursday (Besant, 1906). In 1504 the London butchers supplied six men with bows and arrows, the fishmongers eight men and the poulters four men to wait on the Mayor during the watches on the nights of the vigils of St John the Baptist, St Peter and St Paul. In 1509 four men were provided by the butchers along with other companies to keep watch at Aldersgate (Jones, 1976). There are a number of records from the 1500s relating to the City of London companies being required to supply men or money to equip soldiers needed during the turbulent periods due to the religious upheavals in the country during the 16th century (Besant, 1906).

MEDIEVAL APPRENTICESHIPS

Coming of age in the 12th century according to R de Glanville was 21 for a knight's son, 15 for the son of a free peasant but for the son of a burgess of the town it was when he could count money carefully and otherwise attend to his father's business (Chibnall, 1986). An Elizabethan state paper defined the object of apprenticeship in the following terms: "Until a man grow unto the age of twenty-four years" he has not "grown unto the full knowledge of the art that he professeth".

Apprenticeships were the principal way of artisans being trained in the various aspects of a craft and acquiring the skills necessary to perform the tasks of the craftsman to the accepted standards of that craft. The apprenticeship system for training craftsmen has its roots far back in history. The Romans had apprentices learning their crafts and there are records from ancient Egypt referring to forms of apprenticeship. Apprentices are mentioned in the statutes of London dated

1230. During the 1200s formal systems of apprenticeship became widespread for all crafts throughout the country and this was a means of becoming a freeman of a guild. In most towns it was necessary to become a freeman of the Guild of Butchers to be able to sell meat or open a shop in the town. Initially the guilds were the sole regulators of apprenticeships but this was soon changed with overall municipal control as evident by the numbers of municipal authorities issuing statutes requiring the apprentice to be enrolled with the authority within the first year of the apprenticeship and having the indentures sealed (Besant, 1906; Lipson, 1959).

The period of apprenticeships varied in the medieval period. Initially the period was 'open ended' with many guild ordinances containing a statement to the effect that an apprentice was to "occupy the craft" until the masters of the mistery were able to testify that he was "able and well instructed in the craft". Twelve apprentices were recorded in the Chamberlain's register of the City of London as bound to London butchers during 1309 - 1312 and another 11 butchers obtained their freedom having served an apprenticeship. One apprentice was bound for twelve years and others for nine years and eight years (Jones, 1976). The regulations for the guilds in London under Edward I in 1252, are contained in *Liber Albus* :

> "And that no person shall from henceforth receive an apprentice if he be not himself free of the City, and cause their covenant to be enrolled, of whatever condition such apprentice may be. And that no apprentice, after his term fully served, shall follow his trade in the City, before he shall have been sworn of the freedom, and thereupon enrolled. And that no apprentice shall be received for less term than seven years according to the ancient and established usage." (Riley, 1861)

The term of seven years for apprenticeships was adopted by the guilds in the majority of towns in the country. The Statute of Apprentices (1563) made it compulsory throughout the country for apprentices to be bound for not less than seven years. The apprentice being bound to his master meant exactly that. If for some reason the apprentice ran away his master could have him apprehended and returned. If a boy became apprenticed without the knowledge of his parents the indentures could not be cancelled without the consent of the master (Besant, 1906; Lipson, 1959).

For some reason the majority of the London butchery apprentices came from outside London; in some cases from distant parts of the country, including those listed in the Chamberlain's register (1309 - 1312). When the apprentices had completed their time, only a small number are recorded as becoming freemen. It must be assumed that many returned to their home towns to practise the trade as butchers. Subsequent lists of London butchery apprentices show the same pattern (Besant, 1906; Jones, 1976).

The conditions of an apprenticeship were generally that the master would provide bed and board as well as training "and whatever is needful for an apprentice" (Fig 7.3). The indentures would often require masters to provide clothing. For the apprentice's part the covenant would require obedience, fidelity and good behaviour in not frequenting inns or gaming houses. During his term of apprenticeship he was not to "marry without his master's licence and do all the servile offices about the house and be obedient to his master's commandments and shall and should suffer such correction as his master shall think meet"(illustrations of indenture clauses from records of Leicester, Norwich and York) (Lipson, 1959; Miller & Hatcher, 1995).

Fig 7.3 Due to very restricted accommodation, apprentices and journeymen often had to sleep in the shop.

The master/apprentice relationship was a close one being described as "the master standing *in loco parentis* to the apprentice who lived in his house, sat at his board, and associated with him in the workshop and the home on terms of the most personal intimacy". As the guilds and their members were a dominant part of the town it was expected of all those responsible for training apprentices to endeavour to turn out good citizens as well as good craftsmen. On the completion of the apprenticeship some masters provided the apprentice with a set of tools of the trade which may have been a condition in the indentures (Lipson, 1959; Miller & Hatcher, 1995).

The number of apprentices a master could take on became a matter of controversy in the 1400s and 1500s for a variety of reasons. From the point of view of the apprentice it was considered wrong for a master to take on more apprentices than he could properly support or more than he could manage in their training to a suitable standard. As far as the journeymen were concerned some masters would take on extra apprentices to avoid employing journeymen and with a surplus of apprentices completing their term there were even poorer prospects of employment for journeymen. The attitudes of the masters were divided. Whereas there were some masters who wanted to take on extra apprentices as a matter of economy, many masters and their guilds felt the need to protect the trade in their town. Too many new persons qualifying in the trade could undermine and dilute the livings of those who were engaged in the trade. There are records of craft guilds in different towns restricting the number of apprentices each master was permitted but in some cases the wardens, past wardens and past masters of the company were allowed more than this number (Lipson, 1959).

TRAINING APPRENTICES

The training of apprentices was a two-fold process:

- The master demonstrating a manual operation and the apprentice attempting to carry out that operation under the watchful eye of the master. The apprentice would continue to practise the skills learned to the satisfaction of the master for the duration of the apprenticeship.
- The master would pass on the knowledge of the craft to his apprentices as it had been passed to him by his master. This knowledge would have been reinforced and probably extended during the master's years of experience.

There were almost certainly no written form of instructions or explanations relating to craft activities and even if there were, most craftsmen would have been unlikely to be able to read. The passing of craft knowledge from one to another was by the oral tradition.

ADVANCING THE KNOWLEDGE AND SKILL

The knowledge passed on to apprentices was essentially empirical knowledge acquired over many generations of craftsmen (Fig 7.4). Butchery craft knowledge developed over time and new ideas and methods were passed on by butchers meeting in the markets or travelling from place to place. Butchers from Britain travelling to the Continent would have observed the practices and exchanged know-how with their counterparts in the countries they visited. In this way Continental butchery practices were made known to the English butchers.

Fig 7.4 A drawing of an early 14th century illustration of butchers at work. On the right the slaughter of a pig is taking place, in the centre a pig carcase is being singed to remove the hair and on the left a man is emptying the intestines by running his hand along to squeeze out the contents. The original illustration is in the Bodleian Library, University of Oxford.

One way that butchers travelled was as part of the company of a Lord when he was visiting other parts of the country or journeying abroad. Many of the Norman Lords had estates in Normandy as well as England. In 1119 the Royal Ship "*The White Ship*" in which Prince William, heir to Henry I, was returning from a visit to France, struck a rock off the coast of Normandy and the only survivors were a Knight and the ship's butcher.

With the expansion of the towns, although many of the incoming inhabitants were from the surrounding area, records show that some of the craftsmen and merchants settling in the towns came from more distant parts of the country and even from the Continent. At least 27 aliens from the Continent including Flanders, France and Germany were made freemen of York between 1272 and 1348. It was a similar situation in other towns such as Canterbury, King's Lynn, Newcastle and Southampton. Some of these newcomers enhanced their craft or following by introducing new techniques or a wider knowledge of their trade (Miller & Hatcher, 1995).

Chapter 8

A Profile of the Urban Meat Trade

RURAL ASPECT OF TOWNS

The populations of the towns were not far removed from their rural roots, retaining many of the characteristics of a countryman, a large number of them having moved to the towns during the 12th and 13th centuries. The fields surrounding the towns were part of the heritage of the town's people and represented an essential part of the town's economy. The area within the walls of medieval Leicester was 130 acres whereas the town-fields covered almost thirty times that. In most cases, these fields were cultivated by the burgesses and the town butchers would use some of the fields for holding livestock. In most towns burgesses had rights to pasture animals in the surrounding fields. The Domesday Book records that "all the burgesses of Oxford have common pasture without the wall". A dispute arose in 1513 when the citizens of London found their common fields at Islington, Hoxton and Shoreditch had been enclosed. The citizens set to and removed the hedges and filled the ditches that enclosed the fields and won the day, the act of enclosing these fields being abandoned. A similar incident occurred in 1549 at Bristol with the same result (Lipson, 1959). Pigs were kept in the towns and there were numerous ordinances to control them. A proclamation in the City of London in 1297 banned pigsties in the streets and during the 13th century four men were appointed to seize and slaughter any pigs found wandering in the streets (Besant, 1906). It can be concluded that significant numbers of livestock were reared by the towns folk which would have meant work for the town butchers when these animals were ready for slaughter.

In Scotland a similar situation pertained with burgesses having rights to a considerable area of land around the burgh. The burgesses would use their land for growing crops and for pasturing animals and they would often enjoy grazing rights over the burgh's common land. Some of the land was kept for woodland to provide the burgesses with fuel and it was also used for pannage. The fleshers of the burgh were employed by the other burgesses to kill and butcher their animals when ready for slaughter. From Martinmas (11th November) to Yule (Christmas) fleshers were required by a burgh law to cut and prepare their meat for the burgesses' larders and during the period they were employed the fleshers were to eat at the burgesses' board (Ewan, 1990).

SUPPLY AND DEMAND FOR THE MEAT TRADE IN THE MIDDLE AGES

The economic expansion in the medieval period caused the growth in the volume of production, increase in urbanisation due to the size and number of towns and the increase in the markets and fairs, which in turn further stimulated the economy. There was also an improvement in marketing efficiency and the improvement of transacting (especially with the increase in the use of money). There were large numbers of merchants facilitating the expansion from local or regional trade into national and international trade. There was also the improvement in the transport of goods including a greater use of horses for the purpose (Donkin, 1976; Miller & Hatcher, 1995).

For an expanding meat trade the two fundamental requirements were an increase in meat supplies and a larger consumer market to serve.

The increase in supplies of mutton is evident from the considerable increase in the sheep flocks to supply the wool both for the home cloth market and the export of wool and cloth. Not only were there the great sheep flocks of the monasteries and those of lords on their demesnes but the peasants also kept a few sheep for the wool income which accounted for a not inconsiderable proportion of the national sheep flock. This proportion in the numbers of peasants' sheep increased during the reign of Edward III (Power, 1941). The increase in the numbers of sheep producing fleeces meant an equal increase in the mutton carcases available for the butchers. Tanning was a thriving trade and in some towns, particularly those in the West Country, there were large numbers of tanners to meet the demand of the export trade in hides. With all the additional hides there were also additional beef carcases for the butchers. This is supported by evidence of livestock numbers that clearly indicate a considerable rise in livestock from the Domesday survey to the early 1300s. The improved facility for buying and selling produce through the markets enabled farmers to specialise so that the regions more suited to pastoral farming concentrated on stock rearing which further increased the availability of slaughter stock. Trow-Smith (1957) estimated from the amount of wool produced that the sheep numbers for England and Wales in 1310 were about 12 million; he stated that this was a very rough figure due to the nature of the evidence on which the estimates were based.

An important fact to consider in contrast with the present day is that the proportional value of the carcase was very much lower compared with the other products. A bovine hide was worth about a third of the animal's total value. Apart from the hides and wool fells there was a greater demand for horns and hooves for the manufacture of various products such as buttons and combs, and fats and tallow were of very good value because of a rising demand for candles and grease for general purposes. Many of the manufacturing crafts relied on animal products for their raw materials, emphasising the importance of animals beyond the provision of meat. The make-up of the guilds of any medieval town will show a large proportion of craft guilds that worked principally with animal products which were the raw materials of their trade.

As is generally the case an expanding economy increases the wealth of many people and an increase in meat consumption is commonly part of the rise in opulence that follows. The increase in wealth during the 12th to 14th centuries was not distributed evenly, which seems to have been the pattern throughout history. The lords of the manor and the lesser landowners were able to increase their income considerably and the astute merchants also amassed fortunes. The local traders, craftsmen, carters, etc., will have profited, affording their families more affluence. At the lowest level the smallholding peasant suffered from pressures to pay higher rents and many had their land reduced through enclosures resulting from the moves to increase farming productivity. The rise in population also put pressure on these peasants and increased the numbers of landless peasants who had a struggle merely to survive (Lipson, 1959; Trevelyan, 1949). As feasting was a major feature of medieval life, the increase in the wealth of many resulted in even more lavish feasting which led to large numbers of people taking advantage of the hospitality of the baronial halls (Fig

8.1, Fig 8.2). A series of bad harvests resulted in the need to restrict some of the extravagances. Such was the necessity for some action, that a statute of Edward II in 1336 stated that:

> "No man shall cause himself to be served in his house or elsewhere at dinner, meal or supper, or any other time with more than two courses, and each mess of two sorts of victuals at the utmost be it flesh or fish, with the common sorts of pottage, without sauce or any other sort of victuals; and if any man chose to have a sauce for his mess he well may, provided it be not made at great cost: and if the flesh or fish be mixed therein, it shall be of two sorts only at the utmost, either fish or flesh and shall stand instead of a mess." (Curtis-Bennett, 1949)

Fig 8.1 Drawing of part of the Bayeux tapestry, a celebration of the conquest of England in 1066 by William I, showing cooking and serving food. On the left a pot is suspended over a fire, probably containing pottage or boiled meat; next is the baking of bread in an oven and then there are two men handing to those serving the food skewers on which pieces of meat and small birds have been cooked.

Fig 8.2 Drawing of part of the Lutteral Psalter, 1340. On the left is a cook removing meat from the boiling pot, using a flesh-hook and a ladle perforated to strain the liquid. In the centre is a butcher chopping a suckling pig in two and the serving men are collecting the prepared dishes to take to the table.

The range of poultry available for the table was extended in about 1520 by the introduction of turkeys from the New World. How they came to be called turkeys is the subject of conjecture, one suggestion being that a Turkish merchant ship plying its trade through the Mediterranean put into Seville and the master seeing a flock of turkeys that had arrived from the New World bought them and carried them on to England. They were bought by the English traders and because they had been obtained from a Turkish merchant these strange large bronze coloured birds were called 'turkie fowles'. In 1545 Archbishop Cranmer promulgated rules for clerical diet which included the "Turkey-cocke" classified among the "greater fowles" of which "one in a dishe was permissible for an ecclisiastic".

PROFILE OF MEDIEVAL URBAN CONSUMERS

Whilst the trade boom of the 1100s and 1200s provided opportunities for those capable of exploiting their entrepreneurial abilities as merchants, traders or in the craft industries, there were many for whom the alleviation of poverty was slight or non-existent. Many of the smallholding peasants did not find it easy even to achieve a subsistence level of existence. For the landless peasants the scarcity of even casual work forced many to flock to the towns in search of some work and income swelling the numbers of urban poor. A large section of the town populations had very low incomes even at the standards of the time. The graduated poll tax in King's Lynn for 1377 put servants, labourers, spinners, tapsters and sailors at the lowest level. A sizeable proportion of the population of the medieval towns was the destitute who would be existing in the direst circumstances, suffering malnutrition or near starvation with inadequate clothing to cover their bodies and no place to shelter. William Langland (1332 – 1400) in "*Piers the Plowman*" listed the most vulnerable which included "the old and infirm, expectant mothers who can no longer work, the blind, the disabled, victims of robbery or fire or unjust litigation and those families burdened with so many children that with their meagre earnings they were unable to feed and cloth them" (Miller & Hatcher, 1995).

The burgesses, tradesmen and craftsmen made up the more substantial citizens of the towns. Taxation records, which exclude the very poor, give some indication of the relative wealth of these citizens but it is no indication of their incomes. Taxation was based on the value of the possessions of the citizen. A surviving record for King's Lynn in the late 1200s listed most of the taxpayers having goods worth less than £5, and 25% with goods less than £1 whereas at the other end of the scale there were a number with goods worth up to £100 and four with goods between £100 and £250. The records for Colchester in 1301 had more than half of the taxpayers having goods valued at less than £1 and there were only six with goods at £5 or more, these being a mercer, two butchers and three tanners. In London in 1332 the citizens paying the highest tax were two corn merchants, a fishmonger and a butcher, Nicholas Crane, the first butcher to become an alderman of the city. An entry in the Bridport, Dorset, tax return itemises the value of possessions for one of the wealthier citizens who owned 1 cow, 2 hogs, two brass platters, some hides and some furniture, valued at a total of £4 - 8s. This helps to put the previous values more into perspective (*Ibid*).

The households of the towns constituted a major part of the town butchers' customers and there were the people from the close surrounding areas who would have come into the town especially on market days. The 1363 Act of Diet and Apparel of Servants stated the food that the servants of the nobility, tradesmen and artisans should receive each day, which included meat or fish once a day. Servants would have included apprentices and journeymen; in fact any ordinary employee was a servant. The meat purchased for the servants would have been included in the meat bought for the household of their employer (Hammond, 1993).

The urban populations in Scotland in the Middle Ages would seem to have had a plentiful amount of meat in their diet which was higher than that of the rural population. The quantities of fish and meat consumption was commented on by Aenius Sylvious in the 15th century (Ewan, 1990). Some houses had quite substantial meat supplies. Two priests residing at Mundens Chantry at Bridport, Dorset, spent about 80% of their budget on food, much of it on the basics consisting of bread, vegetables and ale but fish and fresh meat took a large portion of the budget. The two priests often had guests and in January 1455 they purchased extra food, including a sucking pig, a goose and two cocks when they entertained six guests. The additional food cost 2s - 3½d. (*Ibid*).

Generally the manor houses and other large establishments would have been supplied with meat from their estate but there is some evidence that butchers would be called upon for some bulk supplies, especially when a feast was being organised. The household book (1412 - 13) belonging to the household of Dame Alice de Bryene of Acton Hall, Suffolk, shows that apart from supplies from her estates, regular purchases of food were made including carcases of beef, mutton and pork, plus bacon. Gifts of meat were made to King Edward III and his Queen in 1328 by the City of London which was supplied by London butchers and poulters. The gift to the King consisted of "10 carcases of beeves, price £7 - 10s; 20 pigs price £4; 24 swans price £6; 24 bitterns and herons, price £4 - 4s; 10 dozen capons, price 50s". The gift to the Queen consisted of "5 carcases of beeves, price 75s; 12 pigs, price 48s; 12 swans, price 60s; 12 pheasants, price 48s." The carcases were bought from Nicholas Derman and the poultry from John Brid and John Scot (Besant, 1906; Hammond, 1993).

The proportion of income spent on food was very high at the lower end of the income scale; in fact obtaining sufficient food left little, if anything, for other things. The priests at Bridport spent well over half of their income on food. Sir Thomas Berkley of Berkley spent 57% of income on food in 1345 and Sir Hugh Luttrell of Dunster, a wealthy knight spent less than half his income on food in the 1420s (Hammond, 1993).

TYPES OF BUTCHERY BUSINESSES

There is no clear evidence of the size and type of medieval butchery businesses that existed but the foregoing evidence indicates that wealthy butchers were not the exception. It is difficult to think in terms of a wholesale butcher but wholesale butchers (then called carcase butchers) were operating in the 18th century but there are no clear indications from earlier periods. It is unlikely that large scale butchers were part of the Anglo-Saxon meat trade but by the 1300s a number of traders were operating in a substantial way of business. The Guild of Pepperers became the Guild of Grocers (or grossers: dealers in bulk or wholesalers) which indicates that the concept of wholesale trading in food existed. It is evident that some butchers traded in bulk meat and whole carcases and were therefore functioning in the nature of meat wholesalers. It is quite clear that Nicholas Derman was able to trade in bulk by supplying the Royal Household with 15 beef and 32 pig carcases in the course of his trading. There were instances where restrictions placed on members of the Guild of Butchers would have tended to frustrate the enterprising butchers. In some cases there were restrictions on the number of apprentices and journeymen they could employ and in other cases restrictions were placed on the numbers of animals they could slaughter each day (Besant, 1906).

Hucksters or chapmen were people who derived a meagre living by carrying goods to the customers' homes or selling in the street. Hucksters were mostly women. Some of them sold bread which was provided by bakers who charged them for 12 loaves and supplied 13; the extra loaf was their profit (the baker's dozen). It is not clear that meat was sold in this way but there is evidence of jobbing or hawking butchers in 1700s who were street sellers (*Ibid*). There is also documentary evidence from the 1700s of hawkers of fresh meat street-selling in the surrounding area of a town, including near-by villages; a practice which would have been highly probable in the medieval period. The problem for the poor in the purchase of food was that the penny was the smallest coin until half pennies and farthings were minted in the reign of Edward I (1272 – 1307). Prior to this a device to overcome the problem was to cut a penny into halves or quarters (Stenton, 1951). A number of butchers in Winchester in the 1300s would not sell less than a penny's worth of meat which amounted to about 2½ lb (Hammond, 1993).

Markets provided an opportunity for butchers from outside the town to bring meat in for sale. The markets were held on one day per week or in some cases more frequently. A number of the early medieval markets were held in the churchyards, generally on Sundays, serving the congregation before and after the services. Many of the charters and authorisations for these Sunday markets were for the sale of victuals which would have provided the poor with a chance to obtain meat, albeit in some cases of a dubious quality (Miller & Hatcher, 1995). Generally beef was the meat for the more wealthy members of society while pork and bacon was the meat of the poor. This may have been due, to some extent, to the poor quality of pork at this time. A number of the pigs would have been fattened on the grain residues of ale brewing.

The burgess butcher, a member of the butchers' guild, having his own shop, would generally have been the high class butcher serving the more affluent of the population, whereas the hucksters, hawkers and many of the market butchers scraped a meagre living selling to the lower end of the market. There has long been the practice, before the widespread use of refrigeration, for butchers to sell the meat they had left at the end of the day cheaply enabling some of the poorer people to afford to buy meat. Many of the wealthier households purchased the cheaper meat for their servants. William Langland did not express a high regard for medieval victuallers in 'Piers the Plowman':

"Punish in the pillories and stools of repentance
The brewers, the bakers, the butchers, the cooks,
For these are the men that do the most mischief
To the poor people that buy by the parcel.
They poison the people privily and often
Getting rich by retail and buying up rents
With what the poor people should put in their bellies." (Coghill, 1949)

A considerable proportion of the meat consumed in a medieval town was sold in a cooked form. There were the taverns and other eating houses where food was consumed on the premises and then there were the cook shops and pie bakers where the food was eaten on the premises or taken away (Fig 8.3). The common town cries of the cooks according to Langland in "*Piers the Plowman*" were "Hot pies, hot! Good pigs and geese! Come and dine! Come and dine!" While the taverner bawled White wine of Alsace! Red wine of Gascony! Wine of the Rhine!" (Besant, 1906). In 1183 Fitzstephen's description of London included;

> "upon the river's bank, amid the wine that was sold from ships and wine cellars, a public cook shop. There daily according to season, you may find great viands dishes, roast, fried and boiled, fish great and small, the coarser flesh for the poor, the more delicate for the rich, such as venison and birds both big and little." (Curtis-Bennett, 1949)

Fig 8.3 Cookshop specialising in tripe. On the left a woman is cleaning and scraping the tripes ready to go in the pot on the right for boiling. There is a funnelled ventilator above the pot to catch the steam and channel it outside. In the background a man is being served with a helping of cooked tripe. A line drawing from an illuminated manuscript from Lombardy, 1350 - 1400.

The town butchers would have been the main suppliers of the meat for these cook shops and pie bakers; in many cases this would have assured the Butchers' Guild monopoly. The reason that every town was well supported by pie bakers and cook shops was that ovens in poorer domestic housing did not exist, added to which obtaining fuel for cooking would have been difficult or expensive. The peasants on the estates usually had their bread, pies, etc., baked in the common bakehouse on the estate. For this there was a small charge; extra revenue for the lord of the manor (Saltzman, 1926).

There were requirements for butchers' shops to be closed and cook shops not allowed to sell meat on Fridays, during Lent and on any other fish days. Due to the power and influence of the medieval church, general compliance was highly probable although there were always those seeking to find a way around the ruling. According to William Caxton's "*The Description of the Britain*", 1480, there was the belief in Ireland that barnacle geese grew on trees therefore Irish monks regarded it as permissible to eat the flesh of barnacle geese on fish days (Fig 8.4) (Collins, 1988).

Fig 8.4 There was a belief among the Irish monks that barnacle-geese grew on trees and therefore they were allowed to eat the flesh of the geese during lent. (From Topographical Hibenica by Gerald of Wales, 1146 - 1220.)

From time to time town ordinances and statutes of the crown were made to control prices when certain provisions were in short supply but although it was easy to make laws there was little or no organised policing and enforcement to ensure these laws were obeyed.

MEAT COOKING IN THE MIDDLE AGES

The principal methods of cooking meat in the Middle Ages were stewing or boiling and spit roasting. A standard method of cooking meat was to skewer cut pieces of meat on a long metal skewer and cook it over a wood or charcoal fire, as illustrated in the Bayeux Tapestry. In some cases the fire was on a raised brick or stone surface. When cooked the meat was pushed off the skewer onto a dish and served. There were a range of spits of different sizes; small spits for meat joints or poultry and larger spits for whole carcases or several meat joints or chickens (Fig 8.5). These spits were turned in various ways, mainly manually or in some situations by a descending weight on a cord that through a series of pulley wheels would slowly turn the spit. The basic firedog which originated in the Iron Age was in use in the Middle Ages, although often of more elaborate design and supporting several spits (Wright, 1964). A shallow dish or tray was commonly placed under the meat turning on the spit to collect the fat and a large spoon or ladle would be at hand with which to baste the meat with its own fat. Gridirons were in use which were similar to those from the Roman period and were used to support pots over the fire or for grilling steaks (Ainsworth-Davis, 1931). Boiling or stewing meat was common either for great banquets or the peasants fare. Meat when boiled was referred to as 'sodden' and would have been taken piping hot from the pot, using flesh hooks (Fig 8.6, Fig 8.7). Adding vegetables to the meat in the pot produced pottage or soup. A variety of pottages were made using different vegetables and herbs to serve at banquets. The term 'pot herbs' (referred to in Langland's "*Piers the Plowman*") was used for a

Fig 8.5 Roasting birds and boiling pottage or meat outside the Saltire Inn *c.* 1340 . Cooking often took place outside or at least in an outbuilding separate from the main building because of the danger of fire. The original is in the Bodleian Library, University of Oxford.

Fig 8.6 Drawing of an illustration in a 13th century manuscript showing meat being served up from the large cooking pot. The meat is being lifted out of the pot using a flesh hook. On the left a sheep is being killed, which may indicate that in this case animals are slaughtered, prepared and their meat cooked at the same time and in the same place. The hook suspending the cooking pot is on a ratchet enabling the height above the fire to be adjusted. Original in the Pierpont Morgan Library, New York.

Fig 8.7 An impression of a medieval flesh-hook that was used for removing meat from a pot in which the meat was being boiled.

collection of vegetables suitable for pottage. For the poor, pottage was their main source of sustenance very often a pease pottage. Andrew Boorde's "*Compendyous Regyment or Dyetary of Health*", 1542, contains the following: "Potage is not used so moch in all Crystendom as is used in Englande. Potage is made of the lyquor in whiche fleshe is soden in, with puttyng to chopped herbs and otemel and salt. Fyrmente is made of whete and mylke, in whiche yf flesshe be soden it doth nourysshe, and it doth strength a man". It was already the fashion of eating collops (slices) of bacon with eggs in the Middle Ages (Wilson, 1973). Chaucer described the table of the poor widow in 'Nonne Prestes Tale' thus:

"Hir bord was served moost with whit and blak
Milk and broun breed, in which she foond no lak
Seynd bacoun (smoked bacon), and somtyme an ey or tweye (egg or two)."

Fig 8.8 Cardinal Wolsey's kitchen at Hampton Court.

Andrew Boorde had a high regard for bacon and eggs: "Bacon is good for carters and plowmen, the whiche be ever labouringe in the earth or dunge. I do say that colloppes and egges is as holsome for them as a talowe candle is good for a blereyed mare" (Boorde, 1542). A list of kitchen equipment was drawn up in 1403 as that necessary for a two-day occasion in Savoy. The list included the provision of good cauldrons to boil large cuts of meat, a great number of moderate sized ones for pottages or for other cooking uses, a great many large and ordinary sized boilers, suspended pans for cooking fish and a dozen good big mortars. Also needed were 20 large frying pans, 12 great kettles, 50 pots, 62 handled pots, 100 hampers, 12 grills, 6 large graters, 100 wooden spoons, 25 holed spoons, 6 pot-hooks, 20 oven shovels, 20 roasters with turntable spits and those with spits mounted on andirons (firedogs) (Fig 8.8) (Hammond, 1993).

Chapter 9

Markets and Fairs

MEDIEVAL COMMERCIAL TRANSACTIONS

The growth in the number of markets and fairs during the 1100s and 1200s in itself improved trading efficiency by virtue of the fact that markets and fairs were more accessible to both the producers and the buyers. The improvements in transportation and the increase flow of money all helped to facilitate the expansion of trade. The money supply during William I's reign has been estimated between £25,000 - £37,500. Estimates show dramatic increases to £250,000 before the end of the 1100s, £600,000 during the 1200s and over £1,000,000 by the beginning of the 1300s. This growth in the money supply was beyond that which could be accounted for in respect of population growth and was largely the result of increased trading activities (Miller & Hatcher, 1995). Coinage was based on the silver penny that had its origins in the 8th century when Charlemagne introduced the standard of 240 silver denarii to weigh one pound. Between 775 and 780 official coinage began in Canterbury and as there were strong trade links with the Frankish kingdom, they adopted the Frankish silver denarius as the standard. The denarius became the Anglo-Saxon steorra (sterling) with 240 steorra equalling a pound of silver hence the present day pound sterling (Fisher, 1973). The sterling became the penny and subsequently the currency being defined in the values £.s.d. or l.s.d. (Latin: *librae - solidi - denarii.*).

Apart from all these improvements there were still constraints on trading due to the method of counting and calculation in the Middle Ages. The introduction of the Hindu/Arabic numbering system was not until the 16th century. Prior to this it was the Roman numbering system that existed. Two important developments of the Arabic system were (i) the zero and (ii) the positional notation in which a numeric character assumes a different value according to its position (i.e. positioned from the right: units, 10s, 100s, etc.) (Encyclopaedia Britannica CD 1999). While the Roman numerals can be used to represent quantities etc. the problem arises with regard to commercial calculations; indeed any form of calculating, the result being that medieval trading transactions and accounting were a much more difficult process.

The most important device for the purposes of accounting and calculation was the counting board with the casting counters or jettons. The casting counters were round metal discs similar to coins but to distinguish them they had a hole punched through the middle. They were usually made of copper. The counting board was divided by a series of lines or grooves. Casting counters were placed on the board, each section giving a different value to the counter. Adding and removing counters and moving them to different positions on the board was a method of calculating that was very efficient. Where there was a permanent room or counting house for the calculating there would be a table with the table top marked off as a counting board. The portable counting board was a sheet of cloth marked off as a counting board which could be spread on a table or other flat surface for the calculating to be carried out. Counting boards were used in the royal treasury and the chess-board-like appearance of the counting board gave rise to the name exchequer for the office administering state revenues (Lipson, 1959; Stenton, 1951).

Tallies were one of the principal forms of documentation in relation to medieval transactions. They were used as receipts, bills, records of debts, etc. Tallies were made of wood which had the advantage of being durable. They were flat, about 80mm - 160mm long and 6mm - 12mm wide. The top part was used to write the names of the parties to the transaction and notches were cut into the remaining part, each notch representing a monetary value (Fig 9.1, Fig 9.2). The wider the notch the higher the value; a single cut represented one penny. The tallies were so fashioned along the grain of the wood that when the notches were all cut, the part of the tally containing the notches could be split longitudinally so that each piece had identical notches. This guarded against fraud or forgery as the two pieces from the same tally would match perfectly. When the matching of tallies had taken place they were said to have tallied: hence the matching of invoices, weight notes, statements, etc., is still referred to as tallying. The use of tallies was abolished in 1783 but there were still some in use up until 1826 (Lipson, 1959).

Fig 9.1 A tally for 6s. 8d. issued by the treasurer of Edward I to the Sheriff of Lincolnshire.

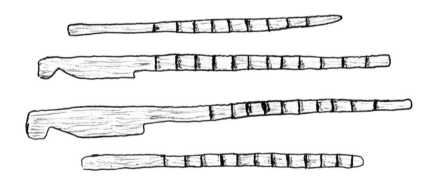

Fig 9.2 An example of 14th century wooden tallies. Each notch cut into the tally represented a monetary value or an item that had been traded such as an ox, sheep, pig, hide, etc. The notches were first cut and then the wooden tally would be split longitudinally into two, which could be identified one with the other. One would be for the seller and the other for the buyer, which they would retain until the day of settlement.

Credit trading was a feature of the medieval economy but to what extent is not clear. There are records showing debts owed to and by traders. For some commodities it was considered necessary for the transactions to be in cash, Court Rolls in the City of London in the early 1300s required that bakers paid cash for their wheat and butchers paid cash for their animals. The fact that these ordinances existed is evidence that credit trading in these commodities was practised (Besant, 1906).

MEDIEVAL MARKETS

The build up of a network of markets during the medieval economic boom of the 1100s and 1200s was an essential part of the expansion of trade. Markets and fairs were the principal way in which buyers and sellers could come together to transact their business. Another important feature of this development of the market network was the improvement of market intelligence. Market intelligence is today fundamental to the working of a free market. Modern traders would be at a loss without the availability of information on prices, supplies, etc., of the commodities in which they deal. Before 1100, although many markets existed, there were parts of the country where villages were remote from any markets, therefore the villagers were heavily constrained in selling or buying goods or produce if markets were not available in the immediate locality. The network of markets built up to a peak between 1100 –1300 and could be compared to the great French markets of Champagne and Lyons (Lipson, 1959). This marketing network facilitated the balancing of supply and demand. Buyers had a better knowledge of where they could obtain the goods or produce they required and sellers had a market place where potential buyers would be present.

In most cases the market or fair was the only legal place for sales to be made. For a sale to be legal outside of a market it would normally require two or three witnesses. The day of a market could not be changed except by royal sanction and the rights and privileges pertaining to a market charter were jealously safeguarded (*Ibid*).

Markets and fairs could only be held in the burghs in Scotland giving the burgh control over market trading and therefore reinforcing the burgesses' trading monopolies (Ewan, 1990).

A number of the early markets were held in churchyards so that the traders were able to take advantage of selling to the gathered congregation (Fig 9.3). All Saints churchyard at Northampton was used for this purpose until it was banned in 1235. There was a court leet reference to the sale of fish in the churchyard at Walsoken, Norfolk, in 1299 and in 1306 there was a market in the Crosthwaite churchyard, Cumberland for food which included meat and fish. Sunday was often chosen as the day for food markets. William I granted a charter for a Sunday market to Battle Abbey. There was opposition to holding markets in the churchyard, considered by some as a desecration. There was an episcopal charter to Wells in 1201 directed at traders which stated; "by no means presume to enter, or desecrate, the church of Wells or the church porch to sell their merchandise". The Statute of Winchester issued by Edward I in 1285 required "from henceforth neither fairs nor markets be kept in churchyards for the honour of the church". In spite of this the practice continued and the accusation of desecrating the Sabbath was added by the opponents of Sunday markets. A petition to Parliament in 1449 complained that "For great earthly covetise the

Fig 9.3 An impression of a market held on Sunday in a church yard. The vendors set up their stalls to catch the congregation as they left the church after the service. Some clergy were opposed to this type of market regarding it as sacrilegious.

people is wilfully more vexed and in bodily labour defouled than in other festival days, as in pitching and making their booths and stalls, bearing and carrying, lifting and placing their wares onward and homeward, as though they did nothing remember the horrible defiling of their souls in buying and selling, with many deceitful lies and false perjury, with drunkenness and strifes, and so specially withdrawing themselves and their servants from divine service". A Sunday market in Norwich for the sale of victuals was granted in 1380 and the order rescinded in 1422. A statute of Henry VI revived the old enactment for the Sunday market for 'necessary victuals' (Lipson, 1959; Miller & Hatcher, 1995).

There was the encouragement for the local lords and the crown to set up markets because it gave them an income from the tolls paid by the traders (Fig 9.4). There were about 300 officially authorised markets in England before 1200. In the period 1200 - 1274 there was the foundation of 425 markets and 249 were founded in the period 1275 - 1349 (Miller & Hatcher, 1995).

Many of the markets in this period were in villages that were growing into towns but a large number were held in average villages. Apart from those formally founded there were many informal markets that were also held in the churchyards or other convenient spaces in the villages. There is

Fig 9.4 Drawing of a medieval illumination depicting officials checking the weights and measures in a market place.

very little documentary evidence of the nature of these markets but there is reference to a market in court proceedings in the reign of Edward I; '... market held every week on Wednesdays, to which all of the people of the countryside used to come to sell and buy oxen and cows, sheep and other kinds of animals, wheat, rye and barley, etc., sendal, silks and other kinds of textiles'. There were pleadings before the Shropshire justices in 1256 relating to competition between the neighbouring markets of Hawkesbury (Gloucestershire) and Sherston (Wiltshire), both being no more than villages according to the 1334 tax assessments. One function of these small markets was for villagers to sell their produce, including meat, to the people from the surrounding area and traders from the larger towns. Buyers of meat at village markets may have been town butchers or traders buying on behalf of town butchers. There would have been some meat bought to be hawked around the town by hucksters. Some merchants (or dealers) present at these village markets bought up produce and livestock which they took on to the larger markets for resale. This fact was noted at the time of Henry III with produce being bought at Hawkesbury for resale 20 miles away in the Bristol market (Miller & Hatcher, 1995).

A major source of contention that arose when new markets were founded was the effect on the trade of existing markets due to the proximity of a new market. Burgesses of towns were automatically opposed to the establishment of a market or fair in the vicinity of their town. Bracton, a lawyer in the 1200s, established that a market would not affect the trade of an existing market providing it was not less than $6^2/_3$ miles distant. This was said to be based on the premise that a reasonable day's journey (on foot) was 20 miles and dividing this into three, the first part was to get to the market, the second part to transact business at the market and the third part to return home, equalling $6^2/_3$ miles for the journey to and from the market. This was the basis of Edward III's charter to London in 1327 prohibiting any market being established within 7 miles of the city. In many parts of the country this did not apply, as in Derbyshire in about 1300 where the numerous markets considerably overlapped the $6^2/_3$ mile radius around each one. It was claimed that as long as the markets in close proximity were held on different days they would complement each other by attracting more merchants into the area (Donkin, 1976).

Some of the controversy over competing markets turned into physical violence. The monks at Ely set up a market at Lakenheath and refused to acknowledge the king's writ or the protests of the abbot of Bury St. Edmunds. The abbot sent word to his bailiffs "to take men of St. Edmunds with horse and arms and destroy the market; all whom they found buying or selling they should bring away in bonds." The abbot's bailiffs descended on Lakenheath with almost 600 men but the people in the market were warned in advance and had dispersed. The bailiffs' men turned over the butchers' shambles and the stalls in the market and carried them away and they also seized their cattle (Lipson, 1959).

During the 1300s there was an increase in the activities and the role of merchants. The growth in trade and the network of markets facilitated more specialisation in parts of the country, such as parts of the north of the country becoming more orientated to cattle rearing. This enabled the entrepreneurial merchants to trade in a variety of commodities. William Durham of Darlington exported wool from the north to the Low Countries and dealt in grain and was involved in procuring livestock for the Durham Priory. There was at this time a rise in livestock traders or dealers referred to as 'merchants of beasts' (Miller & Hatcher, 1995).

SMITHFIELD LIVESTOCK MARKET

There was a regular market for the sale of horses, cattle and other livestock at Smithfield (Smoothfield) from the Anglo-Saxon period and it was also a place of execution. Smithfield was the site chosen by Rahere in 1123 for the founding of a hospital and a priory dedicated to St Bartholomew. Rahere had been a minstrel or a jester at the court of Henry I. In 1120 he went on a pilgrimage to Rome during which time he became ill with a malarious fever and had a vision of St Bartholomew. Rahere recovered from his fever and dedicated himself to these foundations and became the first Prior of St Bartholomew (Thornbury, 1987). There was to ensue a close relationship between the priory and the market.

The Smithfield area in 1100 was described as a flat barren heath covered with springs and ponds and the occasional clump of trees. The site where the priory was built had been the place of executions so the execution site was moved to a position between "the horse pond and Turnmill brook" and was known as The Elms. The site is now occupied by the top part of Smithfield meat market. Some eminent people were executed at The Elms in the medieval period. William FitzOsbert (also known as William Longbeard) who sided with the craftsmen against the authorities was hanged in about 1200 and it was here that the Scottish patriot Sir William Wallace was executed in 1305. Roger Mortimer was hung, drawn and quartered in 1330 for his part in the murder of Edward II. In 1388 Tyburn replaced The Elms as the principal site for hangings. Smithfield continued to be the place of executions by burning and boiling in oil (Besant, 1906; Thornbury, 1987).

During the medieval period Smithfield market expanded into the largest market for livestock for slaughter in the country. This was due to the growth of London as an urban and a commercial centre. The population of London in 1200 was about 30,000 (estimate) and about 50,000 in 1334 (estimate). The population had spread beyond the walls of the city to the west reaching as far as the palace of Westminster. Much of the population growth was due to migration from rural areas. By comparison there were few towns in the country that had a population above 5,000 (Donkin, 1976). Apart from the large population requiring meat there was also the wealth to attract the suppliers. Assessments of wealth of towns for tax purposes in 1334 put London at £11,000. The next highest was Bristol at £2,200 with York, Newcastle upon Tyne, Boston, Great Yarmouth and Lincoln above £1,000 and all others below £1,000 (Glasscock, 1976).

Riley states in 'Introduction to *Liber Albus*' "From the frequent mention of pigs, it would seem probable that pork was more extensively consumed than any other kind of butchers' meat. In Edward IIIs reign lambs were mentioned as being brought by boat to St. Boltoph's wharf near the Tower" (Riley, 1861).

THE LONDON MEAT MARKETS

While Smithfield was the livestock market for London there were three principal dead meat or flesh markets in the City to supply the needs of the population in the medieval period. These were St. Nicholas Shambles, East Cheap and Stocks. Late in the medieval period Leadenhall market became prominent as a flesh market (Fig 9.5).

St. Nicholas Shambles was a series of butchers' stalls and shops adjoining Newgate market collectively called West Chepe. The flesh market was adjacent to the parish church of St. Nicholas Shambles in which there was a chapel dedicated to St. Luke the evangelist, the patron saint of the Butchers and it was where the butchers stored their chests and hearse cloth. John Godbehere, a butcher, gave a silver gilt chalice for the side alter of St. James and in his will dated 1460 he asks to be buried in the church before the alter of St. James (Combes, 1997). The site of St. Nicholas Shambles, a Saxon church, was excavated in 1975-9 and the site is now occupied by the British Telecom Centre.

An account of Farringdon Ward Within from Stow's 'Survey of London' reads as follows:

> "From the conduit by St Paul's Gate on the north side is a large street running west to Newgate, the first part whereof, from the conduit to the shambles, is of selling bladders there, called Bladder Street. Then behind the butchers' shops be now divers slaughter houses inward, and tippling houses outward. This is called Mountgodard Street of the tippling houses there... Before this Mountgodard Street stall boards were of old time set up by the butchers to show and sell their flesh meat upon, over the which stall boards they first built sheds to keep off the weather; but since that, encroaching by little and little, they have made their stall boards and sheds fair houses, meet for the principal shambles. Next is Newgate Market, first corn and meal, and then other victuals, which stretcheth almost to Eldenese Lane." (Stow, 1598)

East Cheap (East Chepe) Market or Shambles was the flesh market for supplying the eastern half of the city while Nicholas Shambles supplied the western half. Until the opening of Stocks Market, East Cheap and Nicholas Shambles were the only places in the city where fresh meat could be sold retail. This restriction was reinforced in an ordinance of 1277. Some butchers attempted to set up stalls in the Poultry in 1345 and in consequence their meat was confiscated. One course taken to regulate the markets in 1244 by the King's Justices was to require all the butchers' stalls in both Nicholas Shambles and East Cheap to be numbered and a return made of the stall holders. As these stalls were standing in the King's highway there were attempts by the sheriffs to claim rent from the butchers (Jones, 1976). Leading from East Cheap was Pudding (or Podying) Lane along which the East Cheap butchers carried the entrails from their slaughtered animals to the dungboats on the Thames.

Fig 9.5 Map of the City of London based on an engraved map of the City before 1550 (facing page).

A. Smithfield Market.
B. St Nicholas Shambles. Site is now Newgate Street.
C. Stocks Market. Present site of the Mansion House.
D. Leadenhall Market.
E. Queenhythe. On the west side was Brookes Wharf from where the butchers of St Nicholas Shambles disposed of their waste.
F. Rother Lane or Red Rose Lane, later Pudding Lane where the East Cheap butchers carted their waste to load onto the dung boats near London Bridge.
G. The Fleet (Flete) River which the butchers used at one time to wash the entrails from the slaughtered beasts.
H. Bridewell Palace of Henry VIII, later to become the house of correction for the undeserving poor; the first workhouse.
I. Baynard's Castle.
J. St Paul's Cathedral showing it with its tall spire which was destroyed by fire in 1561 and never replaced.
K. The Augustinian Priory of St. Bartholomew now the church of St. Bartholomew the Great.
L. Lud Gate.
M. New Gate.
N. Alders Gate.
O. Cripple Gate.
P. Moor Gate.
Q. Bishops Gate.
R. Cheapside.
S. Poultry.
T. Cornhill.
U. Threadneedle Street.
V. East Cheap, an area for butchers' shops.
W. London Bridge.
X. Holborn.
Y. Fleet Street.

Stocks market (Le Stokkes) was on the site now occupied by the Mansion House. The Stocks market house was built in1283 by Henry Walles, then mayor, for the sale of meat and fish in the midst of the city. Stocks market house was so named as a pair of stocks for the punishment of offenders previously stood on the site (Jones, 1976). Stow states; "in the year 1543 … there were in this Stocks Market, - for Fishmongers twenty five boards or stalls, rented yearly to £34-13s-4d; there were for butchers eighteen boards or stalls rented at £41-16s-4d" (Stow, 1598).

Leadenhall was a mansion, so named because of its lead roof, which belonged to the Neville family in the 1309 and was obtained by the city in 1411. It was converted into a granary and market in 1445 by the Lord Mayor, Sir Simon Eyre. Leadenhall was the market for foreign traders, those coming in from outside the city. It was a market for food in general, including poultry and fish, but foreign butchers were not admitted there to sell flesh until 1533. Stow writes;

> "The foreign butchers for a long time stood in the high street of Lime Street Ward on the north side, twice every week, namely, Wednesday and Saturday, and were some gain to the tenants before whose houses they set their blocks and stalls; but that advantage being espied, they were taken into Leadenhall, there to pay for their standing to the chamber of London." (Stow, 1598).

Stow additionally states;

> "it was enacted (1533), that butchers should sell their beef not above a halfpenny the
> pound, and mutton a half penny half farthing. Which act being devised for the great
> commodity of the realm, as it was then thought, has since proved otherwise; for
> before that time a fat ox was in London for six and twenty shillings and eight pence
> at the most, a fat wether for three shillings and four pence, a fat calf for the like price,
> a fat lamb for twelve pence, pieces of beef weighing two pounds and a half at the
> least, yea three pounds or better, for a penny, on every butcher's stall in this city, and
> of those pieces of beef thirteen or fourteen for twelve pence, fat mutton for eightpence,
> at the dearest. What the price is now (1598) I need not set down. Many men thought
> the same act to rise in price, by means that graziers knew or supposed what weight
> their beasts contained, and so raising their price thereafter, the butcher could be no
> gainer, but likewise raising his price. The number of butchers then in the city and
> suburbs was accounted six score, of which everyone killed six oxen apiece weekly,
> ...or seven hundred and twenty oxen weekly." (*Ibid*)

In the latter part of the medieval period the rising population and increasing wealth of London
considerably increased the demand for meat, putting pressure on the municipal authorities to
ensure that there was an adequate supply. It was for this reason that the foreign butchers were
given increasing facilities and more times during which they could sell meat in the city. To a lesser
extent, foreign butchers were increasing their part in the supply of meat in many towns throughout
the country during the latter medieval period. An effect of this was to reduce the control of the
trade by the butchers' guilds.

FAIRS

Fairs were another major development of commercial activity in the Middle Ages and were generally
established by royal charter. The fairs were usually held once a year on the occasion of a religious
festival or other prominent dates in the religious calendar and could last for as long as a month.
The tolls collected from the merchants at the fair either went into the local coffers or to the church.
For the larger more important fairs merchants would travel not only from all parts of the country
to attend but also from other countries to sell their spices, cloth, silks and trinkets; indeed there
was a wide range of commodities of all sorts, including livestock. Markets differed from fairs in
that they were held on a regular basis, usually one or more times per week and were much less
extensive in the commodities available.

    A number of the fairs had an emphasis on one commodity and were held at the time of year
when that commodity was most readily available. One such fair, held under a charter granted by
Henry I in 1133 to the Augustinian priory of St Bartholomew the Great, was St Bartholomew's
Fair which was held annually on Bartholomew Tide at Smithfield (Thornbury, 1987). This fair
became the greatest cloth fair in the country and, according to Stow "to which the clothiers of all
England and the drapers of London repaired, and had their booths and standings within the
churchyard of this priory" (Stow, 1598). St Bartholomew's Fair attracted many that were out to

make some money from the merchants and others attending the fair. There were the entertainers, musicians, dancers, jugglers, and there were those supplying food and drink to the people at the fair (Thornbury, 1987). Many London butchers did very well with this great influx of people. The fair was to become notorious because of the riotous behaviour that commonly occurred during the time of the fair.

Although there were many smaller fairs that did not require too much advanced planning, the large fairs were a different matter. They could be compared with the county shows of today for which planning and organisation is a major task. The Stourbridge Fair was a great international fair which began in 1211 when permission to hold the fair was given to the Leper Hospital at Stourbridge by King John. The fair which was held from 8th September, lasting for three weeks, needed a great deal of planning and organisation as the following account relates;

> "The temporary wooden buildings were commenced by custom on St Bartholomew's Day, August 24th, and the builders of these houses were allowed to destroy corn grown on the spot, with impunity, if it were not cleared before that day. On the other hand the owner of the field was empowered to destroy the booths on Michaelmas Day, if not cleared by that time. The space allotted to the fair, about half a square mile, was divided into streets which were named, sometimes by nations, and in each of these streets some special trade was carried on, the principal being foreign spices and fruits, ironmongery, fish, metal goods, cloth, wool, leather, and latterly books. Nothing was too cumbrous or too costly for a medieval fair, because the dealer, if he could not find customers there, could find them nowhere else. There were few householders possessed of any wealth who did not either purchase or give a commission for Stourbridge Fair. There were assembled merchants of the East and the West, traders of the Levant, Venetians and Genoese, Spaniards with jennets and war-horses, and iron from the 'crane of Seville'." (McDougall, 1929)

An important accommodation that had to be considered in the planning of a major fair was space for parking the wagons that brought the goods and produce into the fair and those of the buyers ready to cart their purchases away. Added to this was the need for accommodation and grazing for draught animals, also the pack animals and those ridden in by the merchants and their servants. In some cases, quantities of oats would have been accumulated at the site of the fair to provide feed for the horses (Miller & Hatcher, 1995).

With the great influx of people for the fair there was the demand for food. Butchers had stalls selling meat and there were the stalls for cooked food and bakers selling pies; all adding to the level of meat consumption. This would have been a very profitable boost for the local butchers.

As far as livestock was concerned the fairs were a good venue for farmers to offer breeding stock or store stock for sale. The autumn fairs were appropriate for the larger households to buy animals for slaughtering and salting to stock up their larders for the winter (*Ibid*).

A major livestock fair in the North of England was the Stagshaw Bank Fair, close to Hadrians Wall, north of Corbridge, Northumberland. The fair was in existence in 1204 according to records, being held annually at midsummer and was a major destination for Scottish livestock exported to England. A second fair was held at Whitsuntide from 1480. There was also a weekly market from 1293 (Bonser, 1970).

Chapter 10

Medieval Statutory and Other Controls of Meat Trading

STATUTES TO CONTROL THE NUISANCE OF SLAUGHTERING

Problems arose where trading activities created a nuisance for the local community, particularly with regard to slaughtering with the concomitant smells, noise of animals, effluent and other waste discarded in the streets. There were many statutes aimed at the elimination of the nuisance caused by slaughtering and the disposal of the unwanted offals. The fact that statutes were enacted from time to time covering the same problems indicates their lack of effectiveness. There were attempts to legislate for the prevention of slaughtering taking place within the town and for stipulating a place for the slaughter of animals outside the town walls and in some cases only allowing slaughter to be carried out some distance from the town. This meant that butchers had to cart their carcases to their shops in town, adding to their costs.

The following command was given by Edward III in 1362 to the Mayor and Sheriffs of London, upon a great Contagion in the City:

> "Because by reason of killing great Beasts, &c. from whose putrefied Blood running down the Streets, and the Bowels cast into the Thames, the Air of the City is very much corrupted and infected, whence abominable and most filthy Stinks proceed, Sicknesses and many other Evils happen to such as have abode in the said City, or have resorted to it; and greater dangers are feared to fall out for the time to come, unless Remedy be presently made against it; Wee, willing to prevent such danger, and to provide as much as in Us lies, for the Honesty of the said City, and the Safety of our People, by the Consent of Our Council in our present Parliament, have ordained, That all Bulls, Oxen, Hogs, and other gross Creatures, to be slain for the sustentation of the said City, be led as far as the town of Stretford [Stratford le Bow,] on one part of London, and the town of Knightbrugg [Knightsbridge] on the other; and there, and not on this side, be slain. And that their bowels be there cleansed; and being so cleansed, to be brought, together with the Flesh, to the said City to be sold. And if any Butcher shall presume anything rashly against this Ordinance, let him incur Forfeiture of the Flesh of the Creatures, which he hath caused to be slain on this side of the said Towns, and the punishment of Imprisonment for one Year. This Ordinance to be publicly proclaimed and held; and all Butchers doing otherwise to be chastised and punished according to the Form of the Ordinance aforesaid. Witness the King at Westminster, the 25th of February, 1362." (Fig 10.1) (The Experienced Butcher, 1816)

Fig 10.1 An impression of slaughtering in the streets in a medieval town. On the left a butcher is killing a pig, with a pile of viscera lying on the pathway in front of him. Behind is a large tub in which a pig is being scalded and scraped to remove the hair. On the right is a woman squeezing the contents from intestines to prepare them for use as sausage skins.

There was obviously a lack in the enforcement of this ordinance by the City authorities because in the year 1371 the King issued a further order for the same purpose (Pearce, 1929). Again in 1379 an order of Richard II prohibited the slaughter of animals within the City stating that "no butcher should kill any flesh within London, but at Knightsbridge, or such like distant place from the walls of the City" (Besant, 1906).

A later statute was issued under Henry VII in 1485 banning slaughter in towns:

> "No butcher shall slay any beast within a walled town, except Carlisle and Berwick; on pain of forfeiting for every ox 12d. every cow and other beast 8d. half to the king, and half to him that will sue."

The exception of Carlisle and Berwick was probably due to the risk of cross border raiders (the reivers) (The Experienced Butcher, 1816).

The Franciscans or Greyfriars complained that the butchers of St Nicholas Shambles threw the entrails of slaughtered animals on the pavement causing a great stench. As a result, in 1342, the City granted to the butchers of St Nicholas Shambles a piece of land in Secollane alongside the

Flete river for the purpose of cleansing entrails of their beasts in the Flete. For this privilege the butchers were to maintain a wharf and to render yearly to the Lord Mayor of London a boar's head at Christmas (Pearce, 1929). (The presentation of the boar's head is still carried on today by the Worshipful Company of Butchers but not the maintenance of the wharf.) As a result of complaints of the stench by the Prior of the Hospital of St. John of Jerusalem, the butchers were ousted from the land at Secollane in 1354. In 1355 the butchers purchased some land on the Thames alongside the house of the Dominicans or Blackfriars. The butchers erected a staging from which they could wash the entrails and deposit their waste in the Thames. This was known as Bochersbrigge which in turn gave offence to the neighbourhood with the issue of a writ in 1370 resulting in the place being pulled down (*Ibid*). Sometime following the loss of Bochersbrigge the Butchers' Company acquired property at Brookes Wharf, Queenhithe, in 1392 which comprised of a barrowhouse for the use of the butchers of St. Nicholas Shambles for the disposal of their waste. There was also the acquisition of facilities at Fresh Wharf near London Bridge and a lease on Katherine Lane leading to the wharf in 1402, for the disposal of offals by the butchers of East Cheap (Jones, 1976) Stow in his Survey of London describes the removal of the offals; "Rother Lane or Red Rose Lane, now commonly called Pudding Lane, because the butchers of East Cheap have their scalding house for hogs there, and their puddings, with other filth of beasts, are voided down that way to their dungboats on the Thames." (The intestines of the animals were called puddings hence the name of the lane.) It was required that the entrails for disposal in the Thames be cut into small pieces and taken by boat to be dumped in midstream down river of the Tower at the ebb tide (Stow, 1598).

A complaint was heard before the Mayor, Recorder and five Aldermen 15th February 1370:

> "Brother Robert de Madyngton, guardian of the Friars Minor, complains by Robert de Watlyngton, his attorney, that Richard Bayser, botcher and Emma his wife have built a skaldynghous in their tenement in Pentecostlane in the parish of St. Nicholas Shambles, in which they slaughter pigs and many other animals and the water mixed with blood and hair of the slaughtered animals, and other filth from the washing (lotura) of the carcases, flows into the ditch or kennel in the street, through which it is carried into the friars' garden, causing a stench in many places there." (Chew & Kellaway, 1973)

The Plea and Memorial Rolls, 1422, contain a complaint made by the Warden and Convent of Friars Minor also by the Rector and parishioners of St Nicholas Shambles that the lane used by the Friars was full of dung and entrails thrown there at the weekly butchering, preventing passage through the lane and the place was filled with horrible stenches (Sabine, 1933).

Selling meat in the streets of Edinburgh became such a nuisance that a mid-1500s order provided that:

> "no fleshers break nor sell flesh upon open street, nor yet in vennels, especially in Merlin's Wynd; nor cut, carve, blaw, nor slit, nor hold the same within their houses, but be brought to the open market" (The Scotsman, 1902).

A 15th century Statute of the streets of London contains several clauses forbidding butchers to:

> Scald hogs save in a common scalding house.
> Cast offal in the public way.
> Drive offal carts through the streets before 9 pm or after 5 am. (Hammett & Nevell, 1929).

There was an order of the City of London Court of Aldermen on 14th June, 1425, to the effect that butchers remove the offal of the beasts slaughtered by them, at morning and night, and in closed carts so as to cause least annoyance (Jones, 1976).

The objection to the obnoxious stench was compounded by the belief that the foul air rising from the rotting entrails, blood and other filth discarded by the butchers contained miasmas, the source of contagion and therefore the cause of many diseases.

These problems were to some extent due to the disregard for local inhabitants by a number of butchers but on the whole they were related to the nature of the slaughtering trade. Such problems arose in all the towns throughout the country. The special problem with London was the large concentration of slaughtering due to the number of animals needed to be slaughtered in order to meet the demand of the population of the city. According to Sabine (1933) the number of complaints regarding animal refuse in the streets increased during times of plague or other epidemics, the common belief being that the stinking animal waste produced miasmas which were the cause of many diseases.

STATUTES AGAINST THE SALE OF UNFIT MEAT

Throughout history there has been a need for laws to prevent the sale of unfit meat by unscrupulous butchers, thereby protecting the public. It was generally found practical in the past to employ butchers to inspect meat in the markets. The butchers' guilds were often responsible for enforcing laws relating to unfit meat. It would have been the responsibility of their officers (the beadle and the wardens) to patrol the markets and inspect meat presented for sale. Certain disease conditions would have been obvious in the carcase such as measly pork (*Cysticercus cellulosa*) while many other conditions were often quite vague but the experienced butcher would been well able to recognise signs of putrefaction, a fevered carcase, signs of dropsical or oedematous animals, etc. The Wardens of the Butchers' Company of London petitioned the Court of Aldermen in 1484 for the authority to examine pigs brought into London for sale and to seize any that were measled. The Wardens claimed that no one was more experienced than themselves in judging if flesh was clean and wholesome for 'man's body' (Jones, 1976). The office of bailie for the administration of justice was part of the Scottish system, the bailies being appointed by the crown and next in line was the sergeand. The sergeands were responsible for the supervision of the markets and the examination of bread, ale and meat. In this the sergeands were assisted by apprisers of flesh who were required to be on hand every market day to watch over the quality and price of meat (Ewan, 1990).

An act of Henry III in 1266 forbade the sale of unfit meat and the 15th century Statute of the streets forbade butchers from selling measly or unwholesome pork.

In the reign of Edward II, inspectors of the markets of the City of London were appointed who were sworn to survey meat. Records show that on 1st November 1319, "the sworn Wardens of flesh meat brought to the Shambles called Les Stokkes seized two carcases putrid and poisonous taken from William Sperlyng of West Hamme, he intended to sell the same at the said shambles." It was found by a jury consisting mainly of butchers that the said carcases were putrid and poisonous and had died of disease. This resulted in the Aldermen ordering that the said William Sperlyng be placed in the stocks and the 'meat burned under him' (Fig 10.2).

Fig 10.2 The punishment for selling unfit meat was for the butcher to be placed in the stocks and the unfit meat to be burned under his nostrils.

The success of this prosecution may have engendered enthusiasm among the sworn Wardens of flesh meat as there followed more seizures of meat and prosecutions. It was further recorded that on 25th July 1320, William Le Clerk was brought before the Mayor and Aldermen charged with having unfit meat for sale and receiving the same sentence of standing in the stocks and the meat burned under him. In 1350 Edmund de Ware and Reginald Bridel suffered the same fate; likewise John Russell in 1366 for offering for sale 37 pigeons which were 'putrid, rotten, stinking and abominable'. It was a jury of cooks that found the meat offered by four butchers in 1374 to be unfit and they were sentenced to the pillary (Pearce, 1929). 'Strype's edition of Stow' quotes the penalties of selling unfit meat given by the clerk of Smithfield in 1468:

> First offence, grievously amerced.
> Second offence, the pillory.
> Third offence, imprisonment for a year.
> Fourth offence, outlawry.

The penalty of the pillory was replaced by a fine, when in 1452 William Scalon was fined £20 for offering for sale the carcases of two oxen that were in an unfit condition. A variation of the punishment of the pillory was that ordered for John Pynkard in 1517 for offering for sale four flitches of bacon that were putrid. He was put on his horse to be led from Newgate to Leadenhall with two of the flitches fastened on him and the other two carried before him with a notice on his head which read "For puttyng to sale of messell and stynkyng bacon". This method of exposing the offender and his offence became a more common practice in the 16th century (Jones, 1976).

The authorities in the 1500s did not regard all the meat seized to be unfit for human consumption *per se*. Records show that in 1543 one of the City serjeants was ordered to assist Wardens in their search for unfit meat and that the meat seized be distributed to prisoners of Newgate and Ludgate and the inmates of the Bethlehem asylum (*Ibid*).

The Incorporation of the Fleshers in Edinburgh in 1488 obtained approval of their seal of cause which contained stringent rules for the conduct of their craft. The deacon and members of the craft "are daily to search the craft gif ony of them owther buys or sells ony infectit flesche or fish" and "if any tradesman is found guilty he is to be depryvit of his Fredome, the goods to be escheit to the seik folk in alms houses, and he is to be banished the toun and craft be the officiars for evir mair."

In the 16th century complaints were received from factors dealing with exported hides and skins that the fleshers were sending hides that were missing part of the hide; in some cases as much as a quarter. This led to an order that provided for the appointment of searchers (inspectors) who were paid six pennies per score of hides which they had to check to see that the flesher had not cut away any part of the hide and still sold it as "haill and intear" (Scotsman, 1902).

There were laws on the sale of unfit meat in mainland Europe during the medieval period. The 1276 charter of Augsberg (Germany) contains the following reference to the sale of meat:

> "If a butcher kills a measly hog he shall sell it to no one without a statement of this fact. Inflation of meat and placing straw in the abdomen is forbidden."

In Stettin (Germany) a statute of 1312 prescribed that the tails should be left on the carcases so as to detect cow meat from steer meat, goat meat from mutton and the meat of bucks from that of wethers (sic). Berlin City Ordinances of 1343 forbade the sale of milch cows, animals torn by dogs and also diseased, malodorous and unclean animals. A system of meat inspection was established in Passau (Germany) in 1394. A meat trader by the name of Begendurf was imprisoned for attempting to sell hogs containing bladder worms (*Cysticerci*), which had been punctured to deceive the meat inspectors. Some of the penalties were extremely severe e.g. regulations for the Kingdom of Naples and Sicily provided that butchers must not slaughter sows or boars for pork or deal in animals that had died a natural death:

First offence, fine of a lire of gold or corporal punishment.
Second offence, cutting off a hand.
Third offence, hanging. (Young, 1929)

The city records of Aberdeen in 1399 state that there were four *appreciators carneium* (meat inspectors) to inspect the meat sold in the town (Leighton & Douglas, 1910).

According to the *Liber Albus* a regulation was made during the reign of Richard II to the effect that all butchers keeping shops should close them at dark and not sell their meat by candle-light (Riley, 1861). This was obviously to protect buyers from having poor quality meat, or indeed, unfit meat foisted upon them. Pork and beef was seized from John Estmar, John Perer and Reginald atte Watre, foreign butchers of Les Stokkes on the 25th November 1320 because they had exposed this meat for sale by candle-light after curfew had rung at St Martin's le Grand (Pearce, 1929).

REGULATION OF MARKETS AND FAIRS

There were numerous statutes and local ordinances along with the charters conferring rights and responsibilities for markets and fairs aimed at the regulation and the application of the rule of law to trading activities. Although statutes or ordinances were made to restrict or prohibit an activity, it does not follow that the object was achieved. It was often the case that the means for enforcement was either inadequate or non-existent. From a historical viewpoint it is evident that the activities the statutes were intended to prevent would have been commonly practised. For those who were instrumental in compiling these laws it was more often in hope than in expectation.

Where the enforcement of regulations resulted in commercial advantage it was more likely to be carried out to good effect. This would be the case where the confidence of trading in a market or fair could be at issue or any matter that may have affected the returns from markets or fairs to the charter holders. It was in the interest of charter holders to protect the standing of their market or fair.

The same was true of the guilds regulating the trade in the towns. The officers of the guilds were active in ensuring that no illegal trading took place and that the members of the guilds conformed to the standards and conditions laid down by the guilds.

Laws to regulate trade activities were invariably related to a town or locality and the enforcement was the responsibility of the municipality or local lords. The obligation for enforcing some of the laws fell to the guilds, particularly where they were related to the way in which their members carried out their trade. In some cases the guild officers and members were expected to ensure the good behaviour of their employees, especially the apprentices.

LAWS TO REGULATE TRADING ACTIVITIES

Some of the laws put in place to regulate trading would have been contrary to the principles of a free market and could have frustrated commercial enterprise. In spite of these laws many traders were successful and in some cases merchants became very rich, which implies that enforcement may not have been very effective.

It was made unlawful in the medieval period to forestall, regrate or engross (ingross). These restrictions seemed to apply more to food supplies than to other goods.

The act of forestalling was for a trader to buy up goods ahead of the market. An example of this would have been where a butcher intercepted and bought cattle or sheep being driven to market or went to the farms and bought animals that would have gone to the market. In addition to this practice being seen as unfair to the competitors, it also deprived the market charter holder of the market tolls. Apart from the other advantages of the markets and fairs, transactions taking place there were deemed as legal whereas transactions outside a market could put in question the ownership of the goods or animals without witnesses to the transaction. A Charter granted by Henry III in 1268 to the City of London stipulated that "no merchant or other do meet any merchants coming by land or water with their merchandise or victuals" in order to buy their goods before they had been put up for sale in the city (*Ibid*). Ordinances in *Liber Albus* for 1284 included one forbidding forestalling. A mandate to the Mayor and Sheriffs of London in 1315 required them to appoint inspectors of the meat markets to prevent forestalling. The penalty for a forestaller was the seizure of his goods and the loss of his civic rights (Riley, 1861).

The medieval records in the "Little Red Book of Bristol" includes the derogatory description of a forestaller:

> "a manifest oppressor of the poor and a public enemy of the whole commonality and country, who hastens to buy before others grain, fish, herrings or anything vendible whatsoever coming by land or water…making gain, oppressing his poorer and despising his richer neighbours, and who designs to sell more dearly what he so unjustly acquired." (Lipson, 1959)

Forestalling was also illegal in Scotland. The records of Aberdeen contain numerous references to individuals being found guilty of this offence. Tanners were major culprits in buying hides before they reached the Aberdeen market (Ewan, 1990).

Regrating was where a trader bought commodities in the market to resell at a profit. To prevent regrating there was a London ordinance forbidding retail dealers to buy victuals before sunrise under the penalty of forfeiture of their purchases. The same restrictions applied in many towns such as York, Norwich, Bristol, Chester and Southampton with sales not allowed until the market bell had rung (*Ibid*). The citizens of Worcester in 1221 complained that the men of Droitwich came to Worcester market early while the Worcester people were at church, bought up the food and when the Worcester people came out of church the Droitwich men sold them the provisions at inflated prices. Butchers' wives at Leicester were forbidden to buy meat and sell again in the same market unless it had been cooked (Stenton, 1951).

Engrossing was an endeavour to profit by buying up quantities of a commodity to keep in store with the prospect of the price of that commodity rising due to a shortage. Records of London and Bristol contain ordinances that retailers of victuals should not conceal any of their stock and should not store victuals from one market to sell at a higher price at another market. The penalty being the forfeiture of their stock

Laws placing restrictions on the sale of fat and tallow was a feature of the medieval period due to its importance for candles and other industrial use. An ordinance of London in the reign of Edward III prohibited the sale of suet, tallow or lard by butchers. These restrictions are contained in *Liber Albus*:

"And that no butcher, or wife of a butcher, shall sell tallow or lard to a strange person for export to the parts beyond the sea; by reason of the great dearness and scarcity that has been thereof in the City of late." (Riley, 1861)

A later Statute of the 15th century forbade the export of tallow from the city for fear of causing a rise in the price of candles. Many ordinances of the towns contained a clause forbidding the sale of tallow by butchers except to tallow chandlers or candle makers (Pearce, 1929).

Edinburgh Magistrates in the 16th century issued an order to the effect that Fleshers were required to sell their tallow to the "candlemakers and neighbours, and no others, and their houses and booths where tallow users are to be made patent for buying". (The Scotsman, 1902)

The Mayor's Court Rolls for The City of London contain an entry for 1306 requiring butchers to pay cash for the animals supplied and not to delay payment as this was to the detriment of the farmer or peasant who sold them the animals (Lipson, 1959). This ordinance was endorsed in *Liber Albus*:

"and whereas some butchers do buy beasts of country folks, and as soon as they have the beasts in their houses kill them, and then at their own pleasure delay the peasants their pay; or else tell them that they may take their beasts. Penalty – pay double value if not – pillory." (Riley, 1861)

Certain restrictions on the sale of woolfells are contained in *Liber Albus*:

" And that no butcher shall sell woolfells so long as they are on the living animals, but that he shall carry the skins, together with the flesh, to the market, in manner as is ordained; and he shall sell none of such skins and hides in his own house or elsewhere in secret; but only in the king's market, and then after prime has rung out, under pain of losing the article, whether the same shall be found in the hand of the vendor or of the buyer." (Riley, 1861)

In the medieval period cattle stealing had been rife in Scotland, particularly in the Highlands, the Southern Uplands and the Border country. It was such a way of life that the cattle reivers (rustlers) were often the victims of cattle stealing. An act of Scots Parliament in the reign of William the Lion in 1175 laid down heavy penalties for the purchase or possession of stolen cattle. The buyer was required to obtain from the seller a form of guarantee that the cattle were not stolen or a guarantee of the seller's good faith by a third party. There were also heavy penalties if the guarantees were invalid (Haldane, 1968).

RESTRICTIONS FOR FOREIGN BUTCHERS

Foreign butchers were those from outside the town, not members of the butchers' guild and not having the freedom of the town as traders. Initially the guilds' endeavours were to exclude all foreign butchers or at least allow them only to sell their meat to the guild butchers who then sold it retail to the townspeople. As there were occasions when guild butchers could not meet the demand and higher prices charged for meat caused unrest in the town, the municipal authorities permitted foreign butchers to sell their meat in the town markets. Town ordinances were drawn up which, while allowing the foreign butchers the rights of retail selling, imposed limitations compared with the rights of guild butchers.

Ordinances governing trading in the City of London during the reign of Edward I contained among its many clauses one prohibiting guild members from entering into a partnership with a foreign trader and a clause requiring foreign butchers to bring into the city the hides and skins of their carcases. It was ordered that foreign butchers only sell their meat by retail until noon and after that "by wholesale until Vespers rung at St Paul's; by which time they must have finished the sale of their meat, without carrying anything away to salt or store, under penalty of forfeiting the same". The time restriction on foreign butchers selling meat retail was extended to Curfew at St Martin's le Grand during the reign of Edward III (Besant, 1906).

The restrictions on foreign butchers are endorsed in *Liber Albus*:

> "And all foreign butchers shall come into the City with their meat for sale, and bring the hides and pelts of every beast together with the flesh, under pain of losing the price of such hide: that is to say, for the price of an ox-hide two shillings and sixpence, for the price of a cow-hide two shillings, for the pelt of a woolled mutton sixpence and for the pelt of a mutton without wool one and half pennies. And then he shall stand to sell his meat there in pieces, both small and large, just as he shall please to cut, until high noon (according to Riley between 1pm and 3pm); so that by such time he shall have fully made his sale, without getting rid of any meat, or harbouring it either secretly or openly, or putting it in salt or otherwise. And if such shall be found in town carried into the house where he is staying after an hour that is forbidden, the same shall be forfeited unto the sheriff." (Riley, 1861)

It is apparent that in the 16th century foreign butchers were selling meat in Edinburgh because in 1558 an order of the Magistrates restricted the fleshers to selling flesh only at the "over end of the Tolbooth" and that no "unfreeman sell flesh anywhere but in the Vennel or in the South part of the Cowgate that leads from the common causeway of the Bow to the Blackfriars" (The Scotsman, 1902).

WEIGHTS AND PRICES

The value of having a standard system of weights and measures was long recognised, even in the time of the ancient civilisations. During the reign of the Anglo-Saxon King Edgar there was the aspiration that "one measure and weight should pass throughout the king's dominions such as is observed at London and Winchester". Contained in the Magna Carta was the clause that there be standard weights and measures throughout the realm. It was enacted in Parliament in 1340 that "from henceforth one measure and one weight shall be throughout the realm of England". Because of complaints that these requirements were not being kept, standard balances and weights were sent to every county and in 1361 Justices of the Peace were empowered to inquire into infringements of the statutes (Lipson, 1959).

The steelyard became a common piece of equipment for butchers for weighing carcases, quarters or other large pieces of meat as it was the most suitable for this purpose. The term steelyard originated from the place of that name in the City of London alongside the Thames occupied from the early 1300s by the Hanseatic League, a consortium of German merchants. The name comes from the German *stālhof* (pattern + courtyard) which became 'steelyard' or 'stiliard' and as the place had numbers of scales for weighing imported goods, the name steelyard or stiliard was given to the scale.

Attempts to regulate prices were frequent, particularly the price of food, to protect 'the poor commons' from extortion. The aim of the medieval legislators was to achieve a 'just price' that was equally fair to vendor and purchaser. There are records of laws regulating the price of victuals in many towns such as Chester, Coventry, Bristol and London and as new towns received their charters it was a usual practice to adopt the systems of laws and administration of the established towns (Lipson, 1959).

A statute was issued under Edward VI to prevent conspiracy to raise the price of meat:

> "If any butchers shall conspire not to sell their victuals but at certain prices; every such person shall forfeit for the first offence £10. to the king, and if not paid in six days, he shall suffer twenty days' imprisonment, and shall have only bread and water for his sustenance; for the second offence £20. in like manner, or the pillory; and for the third offence £40. and pillory and loss of an ear, and to be taken as a man infamous, and not to be credited in any manner of judgement." (Young, 1929)

A 1378 ordinance of the City of London setting the prices to be charged by cooks and pasterers or piebakers included the following:

Best roast pig - 8d	Best roast goose - 7d
Best roast capon - 6d	Best roast hen - 4d
Best roast pullet - 2½d	Best roast rabbit - 4d
Best roast river mallard - 4½d	Best roast dunghill mallard - 3½d
Best roast teal - 2½d	Best roast snipe - 1½d
Five roast larks - 1½d	Best roast woodcock - 2½d
Best roast partridge - 3½d	Best roast plover - 2½d
Best roast pheasant - 13d	Best roast curlew - 6½d
Three roast thrushes - 2d	Ten roast finches - 1d
Best roast heron - 18d	Best roast bittern - 20d
Three roast pigeons - 2½d	Best capon baked in pastry - 8d
Best hen baked in pastry - 5d	Best lamb roasted – 7d

(Riley, 1861)

THE REVOLT OF THE LONDON BUTCHERS

In the early 1500s a shortage of meat in London and the consequent high prices resulted in orders to control the price of meat. In 1529 the London butchers were ordered by the Privy Council not to sell beef above ½d lb, veal not above $^5/_8$d lb. and mutton not above ¾d lb. This attempt at price control was reinforced by the requirement to sell meat by weight instead of by the piece. An Act of Parliament in 1533 began with the statement that 'poor people could not gain sufficient money by their labour to provide their common victual of beef and other flesh owing to its excessive price'. The main clause of this Act was that as from 1ˢᵗ August 1533 all meat was sold by weight and in proportions requested by the buyer. (The tradition had been for the sale of meat by the piece or by the pennyworth.) It included the maximum prices which were; for beef and pork ½d lb. and mutton and veal $5/_8$d lb. The proclamation of this act included a statement to the effect that by reason of equity the graziers and farmers should sell animals to the butchers at such prices in order that they could make a living selling the meat by weight at the regulated prices. The freemen of the Butchers' Company refused to sell meat by weight to the citizens of London in accordance with the Act. This action by the butchers did not please Henry VIII and the freemen of the Butchers' Company were ordered by the Court of Aldermen to appear before the Common Council whereby they were disfranchised, losing all their privileges and liberties as freemen; an action unprecedented in the annals of the Craft Guilds.

The municipal authorities allowed foreign butchers full freedom to sell meat in the City in an attempt to thwart the Butchers' Company. In July, 1534 the municipal authorities felt that the wardens of the Butchers' Company were no longer to be entrusted with the supervision of the meat markets and this task was given to the officers of other companies, e.g. Grocers, Mercers, Drapers. There continued from this time a series of orders issued for further sets of prices and the suspension of the requirement to sell meat only by weight in accordance with the 1533 Act and a subsequent Act of 1534. A constant complaint of the butchers was that they were tied to the set prices for the sale of meat whereas the price of livestock fluctuated. To counter this a proclamation in 1549 set the prices for cattle and sheep, with an adjustment of the price according to the season.

In October 1534 the members of the Butchers' Company petitioned for their restoration as freemen as they were prevented from engaging servants which restricted their capacity to supply meat to the citizens. In December the Butchers were reinstated to their former freedoms and liberties. The order in 1557 for the maximum prices of meat was 1¼d lb for beef and pork and 1½d lb for mutton and veal which was more than double the prices for 1534. By 1581 the authorities were taking a more balanced approach with their instructions to those supervising the shambles in that none of the butchers "do utter and sell any kind of flesh meat at excessive prices, but at such a rate as is convenient and as they may reasonably afford to live on". From this time there ceased to be a regular issue of orders setting the price of meat and the confrontation between the Butchers' Company and the Authority receded.

Although orders fixing prices affected other City Companies such as the Poulters and Bakers, none had such an outright confrontation with authority as did the butchers (Jones, 1976).

COURTS OF PIE POUDRE

The courts of pie poudre were to settle disputes in fairs or markets. The right to set up a court was usually contained in the charter granted for the fair or market. The term pie poudre means 'dusty feet' which relates to the merchants attending the fairs or markets being people always on the move and therefore needing immediate settlement of a dispute (Courts of instant justice). The disputes dealt with by the courts generally related to debts, contracts and standard of goods sold. It could also deal with acts of disorder including "annoying the beasts in the market with carts" (records of Leicester).

Part III

1550-1750. Paving the Way for Improvements in Livestock Production, Technology and the Commercial Expansion of the 19th Century

Chapter 11

Standing of the Guilds and Their Function: 1550-1750

INTRODUCTION

This was the period of Elizabeth I and the Stuart kings. The defeat of Richard III at Bosworth Field in 1485 by the Earl of Richmond, who was then crowned Henry VII, marked the end of the internal conflicts between the Houses of Lancaster and York. The break with Rome by Henry VIII and the dissolution of the monasteries brought about an upheaval in the rural economic structure. The establishment of Anglican Protestantism resulted in a period of religious persecution, firstly of the Catholics and then the Protestants when Mary Tudor came on the throne. With the accession of Elizabeth I there was a period of stability which was conducive to economic, commercial and industrial development.

Under Elizabeth I began the age of Mercantilism with England becoming a formidable maritime nation in the forefront of discovering new territories, exploiting their commercial advantages and developing global trading. A consequence was an expansion of the wealth of the country, a fact which commonly led to an increase in the demand for meat. The effect of the development of the maritime capability in the longer term was as an essential factor in the establishment of the imported meat trade in the latter half of the 19th century.

The union of the English and Scottish crowns in 1603 brought peace and stability to the border country and paved the way for freer trade between the two countries. Trading in cattle began building up, leading to the very large droves of cattle moving south in the 1700s.

The period 1550 to 1700 saw the defeat of the Spanish Armada, the ravages of the civil war and the rule of Cromwell, followed by the restoration of the monarchy. During the reign of Elizabeth I, there was a strengthening of local administration and law centred on the Justices of the Peace and greater supervision by the Privy Council. The latter half of the 17th century saw the devastation caused by the plague and the great fire of London.

As at all times, the basis of meat industry trading was related to the commercial, social and agricultural environment. There had been dramatic changes during the medieval period in trade and other commercial activities, including the growth of markets and towns. These developments were to continue along with a growth in prosperity, but as is often the case, this prosperity did not improve the plight of the poorest of the nation. Meat was at most times regarded of considerable importance as part of the diet. This is borne out by attempts by authorities to control the price of meat from time to time and of opinions expressed as to the importance of the lower classes being able to afford meat. It would follow that a good proportion of the increase in the disposable income of many of the town's people would swell the coffers of the butchers. For those merchants and tradesmen enjoying a degree of affluence, the butcher could provide many of the luxuries to grace their tables.

Fig 11.1 A drawing of the illustration for November from the mid 17th Century Mummer's Almanac. A predominant activity for November is the Autumn slaughter of cattle, sheep and pigs. In the foreground a slaughterman is about to stick a pig, with the woman standing ready to catch the blood in a pan. In the background is a butcher dressing a beef carcase which appears to be very fat. On the nearby table a woman is dealing with the paunch (stomach).

DISSOLUTION OF THE MONASTERIES

Whatever criticism there may have been of the way the monasteries conducted their affairs, they were considerably involved in the agricultural, commercial, social and political affairs of the country and their dissolution resulted in an upheaval. It took many years for the country to adjust to the new situation.

With regard to agriculture, the large monastic houses owned extensive estates which were either sold off, gifted to those in allegiance with the king having done him some service, or some estates became royal estates. The monastic houses were involved in a range of commercial activities, in particular the production of wool, its collection and its sale and export. There were many English merchants in the wool trade at this time who probably gained some advantages by the dissolution. There was also the problem of a number of charters granted for fairs and markets which were held by monastic houses.

Monasteries were a haven for many destitute and sick people in the country. Some of the monastic hospitals in London were able to continue their function, such as the St Mary of Bethlehem hospital for the mentally ill (Bedlam) and the St Bartholomew's hospital taken over by the Lord Mayor and refounded by Henry VIII in 1544. This refounding was commemorated in 1702 with a statue of Henry VIII placed above the gate built as the main entrance to the hospital from West Smithfield (Weinreb & Hibbert, 1983).

There were various attempts to provide for the destitute, relying initially on local goodwill. The Act of 1531 was for the licensing of beggars which would be the aged and infirm. A further Act of 1536 required that town and parish authorities collect alms voluntarily given. The 1572 Act instituted a compulsory assessment for alms giving. The 1598 and 1601 Acts established the system that was to last until the 19th century and placed the obligation for the relief of the poor on the parish. Parishes were required to provide overseers of the poor and to raise funds for the relief of the poor by local rates. The payment of these rates fell mainly on the traders and other businessmen in the parish. It was the practice of many of the town guilds to give succour to members or the families of members who, for some reason, had become impoverished. Children of the poor and orphaned children were generally put to apprenticeships when they were of age. This system of parish apprenticeship frequently resulted in the apprentice being bound at the age of seven and the term of servitude expiring at the age of twenty-one for women and twenty-four for men.

Of the able bodied poor there was a distinction made between the industrious poor who were unable to gain paid employment and those who were idle by inclination. For the former it was incumbent on the aldermen and others holding municipal office to obtain some form of work with remuneration. For the latter, generally referred to as rogues and vagabonds, the Act of 1576 ordered the building of houses of correction. The most famous of these was Bridewell in London which had been originally built as a palace for the king but had ceased its royal role early in the 1500s. The term 'Bridewell' was often used in other parts of the country to refer to houses of correction. These houses of correction became the workhouses (Lipson, 1959).

Prior to the 16th century the maintenance of roads was the responsibility of the monastic houses and the manorial courts. After the dissolution of the monasteries it was necessary for an alternative system. The 1555 statute imposed the responsibility on each parish to maintain the roads within their boundaries. This was effected by a farmer supplying a cart and horses plus two men and each householder to labour on the roads for four days. In 1563 the period was raised to six days (*Ibid*).

The Butchers' Company of Newcastle-upon-Tyne along with eight other companies leased the former Dominican monastery from the corporation. This became the butchers' meeting house (Dodds, 1917). The church of St Nicholas by the Shambles in London was demolished after its parish was combined with the parish of Christ Church, leaving the parsonage house vacant. This building was leased in 1548 to the Butchers' Company for use as their hall on an eighty-year lease at £6 per annum.

With the dissolution thirty abbots and priors lost their seats in the House of Lords resulting in the dominance of the secular lords (Weinstein, 1994).

THE RISE OF CAPITALISM AND ITS EFFECT ON THE CRAFT GUILDS

The craft guilds enjoyed the peak of their influence over the trade and administration of the towns from 1200 when they began to replace the Guild Merchant in that respect. By the 1400s the power and influence of the craft guilds began to decline which was partly due to conflicts between the municipal authorities and the guilds. A major cause of the decline was the rise in capitalism from the 1400s, which, while mainly affecting the industrial guilds, tended to weaken the whole guild system. It was the successful merchants who were the financiers and capitalists in the medieval period. Merchants dealing in wool and cloth engaged spinners and weavers in the villages, supplying them with wool and taking from them the finished cloth. Other industrial activities such as the tanning of hides were organised away from the towns and therefore beyond the restrictive influence of the guilds. These capitalistic enterprises produced greater bulk of materials and goods at lower cost resulting in undermining the industrial craft guilds of the towns.

The successful merchants were the appropriate people to become involved in this early move towards capitalism as they not only had the financial resources but also the contacts with the producers and knew the markets, both national and international. Their other major advantage was their entrepreneurial drive that had made them successful as merchants. Many landowners were in the position to invest in this capitalism but there were few with the commercial aptitude and incentive of the merchants.

This establishment of capitalism and industrial organisation continued to develop during the Elizabethan and Stuart periods and was the foundation on which the industrial revolution was to be built.

The weakening of the industrial guilds had the effect of diminishing the collective influence of the urban guilds.

ATTEMPT TO RE-ESTABLISH THE INFLUENCE OF THE GUILDS IN THE 17TH CENTURY

There was a degree of reinstatement of the guilds under James I with the numerous grants of incorporation to the old established guilds or those newly formed. Of these many grants of incorporation, the butchers of London received a charter in 1605 and a charter was granted in 1621 to the butchers of Newcastle upon Tyne. Other butchers' guilds throughout the country were also receiving charters during this period.

The standard of manufactured goods had, in many cases, become very poor and there were petitions exhorting the government for the regulatory function of the guilds to be reinforced. It was seen as important that the guilds had control over craft practices, the standard of workmanship and the apprenticeship system. Another factor supporting the guild system was that a major proportion of municipal revenues was derived from the taxes on the burgesses and tolls from the markets.

THE POSITION OF THE GUILDS OR COMPANIES IN THE 16th & 17th CENTURIES

The medieval development of the guilds from the fraternities of craftsmen or tradesmen was to regulate the trade and protect those engaged in the mistery from unreasonable, free for all, competition. The guild system was oligarchical in that it conferred a monopoly of the trade on the craft guilds and the control and employment of workers in the mistery but was accompanied by the equality of privileges for the members of the guild. This was the principle but there were occasions when there was not total equality for all members of the guild. In some cases guilds became closed shops with little chance of persons other than the sons of guild members or the husbands of guild members' daughters becoming freemen of the guild. There were also times when municipal authorities considered that some guilds were misusing their monopolistic control to the detriment of their town and its people.

There were basically three types of guilds; the guilds of merchants or traders, the guilds of purely industrial crafts and the craftsmen who also sold their goods directly to the people.

Whereas the small trader who sold his wares from a stall in the market could be categorised as a merchant, the term merchant usually related to the individual trading in bulk goods. The merchants who dealt in bulk goods would have acted as wholesalers and were in some cases importers or exporters. It was usually among the merchants that the richest burgesses of the towns were to be found and they invariably had the most influence over municipal affairs, including being strongly represented by aldermen and mayors.

The purely industrial crafts such as those of the weavers, dyers and leather curriers, were very vulnerable as the work could be carried out away from the town and controlled by the merchant capitalists who undermined their guilds.

The craftsmen traders, for example the butchers, the bakers and indeed the candlestick makers, also the tailors and cordwainers (shoemakers), needed to have premises in the town for use as a work shop, store and for sales. In view of the importance to the town's people of the service provided by these craftsmen, their guilds were sustained while the industrial guilds were declining.

The butchers' guilds were high on the list of the craft guilds with wealthy members and members serving in municipal office. Records show that the butchers of Leicester provided the town with a number of its mayors. During the Tudor period, butchers of Leicester filled the mayoralty eight times between the years 1548 to 1592. A number of these mayors were from two families of butchers, the Stanfords and the Freakes, both being wealthy families of Leicester at the time. It was shown by an assessment for subsidy in 1590 that the wealthiest burgesses of Leicester were butchers and tanners, with John Stanford topping the list. An important contribution to the rise in the prosperity of the butchers was a number becoming graziers as well as butchers. Leicestershire and surrounding areas were becoming established as the principal grazing land for livestock in the country and the value of meat and the butcher's animal was increasing (Hoskins, 1950). What happened at this time was a prelude to the further developments 200 years later with the Leicestershire farmer Robert Bakewell's longhorn butcher's beast and his Dishley Leicester sheep.

An analysis of inventories according to occupation made between 1660 and 1740 show butchers high on the list in respect of the total value of the inventories, being above the other crafts but below innkeepers and merchants. The grazier-butchers were among the most wealthy traders in the 16th and 17th centuries, as in Newcastle-upon-Tyne according to inventories a number of them exceeded £2000 putting them up with the more successful merchant-venturers of that town (Everitt, 1990).

THE GUILD SYSTEM IN SCOTLAND

The guild system in Scotland did not develop as early as in England and the rest of Europe, with the earliest records of incorporations dated in the middle 1400s. Due to the slower development of urban institutions in Scotland, the guilds flourished during the 1500s and 1600s while those elsewhere were going into decline. The number of incorporations in each town in Scotland were less than in England with each guild embracing several of the trades that would be represented by separate guilds in the larger towns of England. The guilds for the butchers were the Fleshers' Guilds which included the handling and sale of fish and poultry as well as red meat. The seal of cause of the Fleshers at their incorporation laid down some very stringent rules for conduct by members of the craft. In Edinburgh, there were fourteen incorporations that went under a banner known as the 'Blue Blanket' in which the "powers and prerogatives of the crafts thereof" were set forth. Records show the existence of similar groupings of companies, including guilds of fleshers in Glasgow, Dundee, Aberdeen and Selkirk (Leighton & Douglas, 1910). The number of incorporations in many of the towns was around seven. It was not until 1621 that the first guilds were incorporated in Dumfries.

The councils administering the burghs were dominated by the merchants in the 16th century which prompted attempts at greater democracy. In Perth, half the council members were from the crafts but generally council members were only chosen from the wealthiest members of the high status crafts. A revised constitution for Edinburgh in 1583 allowed middle ranking burgesses to hold the lower administrative posts but were excluded from the controlling body of the burgh. In the early 1600s the Aberdeen council consisted of seventeen merchants and two craft members. In the late 1500s there was a series of strong protests by the fleshers and baxters (bakers) over the merchant dominated councils fixing the price of victuals during a period of high inflation (Whyte, 1995).

Fig 11.2 A butcher's shop in the High Street, Edinburgh. In front of the shop is a cradle used for the bleeding and skinning sheep. The drawing is based on a print by Paul Standby, 1750, Department of Prints, British Museum.

These associations of the guilds in Scotland gave rise to the establishment of the Dean of Guild Courts, which dealt with trade disputes, but after their establishment they became the main courts for jurisdiction in the burghs. These courts dealt with general disputes, such as the case brought before the court in Edinburgh in 1591 regarding one of the occupants of a tenement who created an inside toilet by the simple expedient of cutting a hole in the floor, much to the annoyance of the tenant below. These courts were given responsibility for the regulation of weights and measures. The power of these courts declined with the institution of other courts and the introduction of imperial standards of weights and measures in 1824. After 1834 the Dean of Guild Court was only able to act in disputes concerning the structure of buildings (Close, 1997).

THE GUILDS IN CONTINENTAL EUROPE

The guilds on the Continent developed in the medieval period largely in parallel with the English guilds although in some parts of Europe they came into prominence earlier. The Guild Merchant originated in Continental Europe. Records show the existence of craft guilds in most of the major towns and cities of Germany, Italy, France, Switzerland, Flanders and Holland.

The Guild of Butchers of Antwerp was the richest of the guilds and wielded considerable municipal power. Their influence was such that in 1585 a plan by the Dutch to flood the polders north of Antwerp as a defence strategy against the invading army of the Duke of Palma was vetoed by the Guild of Butchers. The reason that the butchers were against flooding the polders was that it would have resulted in putting under water the fields in which they grazed their cattle.

In the years 1501 – 1504 the butchers' guild had a magnificent hall built, the 'Vleeshuis' which became the tallest building in Antwerp. The ground floor served as a market for the sale of meat with space for 62 stalls. The siting of the building was close to the Scheldt River to allow the easy disposal of blood and effluent. The steps leading up to the building were called Bloedberg (Blood Hill). The butchers would not trade in Grote Markt (marketplace) where the other guilds traded and ensured that the Vleeshuis was the only place in Antwerp where meat could be sold. Above the meat hall there was a banqueting hall, meeting rooms and a chapel. The present day use of the building is as a museum.

THE ROLE OF THE GUILD IN MEAT INSPECTION.

As in the medieval period, officers of the butchers' guilds carried out the responsibilities of meat inspectors or market inspectors. The records of Leicester give the names of butchers holding the post of meat testers for a year in the 1500s. Philip Freake held the office three times and his son John was a meat tester in 1590–91 and the following year 1591-92. There were three meat testers appointed each year (Hoskins, 1950).

The stewards of the Butchers' Company of Newcastle upon Tyne were responsible for the inspection of meat offered for sale and would seize and destroy any they deemed unfit for human consumption. In the 1636-37 records of the company there are several references to the destruction of meat for which purpose the accounts refer to a tar barrel. For example one entry reads "Itm pd for carrying upp a tarr barrell to burne Edward Langland's beife ..." (Dodds, 1917). The way the meat was burnt is a matter for speculation but it is most likely that it was the tar rather than the barrel that was used; perhaps it was smeared over the meat. Professor Swatland, University of Guelph, Canada, suggests that what was used was not tar as we use today on roads and roofs, but Norway Tar, a pine tar. This would have been available from the ship chandlers, especially in Newcastle which was a thriving port. By covering the meat with the tar it would have caused it to burn readily and perhaps more important, the tar was to cover the dreadful smell of burning meat. Pine tar gives off a very pleasant smell.

When the markets of London were re-established after the great fire of 1666, the Market Act of 1674 preserved the position of the Master, Wardens and Assistants of the Butchers' Company as the inspectors of meat and supervision of meat trading generally. Any meat they considered unwholesome and unfit for food they were empowered to seize and to proceed against offenders.

The practice originating in the medieval period of parading a butcher guilty of selling unfit meat through the street with the meat hung around his neck continued as a penalty. Such was the punishment of George Slater as late as 1650. Robert Austen was fined for selling measled pork in 1587 and John Austen for selling a carrion hog in 1599 (Jones, 1976).

Meat that was seized could be disposed of by burning or dumping in the Thames, although at times it was given to the prisons to feed the inmates. A quantity of carrion beef that had been sold by Thomas Thorowgood in Leadenhall Market in 1564 was seized and distributed to the prisoners of Ludgate, Newgate, and the inmates of Bedlam. Some mutton that had been sold by John Boone of Tottenham was seized by the Wardens who described it as "scarce fit for any Christian to eat" and was, nevertheless, sent to the prisons. Measles in pigs (*Cysticercus cellulosae*) was one of the most common causes of pork being found unfit. The probable reason was that measles is the cystic stage of a tapeworm of man and as many pigs were reared in towns with their habitation being close to the human population, cross infection was highly likely.

APPRENTICESHIPS

The Act of 1563, the Statute of Apprentices, made it compulsory throughout the country for apprentices to be bound for not less than seven years and it was unlawful for any person who had not served such an apprenticeship, to set up or exercise any occupation, art or mistery. The Act also prohibited the employment of a person in any occupation who had not served a seven-year apprenticeship in that art or mystery. To protect journeymen from the competition of cheap labour, the number of apprentices to journeymen was fixed. The Statute of Apprentices instituted national legislation for apprentices that had formally been regulated by local ordinances of the guilds and municipal authorities.

The Elizabethan government was very much inclined towards the merits of the apprenticeship system because it regarded it important to protect the skilled worker and as an essential way of maintaining the level of craftsmanship necessary to provide the standard of services and manufactures for the public. This concept is borne out by an Elizabethan document dated about 1573:

"The prentice that is bound for less than seven years doth not commonly prove to be an expert artificer, so that thereby ignorance and imperfection in divers arts and occupations do enter; yet many are bound for five, four, three, yea two years or less, and then take upon them to bring up others under them, whom they make as evil and as unskilful workmen as themselves, which doth not only impair good and perfect workmanship or knowledge in occupations, but also is a means whereby the number of artificers do so multiply that one of them do as it were eat out and consume another" (Lipson, 1959).

After the Civil War (1642 – 1651) there were many discharged soldiers whose apprenticeships had been interrupted and others who had missed the opportunity to become bound as apprentices. An Ordinance of the Commonwealth (1654) allowed ex-servicemen to be admitted to any occupation, art or mystery.

After the Restoration in 1660 there were a number of Acts for the regulation of trade with apprenticeship remaining obligatory. The 1700s saw a change of attitude which is embodied in the maxim "Trade ought to be free and not restrained" contained in the 1702 House of Commons Journals. There was the contention that some unskilled or semiskilled occupations did not warrant an apprenticeship. There were also arguments that the rigid adherence to the seven-year apprenticeship was a constraint on trade. A parliamentary committee looking into the laws on trade considered, "since the improvement of the trade in general, it is found that all manufactures find their own value according to their goodness". Although this attitude of parliament was towards relaxing the application of the law regarding apprenticeships, a number of local authorities still pursued enforcement. In the early 1700s, indictments were brought against a number of people for the unlawful exercise of a trade or mystery, including a butcher, a fellmonger and a tallow chandler in Hereford (*Ibid*).

An apprentice could put his apprenticeship term in jeopardy by getting married as the following entry in the London Butchers' Company records shows: "Item of Henry Fesie for setting his apprentice to worke being become a forreyner by marrying within his time, fine 3s – 4d." (Pearce, 1929).

Lists of apprentices for the 16th century show that twenty to thirty butchery apprentices a year were being registered in the City of London. A notable fact was that very few of the apprentices were from London, the majority coming from other parts of the country; some from as far as Wales, Devon, Cumberland and Durham. Another point of interest was that only a small number of the fathers of the apprentices were butchers, the rest being in a variety of occupations e.g. mercers, woolmen, carpenters, bakers, farmers, husbandmen, yeomen. As the first son was in line to take over from the father, the other sons were often put to other trades (Jones, 1976).

After the Butchers' Company received their charter of incorporation in 1605 the number of apprentices bound each year rose to about sixty with the same proportion coming from all parts of the country and the majority of their fathers being in occupations other than butchery. There was a marked discrepancy between the numbers of bound apprentices and the number that became freemen or continued employment as journeymen. It can be assumed that the majority of the apprentices, on completion of their time, returned to their own part of the country to take up the trade (*Ibid*).

The profile of apprentices of the Butchers' Company of Newcastle upon Tyne differed from that of London in the 1600s in that many of them came from Newcastle while those coming from elsewhere were mainly from Northumberland and Durham. There were more apprentices in

Newcastle whose fathers were butchers than was the case in London. The charter of the Butcher's Company of Newcastle laid down the minimum term of apprenticeship as eight years which condition remained until 1834 when it was reduced to seven years. It was also in the charter that a second apprentice could not be taken on until five years of the first apprentice's term had expired. The son of a freeman of the Company could be enrolled on the company's books soon after his birth to entitle him to take up his freedom on attaining the age of twenty-one under the patrimony clause. A number of sons of freemen became freemen and practised the trade of butcher without having been registered as an apprentice. The same also applied in London. Some of the Newcastle apprentices had wayward tendencies in the 1600s and were wont to frequent gaming houses playing at dice, cards, shovelboard, billiards or quoits. To obtain proper respect for their elders, apprentices were obliged to take their caps off to free brothers in the street. Fines for misdemeanours of an apprentice were recorded and he would be required to pay the fines when he had completed his apprenticeship and taken up his freedom (Dodds, 1917).

A number of the masters to which these apprentices were bound were women who were generally the widows of freemen of the guild. There was nothing to prevent women obtaining the freedom of the Butchers' Company in the same way as men. In London in 1585 John Shaw was apprenticed to Ann Taylor, in 1586 Johanna Best and Mary Frend each had an apprentice and in 1587 Johanna Lambert had two apprentices. There were, from time to time, female butchery apprentices; Hester Maynard served her apprenticeship with Francis Baker and was admitted to the freedom of the company in 1742. (Jones, 1976) Under the charter of the Butchers' Company of Newcastle upon Tyne, the wife of a free brother became a free sister and if her husband died she was entitled to carry on his business as a master butcher (Dodds, 1917).

The Guilds or Companies supported scholars pursuing general education. The records of the London Butchers' Company include the following entries:

> 1595 "Item given to Thomas Merest, a poor scholler in Cambridge, 13s – 4d."
> 1606 "An annual pension of 4 marks (£2-13-4) is awarded to Ralphe Cooke, the son of Richard Cooke in Eastcheap, Butcher, towards his mayntenance and educacion in the Universitie." (Pearce, 1929)

BEHAVIOUR OF BUTCHERS IN THE 16TH & 17TH CENTURIES

The Butchers' Companies as with other companies always endeavoured to maintain certain standards among their members. To this end regulations were passed and any member not complying was usually subject to a fine. The Butchers' Company of London were obviously particular about the dress of their members on certain occasions to which the following entries in the records attest:

> 1584- *"Item of Olyver Mason for coming to the election of the Wardens in his frycecoate and hatt"* – fine 3s – 4d.
> 1586- *"Item of Thos. Shipton for coming in a cloke without a gowne"* – fine 6d.
> 1598- *"Item of Peter Snell for coming before the Wardens in his cloke"* – fine 20d.
> 1598- *"Item of Mr. Lowes for not coming in a satten doublet and a decent gown at the election day"* – fine 12d.

1600- *"Item of Richard Milles for sitting in his hat"* – fine 12d.
1616- *"Item of Mr. Gawrite for undecency in apparell at Pawles"* fine 12d.

From the middle ages members of the Butchers' Company were expected to control the behaviour of apprentices and servants but as well as this it seems they were also held responsible for the conduct of their wives. This is borne out by the following entries into the records:

1583- *"Item of Hy. Lambert for words spoken by his wyfe agaynst Mr. Austene"* – fine 12d.
1595- *"Item of Robert Clement for his wife's disobedience to the Wardens"* – fine 5s.
1606- *"Item of George Tailor for wordes by his wife against John Rylie, Bridgmaster"* – fine 3s - 4d

There were also fines for a member playing dice with an apprentice (1577), for non-attendance at meetings, and in one case for "abusing a customer with undecent speeches" (1635) (Pearce, 1929).

The meetings and general activities of the Butchers' Company of Newcastle upon Tyne were not always tranquil according to some of the ordinances contained in the records. Brothers were forbidden to come into the meeting house wearing their aprons and steel, to bring dogs, to take tobacco, make a noise, come drunk, swear or leave the house before the meeting was over, according to the records between 1685 and 1730. The rules most frequently broken were those against reviling and unbrotherly words and against fighting. Few meetings took place in the early 1700s without a quarrel and a fight (Dodds, 1917).

The Butchers' Company of London sponsored wrestling matches at the St. Bartholomew fair annually from before 1500, offering livestock as prizes. This may have been a way of channelling aggressive tendencies away from routine business.

Chapter 12

Meat Consumers and Meat Consumption: 1550-1750

THE CONSUMERS

During the 16th and 17th centuries the structure of meat trading was developing significantly. Some of the developments had commenced in the late Middle Ages but were gathering pace throughout the Elizabethan and Stuart periods.

In the early Middle Ages under the feudal system the villeins (or tied peasants) and free peasants existed largely at a subsistence level and could not have supported a retail type butchery trade in the rural areas. The large households (castles, manors and bishops' palaces) and the monastic establishments would have generally organised their own supply of meat. The animals for slaughter came from their own estates or were bought in from a market or fair, and either one of their servants was a butcher or a butcher was employed to slaughter the animals. The butchery trade existed mainly for the supply of the urban dwellers.

The growing economy and changes in the structure of society were of consequence in the expansion of the meat industry. The emergence of the middle classes, or as they were referred to, the middling sort of people, and the growth of the wage-earning workers, produced more customers with more money to spend on meat.

For the royal court feasting and food consumption in general required large supplies of food and meat. The kitchens and food preparation areas in Hampton Court were enlarged by Henry VIII between 1529 and 1532 to an area of 36,000 square feet. The facilities included a counting house where the Clerk of the Kitchen aided by the Clerks of the Green Cloth (so called because of the green baize covering the tables at which they worked) accounted for the supplies of food. The royal court numbered about 1,200 in the winter and 800 in the summer, most of the court dining in the great hall. In one year the meat supplies amounted to 1,240 oxen, 8,200 sheep, 2,330 deer, 760 calves, 1,870 pigs and 53 wild boar. Some of the meat came from the King's estates but most was bought from local farmers and the markets. There was a whole range of game birds and poultry including swans, peacocks, chickens, quail and larks. Pheasants were readily available from the pheasant yards. Although most of the meat and poultry was roasted some was boiled in the Boiling House or used for making pies. A regular dish, especially for the lower courtiers, was pottage which was a thick broth made with meat and meat stock thickened with oatmeal or barley and seasoned with herbs. Food was served in helpings for four people which were called *messes* (Context, C.O.L.A.S).

The great houses of the large estates, apart from catering for the members of the household, often well in excess of 100, would entertain visiting dignitaries and their retinues, including the occasional visit from the monarch (Brears, 1985). The household of the Earl of Dorset at Speke

Fig 12.1 Drawing based on an illustration of a Tudor cook. It shows the wide range of utensils and ingredients the Tudor cook had readily available. The casks on the right would have contained wines and vinegar and the baskets were filled with fruit and vegetables. The cook is working on a raised hearth with the main fire at the back and smaller fires at the front for cooking or heating the contents of small saucepans, which somewhat resembled working with a modern hob.

Hall, near Liverpool, in 1613 numbered 130 (Hardyment, 1997). Among the top ranking servants was one, Robert Elnor, Slaughterman, who would have been responsible for the slaughter of the estate animals and dressing the carcases, as well as cutting the carcases into joints ready for the kitchens. He would have also prepared the edible offals and the various other animal products for their various uses. Most of the meat for these great houses would be supplied from their estates although there would be occasions when animals for slaughter were bought in, or in some cases carcases were bought in. The 17th and 18th centuries saw the rise in the middlemen, cattle dealers and carcase butchers or meat wholesalers. The clerk of the kitchen was in charge of all the activities to do with feeding the household and organising banquets, which included responsibility for the kitchens, pantries, larders, dairy and cellars. At Speke Hall there were two clerks of the kitchen, Messrs Edward Fulke and John Edwards (*Ibid*).

In Scotland large quantities of meat, particularly beef, were consumed in the houses of the aristocracy. In the early 1600s the supplies of meat to the household of Earl of Angus were most liberal. Large joints of fresh meat were spit roasted over an open fire to be served hot, with the cold remains being served at a later meal. Poor quality meat was cooked slowly with barley and vegetables in a large cauldron suspended over a fire. The large pieces of meat were served on platters as sodden (boiled) beef. Guests visiting the Earl of Angus on the 3rd November 1608 apart from being served lavish amounts of beef, mutton and chicken, were also served such delicacies as partridges, plovers and rabbits. Rabbit at this time was a luxury item, one rabbit being worth the same as four chickens. Rabbits were reared in warrens on estates tended by the warrenders (Geddes, 1994).

Apart from the aristocracy with their very large households there were the country gentry with their estates and somewhat smaller households. One such was Sir William Petre who resided at Ingatestone Hall in Essex with a staff of 21 at an annual wage bill of £51 in 1550. One member of the household was the *acater* who had the responsibility to obtain provisions for the house. (The term *acater* was later changed to caterer.) The animals slaughtered to provide meat for the household in 1552 were; 1 bull, 17 oxen, 14 steers, 4 cows, 29 calves, 129 sheep, 1 teg, 54 lambs, 3 boars, 9 porks, 5 hogs 'killed for bacon', 3 goats, 7 kids, 1 stag, 13 bucks and 5 does. The records for the weekly lists include 'one ox was cut into livery pieces'(usually about 30). These 'livery pieces' were for each of the household servants and the servants of guests. Much of the meat consumed by the household was from the estate and additional meat was purchased from Peter Preston, a local butcher. These more moderate households, as with the great houses, were also subject to visits by eminent people and their servants to whom they offered hospitality. The meals provided on a visit by Lady Darcy, wife of a privy councillor, consisted of:

> Dinner: 16 pieces of boiled beef, 4 pieces of roasted beef, half a calf, 2 pigs, 7 capons, 5 pasties of venison, 12 conies, 20 pigeons, an heronshew, 7 quails, 5 partridges and 2 tarts.

> Supper: 11 joints of mutton, half a lamb, 4 capons, 3 pasties of venison, 9 conies, an heronshew, a peahen, 18 pigeons, 6 chickens, 3 partridges, 2 tarts and a florentine. (Emmison, 1964)

The middling sorts (middle classes) comprised of the professionals (practitioners of law, medicine, etc.), merchants and the more successful traders, master craftsmen and yeomen. The middling sorts would have had a household consisting of their family and a number of servants, with a disposable income enabling them to eat well and provide the butchers with a good trade, especially in the towns.

The growth in wage earning workers was to a large extent due to the growth in capitalism, with the workers having little else to sell but their labour and craftsmanship, particularly in the clothing industry. There were a number of statutes for the control of wages from the Statute of Labourers in 1351 fixing the maximum rates of pay after the Black Death. The enactment known as the Statute of Apprentices, 1563, aimed at just rates of wages and conferred the authority to the Justices of the Peace to prescribe wages for each county at the quarter sessions. There were cases where the statutory rates were exceeded to attract the competent craftsman. Although there were attempts to relate wages to the prices of food it was rarely possible to reduce wages when food prices were generally lower. From at least the early part of the 16th century unscrupulous employers would pay their workers '*truck wages*' which entailed paying part of the wages in provisions which were assessed by the employer at well above the prices current at the time (Lipson, 1959). In the 1500s and 1600s the predominant portion of the ordinary worker's wages went on buying victuals, with bread and meat at the top of the shopping list.

The price of meat was relatively low compared with other food such as fruit and vegetables and sometimes there would be some good bargains. Meat could be sold at very reasonable prices because the other animal products such as skins, hides, horns, wool, tallow etc. were of a high value. There were, of course, times of scarcity due to weather conditions or livestock epidemics. During such times the municipal authorities in the towns would endeavour to enforce price controls, not always with success. The concern by the authorities to keep meat prices down led to them allowing foreign butchers (butchers from outside the town) to trade in the town markets and thereby breaking the guild's monopoly. Cheap meat was often available to the poorer people in the town suburbs or the surrounding villages from the hucksters or carkers (hawkers).

MEAT CONSUMPTION

The sumptuary laws, which were quite strict under Henry VIII, were laws specifying the amount and quality of food that persons could have according to their rank. There was considerable importance attached to food as a mark of status. There was a strict protocol at banquets, not only with the order of seating but also in respect of the type and quantity of dishes served to each order of guests according to their status. It was essentially meat dishes that were rated in respect of a person's status. A usual practice at banquets was for the best dishes to be served to the top table and then passed to the guests next in rank. Guests at the tables at the lower end would be served plainer food (Sim, 1997).

Henri Misson de Valbourg, a Frenchman writing about his travels in England, was astonished by the vast amount of fish and meat consumed, not only by the gentry but also by the middling sort (middle class). He describes a dinner laid on at a tavern which would have cost around a shilling:

> "Generally four spits, one over another, carry round each five or six pieces of butcher's meat, beef, mutton, veal, pork, lamb; you have what quantity you please cut off, fat, lean, much or little done; with this, a little salt and mustard upon the side of a plate, a bottle of beer and a roll; and there is your feast."

Many visitors from the Continent commented on the high level of meat consumption in England during the 16th and 17th centuries. Paul Hentzner writing in 1598 on the English and the quality of their roasts said "they are more polite in eating than the French, devouring less bread, but more meat, which they roast to perfection." (Rye, 1965). Estimates put the diet of the higher levels of society as consisting of 75% meat or more.

According to Stow, 1598, the number of butchers then in the city (of London) and suburbs was accounted six score, of which every one killed six oxen apiece weekly. This would have totalled 720 oxen per week. Add to this pigs, sheep, calves and lambs and it would have amounted to a large quantity of meat consumed in the metropolis. In 1725 the estimated meat consumption for London was 98,000 beeves, 60,000 calves, 70,000 sheep and lambs, 187,000 swine and 52,000 sucking pigs (Besant, 1902).

Meat served at the tables of most levels of society was generally far in excess of what was required and what was left was sometimes eaten by the servants or, in many cases, distributed to the poor. In some cases if the meat was not broken, i.e. the dish was whole and untouched by the carver, it would go to the servants but if it had been broken it would go to the poor. Many of the poorest lived off the leavings of the rich men's tables.

John Murrell's 1650 edition of his *Two Bookes of Cooking and Carving* contain details of what he refers to as a "Small Common Service of Meate":

First Course.
1.   A boyld Capon or Chicken;
2.   A Legge of Lambe farc'd (stuffed) of the French fashion;
3.   A boyld Mallard or Rabbet;
4.   A dish of boild Olives of Veal, or Collops and Egges;
5.   A piece of roast Beefe;
6.   A dish of Chewets of Veal (minced veal pie), or Mutton-pyes, if it be Winter, but if it be Summer an Olive pie (beef olives enclosed in pastry);
7.   A legge of Mutton roasted whole, or a Loyne of Veale, or both;
8.   A Pigge;
9.   A Swan, Goose, or Turkey;
10. A pasty of Venison, or a forequarter of Mutton, or a fat rumpe of Beefe;
11. A Capon, Pheasant, or Hearne (heron);
12. Custard.
Second Course.
1.   A quarter of Lambe;
2.   A couple of Rabbets;
3.   A Mallard, Teale, or Widgin;
4.   A brace of Partriges, or Woodcocks;
5.   A Chicken or Pigeon-pye;
6.   A dish of Plovers or Snites (snipe);
7.   A couple of Chickens;
8.   A Warden (pear) or Quince-Pie;
9.   A sowsed (soused) Pig or Capon;
10. A Cherrie or a Goosberrie Tart, or a Quarter-Tart of Pippins
11. A dish of some kind of sowsed-fish;
12. Lobsters or pickled Oysters. (Ainsworth-Davis, 1931)

A number of entries in Samuel Pepys' diary give details of his dinners, as on 4th April 1662:

"We had a fricassee of rabbits and chickens, a leg of mutton boiled, three carps in a dish, a great dish of side of lamb, a dish of roast pigeons, a dish of four lobsters, three tarts, a lamprey pie, a most rare pie, a dish of anchovies, good wine of several sorts, and all things mighty noble, and to my great content." (Ibid)

Meat was a principal ingredient of the repast of the farm labourer. Thomas Tusser wrote in 1573:

Good Ploughmen look weekly of custom and right
For roast meat on Sundays and Thursdays at night.

A few lines from a poem by Cobbe in 1614:

> When beefe, Bread and Beere,
> Was honest men's cheere,
> And welcome and spare not;
> And John and his Joane,
> Did Live of their owne,
> Full merrily, though but all meanely.

An annual dinner was held on St. Thomas's Day for the inmates of the Temple Hospital, Bristol, which was founded in 1613 for ten poor people. This dinner was known locally as the "Pease and Pork Dinner" consisted mainly of boiled legs of pork and pease pudding.

The inmates of the Ludgate Debtor's Prison received a meat meal on Sundays courtesy of the Butchers' Company according to a pamphlet dated 1710. It states that the kettle-pot man made the Sunday Broth from meat sent in by the Butchers' Company. In one place the pamphlet states that the prisoners were entitled to this weekly dole of food but in another place it suggests the kettle-pot man sold it to the prisoners (Besant, 1902).

In Scotland in the Middle Ages the diet of most Scots was dominated by flesh, cheese, butter and milk, indicating a predominantly pastoral agriculture. By the 1600s, the landowners and the wealthier in society were still consuming large quantities of flesh while the diet of the poor became largely cereal based (Geddes, 1994).

In the past veal seemed to be much more commonly consumed than is the case today, considering the number of recipes for veal, the inclusion of veal dishes on the menus and the numbers of calves in the lists of meat supplies. In the late 1500s there were 1,700 – 1,800 veal carcases sold in Cheap Side, London, every Saturday (Everitt, 1990).

FAST DAYS

The growing consumption of meat, especially meat eating on fish days, resulted in the reinforcement of the laws for the observance of fish days or fast days during the reign of Elizabeth I. This was due largely to the need to maintain a strong and viable fishing fleet as this was regarded as the training ground and the reserve for the British Navy, plus being a source of seamen for the growing mercantile fleet. Another factor influencing the government was the growing demand for beef and mutton resulting in the conversion of arable land into pasture. The fast days or fish days were Fridays, Ember days, Rogation days and the forty days of Lent (Trevelyan, 1960).

There was not an adequate availability of fresh fish for all on fish days and many had to resort to salt fish or stockfish which was dried fish. Individuals, who through infirmity or any other cause were unable to fast, could obtain a licence permitting them to buy and eat meat on fish days. The licence cost 15 shillings (Besant, 1904). To supply such people there were 'lenten butchers' who were permitted to slaughter and sell meat on fish days. There were four lenten butchers in the City of London and one in Southwark. There were prosecutions against butchers unauthorised as lenten butchers for slaughtering and selling meat during Lent (Pearce, 1929). A London woman was committed to the pillory in 1563 for serving flesh in her tavern during Lent.

HEALTHY DIETS

There have long been the advocates of the importance of meat as part of a healthy diet, not least in the 16th century as the following extract from Boorde's "Compendyous Regyment or Dyetary of Health" 1542, attests:

> "Beef is a good meate for an Englysshe man, so be it the beest be yonge, & that it be not kowe-fleshe; yf it be moderatly powdered (salted) that the groose blode by salt may be exhaustyd, it dothe make an Englysshe man stronge; Veal is good and easily digested; Brawn is an usual meate in winter amonges Englysshe men; Bacon is good for carters and plowmen, the which be ever labouringe in the earth or dung… I do say that coloppes (slices of bacon) and egges is as wholesome for them as a talowe candell is good for a blereyed mare… Potage is made of the lyquor in which fleshe is soden (boiled) in, with puttyng-to chopped herbes and otemel and salt. Fyrmente is made of whete and milke, in which the flesh be soden… It doth nourysshe, and it doth strength a man." (Brears, 1985)

MEAT QUALITY

Eliza Smith's advice on assessing the quality of different meats is a good guide to the quality of meat in the early part of the 18th century.

Her advice for the assessment of the quality of different meats was as follows:

"To chuse Beef"

> "If it be true ox-beef it will have an open grain, and the fat, if young, of a crumbling or oily smoothness, except it be the brisket and neck pieces, with such others as are very fibrous. The colour of the lean should be of a pleasant carnation red, the fat rather inclining to white than yellow, and suet of a curious white colour. Cow-beef is of a closer grain, the fat whiter, the bones less, and the lean of a paler colour. If it be young and tender the dent you make with your finger by pressing it, will in a little time, rise again. Bull beef is a more dusky red, a closer grain, and firmer than either of the former; harder to be indented with your finger, and rising again sooner. The fat is very gross and fibrous, and of a strong rank scent. If it be old it will be so very tough, that if you pinch it you will scarce make any impression in it. If it be fresh it will be a lively fresh colour, but if stale of a dusky colour and very clammy. If it be bruised, the part affected will look of a more dusky or blackish colour than the rest."

"To chuse Mutton"

> "Take some of the flesh between your fingers and pinch it; if it feels tender, and soon returns to its former place it is young; but if it wrinkles, and remains so it is old. The fat will, also, easily separate from the lean if it be young; but if old it will adhere

more firmly, and be very clammy and fibrous. If it be ram mutton the fat will be spongy, the grain close, the lean rough and of deep red, and when dented by your finger will not rise again. If the sheep had the rot[1] the flesh will be palish, the fat a faint white, inclining to yellow; the meat will be loose at the bone, and, if you squeeze it hard, some drops of water resembling a dew or sweat, will appear on the surface. If it be a fore quarter, observe the vein in the neck. For if it look ruddy, or of an azure colour it is fresh; but if yellowish, it is near tainting, and if green, it is already so. As for the hind quarter smell under the kidney, and feel whether the knuckle be stiff or limber; for if you find a faint or ill scent in the former, or an unusual limberness in the latter, it is stale."

"To chuse Pork"

"pinch the lean between your fingers; if it break, and feel soft and oily, or if you can easily nip the skin with your nails, or if the fat be soft and oily, it is young; but if the lean be rough, the fat very spongy, and the skin stubborn it is old. If it be a boar, or a hog gelded at full growth, the flesh will feel harder and tougher than usual, the skin thicker, the fat hard and fibrous, the lean of a dusky red, and a rank scent. To know if it be fresh or stale, try the legs and hands at the bone, which comes out in the middle of the fleshy part, but putting in your finger, for as it first taints in those places, you may easily discover it by smelling to your finger; also the skin will be clammy and sweaty when stale, but smooth and cool when fresh."

"To chuse Brawn"

"The best method of knowing whether brawn be young or old, is by the extraordinary or moderate thickness of the rind, and the hardness and softness of it; for the thick and hard is old, the moderate is young. If the rind and fat be remarkably tender it is not boar brawn but barrow or sow." (Smith, 1758)

COOKING MEAT IN THE TIME OF ELIZABETH I AND THE STUART KINGS

The principal form of roasting meat was spit roasting as in the medieval period although there was much development in the types of spit and the way they were operated. There was one method for turning the spit by harnessing it to a tread-wheel in which a dog was placed to keep the wheel and the spit turning. The 1710 inventory of Dyrham Park, Gloucestershire, includes a dog-wheel which turned five spits (Hardyment, 1997). During the 16th and 17th centuries weight driven spit-jacks came into use. These consisted of descending weights driving the spit by a pulley via a mechanism which caused the spit to turn slowly. The next development was the clockwork driven spit (Ainsworth-Davis, 1931; Wilson, 1973); Gervase Markham's instructions for spit roasting meats were:

---

[1] Rot: liver rot caused by liver fluke.

"the spitting and broaching of meat, which must be done so strongly and firmly that the meat may by no means either shrink from the spit, or turn about the spit; and yet ever to observe that the spit do not go through any principal part of the meat, but such as is of least account and estimation: and if it be birds or fowl which you spit, then let the spit go through the body of the fowl, and so fasten it with picks or skewers under the wings, about the thighs of the fowl, and at the feet or rump, according to the manner of trussing and dressing them."

Markham then advises on the fire:

"then to know the temperatures of the fires for every meat, and which should have a slow fire, yet a good one, taking leisure in roasting, as chines of beef, swans, turkeys, peacocks, bustards, and generally any great large fowl, and other joints of mutton, veal, pork, kid, lamb, or such like, whether it be venison, red or fallow, which indeed would lie long at the fire and soak well in the roasting; ..."(slowly absorb a steady heat). For smaller joints of meat or smaller birds "would have a quick fire without scorching, ...".

According to Markham:

"To know when the meat is roasted enough; for too much rareness is unwholesome so too much dryness is not nourishing. Therefore to know when it is in the perfect height, and is neither too moist nor too dry, you should observe these signs ... when the steam or smoke ascendeth, either upright or else goeth from the fire, when it beginneth a little to shrink from the spit, or when the gravy which droppeth from it is clear without bloodiness, then the meat is enough." (Markham, 1615)

The use of ovens for roasting or baking meat had been restricted because the ovens were of brick and stone constructions primarily for baking bread. In the towns ovens were largely owned by the bakers and in the rural areas the great houses and the houses of the gentry would have had a bake-house. For many households the practice grew of taking their meat for roasting or their pies for baking to the local baker who would bake them for a small charge. Apart from the fact that these people did not possess an oven there was the added advantage of it costing much less than the fuel cost for individual cooking. Ovens in the home did not become a common feature until the 19th century (Wilson, 1973).

Cooking meat in a pastry case or enclosed in pastry was a regular method of cooking meat. Raised pies or coffins (pastry cases) were commonly used as a container for the meat during cooking, serving and storage and generally the pastry would not be eaten. Markham discusses types of pastry for different types of meat. For the heavier, coarser meats such as red deer venison, wild boar and swan which are to be kept for some time before eating, he states "they be baked in a moist, thick, tough, coarse, and long lasting crust and therefore of all other, rye paste is best." Markham writes that poultry "that come to the table more than once (yet not many days) would be baked in a good white crust, somewhat thick therefore your wheat is fit for them." According to Markham, for those meats eaten hot these "would be in the finest, shortest and thinnest crust;

Fig 12.2 This drawing of a 1677 illustration shows activities in the kitchen with the woman on the left raising the crust for the sides of a pie. On the right a joint of meat and poultry is being spit roasted and pottage is simmering over the fire.

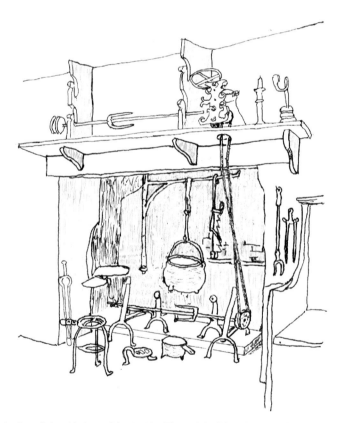

Fig 12.3 A drawing of the hearth in a kitchen of the 1600s. The spit is driven by a clockwork motor from the mantle shelf. There is the ratchet hook for suspending pots above the fire, enabling the pots to be raised or lowered to the appropriate height. There are the firedogs to support the burning wood and cast iron stands on which pots can be placed close to the fire. This is the type of hearth that would have been found in the kitchen of a middling sort of family (middle class).

therefore your fine wheat flour which is a little baked in the oven before it be kneaded is best for that purpose." and:

> "your rye paste would be kneaded only with hot water and a little butter … and it would be made tough and stiff that it may stand well in the raising for the coffin thereof must ever be very deep: your course wheat crust would be kneaded with hot water or mutton broth and good store of butter, and the paste made stiff and tough because that coffin must be deep also; the fine wheat crust must be kneaded with as much butter as water, and the paste made reasonable lithe and gentle, into which you must put three or four eggs." (Markham, 1615)

Where the meat in the pie was to be kept to be eaten cold some days later the meat would be sealed in with melted clarified butter or lard which may have been poured into the pie through a hole in the pastry lid.

Venison was highly regarded by the gentry and hosts would endeavour to serve it as a mark of their esteem. It was often served as venison pasty, the meat being highly spiced and baked in a case of pastry to be eaten hot or sealed in with clarified butter to preserve it for use as a cold dish. There were occasions when the dish served as venison was meat other than venison. After Samuel Pepys and his wife had dined out on 6th January 1660 he wrote of the meal "which was good, only the venison pasty was palpable beef, which was not handsome." (Wilson, 1973). Markham even gives a recipe for disguising beef as red deer venison and the flesh of a ram as fallow deer venison (Markham, 1615). There was also a recipe in the *'Good Huswifes Jewell'* by Tomas Dawson, 1596, for beef pastry baked like venison (Brears, 1985). Treatment for tainted venison was to bury it in the soil overnight or to marinade in a mere sauce which consisted of vinegar, small beer and salt (Wilson, 1973; Experienced Butcher, 1816).

The fat from marrow bones was used in cooking ways which would not be contemplated today. There is a recipe for marrow bone pie in Markham consisting of layers of marrow fat and in between layers of artichokes, potatoes, dried fruits, sugar and cinnamon in a raised pastry coffin. (Markham, 1615) In *'The Compleat Huswife'* there are two recipes for marrow pudding, both containing dried fruit, eggs, sugar and spices as well as marrow fat and a recipe for marrow pasties. (Smith, 1758)

Minced meat in the 16th century as in the medieval period consisted mainly of finely chopped meat, suet, dried fruit and spices. In *'A Book Of Cookrye Very Necessary For All Such As Delight Therein'* (1591) there is a recipe for pies; 1½ lb lean mutton or beef shred fine (minced), 4 oz suet, ground cloves, mace, black pepper, saffron, raisins, currants and prunes (Brears, 1985). Eliza Smith's recipe for mince pies of veal in 1758 had less meat (veal) with double the quantity of suet to meat and relatively larger quantities of raisins, currants plus apples and lemon peel. The spices were cloves, nutmeg and mace, put in along with sugar, and as the pies were filled, into each was to go lemon juice, candied lemon peel, slices of citron, a spoonful of sack (sherry) and a spoonful of claret. In the 18th century it was found that the mixtures containing the foregoing ingredients, less the meat, placed in stone jars with brandy or sherry could be kept for up to four months. It followed that using this mixture as a filling for tarts and pies without the meat was preferred, hence the modern version of mincemeat (Wilson, 1973).

In the Scottish households of the period, soups and broths were a much more common feature of the menu than in England. Elizabeth Cleland's '*A New and Easy Method of Cookery*' (Edinburgh, 1755) has the whole first chapter devoted to gravies, soups, broths and pottages whereas recipes for these are much less in the books of Hannah Glasse (1747) and Eliza Smith (1758).

Broiling or grilling steaks was increasing during this period encouraged by the growing availability of good quality steaks from younger animals. This was usually done on a gridiron over the hot coals or a charcoal fire (Smith, 1758). Gridirons date back to the Roman period: a number have been found during archaeological excavations (Ainsworth-Davis, 1931). Carbonado was described by Markham as a method of broiling meat. Half boiled breasts of mutton, half roasted shoulders of mutton and poultry were considered ideal to be carbonadoed (Markham, 1615).

A recipe for roast fillet gives some further illustration of the historic reference to cuts and names of cuts. This recipe is contained in a book of recipes entitled 'The Queens Closet Opened' published in 1665 and purported to have been transcribed from the recipe book of Queen Henrietta Maria. The recipe:

> "Take a Fillet of Beef which is the tenderest part of the beast, and lieth only in the inward Part of the Surloyne next to the Chyne, cut it as big as you can, then broach it on a broach not too big, and be careful you broach it not thorow the best of the meat, roast it leasurely and bast it with sweet Butter. Set a dish under it to save the Gravy while the Beef is roasting, prepare the Sauce for it, chop good store of Parsley with a few sweet herbs shred small, and the yelks of three or four Egs, and mince among them the pill of an Orange, and a little onyon, then boyl this mixture, putting into it sweet butter, Vinegar, and gravy, a spoonfull of strong broth, when it is well boyled put it into your beef, and serve it very warm, sometimes a little gross pepper or Ginger into your sauce, or a pill of an orange or Lemon." (Isitt, 1987)

SAUSAGES AND PUDDINGS

Sausages certainly date back to the Roman period; there were several recipes in Apicius for sausages including blood sausage (black pudding). The recipe books for the 17th and 18th centuries contain a variety of recipes for sausages and puddings such as liver puddings, blood puddings and hog's puddings. The term puddings was used for the animals' entrails. The scraped and cleaned intestines were used as containers or casings for a range of recipes, both sweet and savoury. These products were cooked in their casings hence they were called puddings. Markhams' recipe for bread pudding consisted of two loaves of white bread (grated), dates, a great store of currants, twelve to fourteen eggs and plenty of suet, to which was added powdered cloves, nutmeg, mace, cinnamon, saffron, salt and sugar; all to be mixed well and filled into farmes (casings) and boiled. Rice pudding containing rice, milk, cream, eggs, cloves, mace, currants, dates, sugar and salt were also filled into farmes and boiled (Markham, 1615). The wider casings obtained from the large intestines were used for the bulkier recipes and the narrow small intestines used for sausages.

A recipe by Markham for sausage links begins with a large chine of pork, the lean cut into thin slices and the fat likewise and then placed in layers; alternate layers of lean and fat, with the first and last layers being lean. The whole was then cut thoroughly into very small pieces and mixed with salt, pepper and shredded sage. The recipe then follows:

> "Then take the farmes (casings) made as long as possible, and not cut into pieces as for puddings, and first blow them well to make the meat slip, and then fill them: which done, with threads divide them into several links as you please, …" For cooking Markham recommended the links be fried, broiled on a gridiron or roasted about a capon. (*Ibid*)

The meat content in Eliza Smith's recipe for sausages was 3lb of lean pork and 3lb of fat. The seasoning consisted of salt, pepper mace, nutmeg, cloves sage and rosemary. The recipe also includes 6 eggs. Her recipe for very fine sausages is for the meat to be cut from either a leg of pork or of veal and all the fat and skins removed from the lean meat. To every pound of lean meat was added 2lb of beef suet and the whole chopped very fine. Then was added a large handful of finely shredded green sage, grated nutmeg, salt and pepper. The sausage meat was not put into skins but was rolled into lengths of a finger and two fingers thick and fried in clarified suet which had to be boiling hot before being put into the sausages. These recipes would have had a very high fat content (Smith, 1758).

Hannah Glasse also gives a recipe for pork sausages and suggests that "Beef makes very good sausages." Her recipe for black puddings starts with boiling a peck of groats for half an hour followed by two quarts of blood from a freshly killed pig the blood having been stirred until it was cold. Then the blood and groats were mixed together with salt, mace, nutmeg, cloves, sweet marjoram, thyme and pennyroyal. The following day the leaf fat from the hog's carcase was diced and added to the mixture. Scraped and washed guts were filled with the mixture and the puddings boiled softly for an hour. In Scotland they made puddings with goose blood (Glasse, 1747). Sausage seasonings used today will consist of salt, pepper, mace and/or nutmeg, often with sage or thyme and occasionally some of the spices or herbs aforementioned. Mincing meat in the 17th and 18th centuries would have been done by chopping the meat very fine with a knife. If the meat was required to be a finer texture for paste or pâté then it would be ground using a pestle and mortar. The kitchen equipment listed in *"A Perfect School of Instructions for Officers of the Mouth"* by Giles Rose (1682) includes a chopping knife, a mincing knife, a stone-mortar and pestle, and small and great larding pins.

Sausages were the province of the cooks at this time and it would seem from the evidence that it was not until the 19th century before butchers became involved in making sausages. Some women street traders made and sold sausages. The following is the cry of the sausage sellers taken from a very rare sheet of woodcuts in the British Museum with figures of the criers; said to be the same date as Ben Jonson's fish wives:

> "Who buys my sausages, sausages fine,
> I ha' fine sausages of the best;
> As good as they are as ere was eat;
> If they be finely drest.
> Come, mistris, buy this dainty pound,
> About a capon roast them round." (Hindley, 1885)

MEAT PRESERVATION IN THE 16ᵗʰ & 17ᵗʰ CENTURIES

Salting or curing meat was still the main method of preservation. The recipes of the period for curing meat showed considerable importance for the type of salt used. Bay salt was so named originally for salt coming from the Bay of Bourgneuf but became the name for all the salt from the salt pans around the Bay of Biscay, much of it coming from the La Rochelle area. Bay salt was favoured for being large grained and having a sharp sweet taste. The finer white salts were considered to create a barrier at the surface of the meat preventing further penetration of the cure (Wilson, 1973). The inclusion of saltpetre was common in the curing recipes sometimes as both saltpetre and the unrefined petre-salt. Sal prunella is produced by heating saltpetre and is moulded into small cakes. Much of the nitrate is converted to nitrite therefore being more immediately effective in the curing process. An advantage of using saltpetre in the curing process was that the nitrate would be converted to nitrite which has an inhibitory effect on bacteria, increasing the preservative effect of the cure. Another important advantage of nitrite is that it combines with the red pigment in muscle, myoglobin, to produce the attractive pink colour of the cured meat.

In Eliza Smith's recipe to salt hams, a peck (2 gallons) of bay salt, four ounces of saltpetre and three pounds of brown sugar were dissolved in water to make a pickle (brine), it being strong enough to float an egg. Middling hams were to lie in the pickle for three weeks and large ones for a month. When they were taken out of the pickle they were dried with a cloth and then rubbed in with bay salt and she states

> "hang them up to dry, and smoke them with sawdust every day for a fortnight together; the chimney you hang them must be of moderate heat".

Eliza Smith's book also includes a Westphalian bacon recipe. The pickle was made of one gallon of pump water, half a gallon of bay salt, half a gallon of white salt, pound of petre-salt, quarter pound of saltpetre and a pound of coarse sugar; boiled well together. When it was cold the pork would lie in the pickle for a fortnight then it was taken out and dried over burning sawdust (Smith, 1758).

Some advice is given by Eliza Smith in choosing hams. She writes "take a sharp pointed knife, run it into the middle of the ham on the inside under the bone, draw it out quickly and smell to it; if its flavour be fine and relishing, and the knife little daubed, the ham is sweet and good; but if on the contrary, the knife be greatly daubed, has a rank smell, and hogoo issues from the vent it is tainted." (This would seem to be a test for bone taint.) She continues regarding the fat that "if it appear white and be well scented, it is good; but if yellowish, or a rusty colour, and not well scented, it is either tainted or rusty (rancid), or at least, soon will be so." (*Ibid*).

Brawn, although being a speciality, was prepared by a method which included pickling or sousing the cooked meat. Brawn during this period was very different from the brawn of today. Brawn was made from the carcase meat, preferably of an old boar. In fact the term brawn is an alternative to boar for a male pig (Culley, 1807), and Brawner is the term given to older boars no longer required for breeding and therefore castrated to fatten for slaughter. Eliza Smith and the Experienced Butcher refer to the best brawn from old boars being made from the meat of old boars, 5 to 6 years old, whereas brawn made from the carcases of barrows (male castrated young) or sows would be more tender but not have the true flavour (Smith, 1758; Experienced Butcher, 1816).

A recipe for making brawn given by Henderson is for the boar's flitches only, without the ham or shoulder. His recipe reads:

> "After the boar is killed, the flesh is sliced off the backbone and ribs, and afterwards sprinkled with salt; and it must then be laid in a tray till the blood be drained from it; give it a little more salt, and let it be rolled up as hard as possible (as tight as possible)". The recipe states that the roll should be nine or ten inches diameter and then boiled in a copper till it is "so tender that you can run a straw through it, and when cold it is put into a prepared pickle". (Henderson, 1814)

The alternative to curing in a pickle would have been to souse in vinegar. The reference to the brawn being rolled up as hard as possible was an important part of brawn preparation. It has been similarly instructed that it be rolled very tightly with a cloth tape requiring two strong men to pull the tape sufficiently tight (Stead, 1991).

Potted meat was a means of preserving meat that became more common in the 16th and 17th centuries. The principle was that the prepared meat was cooked thoroughly therefore destroying all the spoilage organisms and then packed into earthenware pots or alternatively cooked in the pots. The cooked meat was pressed down tightly in the pot and then sealed by using melted clarified butter or pigs fat. Sealing with fat not only created a barrier against microorganisms but the fat was also impermeable to air and therefore to oxygen. Earlier in the medieval period pastry coffins were used for potted meat but by the end of the 16th century the trend was towards earthenware pots. Potted meats were popular for taking on long journeys. Hannah Glasse gives several recipes for potted meats; the one for potted pigeons or fowls, states "that the meat being cooked very tender and drained dry of any gravy is then packed close in a pot and sealed in with clarified butter near an inch thick" (Glasse, 1747). Although the cooking temperatures would have been sufficient to kill normal bacteria they would not have been high enough to kill the spores of *Clostridium botulinum* and the conditions of much of the potted meat would have provided an ideal medium for the germination and anaerobic growth of the organism and the production of its lethal toxin. There are records of botulism in Germany in 1785 associated with sausage and other meat products (Burrows, 1973). It is possible that some persons eating potted meat could have died of botulism and some innocent cook accused of poisoning them.

Icehouses began to appear in Britain in the 17th century but the initial purpose was not for the storage of perishable food but to enable the people in the grand houses to have ice in the summer to cool their drinks and to make sorbets and even ice-cream (Fig 12.4). An icehouse was built at Greenwich in 1619, the first recorded in London, and was followed by many others, including one at Hampton Court in 1625. The early icehouses were generally of brick construction, conically shaped and built into the ground to provide insulation and often further insulated by a thatched cover. A drainage opening at the bottom of the icehouse would allow the water from the melted ice to seep away. The icehouses were progressively filled in the winter with ice and snow and due to the weight as it became filled, the ice would become a solid block which was an important factor in it remaining frozen until late summer (Buxbaum, 1992).

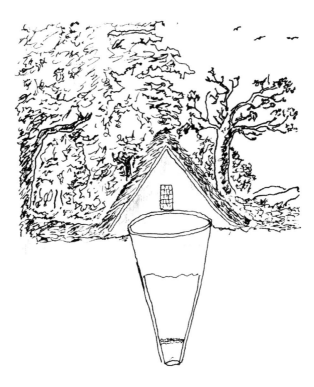

Fig 12.4 A drawing based on an engraving of 1683 of an Italian conical shaped ice-well which was protected by a thick insulating thatched roof, as described by John Evelyn.

Chapter 13

Meat Supplies and Marketing

BUTCHERS' BEASTS

The increase in the number of those deemed the 'middling sorts' (middle classes) and their growing affluence resulted in a greater demand for better quality butcher's meat. An effect of more affluence is often that eating becomes very much a source of enjoyment rather than a means of sustenance. It followed with an expanding demand for good quality meat. Butchers were therefore in the market for well-fed and well-finished animals for slaughter and not just the cull dairy cows (kine) or cull sheep from the wool flocks.

This demand for better butchers' animals led to efforts for the improvement of livestock. Improvement of livestock is twofold, genetic improvement and better standards of husbandry; particularly the feeding regimes.

Genetic improvement can be accomplished either by a system of selection or by bringing into a herd animals with better growth performance or larger animals with a better conformation. There is much evidence of the importation of the larger Dutch cattle which were influencing the cattle herds in many parts of the country in the latter part of the 16th and through the 17th century.

There was of course the better feeding of the animals destined as good quality butchers' animals but another factor which aided this was the enclosures. The enclosure of common land converting it into private property started in the 14th century and became much more widespread during the 15th and 16th centuries. This brought about the gradual transformation of the countryside from the open field system, introduced during the Saxon period. The problem with the open field system, with its common land for grazing, was lack of land management. While the enclosures deprived many peasants of their grazing rights, the enclosed land would have enabled much more effective management of the pasture and control of grazing; therefore improvement of the stock. The following verse by the Elizabethan agricultural writer Thomas Tusser underlines this fact:

> More plenty of mutton and beef,
> Corn, butter and cheese of the best,
> More wealth anywhere (to be brief)
> More people, more handsome and prest,
> Where find ye, (go search any coast)
> Than there, where enclosures are most.

The decline in feudalism, or more particularly seigniorage and the rise of the yeoman farmers and gentlemen farmers, was changing the situation as far as livestock production was concerned.

Graziers who were specialising in the supply of well finished fat animals for the market were becoming more common. Some butchers had additionally taken on the business of graziers which apart from expanding their profits gave them a reserve or stock of slaughter animals. Graziers were often also cattle dealers, or at least cattle dealers would need to have a working relationship with a grazier to provide for holding stock bought from markets, fairs, etc.

INCREASE IN THE SIZE OF LIVESTOCK

There were notable improvements of cattle and sheep through the 1500s and 1600s with the selection of breeding stock by a number of breeders such as the Yorkshire farmer Henry Best around 1640 and John Franklin around 1670. There followed quite a number of noted successful breeders of livestock by the early 1700s and in 1720 Daniel Defoe spoke of the rich graziers of Leicestershire (Darby, 1976c). These were the foundations on which the late 18th century livestock improvers were to build, e.g. Bakewell, the Colling brothers (Robert and Charles) and Culley. Evidence for an increase in the size of cattle from the latter 1500s is supported by archaeological reports of bone assemblages. The documentary evidence for the weights of cattle during the 16th and 17th centuries is sparse and where it exists it is not clearly defined. Where weights are given it will normally be for the carcase; weighing live animals was rarely practised. Weights were usually given in stones but apart from the standard stone of 14 lb there was also a 16 lb stone called the Dutch stone or Scotch stone. In the South West, Wales and the North West of the country the score (20 lb) was most often used for quoting the weights of livestock. The 8 lb butcher's stone (Smithfield stone) was commonly used in relation to the weight of carcases. The 8 lb stone was more commonly used in London and the Home Counties and was in use before the end of the 18th century. The value of using the 8 lb stone for weights of carcases was that there would be approximately 8 lb of a carcase for every 14 lb of the beef animals' liveweight (i.e. a killing out yield of 57%). The butcher's stone continued to be used for price quotations on Smithfield Market until the outbreak of the second world war.

The weights of cattle were relatively low in the middle of the 16th century according to some figures given by Thorold Rogers. In the case of an ox bought in 1546 the carcase weighed 426 lb (775 lb liveweight approx.), 21 oxen and steers bought for the Navy in 1547 averaged 307 lb (558 lb liveweight approx.), 142 oxen averaged 443 lb (805 lb liveweight approx.) and 483 oxen were bought in 1548 averaging 440 lb (800 lb liveweight approx.) (Rogers, 1866).

There were records showing the price of cattle per head and the price paid by King's College, Cambridge for beef given in price per 14 lb stone, which can be assumed were dressed carcases (*Ibid*). From these figures the following are estimates of liveweights and carcase weights working on the yield of a dressed carcase being 55% of the liveweight and the price of the meat equalling the cost of the live animal: the carcase butcher/slaughterer would have made a profit from the 'fifth quarter' e.g. the hide, horn, fats and other offals.

Estimates of liveweights and carcase weights from prices of oxen and carcases are shown in Table 13.1.

The sale in 1642 at Hickstead of eight fat oxen at £11 each with carcase beef at 24s cwt at this time, would have indicated carcase weights of 1,027 lb and live weights of 1,867 lb (*Ibid*); some

Table 13.1. Estimates of liveweights and carcase weights

Years	Ave. price per head	Price per 14lb stone	Est. carcase weight	Est. live-weight
1593 - 1602	103s – 10d	2s – 3d	646 lb	1175 lb
1623 - 1632	146s – 7d	2s – 6¾d	800 lb	1454 lb
1653 – 1662	143s – 5d	3s – 5d	587 lb	1067 lb
1693 - 1702	166s – 8d	3s – 6d	667 lb	1212 lb

very large animals. In 1704 a partnership of Henry Dunnalle and Isaac Holford undertook to supply on demand naval victualling yards with cattle, not less than 6 cwt at 20s per cwt and to include the kidney and suet. This latter clause confirms that it was for the supply of carcases. With carcases at a minimum of 672 lb the liveweights would have been 1,222 lb or more (Chartres, 1990). By the end of the 18th century the slaughter weights of cattle had increased quite considerably. Even so the extremely high weights as exemplified in the following details given by George Culley were for specially fattened animals and would have been well above the average but they still indicate the extent of the improvements (Culley, 1807). These animals being specially fattened would have carried a great deal of fat in the carcase; i.e. subcutaneous fat, intermuscular fat, kidney and channel fat. Such animals would have had a much higher yield of dressed carcase to live weight, probably well above 60%. Well fattened animals could have had a dressed carcase yield of up to 70%; the dressed carcase yields of 15 of the winning fatstock cattle at the Smithfield Show of 1936 were all between 62% and 66% (Gerrard, 1956). Indications from some of the weight figures given in Youatt are that older animals when fattened to the level desired in the past could have resulted in dressed carcase yields of 70% or 72% (Youatt, 1834). The estimated live-weights in Table 13.2 are based on a dressed carcase yield of 66%.

Table 13.2 Estimated liveweights

Year of slaughter	Age of Ox	Carcase weight		Est. liveweight
1779	6 years	151st - 10lbs	2124lbs	3218lbs
1787	7 years	152st – 9lbs	2137lbs	3238lbs
1787	7 years	152st – 8lbs	2136lbs	3236lbs
1789	5 years	150st - 4½lbs	2104½lbs	3189lbs

(Culley, 1807)

With regard to the older cattle and working oxen, Lord Somerville maintained that an ox needed to be worked hard from four to six years old to attain fullest size. If the ox was kept idle until he was six he would be stinted in his growth. Lord Somerville added that an ox reached full stature at six years old unless he was naturally disposed to be more than ordinary size, when he would continue to grow for another half year (Youatt, 1834).

Progressively through the 19th century cattle were slaughtered at younger ages and therefore lower weights and working oxen were less in number. Some slaughter weights of shorthorn cattle from the early 19th century are shown in Table 13.3. The estimated liveweights are based on a dressed carcase yield of 64%.

Table 13.3 Slaugher weights of shorthorn cattle

Year of slaughter	Age of animal	Carcase weight		Est. liveweight
1814	Steer 3yr – 9mths	101st	1414 lb	2209 lb
1815	Steer 3yr – 11mths	112st – 7 lb	1575 lb	2461 lb
1815	Heifer 3yr – 8mths	89st	1246 lb	1947 lb
1817	Steer 3yr – 2mths	95st – 10 lb	1340 lb	2094 lb

(*Ibid*)

Fig 13.1 An engraving of a Devon steer from about 1800, which would have been of an animal before the 19th Century improvement of the breed.

Fig 13.2 An engraving of a six year old oxen that had had heavy work for two years which would have resulted in growth to maximum size (as stated by Lord Somerville). The animal looks to have the conformation of an oxen fattened ready for slaughter. It would probably have weighed around 1½ tons (Horne, 1810).

Fig 13.3 An engraving of a Lancashire Long Horn. This was the same type as the Craven Long Horns from which Bakewell selected his animals to establish the Dishley Long Horn breed. At the end of the 18th Century the Lancashire Long Horns dominated the cattle numbers in the grazing areas of Lancashire, Leicestershire and Warwickshire (Horne, 1810).

Fig 13.4 An engraving of a Dutch Short Horn. Most of its numbers were in the Eastern Counties but their influence by cross breeding was extensive across the country (Horne, 1810).

INTRODUCTION OF NEW FEEDING RÉGIMES

While much of the increase in weights was due to the selection of better breeding stock, there was a marked impact brought about by improved fodder crops and better feeding during the winter (Everitt, 1990). In a report by the Commissioners for Trade and Plantations in 1702 they stated "the lands in England have been very much improved since the year 1670 by clover and other grass seeds" (Lipson, 1956).

During the Elizabethan period, turnips were grown in the gardens. There were a number of people who had observed during visits to Holland and Flanders how turnips could be grown in the field to much advantage. Turnips could provide feeding for cattle and sheep, especially winter feeding, as it could change the normal weight loss over winter into a weight gain, which would have a considerable affect on the ultimate weight of the animal. This winter feeding could also provide sheep and cattle suitable for slaughter during the winter months avoiding the acute shortage of fresh meat in the winter, which was the medieval norm. One of the early proponents of the turnip as a field crop was Sir Richard Weston which he publicised in his book '*A discours in Husbandrie, 1652*'. Worlidge in his '*Systema Agriculturae, 1669*' states that turnips were being grown in fields in parts of England but deplored the fact that they were not more widely used (Lipson, 1959). Jethro Tull (1674-1741) founded systems of cultivation that were to change the whole pattern of agriculture. Among his innovations were horse hoeing for cleaning the land and the invention of the corn drill. He pioneered the growing of turnips as a field crop, which along with the improvement in growing crops generally, enabled the winter feeding of stock to become a practical reality. It was a contemporary of Jethro Tull, the Viscount Townshend (Turnip Townshend), who popularised the use of turnips for feeding sheep and lambs. He also introduced clover as a field crop for feeding sheep (McDougall, 1929). The major advantage of turnips and clover was that they provided a good rotation crop which avoided the wasteful necessity of leaving fields fallow and gave the farmer extra profit on his livestock and a valuable bonus of the extra manure for the fields. The benefits of turnip growing were slow to be taken up outside Norfolk (Evelyn, 1972), 1760 was the year that farmers started to use oilcake for fattening cattle (Stratton & Brown 1978).

The other development that received much attention in the first half of the 1600s in particular parts of the country was the establishment of water meadows. The meadows were subjected to controlled flooding or there were a series of channels or ditches forming a network across the fields carrying water from a nearby river or stream. The effect was to produce a lush and thick sward which greatly increased the stocking level of the meadows. Some farmers combined water meadows with a sheep and barley enterprise by grazing a flock of sheep on the water meadow by day and folding them on the barley fields at night for the benefit of their manure. Water meadows were advocated by a number of agriculturists of the day such as Sir Richard Weston of Sutton, Surrey, Walter Blith and John Worlidge; Robert Bakewell established some water meadows at Dishley (Darby, 1976c).

FAIRS

Fairs continued to flourish during the period 1550 – 1750 for the annual buying and selling of certain goods. A number of fairs became specific in what was traded. In respect of livestock there were fairs for cattle, fairs for sheep and fairs for horses. There was an extensive chain of fairs throughout all the regions of England and Wales with cattle being the main commodity, running into many thousands. Many of the animals were bought for feeding on and fattening and not immediately destined for slaughter. At Bowes Moor, Yorkshire in the early 1600s, up to 20,000 cattle were sold annually (*Ibid*).

A large number of cattle offered at the English fairs were from Wales and Scotland. Fairs for the sale of Scottish cattle in the 16th century were held at Elycht, Brechin and Forfar, with cattle fairs at Garioch and Buchan early in the 17th century. It was from these fairs that cattle were bought by the drovers to take to the fairs in England. An Act of Parliament in 1672 granted the Earl of Perth the right to hold an annual fair at Crieff. As the demand for Scottish cattle by the drovers grew the Crieff Cattle Tryst became the largest cattle fair in Scotland by the end of the 1600s. The number of cattle sold in the autumn of 1723 was 30,000 according to J. Mackey in '*Journey Through Scotland, 1723*'. After the collapse of the 1745 rising there was a shift of cattle sales away from Crieff to the Falkirk Tryst (Haldane, 1968).

Knighton Fair was a major collecting point for the sale of thousands of Welsh cattle, many of which were bought for droving to the South East counties of England. Large numbers of the Welsh cattle passed through the fairs at Leominster, Hereford and Gloucester.

There were fewer sheep fairs than cattle fairs but large numbers of sheep were sold through these fairs. The principal fairs were situated near the main production areas such as the marshland pastures, the southern downlands, the fells and wolds of the north or in the vicinity of the moors and upland pastures of Wales. In 1632, 3,800 sheep were sold at the Machynlleth Fairs, Montgomeryshire, 15,000 – 16,000 were sold at Stow–on–the–Wold in the early part of 17th century and 30,000 were sold during a single part of the 1683 Weyhill Fair (Everitt, 1990).

The time of year for holding the cattle and sheep fairs was, by the nature of their production, seasonal. The peaks for cattle fairs were in May for the sale of dairy cattle and store cattle, and October for the sale of fat cattle ready for slaughter or for stall feeding through the winter. The same seasonal peaks occurred with sheep fairs (*Ibid*).

LIVESTOCK AND GENERAL MARKETS

Most of the markets for livestock were held once per week whereas the markets for meat were usually daily. Markets were held in the market towns under the charters granted to those towns as compared with many of the fairs which were held in a variety of places including open fields, as is the example of the great international Stourbridge Fair. During the Tudor and Stuart periods there were some 760 market towns in England and 60 in Wales. There was however a significant decline in the number of markets in England by 1720, down to 574 but partly regaining the numbers to 660 by 1792 (Chartres, 1990). In Scotland the market towns were the burghs and there were 270 new baronial burghs founded between 1500 and the Union of 1707 (Whyte, 1995).

Markets were generally held for a wide range of products, both agricultural and industrial, with livestock forming a major part of the markets. In many cases the numbers of livestock entering the markets were rising as the populations of the market towns were increasing. This necessitated moving the livestock section of the market to part of the town where there was more space, usually on the edge of town. In Liverpool the general market was held round the White Cross along the High Street where the corn dealers gathered with the butchers' shambles nearby. The market also extended along Castle Street and Dale Street. The cattle market was held in this part of town but about 1570, due to the pressure of population growth, the market was removed first to Castle Fields and then to Chapel Street. In Canterbury there was erected a 'Bull Stake' that was for the purpose of bating and chasing bulls "used by an ancient order and custom of the City by the City butchers before their killing, not for pleasure, but to make them proper meat and fit to be eaten" (Everitt, 1990).

Towards the end of the 1500s there was a tendency for specialisation by a number of markets concentrating on a particular type of product offered for sale, much in line with the specialisation taking place in the areas of agricultural production. Out of the total of 800 markets in England and Wales, about 300 tended to specialise, with 133 predominantly for the sale of corn, 92 for the sale of cattle, 32 for the sale of sheep, 14 for the sale of swine, 13 for the sale of horses and 21 for the sale of poultry and wildfowl (*Ibid*).

During the period 1550 – 1750 in many of the market towns the market house was rebuilt or in some cases newly built. They varied from a plain open building with a roof for some protection from the weather for the traders to transact their business, to others that were more elaborate with rooms above for administration purposes and were often used as guildhalls. In many cases they also served as a courthouse, complete with a prison cell; the mayor's court would often be held in the market building. An important function of the market house was to accommodate the common beam (scale) which was a statutory obligation for the market authorities to provide, along with the necessary weights. It was usually the custom to levy a toll for weighing the goods. Wool, corn, etc., were sold by weight in bulk quantities (*Ibid*). The evidence points to butchers not selling by weight; indeed there is some evidence for a reluctance to sell meat by weight (see chapter 10) although the scale seemed to be standard equipment for the Romano butchers.

MEAT MARKETS

The sale of fresh meat from 1550 - 1750 was from markets or shops. The markets were in some cases housed in a building, as was the Stocks Market in London, or simply a row of stalls or shops referred to as the shambles (as in Aberdeen, Crediton and York) and sometimes as Butchers' Row (as at Exeter and Banbury). Butchers' shops would be open daily for sales as were many of the stalls rented in the shambles or markets. There were some cases whereby butchers would rent stalls at a weekly market to sell their meat; these usually being foreign butchers (butchers from outside the town and not members of the butchers' guild). There were as many as thirty butchers renting stalls for the Tuesday market at King's Lynn. Shops were of a more permanent nature and offered more space for butchering than the stalls in the shambles. They were usually fitted with a pentice or a wooden canopy extending from above the front part of the shop for several feet above the street as a cover for any sales activity in front of the shop. New shops at Crediton were let at rents between 40s to 56s per annum; three were taken by Robert Acourt, a butcher, and two were taken by Edward Baylie, also a butcher (*Ibid*).

A number of village markets founded in the 13th and 14th centuries that had ceased to function were revived in the 16th or 17th centuries. One such was at Westerham, Kent, where the original market granted in about 1337 was no longer held at the beginning of the 17th century. Two local tradesmen, Richard Dawling and Raphe Twigg gained the support of others and resurrected the market in1620. They also built a stone market house and 13 shops or shambles on a site in front of The George and Dragon. This enterprise led to Westerham becoming a centre of the Kentish cattle trade (*Ibid*).

Smithfield Market continued to be the main livestock centre for London. The market days were Wednesdays and Fridays, but as the pressure on the market increased an extra market day, Monday, was included in 1612 (Jones, 1976). The numbers of livestock sold in Smithfield in the year 1732 were 76,210 cattle and 514,700 sheep, according to '*McCulloch's Dictionary of Commerce*' (Youatt, 1834). This was an average of 1,466 cattle and 9,898 sheep per week spread over the three market days. There were restrictions imposed on the non-freemen butchers who were usually not allowed to trade in the market for an hour after it opened. Freemen butchers traded from the time it opened having advantage of first choice. This resulted in some of the non-freemen butchers going to Barnet cattle market, some 10 miles to the north to buy their animals. Some London butchers became graziers and were accused of hiring the best marshes and meadows within 5 miles of Smithfield which enabled them to influence the price in the market (Jones, 1976).

The London meat markets of St. Nicholas Shambles, Stocks, Leadenhall and East Cheap flourished until their destruction by the great fire of London in 1666 (Fig 13.5, Fig 13.6,Fig 13.7). Trade in East Cheap and St. Nicholas Shambles declined in the period before the fire due to country butchers (non-fee butchers from outside the City) being allowed to sell meat in Leadenhall. The object of the City authorities in allowing the country butchers in, was to increase the supply of meat to the citizens, which in turn reduced the prices. This resulted in an on-going hostility between the free butchers and non-free butchers (Jones, 1976).

By the beginning of the 17th century St Nicholas Shambles had encroached on much of the space of the other trades represented in Newgate Market. There was a row of butchers' shops facing Christ Church on the north side of Newgate Street and backing onto these shops was another row of butchers' shops facing Mountgoddard Street running along the south side of the shambles. Behind the butchers' shops were the slaughterhouses. The shambles had begun by the butchers simply putting up their stall boards but over a period of time they covered them in with sheds and subsequently built fair houses over the stalls (Stow, 1598). The market at East Cheap consisted of butchers' shops on both sides of the street with the butchers and their families living above the shops. There was a large scaldinghouse in Pudding Lane used extensively by the East Cheap butchers which may indicate that East Cheap was the main market for pork. Stocks Market (Le Stokkes) was in a purpose-built building and butchers rented the spaces for their stalls. Spaces for stalls were rented in the same way in Leadenhall Market which was contained in a converted mansion house (Pearce, 1929).

For some of the markets the butchers' boards and hanging meat displays encroached upon the already narrow streets, as with St Nicholas Shambles, resulting in occasional accidents between the butchers, their meat or their customers and the passing traffic. This is well illustrated by Samuel Pepys in an entry dated 15th December 1662 in his diary:

> "Driving back through the back side of the Shambles in Newgate Street, my coach plucked down two pieces of beef into the dirt, upon which the butchers stopped the horses, and a great rout of people in the street crying that we had done him 40/- and £5 worth of hurt; but, going down, I saw that we had done little or none, so I gave him a shilling for it, and they were well contented."

Fig 13.5 St Nicholas Shambles.

Fig 13.6 East Cheap Market as per Stow 1598.

Fig 13.7 Leadenhall Market.

These three drawings are based on a series of illustrations produced by Hugh Alley dated 1598. The originals are in the Folger Shakespeare Library, Washington. Although the drawings are stereotypical they show clearly the beef carcases hung on a beef tree. Apart from hanging the carcase the beef tree was used to spread the carcase, which made it easier for evisceration. Much of the beef shown on display had been chopped down into sides and also cut into quarters. The drawing of Leadenhall Market emphasised its role as the market for foreign traders coming from Kent, Essex, Middlesex and Surrey.

The great fire of London destroyed the meat markets but stopped just short of Smithfield Market at Pye Corner and Cock Lane. In the rebuilding after the fire Newgate Market was built on the present site of Paternoster Square to replace St. Nicholas Shambles. Stocks Market was rebuilt on the same site and called Woolchurch Market, which was enlarged from the original Stocks Market. In 1733 this market was removed to a bridge built over the Fleet Ditch from Fleet Street to Holborn, which became known as the Fleet Market. Mansion House was built on the site of the Stocks Market in 1737 (Weinreb, & Hibbert, 1983). Leadenhall before the fire had been part market and part granary but when it was rebuilt it was entirely devoted to a market for meat, poultry, fish, hides, wool and herbs. Honey Lane Market was built in 1667 just off the north side of Cheap Side on the recommendation of the Common Council. It was built largely to accommodate the butchers who had stalls in Cheapside before the fire (Pearce, 1929). The butchers of Eastcheap resumed the practice of having their stalls in front of their houses which were rebuilt along Eastcheap.

Fig 13.8 A drawing of the Market House and butchers' shambles at Dartford, Kent. The Market House was demolished in 1769. The butchers' shambles with its row of stalls is on the right of the Market House, which was a typical construction built on pillars to provide a sheltered sales area below.

Some of these butchers slaughtered their animals in the street in the early morning. After the fire there was a growth in the number of butchers opening individual butchers' shops throughout the City. Being opportunistic they would utilise any space however small or whatever its position, as the case of the butcher's shop that was in front of St. Ethelburga-the-Virgin, the smallest church in the City (Fig 13.9). The small shop with accommodation over was on one side of the entrance to the church and there was another shop on the other side. By the late 1600s carcase butchers (wholesalers) had become a common feature in the meat trade, a number of them operating in the meat markets selling carcase meat to the smaller butchers.

The Common Council passed the Act of 1672 for the regulation of the market which authorised all butchers who did not have a shop within two miles of the City the right to hire a stall or standing

Fig 13.9 A small butcher's shop built in front of St Ethelburga-the-Virgin in Bishopsgate, London. Drawing based on an engraving by Toms 1736, part of the Devonshire collection at Chatsworth.

in one of the markets. The Act also set the opening times for the markets as 6 a.m. to 8 p.m. in the summer and 8 a.m. to 5 p.m. in the winter. In 1674 it was changed to 6 a.m. to 8 p.m. throughout the year plus an extended time for Saturday until 10 p.m. (Jones, 1976).

The flesh markets in Edinburgh were divided by a magistrate's order of 1558, stating that the free butchers' trade "at the over end of the Toll booth" and the non-free butchers "in the Vennel or in the south part of Cowgate". An order of 1665 covering market hours required butchers to bring their flesh to the market before seven o'clock in the morning and continue until six in the evening on Tuesdays, Thursdays and Saturdays. In the winter the times were changed to eight o'clock in the morning until four o'clock in the afternoon, except Saturdays, when they could continue trading until later. No butcher was allowed to sell meat from his house, which prevented butchers turning their houses into shops. With the growth of Edinburgh and the increasing demand for meat, an Act of the Privy Council and the Lords of Session permitted butchers to trade all days of the week except Sunday and the country butchers to have all the rights and conveniences as the town fleshers; the country fleshers to be accommodated in the poultry market. The wives of butchers were not always demure as indicated by the order of 1594 which read as follows: "Discharges fleshers' wives to come to the market because they are given to flyting, sweyring, and banning" (Scotsman, 1902).

METHODS OF BUTCHERY

One of the objects in the analysis of bone assemblages from archaeological sites is to attempt to assess the methods of butchery used on the meat animals. One problem is that all knife cuts and all

Fig 13.10 (facing page) Map of London as it was rebuilt after the great fire. Based on John Rocque's map of 1746. Key: (A) Porters block; (B) Smithfield Market; (C) Fleet Market; (D) Newgate Market; (E) Honey Lane Market; (F) Guild Hall; (G) Mansion House; (H) Leadenhall Market; (I) East Cheap* Market, (J) Steelyard.

chopping indications on the bones were not necessarily the result of straightforward butchery. Another difficulty is that it requires a large assemblage of bones of the same specie for the archaeologist to have enough evidence on particular skeletal elements for arrival at a positive conclusion. Some indications are quite evident, such as chopping through the neck of the femur, which can be concluded as the method used to separate the major part of the limb from the pelvis; there is the question whether this was before or after the buttock meat was removed.

It is most unlikely that there would have been a national method of butchery at any time for even in the 20th century regional differences of cutting carcases into joints exist but all variations relate to a basic form dictated by the configuration of the skeleton and muscles of the carcase. It is most probable that the more orderly methods of butchery were the product of the towns, especially under the influence of the guilds.

A question often tackled by zooarchaeologists is when it became standard practice to split beef carcases into two sides. Although the Hugh Alley drawings of the London markets (*c.* 1588) are not exact representations they give a clear picture of the type of meat and the cuts of meat hanging in the shops. Apart from whole carcases there are sides and quarters of beef clearly demonstrated. The carcases are held up by a 'beef tree', a strong round piece of wood about a metre long and shaped at the ends to enable each end to be pushed through each hock behind the Achilles tendons of the beast. The 'beef tree' is suspended from the crossbeam of the shop. The 'beef tree' not only supports the carcase but also spreads the legs to open up the carcase. It is used in hoisting the animal after slaughter as it assists evisceration and splitting the carcase. 'Beef trees' were still in use well into the 20th century and were the equivalent of the gambrel used for sheep and pig carcases. Records indicate that country killed beef had been brought into London and other towns from the 14th century mostly by the foreign or non-free butchers. Cutting the beef carcases into sides or quarters would have made them much more suitable for transporting and manhandling onto and off the carts into the markets or shops. Splitting a carcase down into sides and even quartering it would not entail cutting into and exposing the main bulk of meat of the carcase which exposure to the air would speed up the deterioration of the meat. Flitches of bacon were sides of bacon and a flitch is shown hanging in the 12th century manuscript of activities (see chapter 6). Markham's instructions for preparing a pig for spit roasting are "the pig you shall chine, and divide into two parts" (Markham, 1615).

Ordinances for the London Butchers' Company, 1607, indicate the practice of quartering carcases well established at that time. Ordinance 45 requires that "with every forequarter of lambe quartered tenn ribs and with the hinde quarter three ribbes". Ordinance 46 requires that "in the quartering of hogges … with the forequarter or loyne of every hogge 11 ribbes and with the hinquarter or loyne of every hogge twoe ribbes". There is also an implication here that quarters of lamb and pork were common retail cuts.

Two cutting diagrams (see Chapter 16) of about 1800 using the London cut names show the method of cutting was very much the same as the present day (The Experienced Butcher, 1816;

* John Stow (1598) and earlier maps represent East Cheap as two words. John Rocque's map and the latter references have Eastcheap as one word, including the London A-Z.

Trow-Smith,1959). The names of the cuts originate from a much earlier time although the method of cutting may have differed.

A collection of recipes for Queen Henrietta Maria dated 1655 includes the meat cuts 'buttock of beef, rump of beef, surloyne of beef, fillet of beef, shoulder of mutton, leg of mutton, and legge of pork' (Isitt, 1987).

Gervase Markham's recipe book includes the meat cuts 'chine (loin) of beef, leg of mutton, shoulder of mutton, loin of mutton, breast of mutton and rack of mutton' (Markham, 1615).

The records of Ingatestone Hall relating to meat for different meals include; in 1551, 'neck of mutton, loin of pork, breast of pork, neck of pork, leg of pork, leg of veal, loin of veal and breast of veal' and in 1552, 'hindquarter of veal, rack of veal' (Emmison, 1964).

A feast given by the Duke of Norfolk in 1561 included 'forequarter of veal, hindquarter of veal, leg of mutton, loyn of mutton, shoulder of veal and breast and coast of mutton'. The mayor of the new borough of Rochester gave a supper to some of the burgesses in 1460. The meat consisted of 2 necks, 2 shoulders and 2 breasts of mutton (Ainsworth-Davis, 1931).

The establishment of the different cuts indicates a more sophisticated method of cutting and therefore a more discriminatory appreciation of the different parts of the carcase.[1]

THE GROWTH OF THE DROVING TRADE

Throughout most of our history, the only practical way of moving animals has been by droving. Sheep and cattle tracks connected farms with villages, and villages with towns, and were the only link in the majority of cases. Transport of goods to many of these villages in the early days was by pack horse, using these sheep tracks. Good roads did not exist until the construction of the turnpikes, beginning with the Turnpike Act of 1663, but it was not until the late 18th century that many good, well-maintained roads existed. The growing urban demand for meat increased the need to move livestock from the production areas to the areas of population. This meant the role of the drovers becoming more important and their numbers increasing. There had long been a necessity for driving cattle to distant markets and the need to collect animals for the victualling for the army and navy, all of which required the service of drovers. The growth in the population of London, along with an increase in the number of ships for victualling and many other areas of development, increased the demand for meat and led to an expansion of the droving trade as well as droving over greater distances.

The pattern of cattle movement in the 16th and 17th centuries was, in general, a flow from the north and west towards an easterly and south easterly direction. Large numbers of Welsh cattle were driven to the fairs and markets of the border counties (e.g. Leominster, Shrewsbury) and were mainly bought by the graziers of the Midlands for fattening ready for slaughter. Many were sold to the butchers in the Midland towns and manufacturing districts and others were bought by drovers to sell in London. The Midlands graziers also obtained cattle from the North. Some of the cattle from North Wales were driven to South Wales for fattening and subsequently slaughtered to supply the local populations. Cattle were driven annually across Bowes Moor and as many as

---

[1] There are a number of pork cuts illustrated in the reliefs on the Roman butchers' tombs, (see chapter 4) but there is no evidence for any continuity between the craft of the Roman butcher and the medieval butcher.

20,000 were reckoned to come from the North West and probably included cattle from Galloway and Dumfriesshire. Many of these animals were to supply the highly populated clothing dales of West Yorkshire. Irish cattle were shipped to England, estimated at 40,000 head annually, many being fattened in Somerset (Everitt, 1990). Cattle were being shipped from the Island of Skye to the mainland of Scotland by the beginning of the 1500s and cattle from Argyllshire were being driven to the Scottish Lowlands by the 1550s. The trade in cattle from Scotland to England was taking place as far back as the 14th century and a number of Acts of the Scots Parliament attempting to control the trade were largely ineffective. There was a complaint to the Scots Parliament in 1542 that the Customs Officers were not being paid for cattle sold out of the country. Although trading between the two countries improved during Elizabeth I's reign and still more so with the union of the crowns in 1603 there were still restrictions on trade, not least the customs duty. In 1612 duty was £10 Scots per head for cattle (£1 sterling = £12 Scots). A major factor for the improvement of the trade was the quelling of the warring and raiding elements in the border areas in the last quarter of the 16th century. On the English side the defeat of the Earls of Northumberland and Westmoreland broke the power in the north of the Percys and the Nevilles who had dominated the border country. On the Scottish side the raiders who had been firmly established in their strongholds were attacked and evicted. This greatly increased the security of the drovers crossing the border (Haldane, 1968).

A factor that was fundamental to this flow of cattle was the supply of lean store cattle from the Welsh hills, Cumbria, the Scottish Highlands and Ireland so that they could be grown on and fattened within easy distance of the areas where their meat would be consumed. The fattened cattle were not good for droving and their weight loss on long journeys would have been high. The advice given by Thomas Horne underlines this:

> "Beasts are chiefly driven to London for sale; and, where the distance from the metropolis is very considerable, they are liable to many calamities or accidents on the road, besides their diminution in point of weight; which, even under the eye of the most attentive drivers, is necessarily incurred, and is often great: …. It will, therefore, be advisable, where it can be conveniently effected, to dispose of fat stock in such markets as are in the vicinity of, or at an easy distance from the farm." (Horne, 1810)

The soundest economic policy therefore was to drive cattle the longest distance towards their ultimate market as lean store stock so that when fattened they would only have a relatively short distance to travel.

The development of the Scottish droving trade from the early 1500s was significant in the growth of commercial activity in Scotland. Apart from the livestock trade being a major export, droving established a reliable form of communication throughout Scotland and England with drovers being used as couriers and agents. An important contribution to trade was that money in circulation in Scotland was insufficient for the needs of the droving trade and commerce in general. Even at the time of the Union of 1707 it was estimated that there was only between £150,000 and £200,000 sterling in circulation. The drovers would pay for the cattle by giving a small amount of money and the rest as a promissory note or bill of exchange. This enabled drovers to assemble a reasonable size drove largely due to the credit from the farmers. The drovers would often obtain letters of credit from mercantile houses along with a small amount of money to use in putting together a drove. As the length of time taken to complete a drove was invariably many weeks the drovers' bills of exchange would be circulating among the community, often being the most available currency (Haldane, 1968).

Cattle stealing or reiving was a major activity in the Scottish Highlands, Southern Uplands and the Border Country from the early Middle Ages, reaching a peak in the 16th and 17th centuries. In a series of raids in 1602, the men of Glen Garry drove off 2700 cattle from Glen Isla, Glen Shee and Strathardle. There were many casualties (numbers of them fatal) in battles between the cattle reivers and the cattle owners. Attempts were made to prevent the trade in stolen animals by the passing of laws to the effect that the purchase of animals should only be made with the knowledge that the seller was the rightful owner, such as the Act passed during the reign of William the Lion in 1175. In spite of the efforts of successive governments, cattle reiving was an occupation of successive generations of a large number of Highlanders. It was the descendants of these reivers who were most suited to the role of the drover as they knew the country well and were accustomed to the great hardships and privations of spending many days and nights in the open and with little more for sustenance than a bag of oatmeal (*Ibid*).

By the middle of the 17th century an estimated 15,000 Scottish black cattle were being driven south of the border each year, numbers increasing towards the end of the century. During the year from August 1662 to August 1663, a total of 18,574 cattle passed through Carlisle at a toll of 8d per head. There would, of course, have been cattle driven into England elsewhere along the border which added to this number (*Ibid*). Such was the extent of this cattle trade that it affected the prices the English farmers were getting for their livestock. This resulted in pressure on the government, such as a petition from the Grand Juries of Yorkshire in 1665 to the House of Commons, which was a complaint about this trade. In 1666 the import of Irish cattle was prohibited and in 1704 there was an act forbidding the importation of Scottish cattle. The repeal of this act and the Act of Union in 1707 between Scotland and England soon reopened the Scottish cattle trade and one writer of the time stated that by the middle of the 18th century, 40,000 cattle per year were being driven South (Bonser, 1970).

If the cattle in the drove were to arrive at the end of a long drive in a reasonable condition then they had to be driven at an easy pace. The average drove proceeded at about 10 – 12 miles per day in Scotland although Arthur Young writing in 1818 put the figure as high as 15 miles per day (Haldane, 1968). This pace allowed the animals to snatch some grazing from the verge of the track as they went along. Planning a drove needed to take account of a series of overnight stops at the right distances for an adequate, but not excessive, day's drive. At the overnight stops the drovers would sleep outside close to their animals with at least one man keeping watch.

Drovers relied very much on their dogs, whether they were droving sheep or cattle. The dogs used for driving sheep were described by Thomas Horne as being docile and sagacious and that well-trained dogs would keep a flock of sheep together on the road and collect stragglers and bring them back to the flock. The type of dog used for cattle was called the Cur Dog which was larger and more fierce. It was short haired, mostly black and white with half-pricked ears (Horne, 1810). It would sometimes occur that the dogs on a drove from Scotland would be sent back on their own by the drovers because either the men were not returning for a while or they were returning by some other means. This pack of dogs from the drove would follow the route by which they had travelled to England, stopping at the inns and farms where the drove had stopped on the way down. At these places the dogs would be fed and the drovers would pay for this feeding of their dogs the following year on their next drove (Bonser, 1970).

When it came to crossing rivers, providing they were not too hazardous, the drovers would get the cattle to swim across. This was also the case when getting cattle from Anglesey across the Menai Strait to the mainland. The herd would be forced into the water and a few manned boats would push the stragglers back to the main herd. The boatmen sometimes put a rope around the horns of a difficult beast and dragged it to shore (Fig 13.11) (*Ibid*). In Scotland cattle were forced to swim from Skye to the mainland, where the stretch of water was not too great, such as the strait of Kyle Rhea (Haldane, 1968).

Fig 13.11 A drawing of a broad, shallow bottomed boat being loaded with cattle for the crossing from the Island of Skye to the mainland.

The large droves of animals which annually passed along the drove roads resulted in the establishment of numerous facilities to service their needs, such as fields for the overnight stops (stances), stores of fodder to feed the animals, sufficient water for the animals, blacksmiths' shops to shoe the cattle, accommodation for the drovers, etc., all of which provided employment and income for a large number of local people. Good use was made by the drovers of the network of inns through the country, especially those on the drove routes. In 1577 there were over 1600 inns in the 25 English counties. Some inns even had fields nearby in which the drove could graze and spend the night, or they would maintain a supply of fodder to feed the animals (Everitt, 1990). During the 17th and 18th centuries, drovers were the most regular and reliable travellers crossing the country apart from the stage coaches. In view of this the drovers would carry news of what was happening in the outside world to the towns and hamlets on their route. Welsh drovers were often employed to act as agents for people transferring money to London or to pay their debts. Many drovers acted as Government Agents during the reign of Charles I, transferring Ship Money collected in Wales. Rather than run the risk of carrying a great deal of cash, these drovers would use this money to pay for stock in Wales and on reaching London would discharge their obligations as agents with the money from the sale of their animals. Another service the Welsh drovers would often perform was to take charge of young boys from Wales and get them apprenticed in London (Bonser, 1970).

Cattle constituted the main animals for droving in the1550 – 1750 period although there were many droves moving other types of livestock about the country. Sheep were suitable for driving long distances but made slower progress than cattle. Sheep were being driven from the pastures of the southern and eastern counties to Smithfield Market on a regular basis. The average number of sheep offered for sale at the market each week from 1732 – 1750 was 10,908 according to *McCulloch's Dictionary of Commerce* (Youatt, 1834). Pigs were also driven to Smithfield, many droves coming from Suffolk. Occasionally sizeable droves of pigs were moved across the country to feed on the beech masts of distant woodlands. In 1591 a swineherd drove 240 swine belonging to farmers of Oxfordshire and Buckinghamshire to be fattened on the masts of woodlands in Sussex, Surrey and Hampshire, to be returned "well and sufficiently fed for bacon". Flocks of poultry were driven from Hertfordshire, Bedfordshire, Northamptonshire, Suffolk, Essex, and Surrey to the London poulterers in Leadenhall Market and St. Nicholas Shambles (Chartres, 1990).

In 1632 a murrain (probably cattle plague) struck the Welsh cattle herds causing such losses that none were available for the English trade (Bonser, 1970). The devastating murrain or cattle plague that spread from Europe to England in 1745 affected many of the cattle droves passing through England, often with disastrous results for the drovers. A drover, Thomas Bell, was taking a drove of over 1,000 cattle from Scotland to East Anglia and had drawn bills for £1,449 on his partner, Bryce Blair of Annan. Bell had paid for the cattle in the usual way with three months' bills. The drove succumbed to the plague and the animals began dying first in scores then in hundreds. Bell wrote to Blair explaining his plight; "God knows what we shall do, we cannot get money to bear pocket expenses; all manner of sale is over …our conditions are such that several drovers have run from their beasts and left them dying in the lanes and highways and nobody to own them." A further letter in ten days as the situation worsened stated: "All is over now. We can neither pay London bills nor anything else. We have over £1,000 charges in this country and not a shilling to pay it with." His final letter read: "I am positive we have lost £3,000… I shall be home by Candlemas and people may do with me as they will. They shall have every groat we have and we can do no more." The extent of the plague was such that the drovers were forced to guarantee the cattle for a certain period after they had been sold (Haldane, 1968).

DEVELOPING STRUCTURE OF MEAT MARKETING

The structure and organisation of meat marketing, and indeed marketing in general, developed considerably during the period 1550 to 1750. The system that prevailed in the early medieval period whereby the basic foods were supplied locally, was satisfactory for a predominantly rural population and did not require an elaborate marketing organisation. The progression in this period (1550 – 1750) towards capitalism and the industrial revolution established an incentive for expanding livestock production to meet the consequent rising demand for meat and encouraged areas specialising in rearing and fattening cattle and sheep. The development of marketing was needed to support and service the rising urban population and to accommodate the increasing specialisation of the agricultural producers in different areas of the country. A major factor in the development was the emergence of new roles for the people engaged in marketing and the expansion of those roles that already existed, which to a large extent related to the people that had become identified as middlemen.

Drovers. Basically all drovers were people engaged as drivers of livestock beyond the normal movement of stock by the herdsmen. Many drovers would have been part of a gang employed by the master or head drover who hired them, paid them and managed the drove throughout its journey. The head drovers could have many functions and many responsibilities not least the responsibility for what was often a large and very valuable drove. Most of them carried out the function of dealer, buying the animals from farmers or at fairs or markets to form a drove and at the destination of the drove acting as a salesman. It was an important aspect of a drover's ability to be able to obtain an adequate return on the animals of the drove when sold. He had to cover all the costs of a drive that may have taken many weeks over a great distance and cover the loss of any animals during the drive, on top of which there would undoubtedly have been the debts incurred for the original purchase of the animals. To this end they needed a great deal of skill to get these animals to market in good condition after such long journeys, with very few animals lost en route. This was achieved whilst pushing the drove on to make good rate of progress and to reach the markets on time (Bonser, 1970). An activity in which many drovers became involved was being engaged as an agent to buy livestock or to sell livestock on commission. Sometimes drovers were employed to act as agents for the victuallers to the army and navy.

In the course of the burgeoning livestock trade, the size of the droves became very large giving the drovers considerable influence over the markets and prices. In Scotland, Wales and the livestock production areas of England the attendance at the fairs and markets of the drovers was important for the clearance of the livestock presented being cleared. The alternative would have been for farmers to take home unsold animals. Some unscrupulous drovers used their buying power to obtain animals at far less than their real worth. William Bulkey of Brynddu wrote in 1735 regarding a drovers' ring operating in Newborough, resulting in cattle being unsold late in the day and then bought up at very low prices. Most of the cattle markets in the Midlands and the south were dependent on the drovers arriving with their droves and the timing of their arrival (Chartres, 1990). Drovers at many times through history have been required to be licensed. An enactment during the reigns of Mary and Elizabeth I required drovers of cattle to be licensed in writing by three Justices of the Peace. A law was passed in Scotland in 1671 that the Scottish drovers should be licensed and would need to carry certificates of respectability and passes giving names of all their company (Bonser, 1970).

An area of activity of the drovers that seemed to evolve by accident was the development of an unofficial banking system based on the drovers' bills or promissory notes which became a major element of circulating currency. In conjunction with moving large herds about the country drovers were also moving large amounts of money which made the large livestock centres also financial centres in the absence of established banking. These facilities were used by those engaged in the wider fields of commerce, well beyond the business of livestock marketing. Smithfield as the ultimate destination for much of the droving traffic became the major centre for inland bills. Before the Union of 1707 the volume of the Scots' droves made the Edinburgh - London exchanges rate dependent on the arrival of the droves in Smithfield (Chartres, 1990). The Crieff market was the main centre for money circulation in Scotland in the first half of the 18th century and later the emphasis turned to Falkirk. During the visit to Skye in 1772, James Boswell and Samuel Johnson found the tenants paying their rents to the Lairds with drovers' bills (Haldane, 1968).

Graziers. Although the occupation of the grazier was to use their pastures to rear and fatten livestock, they were often in an ideal position to undertake various forms of dealing in the livestock markets. The graziers' open fields were an invaluable asset as they were able to hold stock back until the market was right to sell or they could buy stock cheaply when the market had fallen. While this gave them the scope to maximise their profit it also enabled some to influence the market, especially a small local market. A correspondent in the '*Gentleman's Magazine*', 1755, complained: "The reason why meat is cheap in places remote from the London markets, is, that the farmers sell their fat cattle to the butcher, without its passing through a grazier's hands; and it is the combination of a small number of wealthy graziers that keeps the price up here" (Chartres, 1990).

Carcase Butchers. With the growth of the dead meat sales there was the scope for the establishment of large scale wholesale or carcase butchers. A petition to the House of Commons from the Company of Butchers of London and Westminster in 1707 complained:

> "That by the Carcase or Wholesale Butchers trading they hinder a thousand or more butchers coming to the markets of Smithfield, etc., and so that the grazing part of England for sheep and Lambs is subject to about sixty carcase or wholesale butchers which do govern the markets." (Pearce, 1929)

A London carcase butcher, Prescott, was killing about 12,000 muttons per year in the 1730s (av. 230 per week) (Chartres, 1990).

Dealers Jobbers and Badgers. Much of the dealer's activity would have been buying and selling livestock in the fairs and markets The auction system was not used in the markets until the 19th century; consequently the earlier livestock markets, fairs or trysts were places where sellers of livestock would meet potential buyers to negotiate a sale. In the smaller local markets, the farmers would often sell their fatstock directly to the butchers. In the livestock rearing and fattening areas of the country the livestock for sale would greatly exceed the local demand, creating the need and opportunity for the dealer and of course the drover. In most cases animals could be bought at a much lower price in the local markets than they could be obtained for in the larger markets, especially Smithfield. The art of the dealer was firstly to be a good judge of livestock because butchers were well experienced, of necessity, in knowing the worth of any animals they bought for slaughter. The dealer also needed a good knowledge of the nature of the different markets, price fluctuations, the type of stock presented and the major graziers and dealers active in a market. Badgers were itinerant dealers. Jobbers were another type of dealer. Jobbers operating in and around London bought animals in Smithfield market or the other markets around London to sell again at a profit. They were regarded as having an adverse effect on the market by their manipulations, resulting in allegations from butchers and others involved in the market which were sufficiently strong to lead to legislation in 1670 prohibiting jobbing except in calves and swine. These restrictions seemed to cause more problems than they cured, leading to the legislation being repealed in 1672 (*Ibid*).

Salesmen. In Smithfield market the salesmen had a very important role; whereas there were no salesmen in most of the other markets, their function being fulfilled by dealers, drovers, graziers etc. The Smithfield salesmen sold, on commission, animals sent to them by farmers and graziers.

They also sold on behalf of dealers. The expertise of the salesmen in gauging the strengths and weaknesses of the market, assessing the value of the animals delivered to them and knowing the buyers of Smithfield, made them well worth their commission. The salesmen employed or contracted with graziers to take cattle or sheep from the market that were left unsold or to hold stock for a few weeks in anticipation of the market rising. This side of the salesmen's function gave them greater power in the market but added significantly to their expenses.

Chapter 14

Statutory and Other Controls of Meat Trading: 1550-1750

CONTROL OF NUISANCES

Attempts to control the nuisance from slaughtering in the towns and the disposal of butchers' waste continued with legislation, particularly in the form of town ordinances, from the earlier periods and new ordinances proclaimed between 1550 – 1750.

Ordinances for the London Butchers 1607 reinforced the existing regulations for controlling the disposal of slaughtering waste and for the constraint of any fouling of the streets. Ordinance 50 reads:

> "that the streetes and lanes within the Cittye of London may be better kepte sweete and cleane it is ordered that every person nowe using or exercising or hereafter shall exercise the Art or Mysterye of a butcher within the walles of the said Cittye shall carry the ordure (dung) intrayles and issues of the beasts … to one of the barrowhowses for that purpose auncient tyme used". (Pearce, 1929)

The barrowhouses or 'puddynge' houses were situated on the riverside, one near Queenhithe used mainly by the butchers of Nicholas Shambles and one near London Bridge used by the butchers of Stocks and East Cheap. From the barrowhouses the offals were taken across the river to feed the King's bears in Southwark or carried by barge for disposal down river. The Butchers' Company was becoming more conscious of the need to avoid aggravating residents, as included in the ordinances of 1638 that each butcher must have a tub into which he would place his offal. These tubs were to be hidden behind a door and to be set out after 8 p.m. in the winter and after 9 p.m. in the summer. The Beadle would have had charge of collecting and emptying these tubs. During the plague of 1665 butchers were required to carry their offal tubs to the barrowhouse only between 11 p.m. and 3 a.m. (Jones, 1976). Under Ordinance 51, 1607 it was an offence to allow blood from slain beasts to run in any street or lane (Pearce, 1929).

Effluent from scalding pigs could create a nuisance but was easier to channel into a river if there was one nearby, especially as the bristles were removed because of the ready demand for them. There was a scaldinghouse close to Nicholas Shambles and another in Pudding Lane used by the butchers of East Cheap and the Stocks Market. The scaldinghouse in Pudding Lane was acquired by Robert Harding from the Fraternity of Allhallows in 1551 at which time the butchers were charged 1d. for scalding a hog. The scaldinghouse passed to the Butchers' Company in 1619 (Jones, 1976).

A Scottish Act of Parliament, 4th August 1621, entitled "Ratification of the Act of Secreit

Counsell againis Baxteris, Brewstaris, Fleschoers, and Candlemakers of Ediburt" which referred to the abuse of the fleshers keeping their slaughterhouses or shops within Edinburgh and emptying the filth arising therefrom on the High Street and in open vennels and closes. It was ordained and enacted that "from and after the 1st day of May next to come no fleshers shall be suffered to keep any slaughterhouse within the Burgh but shall provide themselves with slaughterhouses at the North Loch side, where they may have use of water for their business". It is obvious that the lack of compliance with this Act seemed to be the rule, as the Town Council issued a number of orders relating to the part of the High Street or Lawnmarket in which the flesh-market should be held. In 1681 the Town Council entered into a tack (lease) for Robert Hepburn's two tennis courts on which to establish a flesh-market and the ground beneath "for any use the town thinks fit". Part of the petition to support these proposals read as follows: "Having designed to lay down the most effectual ways and methods they can for the cleaning of the City, and finding that the great impediment thereof did stand by fleshers their slaughterhouses within the same, which, being scattered in several parts of the Cowgate, did occasion not only the whole Cowgate, but the closes and vennels upon both sides thereof, to be filled with the excrements and filth of beasts, …" The petition advocated the need for the flesh-market and slaughterhouses to be in close proximity to avoid the inconvenience to citizens by the carrying of carcases of slaughtered beasts any great distance through the streets. The new flesh market and slaughterhouses proved satisfactory to the municipality through to the latter part of the 18th century (The Scotsman, 1902).

Slaughtering in the larger towns was more prone to complaints because of the larger numbers of animals slaughtered to meet the needs of the population. Added to which was the problem of any siting of a slaughterhouse or slaughtering area as this was much more likely to cause a problem in view of the more congested nature of the houses.

One thing that always exacerbated the situation between the local residents and the existence of slaughterhouses nearby was that persons working in the slaughterhouses became inured to the obnoxious aspects of their trade, especially the offensive odours resulting from such activities. The slaughterhouse operators were therefore invariably pressured by the authorities to clean up and carry out the proper disposal of their waste. This also applied to similar trades such as tanning and soap boiling.

SALE OF UNFIT MEAT

Meat identified as unfit for sale was mainly that which had undergone a degree of putrefaction, to have a strong odour, showing signs of slime or stickiness and a change of colour. This was often referred to as carrion meat. The incidence of measles in pigs (*Cysticercus celulosae*) must have been common and widespread, not only in Britain but throughout Europe, taking account of the number of times it is mentioned in any records relating to unfit meat. The ordinances for the London Butchers 1607 include Ordinance 57 which states that no person put for sale "any measled Brawne porke bacon or sowse and any other corrupt stinking or unwholesome vitayles (victuals) whatsoever upon paine of forfeite". The officers of the company were empowered to seize any such meat and condemn it or give it to a prison house and 'to punish the offenders by imprisonment of their bodies by the space of 24 hours' (Pearce, 1929). The possibility could have arisen that an offender had a prison meal which included some the meat seized from him. Using unfit meat to feed prisoners was a case of moral principles giving way to pragmatism.

One penalty for selling unfit meat was that the offender was paraded around the streets sitting on a horse, facing its tail, with some of the bad meat hung around his neck. The Wardens of the Butchers' Company declared the mutton on sale by John Boone in 1623 "was scarce fit for any Christian to eat" for which offence he was paraded on horseback and served a spell in Newgate prison. The seized mutton was sent to the prisons. George Slater was also paraded on horseback in 1650 (Jones, 1976).

Offences for selling bad meat, bad fish, etc., brought before the Manchester Court Leet averaged 10 per year in the period 1650 – 59 and reached an average of 21.4 per year in the period 1740 – 49 but dropped back to 10.4 per year in the period 1750 – 59 (Chartres, 1990).

The incidence of measled pork in London was such that in 1568 the Butchers' Company, with the support of the Court of Aldermen, petitioned Parliament for an Act compelling anyone who sold a hog that was found to be measled after slaughter, to restore to the buyer the full price that had been paid. This petition was unsuccessful. (Jones, 1976)

CONTROL OF MARKET ACTIVITIES

Statutes against forestalling, regrating and engrossing were still in force but the administration of these statutes seemed to be somewhat on the wane during the 17th and 18th centuries. If these statutes had been vigorously enforced they would have considerably constrained the activities of the dealers, drovers, carcase butchers, etc. The trend in the 18th century was towards less regulation and much more of a free market situation.

The authorities continued to apply the statute against forestalling to protect the town markets and the income from those markets as with Ordinance 53 of the ordinances for the London Butchers 1607. It begins; "Item for soe much as forestalling is an injurious thing to the common welth and therefore by the laws and statutes of this Realme of England prohibited and forbidden and yet not withstanding by some evyll disposed persons much used". The ordinance continues by prohibiting any butcher of the city or living within a mile of the city from buying "any manner of Cattell as Oxen Steers Runtes Kyne Calves Sheepe Lambes Swine or other beastes commyng or brought within XV myles of the saide Cittye of London of intente and purpose to be sold in Smythfield markett nor make noe manner of price contract covenaute or bargayne for any such cattell untill the same shalbe brought and putt to sale within the said market in Smythfield" (Pearce, 1929).

In 1580 the London Butchers' Company fined Robert Wood "for forstallynge shepe at Padyngton, beyinge within 15 myles, 6s 8d" (*Ibid*).

The offences for forestalling and regrating tried before the Manchester Court Leet totalled 70 in the period 1650 – 59 with a decline in the numbers through to the period 1750 – 59 when the total was 30 in spite of the rise in the commercial activities. This supports the conclusion that the authorities were becoming less inclined for full enforcement of these statutes (Chartres, 1990).

In 16th century Edinburgh regrating was seen as a detriment to fair meat prices and citizens were often advised by the city fathers not to buy from "coupers (dealers) but from the first sellers and feeders of beasts" (The Scotsman, 1902).

Ordinance 53 of the ordinances for the London Butchers 1607 covers the pernicious effect of engrossing fat cattle which is for gain by raising the price of cattle. The ordinance prohibits butchers of London to buy or contract to buy cattle from any known engrosser and that the engrosser should be punished under the Statutes of the Realm (Pearce, 1929). The engrossers of fat cattle were obviously the graziers with their grazings close to markets. These laws were obviously not pursued with any vigour with numbers of London and Leicester butchers becoming graziers (chapters 11 and 13).

Some sharp practices in the presentation of carcases were obviously adopted by certain butchers resulting in Ordinance 38 for the London Butchers. This ordinance prohibited the great deceit and abuse "by the propping, cutting up and raising of calves' kidneys thereby much impaired and that no person hereafter shall raise the kidney of any calf with a prick or prop". Ordinance 39 is much the same in relation to lambs: "Kidneys of lambes are often tymes found dropped stuffed and raised up sometymes with ragges and cloutes". Ordinance 40 prohibited the inflation of carcases or joints of meat viz. "Item for that many doe blowe and puff upp by devyses sondry kindes of fleshe as beefe mutton veale lambe and porke which fleshe soe blowen and puffed uppe is very deceivable and maketh a shewe to be flesh being but winde and oftentymes unwholesome to be eaten being blowen and puffed up with foule and stincking breathes". Ordinance 44 prohibits any butcher from dressing a yoe (ewe) or wether as lamb for sale as lamb (Pearce, 1929). These same practices were also the concern of authorities in other parts of the country. An ordinance in the records of the Butchers' Company of Newcastle, 1709, states; "If any brother shall blow any meat with their mouths, or shall put any bladders blown into any veal's ears, or use any unwholesome way or means for setting out meat, for each offence 6s. 8d". An ordinance of 1652 states that "some brethren do impose upon people by dressing hogs and other sheep into the form of a lamb, fine 6s. 8d." An ordinance of 1733 required that: "no brother shall stuff any sheep's cods" (Dodds, 1917). The inflation of calf carcases was still practised in the 20th century until it was banned.

There was the continuing friction between the freemen and non-free (foreign) butchers as the butchers' companies were jealous of their monopoly. By the middle of the 1500s the presence of non-free butchers trading in the City of London was accepted as a 'fait accompli' but it did not stop the continuing pressure by the Butchers' Company for restricting the non-free butchers' trade. The counter to the Butchers' Company's demands for constraints on the non-free butchers was the acknowledgement by the Aldermen of the effect of competition in the supply of meat to the City's population. From the early days of the conversion of Leadenhall to a market the intention was that it would be the place for the non-free butchers to trade but they were constantly infiltrating the other markets. In 1548 the Wardens notified the Court of Aldermen that the non-free butchers were selling beef and mutton outside Leadenhall in Newgate, Cheapside and Gracechurch Street. They complained again in 1611 and 1620 that the 1611 order was not enforced. The Aldermen were informed of the setting up of a 'flesh shambles' outside Cripplegate in 1629. A petition of 1645 complained of non-free butchers selling all kinds of meat, including beef, in all the markets, resulting in an Act of Common Council in 1646 which provided for the sale of beef in Leadenhall Market only on Wednesday and Saturday by butchers not having a shop in the City or within two miles of the City but they were permitted to sell all other meat in any of the markets. There continued a series of complaints by the Butchers' Company concerning the disregard by the non-free butchers of the restrictions on them and the lack of resolve by the Clerks of the markets to enforce the regulations. There were instances of extending the non-free butchers' right to trade. The antagonistic attitude of the free butchers towards the non-free butchers and the lack of response by the City Authority was briefly ended by the Fire of London, 1666 (Jones, 1976).

The problem of the encroachment of non-free butchers occurred in most towns but to a lesser extent than in London, due to the size of its meat trade and the extent of the spread of the conurbation beyond the City walls. The records of the Newcastle-upon-Tyne Butchers' Company contain ordinances that restrict their members from dealings with foreign butchers with no indication that non-free butchers were prohibited from trading in the town. The James I Charter of 1621 contains a clause that "no Brother shall be partner with any foreigners called carkers". There were further ordinances in this respect. One dated 1675 ordered "that none of the company shall kill or sell any goods belonging to a foreigner". Another dated 1713 stated "none to buy any goods either quick (alive) or dead of a man not free of the Company" (Dodds, 1917).

Although lenten butchers were officially licensed, the London Butchers were totally opposed to them according to the ordinances of 1607, as stated in Ordinance 66 "lenton butchers by good experience are founde not only Enemyes of the Company of Butchers but to the common wealthe of this lande". The ordinance forbade butchers of the City to serve lenten butchers or let their shop, warehouse or slaughterhouse to lenten butchers (Pearce, 1929). It was different in Newcastle in that the Charter of 1621 states "that before a brother buys or seeks a license to kill livestock in Newcastle during lent he must first get the general consent of the Butchers' Company" (Dodds, 1917).

A close season for pork was subject of legislation. The ordinances of the Butchers of London 1607 relate "that the eating of porke in the hot tymes and seasons of the yeare is thought to be very dangerous to the health of man and a great increase of sicknes". It was forbidden to sell pork from 1st May to 31st October (Pearce, 1929). According to Hannah Glasse pork came into season at Bartholomew Tide (24th August) and held good till Lady Day (25th March). Although this gave an extra month open season compared with the London ordinance, the more significant difference was the timing with one starting in August and the other not starting until October (Glasse, 1747).

Ordinance 41, 1607 states that "newly killed beef that is cut before it is thoroughly cold it will hardly take salt and will long continue sweet and is unprofitable for the buyer". Therefore butchers who cut and sold their beef before it was cold were subject to a fine under this ordinance (Pearce, 1929). It is indicated from this ordinance that the concept among butchers at this time was that before meat was ready for cutting and of suitable quality for eating, the carcases needed to have undergone the post-mortem changes and to have set in the process of losing body heat.

Part IV

**Transition From a Craft Activity to
an International Industry. 1750-1914**

Chapter 15

Developments in Livestock Farming: 1750-1914

THE EFFECT OF THE INDUSTRIAL REVOLUTION

Significant changes to the meat industry were beginning to get underway by the 17th century and were to gain momentum towards the end of the 18th and through the 19th century. One notable fact that emerged during the 17th and 18th centuries was that the meat value of cattle and sheep had risen in relation to their other economic values (i.e. producing wool or milk or as draught animals) giving more incentive to livestock producers to produce better butchers' animals. This was to lead to selective breeding, resulting in better quality animals. The developments in agriculture continued from the 17th century with increased productivity, which in turn gave rise to improvements in stock husbandry.

One very far reaching change that affected the whole commercial and social infrastructure was the industrial revolution of the latter 18th and early 19th centuries. This brought about a change from a predominantly rural economy to one centred on industrialisation. The pattern of population was to change. This had been mainly rural with the majority of the people spread throughout the country, living in villages and hamlets. The effect of the industrial revolution was for a large proportion of the population to become concentrated in the industrial towns and the commercial centres, leading to the great conurbations of today. Arising from this was the stimulus for the continuation of the transition of the meat industry that was underway in the 16th and 17th centuries from the medieval sole trader craftsman system to a highly industrial, extensively organised industry in the latter 19th century with the establishment of a number of large and powerful international companies.

MORE LAND ENCLOSURES AND THE SCOTTISH HIGHLAND CLEARANCE

Further enclosure of land took place in the 18th and 19th centuries, particularly under the Enclosure Act of 1810. This reduced still further the ability for many peasants to subsist in the country, forcing them to move to the new industrial towns to seek work. This latter spate of enclosures made it more difficult for drovers to move their flocks/herds though the countryside.

In Scotland at this time the Highland Clearance was taking place. Until the 18th century most of the land in the Highlands was farmed by the members of the clans on their small plots or crofts. These Highlanders would have a few cattle which they grazed on the hills during the spring and summer. Some of these cattle would be sold to buy extra oatmeal to supplement that which they had grown on their small strips of land and also to pay rent to their clan chief or laird. (For many clan chiefs the commitment of their clansmen to fight for them when called upon to do so was more important than rent.)

During the 18th and 19th centuries this changed with the progressive clearance of these small Highland crofters from vast areas of the Highlands to make way for sheep farming. Flocks of Blackface or Cheviot sheep were brought into the Highlands from the lowlands and the border country to occupy stretches of land that had previously supported large numbers of highlanders. These large flocks could be managed by a small number of shepherds. The significance of the change in the domestic animal population is exemplified by this statistic of Sutherland:

	Horses	*Cattle*	*Goats*	*Sheep*
1798	7,763	24,287	6227	37,130
1808	4,291	17,333	1128	94,570

(Youatt 1834)

The first change leading to the Highland Clearance was the gradual breakdown of the clan system at the beginning of the 18th century. This breakdown was accelerated by the defeat of the Jacobite rising at Culloden in 1746; the aftermath of which an edict was issued prohibiting Highlanders from bearing arms or wearing their clan tartans. Many of the clan chiefs lost their lives at Culloden or they were captured after the battle. Those chiefs that survived could no longer call upon their clansmen to fight for them, which was a major reason for the decline in clan allegiance.

The landowners were faced with mounting financial pressure. The prospect of higher rents from sheep farming and less commitment to their clansmen resulted in them clearing the highland crofters off much of the land to make way for sheep. In some cases whole communities were evicted. This movement increased after the end of the Napoleonic wars when the prices of kelp (ash of burnt seaweed used in glass and soap manufacture) and cattle slumped, making it even more difficult for crofters to pay their rents or indeed even to subsist. Many of the people of the Highlands, displaced through evictions or driven by abject poverty, emigrated to the new lands of North America, Australia and New Zealand, or in some cases they sort employment in the industrial regions such as Glasgow.

The final blow came to the highland crofters in the late 1840s. They had become reliant on potatoes as well as oats as the staple crop for feeding their families. In 1846 the potato blight that had already caused such devastation in Ireland struck in Scotland, causing starvation among the crofter families. They were unable to pay their rents to the landowners and in some cases the landowners kept them from starving by providing oatmeal. The financial position of many landowners deteriorated resulting in a further wave of evictions of the crofters, although many left of their own accord because of their desperate situation. Many of the migrant highlanders who settled in the Americas and the Antipodes were to become stock farmers, exporting meat and wool to the UK.

As a result of this clearance and the build-up of the vast sheep flocks, the highlands of Scotland became important to both the meat industry and the wool industry. There have been substantial supplies of mutton and lamb during the 19th and on through the 20th century and the late season supply of small Scotch lamb has been a special attraction for butchers. Another important development of the highland sheep industry was to provide the first stage in the stratification system. The highland flocks have long been renown for producing the Greyface and Scotch Halfbred ewes which have been so valuable to the Lowland and arable farmers, providing them with ewes for commercial sheep flocks for the production of fat lamb.

Sheep dominated the Highlands until the latter half of the 20th century when foresters lead by the Forestry Commission pushed the sheep off large tracts of the highlands to make way for timber plantations. There were further challenges to the sheep by the growth of deer farming.

DEVELOPMENTS IN LIVESTOCK

At the beginning of the 19th century oxen were still widely used for draught purposes, especially ploughing, although the horse was progressively taking over this role. By the end of the century there were hardly any working ox teams left in Britain.

The rise in the demand for meat had increased the value of the flesh of each slaughtered animal with a shift of emphasis to the production of animals specifically for the butcher. Medieval animal production had been biased towards the yield of wool from a sheep or the potential of a bovine as a plough animal. Robert Bakewell (1725-95) is revered as the main instigator of stock improvement that was to continue through the 19th into the 20th century. He started his work on stock improvement in 1745. Bakewell established a number of criteria forming the basis of his selection which were the proportion of the best parts (best cuts), the texture of the muscular parts or flesh (this based on the fact that the grain of the meat was entirely due to breed) and the potential to fatten at an early age (Youatt, 1834). Bakewell believed that breeding only within the breed was the way to firmly establish the desirable traits.

"The greatest obstacle to the improvement of domestic animals" writes Culley, "seems to have arisen from a common and prevailing idea amongst breeders, that no bull should be used in the same herd more than three years, and no tup more than two; because, (say they) if used longer, the breed will be too near akin, and the produce will be tender, diminutive, and liable to disorders: some have imbibed the prejudice so far as to think it irreligious." Culley considered it fortunate that there were farmers and other breeders not bound by these vulgar prejudices and regarded these notions without foundation. Once Bakewell had established his herds and flocks he kept them closed in respect of breeding and would not introduce any stock from other sources. In this way he was able to progressively improve his animals for the traits he wanted. Culley, in advising farmers to breed from their own best stock added that they should never cross with animals worse than their own, quoting the well established rule; "the best only beget the best; like begets like". (Culley, 1807). It was not until 1866 that Gregor Mendel published 'Mendel's Laws of Heredity' which was the beginning of the science of genetics but it is clear that Bakewell and his followers were applying some of the principles of genetics albeit from their empirical knowledge.

In judging animals for their qualities Culley emphasises the importance of handling animals and not just relying on assessing by eye. He mentions that the farmer or breeder of the time was not ashamed to learn from the butcher to feel with his fingers at different points for the amount of fat covering and the fleshing of a beast (Ibid). In spite of the reluctant breeders and graziers, the impetus was for the production of better butchers' animals and Bakewell's methods were rapidly gaining ground as the way forward.

The main cattle of the Craven district of the West Riding of Yorkshire, Lancashire and Westmoreland were a longhorn variety with the horns sweeping forward either side of the face. It was from these animals that Bakewell selected the original stock to found his Dishley herd of Longhorn cattle (Youatt, 1834). From the sheep flocks of Leicestershire Bakewell selected animals that he considered to have the potential to fatten readily and whose shape would produce the largest proportion of valuable meat and the smallest quantity of bone and offal. From these he established the Dishley or New Leicester breed of sheep. Rather than sell, Bakewell leased the bulls and rams from his new breeds by the season, for which there was a great demand by the farmers (Youatt, 1840).

Fig 15.1 An engraving of a New Leicester Bull. A good example of the Dishley Long Horn breed belonging to Mr Honeybourn, Robert Bakewell's nephew and successor (Youatt, 1834).

Fig 15.2 An engraving of a Short Horn Bull belonging to the Rev. Henry Berry (Youatt, 1834).

Fig 15.3 An engraving of a Hereford Cow (Youatt, 1834).

Fig 15.4 An engraving of an Angus Ox (Youatt, 1834).

Following the lead given by Robert Bakewell emerged many breeders who founded the British breeds of cattle, sheep and pigs which provided good quality meat carcases through the 19th and into the 20th century. Contemporaries and disciples of Bakewell were the brothers George and Matthew Culley who took a farm near Wooler, Northumberland, where they established a flock of Dishley Leicesters. In the course of improving their sheep they crossed them with Teeswater sheep and eventually the Culley sheep were recognised as Border Leicesters, the rams of this breed becoming renown for crossing with mountain flocks (Ibid). The brothers Robert Colling (1749 – 1820) and Charles Colling (1751 – 1836) who were farming in the county of Durham visited Bakewell and became diciples of his methods. The shorthorn cattle of Holderness that had been much improved by the Dutch cattle imports, were already noted as good animals for the butcher and the dairyman. It was from these that the Colling brothers selected animals to found their Shorthorn cattle breed, which became a major breed throughout the world in the 19th century. An outstanding animal bred by Charles Colling was the Durham Ox, said to have a liveweight of 3024 lbs, which was exhibited in many parts of the country to promote the Shorthorn breed. Further development of the Shorthorn breed was taken up by Thomas Booth in the latter part of the 18th century, who concentrated on the beef potential, with the result of defining the beef Shorthorn breed. A contemporary of Booth, Thomas Bates, developed the dairy Shorthorn.

The Hereford breed were the local cattle of Herefordshire, red in colour but distinguished by a white face, throat and belly and in some cases the white extending to the shoulders. According to Youatt the white markings only existed from the late 18th century. (Youatt, 1834) Benjamin Tomkins (1745 – 1815) was one of the early breeders to develop the Hereford breed (McDougall, 1929).

Fig 15.5 Prize Long Horn Bull, Melcombe Emperor (Leighton & Douglas, 1910).

Hugh Watson (1789 – 1865) of Keillor, Forfarshire, started with a herd of eighteen black polled Angus cattle known as doddies and from this small number founded the Keillor breed which became the Aberdeen Angus breed. Because of their potential for early maturity they were quick to fatten and were short of leg with a compact form that was well fleshed with fine grained meat which attracted the butchers. Watson won many prizes for his breed including the prize for the

Fig 15.6 Champion Short Horn Steer, property of King EdwardVII, attended by Uriah Robins (Leighton & Douglas, 1910).

Fig 15.7 A Hereford Cow (Leighton & Douglas, 1910).

best pair of Angus oxen at the Highland Society show at Perth in 1829 (Youatt, 1834). The Aberdeen Angus achieved such merit as a butchers' beast as to be regarded by many as the epitome of the quality beef animal. The breed became prominent, due to the efforts of William McCombie (1805 – 80), at the Royal Smithfield shows, the Chicago fatstock shows and the Paris Exhibitions of 1856, 1872 and 1878 (McDougall, 1929). By the 20th century it became the most frequent winner of the best beast in show at the Royal Smithfield show, supplanting the Herefords and Shorthorns (Trow-Smith, 1980).

Fig 15.8 Champion Aberdeen Angus Steer, Pan of the Burn, Edinburgh and London, 1908 (Leighton & Douglas, 1910).

Apart from the Shorthorn, Hereford and Aberdeen Angus cattle with their widespread national and international success, other breeds had their main support in the locality of their origin. There were the Devon and Sussex breeds which were very similar in appearance, being red in colour and having medium length horns. They had been good animals as plough oxen. These breeds became noted as good beef animals as a result of breeding improvements. The Lincoln Red was a strain of shorthorn most commonly found in the eastern counties, likewise the Red Poll which was noted for its dual-purpose (milk and meat) value. Another noted dual-purpose breed was the South Devon or South Hams which was the largest of the cattle breeds. The Welsh Black cattle being hardy and adapted to the conditions of the Welsh hills, retained their value for producing store cattle for the graziers of England. The Galloway and Kyloe or West Highland cattle were in the same way the best animals to exploit the upland grazing of Scotland, producing good calves for rearing and fattening on the Lowland pastures.

With the wool clip being the medieval criteria for the improvement of sheep it was to some extent contrary to the quality of the carcase produced. Robert Bakewell and the other improvers of the sheep breeds for carcase quality had to accept a reduction in the value of the wool clip. As Culley writes "the wool of this breed hath hitherto been only a secondary consideration; the quantity and quality of the mutton obtained at the least expense of food, was the great object of the first improver; this point gained, a new field opens to the experimental rural philosopher, to cover these good carcases with the most valuable fleeces." According to Culley the weight of wool clipped from the Dishley Leicester was less than that from other long-woolled kinds (Culley, 1807). The other longwools did not achieve the same prominence as the Dishley Leicester and Border Leicester but they were popular in their local areas. The improvement of most of the long-wool sheep was brought about initially by some crossing with the Dishley Leicester. The improved long-wool breeds at the beginning of the 19th century were the Cotswold, Lincoln, Devon Longwool, Wensleydale or Teeswater and the Kentish or Romney Marsh (Wrightson, 1905).

The middle-woolled sheep or down breeds were improved in a similar way to the longwools. John Ellman of Glynde carried on his father's work of improving his flock of Southdown sheep. He

Fig 15.9 An engraving of a New Leicester or Dishley Leicester Ram (Youatt, 1840).

Fig 15.10 An engraving of a Southdown Ewe (Youatt, 1840).

was visited by Arthur Young in 1776 who extolled the virtues of his sheep saying they had the finest wool and their carcases were the best proportioned. The fleshing qualities of the Southdown with the fine grained meat and its potential for early maturity put the rams in great demand for improving the other Down breeds. The improved Down breeds include the Hampshire Down, Oxford Down, Shropshires, Suffolk Down, Ryland and Dorset Horn.

The upland or mountain breed of sheep's chief characteristic and one that had to be preserved above all others was hardiness and capacity to survive on the inhospitable upland areas, moors and fells where the grazing is sparse for long periods. These upland flocks had their lambs later in the year than the lowland flocks. The practice was growing in the early 19th century of crossing a proportion of the ewes to an improver ram (e.g. Leicester), the ewe lambs from this cross going for sale to farmers with better lowland grazing or to arable farmers for breeding ewe flocks for the production of mutton or fat lamb. Wether lambs of this cross were ready for the butcher in two years, whereas a pure upland wether would take three years, according to Youatt (1840). The main upland breeds of sheep in the early part of the 19th century were: in the Scottish Highlands the Cheviot and the Black Face; in the hills and fells of the Northern English Counties the Herdwick, Cheviot, Penistone and Lonk; in the Welsh Hills and Welsh Borders the Welsh Mountain, Radnor Forrest, Clun Forrest and Kerry Hill; and in the West country the Dartmoor and Exmoor (Trow-Smith, 1959).

The improvement of pigs owes a great deal to the importation of pigs from China which began on a large scale in 1770 (Stratton & Brown, 1978). The types of animals that made up the pig population in Britain in the 18th century were very poor meat animals. Most of the references to pork during the middle ages put it in the category of meat for peasants and in particular its main use as bacon to provide meat for the poorer people during the winter. For those who could afford it the first choice of meat was beef, followed by mutton and poultry. This attitude to pork did not engender any real incentive for the improvement of the pig, either in respect of its breeding or husbandry, until the latter part of the 18th century. According to Youatt (1847) the original pigs in Britain were

two

Fig 15.11 An engraving of an Old English Hog (Youatt, 1847).

Fig 15.12 An engraving of a Berkshire Sow. This animal belonged to the Duke of Bedford (Youatt, 1847).

Fig 15.13 An engraving of a Chinese Pig (Youatt, 1847).

types; a large breed and a small breed. The large breed he described as "long in the limb, narrow in the back which is somewhat curved, low in the shoulders and large in the bone; in a word, uniting all those characteristics which are now deemed most objectionable, and totally devoid of any approach to symmetry." He then adds; "They nevertheless have their good qualities, although aptitude to fatten does not rank among the number, for they consume a proportionally much larger quantity of food than they repay; but the females produce large litters, and are far better nurses than those of the smaller breeds."

The state of the pig population in Britain in the 18th century was such that improvement of the stock was necessary if pork was to compete with the other meats. The salient points for improvement were to achieve a more compact shape with better fleshing and above all, a potential to lay on fat. To this end, crossing with the Chinese pig was the answer. According to Youatt they were small in limb, round in body, short in the head, wide in the cheek and high in the chine and above all they fattened readily (Ibid). In the 19th century there was the establishment of many pig breeds but for all of them there had been some crossing with Chinese pigs. There was also, to a lesser degree, the importation of Neapolitan pigs from Italy for crossing with the British stock. Although the Neapolitan pigs were less hardy, this was not detrimental to the cross but there was marked improvement in the fineness of the flesh and the tendency to fatten by the progeny of the cross (Ibid). The most numerous of the old breeds was the Berkshire but the description of its colouring did not correspond with the eventual colouring of the improved Berkshire. It was an animal that could be fattened to a great size as the example of a Berkshire pig owned by Mr Joseph Lawton of Cheshire. The pig was killed on 24th January 1774 by James Washington, butcher of Congleton, Cheshire, and weighed 1410 lb (640kg) liveweight and the dressed carcase weighed 1215 lb (551kg) (Culley, 1807). Horne writes that "the Berkshire is chiefly fattened at the distilleries and that it feeds to a great weight and is good for either pork or bacon" (Horne, 1810). Culley describes a large white breed of Yorkshire with large ears hanging over the pigs face. He writes "They were very plain, thin, awkward hogs, with very long legs." (Culley, 1807). Crossing the Yorkshire with the Chinese and the Neapolitan brought about improvements to the breed (Youatt, 1847).

The following statement by Youatt seems to embody the informed opinion at the time of British pork production:

> "The alterations latterly effected in the breeds of swine have tended materially to improve pork, and render it more sought for and valued. We can recall to mind when the thought of pork was associated in our minds with visions of course-grained meat and oily fat, and forebodings of a fit of indigestion. Nothing could tend more effectually to banish such fancies than a sight and taste of the small, fine-grained joints, delicate as poultry, and of excellent flavour, which have taken the place of those ungainly legs and Brobdignagian loins and hands of olden times."

SPECIFICATIONS FOR LIVESTOCK IMPROVEMENT

Although it was well before the practice of drawing up specifications, the early livestock improvers did have well-defined aims to which they aspired. The broad aims were to improve quality for the consumer and improve the quality from the point of view of the butcher, while still maintaining or improving the economic potential of the animal. As far as sheep were concerned there was still the importance of the wool clip that had dominated the minds of the medieval improvers but in the 18th and 19th century they were already foregoing the level of the wool clip in favour of a better carcase.

The changing attitude towards the carcase values of livestock is indicated in the growing enthusiasm for demonstrating the dressed carcases of prime animals by farmers in the 18th century. Apart from including such facts as age at slaughter, sex of the animal etc., the main economic statistics of the slaughtered animal not only included the weight of the forequarters and hindquarters but also included the weight of the hide and the weight of the tallow (the internal fats, e.g. mesenteric fat, omental fat, etc.). This confirms the relatively high value of the hide and tallow compared with the carcase.

Apart from the economic value of large amounts of tallow there was also the importance for well-finished animals to produce the quality carcases with a plentiful layer of subcutaneous fat covering the outside and fat within the carcase. Marbling fat within the carcase was highly esteemed as an element of good quality (Horne, 1810). An essential criterion for the livestock improvers therefore was to select animals that had a tendency to put on fat and above all, produce early maturing animals. There was occasionally carcases with excess fat such as one of Culley's sheep killed in 1787 that carried 7 inches (18cm) of fat over the loin whereas 2-3 inches (5 – 7.5 cm) would have been normal (Culley, 1807). The following observation by Culley reflects the attitude to fat at the beginning of the 19th century: "I am well informed that when the laborious class find this mutton too fat, they cut off a part of the fattest, with which to make suet-dumplins, or bread paste with it for pies, &c. and not unfrequently make sea or boiled pies of the fattest parts."

The other criteria for improvement, as stated by Horne are: "Utility of form or the nice proportioning of parts to which Mr Bakewell bestowed so much attention" and "the flesh or texture of the muscular parts; a quality which was formerly only noticed by butchers, but a knowledge of which the enlightened farmers or breeders ... acquired from them". Horne then adds "it is sufficient to state, that the best sign of good flesh is that of being marbled, or having the fat and the lean finely veined, or intermixed when the animals are killed; and, while alive, by a firm and mellow feel". He explains "This term implies a skin which feels 'mellow', i.e. soft, yet firm to the touch, and which is equally distant from the hard dry skin, peculiar to some cattle, as it is from the loose and flabby feel of others" (Horne, 1810).

The preoccupation of the market with well-fatted animals brought about the use of the word 'fatstock' as the definition of animals ready for slaughter when presented at the markets. This incentive to livestock breeders in Britain to select animals for their readiness to put on fat persisted through the 19th century with the result that the top British meat producing breeds had the potential for early maturity and a high level of fat growth. The very fat finish of these 19th century animals is well exemplified by the many paintings of prime animals and of cuts of meat of the period. By the mid 20th century the value of tallow had significantly declined and consumer demand was turning to much leaner meat. This meant that the British breeds developed in the 19th century no longer conformed to the changed requirements of the market.

SALE OF CATTLE BY WEIGHT

It is interesting to note that by the beginning of the 19th century a number of farmers were selling cattle by weight as indicated by the following according to Thomas Horne:

> "it was proposed by the late Lord Kaimes, to dispose of every beast by weight, and that such weight be ascertained by the steelyard, as being best calculated for weighing heavy goods; which mode he used with ease and success for many years." (Horne, 1810)

The following method of estimating the weight of a beast by measurement is given in 'The Experienced Butcher':

"by measuring the girth, just behind the shoulder blade, with a cord, and ascertaining the number of feet and inches, it is in circumference, by a foot rule, taking one-fourth of it; and also, by measuring from the fore part of the shoulder to the setting on of the tail, and ascertaining the number of feet and inches the animal is in length, and multiplying one by the other, and allowing 42 lb for every cubic foot of flesh, the precise weight of the beast (sinking the offal) * may be known. The allowance given for a half-fatted ox, must be a deduction of one stone in twenty from that of a fat ox: for a cow which has had calves, one stone must be deducted for that case, and another for not being properly fat."

There were a number of tables published around 1800 from which the weight of an animal could be obtained by cross checking the girth measurement and the length; one in Renton's 'Graziers Ready Reckoner' and tables published by Lord Somerville in 1796 entitled 'The Farmer's, Grazier's, and Butcher's Ready Reckoner'.

The average deadweights of livestock in Smithfield Market in 1830 according to figures given by Youatt were:

	Deadweight	Estimated liveweight
Bullocks	656 lb (=298kg)	1193 lb
Calves	144lb (=63 kg)	240 lb
Sheep	90 lb (=41 kg)	180 lb

PRICES OF MEAT, HIDES AND TALLOW

Weights of prize animals were much higher as the following example indicates:

An ox, 5 years old, bred and fed by Mr Milbanks, of Barningham in Yorkshire, was killed at Barnardcastle, in April, 1798, by Mr Lonsdale; -

	stones – lb	price per stone	£ - s - d
Two forequarters	74 - 8½	4s.	14-18-5
Two hindquarters	75 - 10	5s.	18-18-7
Carcase Total	150 – 4½		33-17-0
Tallow	16 – 0	4s.	3-4-0
Hide	10 – 11	4s.	2-3 0
Overall Total	177 - 1½		39-4-0

(Stone = 14 lb)   (Culley, 1807)

* Note: The term 'sinking the offals' is used when the value of the offals is not taken into account in calculating the value of the carcase against the value of the live animal. In this case the term is used for disregarding the offal weight in the process of estimating the carcase weight.

The prices of meat and tallow were given in the '*Edinburgh Advertiser*', 13th June 1800, and are as follows:

> Smithfield, Monday 9th June. Sinking the offals – per stone of 8 lb
> Beef 5s - 0d to 6s – 8d
> Mutton 5s – 0d to 6s – 6d
> Lamb 5s – 4d to 7s – 0d
> Veal 4s – 6d to 6s – 8d
> Pork 5s – 4d to 6s – 6d
>
> Price of tallow in London
>   3s – 9d per 8 lb stone

SELECTION AND SLAUGHTER OF BUTCHERS' ANIMALS

The following is an early 19th century guide to selecting butchers' animals:

> '*The Experienced Butcher*', 1816 advises against what it states as a former preference for big boned, large beasts, as follows:

> "... it has been ascertained, that this breed is, in point of profit, much inferior to the middle-sized kind".

It continues by advocating the principle adopted by Mr Bakewell of Dishley:

> "... to select the beast that would weigh most in the valuable joints;".

On the external form it advises:

> "Beauty, or symmetry of shape; in which the form is so compact, that every part of the animal bears an exact consistency, while the carcass should be deep and broad and the less valuable parts, such as the head, bones, etc. ought to be as small as possible".

There is also this reference to quality of:

> "The flesh, or texture of the muscular parts" … explained as follows: "Although this quality necessarily varies according to the age and size of cattle, ... it is sufficient to state, that the best sign of good flesh is that of being marbled, or having the fat and lean finely grained or intermixed".

'*The Experienced Butcher's 1816*' guide to assessing an animal:

"First, when the general shape and make of an animal appear best proportioned, each member being comely, and each bone covered with flesh, in the manner required to constitute a perfect shape, it must be concluded that the beast is well fed; especially when his hip bones, or as they are sometimes termed his huckle-bones, are round, his ribs smooth and not sharp, his flanks full, and purse round. When these marks are perceptible, the beast may be handled and his lowermost ribs felt; if the skin be kindly, or mellow, that is soft, yet firm to touch, it is certain that he is well fed outwardly, or, in other words, upon the bones. Next, the hand may be laid upon the hip, or huckle-bones; and if they likewise feel soft, round, and plump, it may be safely concluded, that the animal is well fed, both externally and internally, that is both in flesh and in tallow. Further, he may be handled at the setting on of his tail, which, if it be thick, full, and soft to the touch, is also a proof that the beast is well fed externally; the same circumstance is likewise shewn by the nach-bones, which lie on either side of the setting of the tail, feeling mellow, or soft, and loose. Lastly, the purse may be examined, if an ox, or the navel or dug, if a cow, and, if they respectively feel thick, round, large, and plump, it is a certain proof that the beast is well tallowed within; and, when any of these parts, or members, handle contrary to the rules above mentioned, a contrary judgement must be formed."

'*The Experienced Butcher 1816*' explains that at the time the common mode of selling cattle was by lots and suggests:

"... to prevent confusion between the parties, or loss on the part of the feeder, care should be taken to fix the precise time in which any particular lot is to be drawn, in order that no unnecessary food may be consumed. Formerly, and even now, in some places, it is usual to sell by eye, a method which is certainly unequal, as it respects both farmer and butcher; for, the former, unless he has been accustomed to weigh his beasts during the progressive stages of their fattening, can form at best but an uncertain idea of their weight; while the latter, from his continual practice, is enabled to form a tolerably accurate estimate."

THE ROYAL SMITHFIELD CLUB

In 1793, William Pitt established the Board of Agriculture which started the compilation of county reports that were detailed surveys of agriculture. Its first secretary was Arthur Young who was later also to become the first secretary (honorary) of the Smithfield Club.

The Bath and West Agricultural Society held a show in 1797 at which was displayed the carcase of a New Leicester sheep that weighed 218 lb live with a carcase weight of 160 lb. The thickness of the fat of this carcase was much admired. This could have inspired the setting up of the Smithfield Club.

The Smithfield Cattle and Sheep Society was formed in 1798, the first president being Francis, Duke of Bedford. The Smithfield Cattle and Sheep Society held their first fatstock show in 1799 at Dolphin Yard, part of Wootton's Livery Stables which were adjacent to Smithfield Market. There were no separate classes for breeds at this first show but a distinction was made between the more traditional hay and roots fed cattle and those fed on oilcake and corn. The first entries for pigs in the shows were in 1801. In 1802 the name was changed to The Smithfield Club (Trow-Smith, 1980).

The Smithfield Cattle and Sheep Society, after the first show, began the promotion of feeding trials among its members, which were aimed at demonstrating the amount of weight an animal would gain given unlimited feed. One of the main objectives of the society was to encourage the production of good butchers' animals economically. This was expressed by the Duke of Bedford at one of the Society's dinners, that "the better the grazier understands his business, the cheaper will the market be supplied". He urged members to experiment in stock feeding, record the results, and determine what breeds of stock in particular conditions gave "the most food for man from given quantities of food for animals". The beginnings of the Smithfield shows and their success is a further indication of the growing importance that the farmers and graziers were attaching to the production of good butchers' animals. It was complained in some quarters that this emphasis on mutton carcases was having a detrimental effect on the quality of home-produced wool. For the production of quality wool the Spanish Merino sheep had a very strong following in the country. The supporters of this breed included King George III. This popularity of the breed resulted in the introduction of a class for Merino wethers in the 1810 Show (Ibid).

By 1807 a separate breed class was introduced for oxen or steers of 120 stone or above: it was a requirement that these animals had worked for two years prior to fattening. This requirement for "having worked" was dropped in 1810. There was a female class for fat cows having had three or more calves. In 1818 the breed classes for cattle were dropped, to be replaced by age and weight classes for all breeds. In 1841 steers were defined as under four years and oxen as over four years and in the same way females were defined as heifers up until four years old and then they were classed as cows (Ibid).

DEVELOPMENT OF THE CLUB THROUGH THE 19TH CENTURY

From the original site for the Show in Dolphin Yard it moved first to Swan Yard and then in 1806 to Sadlers Yard in Goswell Street close to Charterhouse. In 1839 the Show moved to Baker Street Bazaar which gave it room to expand and for the introduction of farming implements (Ibid).

The development of railways from the 1840s had a marked effect on the condition of the animals arriving for the Show. Not only did this speed up the journey but it considerably reduced their weight loss in getting to the Show. Prior to the advent of the railways some animals were transported by horse-drawn wagons over long distances to avoid their weight loss and there were cases of animals destined for the Show being transported by canal barge, but for many it meant being driven. It was recorded in 1805 that a Devon ox was driven 126 miles to the Show. As the network of railways spread, livestock producers from more distant parts of Britain were encouraged to send animals to the Show.

In 1855 the Metropolitan Cattle Market was opened to replace the Smithfield live market. The Smithfield Club debated the prospect of a purpose built exhibition hall in which to hold the shows. This resulted in the building of The Agricultural Hall at Islington, close to the Metropolitan Cattle Market, which was to be run by the newly formed Agricultural Hall Company. The first chairman of this company was Jonas Webb, a prominent and highly respected livestock breeder and farmer. Sadly, Jonas Webb died in the same year of the first Smithfield Show held at The Agricultural Hall, which was in 1862 (Fig 15.14) (Ibid).

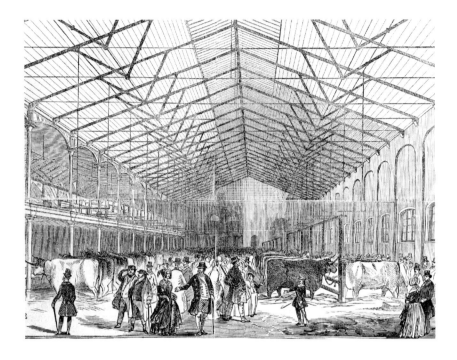

Fig 15.14 Smithfield Prize Cattle Show, 1845. One of the earlier shows of the Smithfield Cattle Club. (*Illustrated London News*, Dec.13, 1845).

In 1862 the male championship for cattle was, for the first time, won by a cross-bred steer; a three and half year old Devon-Shorthorn cross. By the 1860s the ages of the entries were generally lower. An epidemic of rinderpest caused the 1865 Show to be put back for a week and in 1874 a bad London fog caused the deaths of many animals (Ibid).

Classes for carcases were introduced in 1895. There was a class for steers under two years, a class for steers between two and three years, one class for longwool sheep and one for shortwool sheep. The animals were shown alive on the Monday and then slaughtered to be returned to the show for judging as carcases. This carcase assessment was first carried out by two judges; a London butcher and a farmer-grazier. They could not agree and this eventually led to butchers only being appointed as carcase judges. The early carcase judges complained that the farmers were producing over-fat animals which were unprofitable, if not unsaleable. These contentious arguments over excess fat were to rumble on through the 20th century. Carcase classes enabled the butchery trade, through the judges, to indicate the type of animals they wanted; young animals of a reasonable size which were tender and not over fat (Ibid).

Chapter 16

Slaughter of Animals, Meat Cuts and Meat Quality

SLAUGHTERING ANIMALS IN THE EARLY 19TH CENTURY

The first stage was getting the animals to the place of slaughtering. '*The Experienced Butcher, 1816*', suggests care in guarding against the excesses of the drovers, and quoting from '*The Literary Miscellany*':"... it is not uncommon, in driving a number of sheep, when one is untractable, to break its leg ... This is a cruelty, we will hope, not often practised."

   Apart from the cruelty aspects, '*The Experienced Butcher*' quotes from the writings of a Dr Buchan, a medical man, on the effect of bad droving on carcases:

> "Animals are often rendered unwholesome by being over-heated. Excessive heat causes a fever, exalts the animal salts, and mixes the blood so intimately with the flesh, that it cannot be separated. For this reason, butchers should be severely punished who over-drive their cattle. No person would choose to eat the flesh of an animal which had died of fever; yet that is the case with over-drove cattle; and the fever is often raised even to the degree of madness."[1]

'*The Literary Miscellany*' describes another cruel practice of some butchers as:

> "... to tie two calves together by the legs, and to throw them across a horse, in which manner they are suspended for two or three hours together, and still longer, if the inhuman wretch has business on his way home, or invited to lounge at a favourite alehouse."

'*The Experienced Butcher*' again quoting Dr Buchan said:

> "... he seems to think, that the reason why the cellular membranes of the joints of veal are so frequently filled with blood, may, in some measure, be owing to the practice of carrying calves from a great distance to market, by which means their tender flesh is bruised, and many of their vessels burst."

---

[1] Note: The description of blood being intimately mixed with the flesh would indicate congestion of the carcase, the sign of fever but it may be that in some cases of bad droving the animals were stressed and therefore produced dark cutting carcases.

On fasting the animals prior to slaughter, '*The Experienced Butcher*' states:

> "Animals are usually fasted, that is, kept without food for some time before they are killed. Oxen usually fasted three or four days; calves, sheep, and pigs, each of them a day."

The author of *Domestic Cookery* (1812) writes:

> "The flesh of cattle that are killed when not perfectly cleared of food, soon spoils. They should fast twenty-four hours in winter and double that time in summer, before being killed."

'*The Experienced Butcher*' advises:

> "This practice too, should have its limitations and rules of mercy. Fasting too long must be very painful to the animals; and, in many instances, make them restless and feverish, and perhaps hurt themselves by fretting about."

The siting of a slaughterhouse, according to '*The Experienced Butcher*':

> "... should be as retired as possible, that the public may not be inconvenienced by the noise, the sight, or smell of it. To secure the latter point, it should be placed so as to be effectually drained, and for this purpose an elevated situation is best."

It goes on to say that if the drains are properly constructed they could be used for agricultural purposes by directing the drainings over pasture lands or by supplying a reservoir with litter or earth, and lime, to turn it into manure. With regard to the smell, Tissot in his 'Essay on the diseases of Literary and Sedentary Persons', writes:

> "... they should fix themselves at a distance from places which emit unwholesome exhalations such as slaughter-houses, the shambles, tanners' yards &c."

ATTITUDES TOWARDS BUTCHERS IN THE 18TH & 19TH CENTURIES

The antagonism against the butchery trade by the Animal Rights groups is not new. The author of '*The Experienced Butcher*' quotes from a number of sources derogatory statements regarding the profession of butchers, for example:

> "Butchers, whose employment is violent, bloody, and cruel; which practices, actions and motions of the human body, by the repeated strokes of violence, and by the conversations of their school-fellows in all base lessons, language, and methods; never fail to stamp the signatures of brutality and inhumanity, and diffuse their own propertys to the intellectuals:".

It also quotes:

> "It seems generally understood that our legislature has affixed such an imputation of proneness to shed blood, upon persons who slaughter brute creatures for a subsistence, that by the laws of England no butcher is permitted to serve on a jury when sitting on the life of a fellow subject. ... It seems to be a very general opinion, that the English law will not accept the evidence of a butcher in any trial wherein life is concerned, under the idea that butchers are, from the nature of their business, apt to be less feeling and humane than other classes of men."

The author of '*The Experienced Butcher*' continues with various accounts in support of the butcher not least the following:

> "If the occupation of a butcher be cruel, what are we to say of those who set him to it, who purchase meat so cruelly slaughtered, and who send their animals to be slain? It is a maxim in law, Qui facit per alteram, facit per se (He who does a thing by another, does it himself)." '*The Experienced Butcher*'

The following is a poem extracted from that same book:

> Yon lattic'd window and yon lattic'd door,
> Where spreading elms afford a shade before,
> Where two upright posts, with transverse beam,
> With iron hooks, arrang'd in order, gleam,
> Bespeak the butchers shop, where victims bleed,
> That man upon the flesh may freely feed.
> He deals in slaughter and blood, 'tis true,
> He slays his thousands, - but it is for you.
> Man, who condemns the butcher's harden'd heart,
> As instigator, bears the heavier part,
> If aught of blame from out the practice grows,
> Which Providence Supreme to man allows,
> Of flesh and fruit we have the grant to eat,
> The great commandment is - with mercy treat.
> O, Thomas Clement, would that all who cry,
> Against the horrors of the butchery,
> Had manners gentle, and their hearts as kind,
> Their lives as blameless, well-inform'd the mind.
> Search through the village with your utmost care,
> Bring whom thou wilt with Clement to compare,
> I'll take the butcher against all the field,
> In worth and mercy he to none will yield.

PENALTIES FOR CRUELTY

An early piece of legislation against cruelty to animals was enacted during the reign of George III:

> "If any person, hired to drive any cattle within the bills of mortality, shall, by negligence or ill usage in the driving such, be the means that any mischief shall be done by any such, &c. committed to his care; or if any such driver shall, in any wise, misbehave himself in the driving, care, or management of any such cattle, by improper driving, treating, or using of such, he shall forfeit, not exceeding 20s. or less than 5s. and, on nonpayment, be committed to the house of correction to hard labour, not exceeding one month."

The following was recorded in the Address of the Society for the Suppression of Vice, 1803:

> "A drover, who was found treating his sheep with extreme cruelty, was apprehended by a member of the Society, and carried before a sitting alderman, who convicted him in the penalty of twenty shillings; which, being unable to pay, he was sentenced to one month's imprisonment in Bridewell, and the case being attended with circumstances of aggravated cruelty, he was wholly deprived of his number. ... Another case of great barbarity to an ox, was noticed by the Society. The drover, after a very determined resistance, was apprehended by a member of the Society, and taken before a magistrate in Bow Street, who convicted him in the penalty of twenty shillings; and, on account of his resistance, wholly deprived him of his number."

Each drover in London wore a number on his arm which was his licence to work as a drover in London, therefore losing his number meant losing his livelihood.

A report in the *Cambridge Chronicle* for Feb. 10, 1815:

> "Thomas Briercliffe, a butcher of Little Bolton, Lancashire, on the laudable prosecution of the humane municipal officers of that place, was, at the last quarter sessions, sentenced to three months' imprisonment, for cruelly maiming and torturing a sheep; the court deeply regretting that they were not authorized to inflict the additional punishment of whipping."

ADVICE FOR THE BUTCHER

'The Experienced Butcher' gives the following advice to butchers:

> "First, that, in slaughtering animals, everything should be so ordered to give the animals the least pain possible, and that it should be conducted with the utmost regularity, with as little noise and brutality as may be; and the greatest cleanliness should be observed both in respect of the appearance and the smell. It is an old saying, that cleanliness is next to godliness and I believe that it is much connected with it, and, included in that,

with morality and humanity. Secondly, let your other occupations and amusements be of a nature to counteract any disposition to cruelty. Above all, let him (the butcher) avoid all those amusements, (falsely so called) the very essence of which is cruelty; as bull-baitings, cock fighting, racing, shooting, and hunting."

It is interesting to note in relation to the foregoing that at the beginning of the 19th century cruel sports were commonplace, many cruel penalties were exacted by the courts of law and slavery had not as yet been abolished; whereas debate on the humane slaughter of animals was very much in evidence. It was not until an Act of Parliament in 1835 that bull-baiting was abolished.

PITHING AS AN ALTERNATIVE MEANS OF STUNNING

The general method of killing oxen in England, according to '*The Experienced Butcher*', is by striking them on the forehead with a poleaxe to knock them down, and then cutting the throat.

"But, in this way, the poor animal often has to receive many blows before it is brought to the ground. The Jews, when they kill an animal for food, tie all the legs together, and bring it down to the ground, then turn the head up upon the horns, and, with a long knife, cut across the throat, that all the blood may come out at once. This method, likewise, may occasion considerable pain to the animal."

In an attempt to find a more humane and more convenient method of slaughter, Lord Somerville proposed the method used on the Continent of pithing or laying cattle. To this end Lord Somerville took a man to Lisbon to learn the method. The method is described by '*The Experienced Butcher*' thus:

"A line being drawn from ear-root to ear-root of a bullock, at about an inch and a half distance from the horns, the centre of this line would be the place where the instrument should enter. The knife or awl-shaped instrument, should have a guard for the hand, and the point perhaps be curved upward, to secure that direction in the hollow of the skull. No great force is necessary in the operation, which is extremely simple and easy of performance."[2]

Mr Marshall in his 'Review of Reports to the Board of Agriculture, from the Western Department of England' published in the *European Magazine* 1810, pursues the view of pithing being more humane than poleaxing. He writes concerning the brutality of poleaxing:

"Could death be inflicted with certainty, by a single blow, this charge could not be brought against the present practice. In slaughter-houses in the metropolis, where

---

[2] Note: This method of pithing entails the instrument enterering the spinal canal through the gap between the atlas and the occipital bone of the skull severing the medullar oblongata. While this would totally immobilise the animal resulting in paralysis with many body functions ceasing, it would not render the animal immediately unconscious but this fact would not have been understood at the beginning of the 19th century. This meaning of the word pithing differs from its present day meaning.

through constant habit, the knocking-down art is best understood and executed, some degree of certainty may be approached. But not so in the country; where I have seen many savage blows given before the animal fell; and where I have known the head of a victim so much bruised and swollen, by repeated strokes of the executioner, that his instrument no longer had any effect; the mangled wretch being obliged to be shot, in that horrible state of torture!"

Mr Marshall goes on to suggest that there be established properly trained anatomical pithers so that pithing could become the standard method of slaughter. He adds to his recommendations:

"And let it be deemed murder (and a suitable punishment assigned for it) to slaughter domestic animals in the present barbarous manner."

These efforts to get pithing accepted as a method of slaughter to replace poleaxing did not succeed and as late as 1880 the then president of the Smithfield Club, the Earl of Powys, offered a prize of £20 for the best instrument for pithing. After three years the judges concluded that none of the instruments submitted were suitable.

SLAUGHTERING PRACTICES AT THE END OF THE 19TH CENTURY

At the end of the 19th century, as at the beginning, there was still a great deal of dissatisfaction with the use of the poleaxe. The poleaxe was still the most common method used for slaughtering cattle at the end of the 19th century. Slaughtermen working in the larger abattoirs were highly skilled being able to fell a beast with a single blow, driving the bolt of the poleaxe through the frontal bone of the skull and into the brain. The bolt is at the back of the poleaxe opposite the axe blade and is cylindrically-shaped solid steel with a concave hollow at the end which aids cutting through the bone of the skull.

In most cases cattle were slaughtered by the animals being stunned with a poleaxe, pithed and then bled. It was necessary to hold the animal's head still for the slaughterman to deliver a blow in the correct spot and at the correct angle with the poleaxe, to render the animal unconscious. The animal's head was held by a rope tied round the base of the horns, the end of the rope passed through a cattle ring fixed to the wall or floor and the slaughterer's assistant using the rope to pull the animal's head close to the ring. In the case of polled cattle a halter was used. Pithing was carried out by passing the pithing cane through the hole in the skull made by the poleaxe, destroying the medulla oblongata, with a vigorous movement of the cane. This resulted in a violent kicking of the beast for a few seconds and thereafter there would be no more limb movements, making it easier and safer for the slaughtermen to bleed and skin the animal. To bleed the animal the slaughterman severed the blood vessels in the neck (jugular vein and carotid artery). Bleeding took place with the animal lying on the floor so that it was necessary to use a large shallow dish if blood was to be collected. Most of the flaying and evisceration was carried out with the body on the floor and completed as it was hoisted onto the overhead rail. It was common for animals to be led into the slaughterhouse while slaughtering was taking place. Sheep and lambs were usually slaughtered and skinned on a cradle. The cradle generally consisted of an open framework on four legs about

Fig 16.1 Scalding Tank in an Irish bacon factory. The temperature of the scalding tank was 140°-150°F (60°-65°C). Note the mechanical pig scraping machine (Douglas, 1905).

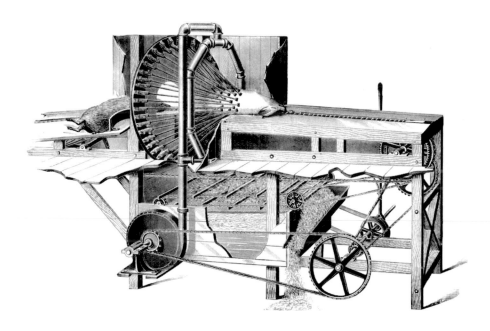

Fig 16.2 Pig Scraping Machine with a throughput of eight pigs per minute (Douglas, 1905).

Fig 16.3 Pig Skinning in a Scottish slaughterhouse. Scottish bacon products were mostly prepared skinless (Douglas, 1904).

Fig 16.4 Scuttling Table in an Irish bacon factory, for scraping pigs free of hair. In the foreground is the base of the singeing stack (Leighton & Douglas, 1910).

18 to 24 inches high. Sheep and lambs were killed by cutting their throats to sever the main blood vessels in the neck. If they were stunned, a hammer or mallet was used.

The problem lies with the poleaxe when it was used by less experienced butchers or trainees and there was the occasion that miss-hits resulted in several blows being delivered to fell an animal resulting in much suffering. In Germany at this time they used a special apparatus for trainees to practise on before they were allowed to fell a beast (Leighton & Douglas, 1910).

Although the larger pigs were stunned using a poleaxe the smaller pigs could be stunned with a pig mall or mallet but in many slaughter houses these animals had their throats cut severing their carotid artery, the loss of blood causing loss of consciousness followed by death.

Fig 16.5 Scud or Pig Scraper and a Bell Pig Scraper. The hook on the back of the scud was for pulling off hoof covers (Douglas, 1905).

In the bacon factories pigs were generally shackled by one hind leg and hoisted to the overhead rail where the slaughterman stuck each pig by a longitudinal incision in the neck severing the arteries; they then passed into the bleeding-passage. When pigs were stunned it was usually with a mallet or mall. In bacon factories pigs were scalded in large tanks with the water being piped to the tank from the factory's boiler. By contrast, in many small slaughterhouses wooden tubs were used for scalding pigs, the hot water being ladled from a brick built copper. Scraping the pigs was done by hand in small slaughterhouses and bacon factories (effective automatic scrapers were not readily available).

The American packinghouse system for cattle was mechanised and included stunning by a blow from a hammer (about 4lb) (Fig 16.7). The animals were driven along a race into a stunning pen where a gate automatically closed behind each animal. The slaughterman was standing level with the top of the pen ready to deliver the stunning blow with his hammer. When the animal had fallen to the floor at the stunning pen, the slaughterman would pull a lever to allow the front of the floor of the stunning pen to drop tipping the stunned animal on to the slaughterhall floor. The animal was then shackled by one hind leg and raised to the bleeding rail where the carotid artery was severed.

Because of the size and throughput of the large abattoirs in the United States, especially in Chicago, they were the earliest abattoirs to have mechanised equipment.

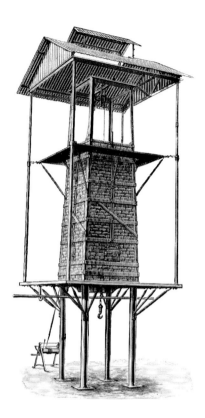

Fig 16.6 Vertical Pig Singeing Stack. It is coal fired and the pig ready for singeing has a 'gob' hook inserted into the angle of the mandible, which is attached to a chain for the pig to be hauled upwards through the furnace. After the pig emerges from the top of the furnace it is lowered into a cold water tank. The pig is then finished off by scraping and cleaning. The old method of singeing was to lay the pig on straw and cover with straw which was then fired. Although singeing was used in some cases to burn off most of the bristles, to be finished by scraping, the Irish bacon factories in the 19th Century scalded and scraped the pigs then singed them. This method was adopted by the Danish bacon factories. The object of singeing was to harden the skin and make the subcutaneous fat firm. (Leighton & Douglas, 1910).

MOVEMENT TOWARDS THE ADOPTION OF HUMANE SLAUGHTER

There was increasing concern through the 19th century over the need for humane slaughter and pre-slaughter care. The development of technology and expanding understanding of animals' physiology made solutions to the humane slaughter more feasible. There were numerous complaints from meat salesmen and butchers that bad treatment of livestock in markets, shipping and short distance droving caused considerable damage to the quality of the carcases.

The situation with regard to slaughtering prompted a number of movements aimed at obtaining more humane methods of killing animals in the slaughterhouses with pre-slaughter stunning as essential in achieving this aim. The Model Abattoir Society founded by Benjamin Ward Richardson in 1886 attempted to use powers contained in the Town Improvement Clauses Act, 1847, to enforce more humane slaughter of animals, but without success.

Fig 16.7 Stunning Cattle in a USA slaughterhouse. Animals were moved along a race, then gates lowered to separate them individually (Leighton & Douglas, 1910).

The Public Health Act, 1875, incorporates provisions of The Improvement Clauses Act, 1847, Section 128 in respect of local bylaws for the licensing, registering and inspection of slaughterhouses and the prevention of cruelty therein. Clauses of the Act are the basis for Model Bylaws issued as guidelines in 1909 by the Local Government Board for the regulation of slaughterhouses by the Urban Authorities (Local Government Board, 1909). The extent by which this was taken up with regard to humane slaughter and the requirement for stunning at slaughter, or indeed if bylaws were introduced, the extent that they were enforced, is not in the records (Leighton & Douglas, 1910).

The British Admiralty set up a committee in 1904 to enquire into the slaughter of animals for food. They issued their report in 1908 containing the following recommendations:

(a)   All animals, without exception, must be stunned, or otherwise rendered unconscious before blood is drawn.

(b)   Animals awaiting slaughter must be so placed that they cannot see into the slaughterhouse, and the doors of the latter must be kept closed whilst slaughtering goes on.

(c)   The drainage of the slaughterhouse must be so arranged that no blood or other refuse can flow out within the sight or smell of animals awaiting slaughter, and no such refuse shall be deposited in proximity to the waiting-pens.

(d)   If more animals than one are being slaughtered in one slaughterhouse at the same time, they must not be within view of each other.

(e) None but licensed men shall be employed in or about slaughterhouses.

It was not until the Protection of Animals Act, 1911, that the RSPCA was able to bring prosecutions for cruelty to livestock prior to slaughter.

There were some bolt apparatus of German manufacture for the stunning of pigs and sheep. The apparatus consisted of a barrel through which runs a bolt. The barrel was fitted to a handle at right angles enabling it to be held so that the bolt was in position to enter the brain of the animal.

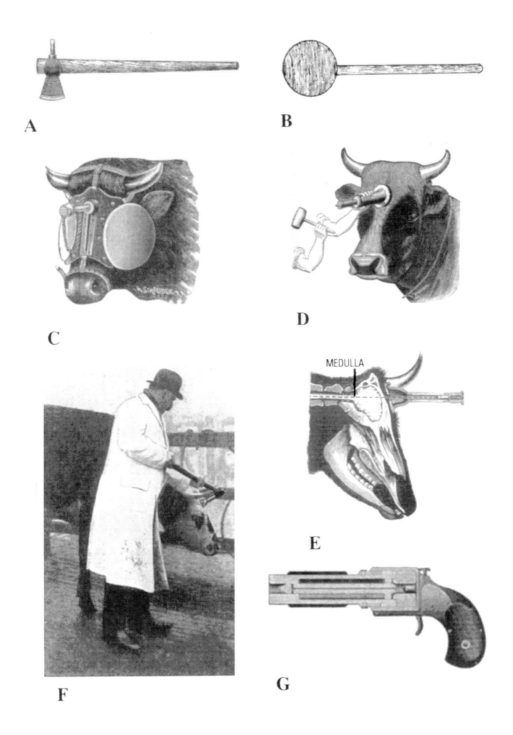

Fig 16.8 Implements for stunning animals.
A. Pole Axe; B. Pig Mall; C. Killing Mask for cattle; D. Greener's Humane Cattle Killer; E. Cross section of the animal's head showing the pathway of the bullet from the Greener's Humane Cattle Killer; F. Demonstration of the RSPCA's humane killer; G. Behr's Captive Bolt.   (Douglas, 1905)

When in position the bolt was driven into the brain by striking the bolt with a hammer. There were a number of killing-masks for cattle which consisted of a leather mask placed on the head of the animal attaching to the horns and having a metal plate with a hole in the centre through which a metal bolt was placed. This hole was in line with the point for penetration of the skull and was driven through the skull with a mallet.

A device commonly used on the Continent, especially in France, was the cattle killing mask; in particular the one invented by the Frenchman Brunneau, called the Brunneau Mask. This mask consisted of thick leather which was strapped onto the animal's head, covering its eyes and having a socket for a bolt positioned at the stunning point on the animal's head. A bolt was placed in the socket and struck with a hammer to drive it into the animal's brain.

DEVELOPMENT OF MECHANICAL STUNNING

Greener's Humane Cattle Killer invented by W.W.Greener was in use in slaughterhouses by the end of the 19th century. It consisted of a short rifled barrel with a chamber into which a small cartridge was placed. The end of the barrel was bell shaped to deaden the sound of the explosion when held against the animal's head. When the cartridge was placed in the chamber it was held in position by a screw cap which contained the firing pin; this pin projected through the screw cap and was protected by a loop when not in use. To kill a beast the instrument was positioned at the centre point between the base of the animal's horns and the tops of the eyes and then fired by striking the firing pin with a mallet. According to the makers, if the instrument was correctly placed the bullet would pass through the animal's brain and into the spinal canal, killing the animal instantly. The entry of the bullet into the spinal canal eliminated any need for pithing the animal. Behr's Humane Slaughtering Pistol was also in use by the end of the 19th century. This worked on the captive bolt principle whereby a blank cartridge was placed in the chamber of the pistol and fired, the explosion driving a sharp pointed bolt forward to project from the muzzle of the pistol, piercing the skull of an animal, entering its brain and killing it instantaneously. A flange on the end of the bolt prevented it leaving the barrel of the pistol and it returned automatically into the barrel thus separating from the animal before it fell. The advantages of the Behr's pistol over Greener's Humane Cattle Killer was that only one hand was needed to operate Behr's pistol leaving the other hand free to hold the animal's head (useful when stunning smaller animals). The captive bolt did not pose a danger to other slaughterhouse workers as was possible using a free bullet.

The RSPCA developed a humane killer consisting of a short revolver barrel, a firing mechanism and a long handle fixed at right angles to the barrel. The humane killer used standard 0.450 revolver cartridges. The nozzle of the barrel was placed in position on the animal's head and on pulling the trigger the gun fired, the bullet penetrating the animal's skull. A satisfactory demonstration was carried out in front of prominent veterinarians at the Metropolitan Cattle Market, Islington, in 1907.

Christopher Cash was involved in the development of the RSPCA humane killer and he later collaborated with George Accles, who was a firearms expert. Between them they produced the Cash Captive Bolt Pistol in 1913 which was to become the dominant cattle stunner in the UK and many other countries throughout the world.

After the success of these instruments had been established, a number of local authorities in Britain made their use compulsory, as did the War Office and the Admiralty in their butchery and victualling establishments but in the majority of cases the slaughtermen did not change from using the poleaxe: reluctance to change being a common characteristic of the meat industry.

RITUAL SLAUGHTER

Jewish ritual slaughter of cattle was usually carried out by tying or shackling the animal's feet together and then throwing it on its side, securing the head for the shochet to cut the blood vessels of the neck and the trachea with a single cut of the shochet's knife. Many attempts were made to find better methods for casting cattle that were less stressful and reduced the chances of the injury and pain caused when heavy animals hit the floor of the slaughterhouse. An appliance patented in the latter part of 19th century by C.Trapp of Strasburg, (slaughterhouse medical officer and veterinary surgeon) had much in common with the casting pens that were to become compulsory in the 20th century. This apparatus consisted of heavy wooden slats fixed to a large frame and attached to a heavy metal frame with deep curved supports. For the commencement of the slaughter process the large wooden frame was upright and there was a narrower slatted frame at right-angles. The animal was led onto the narrow frame or foot board and strapped to the larger frame. The whole appliance with the animal was then swung over on curved metal supports, putting the animal in a prostrate position on the large frame that was then horizontal. The animal's head was held by a rope to the frame for the ritual slaughter. An apparatus devised by Pulverman consisted of a plate with four holes. The animal was led onto the plate to stand with one foot in each hole. The plate was raised to the level of the animal's knees so that it could not move and the animal's throat was then cut from below while it was in the standing position (Harrap & Douglas, 1901).

Ritual slaughter without stunning was banned in Saxony by an order of 1892, and in Saxe-Meiningen by an order of 1891; it was also banned in Switzerland by command of the Republic. A number of other European states allowed ritual slaughter for animals only where meat was destined for the Jewish members of the population.

ASSOCIATION FOR HUMANE SLAUGHTER

At a meeting held on 17th January, 1911, the Council of Justice to Animals was formed with the Duchess of Portland as the first President. The objects of the Council were:

(1)   To promote humane methods in the slaughtering of animals for food.
(2)   To provide for the painless killing, when necessary, of horses, dogs and other animals.

The policy of the Council was to assist the butchers and slaughtermen in the use of the humane slaughter devices which had become available. The Council was later renamed The Humane Slaughter Association.

MEAT CUTS AND MEAT QUALITY (1816)

The cutting diagrams are copies taken from 'The Experienced Butcher'. The following are lists of the cuts shown with some description. Many of the cuts are the same as today but there are a number of interesting differences with either the cut or its name:

BEEF

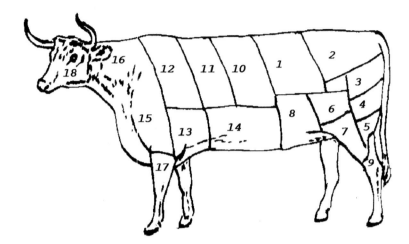

"As an Ox is sometimes ROASTED WHOLE, it may be as well to mention, that when this is the case, the inside is taken out, the head cut off, and the legs above the knees."

1.   The Sir-loin, which consists of part of the loin including one rib and to the chump or huckle bone (hip bone).
2.   The Rump extends from the Sir-loin (the huckle bone being taken out) to the tail. A Baron of beef is two Sir-loins and two Rumps all in one joint.
3.   The Edge-bone, Ridge-bone, Each-bone or Aitch-bone, called also the round, is situated under the rump at the hind part and includes part of the thigh bone (femur).
4.   The Buttock is situated below the edge-bone, and includes the other part of the thigh bone (femur).
5.   The Mouse Buttock or Bed is situated below the buttock and includes part of the upper leg bone.
6.   Veiny Piece, called also, the leg side of the round, below the buttock.
7.   The Thick Flank.
8.   The Thin Flank.
9.   The Leg.
10. The Fore Rib which contains part of the backbone and five ribs.
11. The Middle Rib which contains four ribs.
12. The Chuck which contains three ribs.
13. The Shoulder or Leg-of-mutton Piece.
14. The Brisket.
15. The Clod.
16. The Neck or Crop or Sticking Piece.
17. The Shin.
18. The Cheek.

The heart is esteemed by many as being a little inferior to hare. The best steaks are off the rump. The feet go with the tripe which consists of fore paunches or stomachs.

VEAL

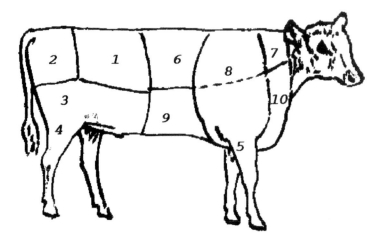

1. The Loin, the best end.
2. The Loin, the chump end.
3. The Fillet.
4. The Hind Knuckle.
5. The Fore Knuckle.
6. The Neck, the best end.
7. The Neck, the scrag end.
8. The Blade Bone or shoulder.
9. The Breast, the best end.
10. The Breast, the brisket end.

The head is normally divided into two halves. The pluck consists of the heart, liver, lights or lungs and the milt or spleen. The feet are sold all together by what is called a gang or half gang.

MUTTON

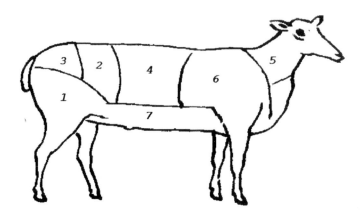

1. The Leg or Jigot. A leg of wether mutton is known by the kernel or round lump of fat on the edge where the leg is cut from the carcase. A Haunch is the leg and chump end of loin cut in one joint.
2. The Loin, the best end.
3. The Loin, the chump end.
4. The Neck, the best end.
5. The Neck, the scrag end.
6. The Shoulder.
7. The Breast.

A saddle is two loins not separated.

A lamb is cut, for the most part, like mutton. A coast of lamb is the neck and breast after the shoulder is removed. A lamb's head and purtenances consists of the head, neck and pluck.

VENISON

1. The Haunch which consists of the leg and chump end of loin.
2. The Neck.
3. The Shoulder.
4. The Breast.

PORK

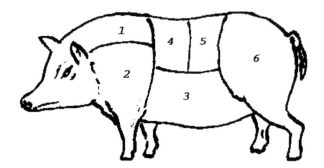

1.   The Spare-rib, so called when the fat and flesh are cut off for salting.
2.   The Hand or Shoulder.
3.   The Belly or Spring.
4.   The Fore-Loin.
5.   The Hind-Loin.
6.   The Leg or Ham.

A neck, in some places, is called a crop. The griskins are the vertebrae or the joints of the neck bones cut into chops. The head, after being divided into two is divided again at the jaw, the upper part being called the face or cheek and the other part the chap. (In some places it is called the chorl.) A flitch or gammon is a side with the leg cut off and the bones taken out. The pluck is also called the harslet.

GUIDANCE FOR JUDGING MEAT QUALITY (1816)

The following is some of the advice given by '*The Experienced Butcher*' for the judgement of meat quality, which will give the reader some idea of the quality and type of meat that the butcher of the day was cutting and selling. It is important for the reader to bear in mind that the general run of butchers' animals were much older and carrying a lot more fat (at this time) than would be the case today. Some of the beef animals would have spent some of their life as working oxen or as breeding or 'milch' cows. Some years after the following was written, a 13 year old Shorthorn cow won second prize at the Smithfield Show.

> "BEEF. If it be really Ox-beef, it will have an open grain; if young, it will have a tender and oily smoothness, except in the neck and brisket, and such parts as are full of fibres; if old, the meat will be rough and spongy. It should be of a fine red colour. The fat should look white rather than yellow; for, when that is of a deep colour, the meat is seldom good. Beef fed with oil cakes is in general so, and the flesh is flabby."

> "Cow-beef is closer in the grain, and the meat is not so firm as ox-beef; the lean is paler and the fat whiter. If Young, the fleshy part, on being pressed with the finger, will leave no dent, but rise up again soon after."

Fig 16.9 Spouting Apparatus. The cylinder is filled and a fine spray of fat is spouted over a carcase to give it an attractive white appearance. This avoided the objectional practice of spouting straight from the mouth.

Fig 16.10 Baron of Beef weighing 200 lbs from a Devon Ox. Bred and fed on a farm of the late Queen Victoria (Douglas, 1905).

"In Bull-beef, the grain is closer still, of a deep dusky red, tough when you pinch it; the fat is skinny, hard, and has a rankish smell."

"Ox-beef is the largest and richest; but, in small families, and, to some tastes, heifer-beef is better, if finely fed. In old meat, there is a streak of horn, or bone, called the crush-bone, in the ribs of beef; the harder this is, the older, and the flesh is not so finely flavoured."[3]

---

[3] Note: In considering the above description, the bone referred to is, most likely, the cartilage of the scapula which progressively ossifies with age.

Fig 16.11 Roasting a Baron of Beef in Durham. Note the screen to protect the woman supervising the cooking from the heat. Based on a drawing by S H Grimm, c. 1778 (Kay Collection, British Museum).

"VEAL. The flesh of a bull-calf is firmer, but not, in general, so white as that of a cow-calf. The leg, or fillet, of the cow calf is generally preferred for the udder (or dug); the fat of a bull calf is harder and curdled.[4] Veal to be delicate, should always look white in the flesh, like rabbit or chicken; nor should it seem much blown up. Hanging in the air will make it look red; but, if you cut into it, the natural colour will be discovered. But the whitest meat is not always the most juicy, having frequently been made so by repeated bleeding, and having had whiting to lick. The meat is best of which the kidney is well covered with thick, white fat. If the bloody vein in the shoulder looks blue, or of a bright red, it is newly-killed: if blackish, greenish, or yellowish, it is stale. The other parts should be dry and white; if clammy or spotted, the meat is stale and hard. The kidney, and the part under it, in the loin, change first, and the suet will not be firm, and the flesh will be soft and slimy. The breast and the neck taint first at the upper end; where, when stale, will have a dusky, yellowish appearance, and the sweetbread on the breast will be clammy. The leg, when fresh-killed, will be stiff at the joint; if stale, it will be limber (flexible) and the flesh seem clammy. In the head, the eyes should look plump and lively; if sunk and wrinkled, the head is stale; and, to be delicate, it should be small and fat. Large, over-grown veal is never good."

"MUTTON. A wether, five years old, is the most delicious. The grain should be fine, the colour a fine darkish red, and the fat white and firm. Ewe mutton is paler in the flesh, the grain closer. If the mutton be young, the flesh will feel tender when pinched; if old, it will wrinkle up and remain so; if young, the fat will readily separate from the

---

[4] Note: the term curdled probably meant lobulated.

lean; if old, it will stick by strings and skins. In ram-mutton, the flesh is close grained and tough, not rising again when dented by the finger, of a dark colour, and the fat is spongy: the flavour is very strong. If the sheep was rotten, the flesh will be pale, the fat a faint white, inclining to yellow, and the flesh will be loose at the bone. If you squeeze it hard, some drops of water will stand on it like sweat."

"LAMB. Fine lamb should look of a delicate, light, bright red colour; the fat white, though not perfectly so as in mutton, nor so close. In the fore quarter, attention should be paid to the neck vein, as in veal; and in the hind-quarter to the kidney."

"VENISON though not commonly among butcher's meat yet, strictly speaking, it is so, for, if killed by the keeper, he is the butcher on the occasion; and the shoulders are frequently sold by keepers, as their perquisite, to butchers and poulterers in London, and exposed publicly for sale. Venison is darker in colour than mutton. If the fat be clear, bright, and thick, and the cleft of the hoof smooth and close, it is young; but, if the cleft is wide and tough, it is old. By putting a finger, or a knife, under the bones which stick out of a haunch or shoulder, the scent will tell whether it be new or stale; and the same of the sides in the most fleshy parts. If tainted, they will look of greenish colour in some places, or more than ordinary black."

Fig 16.12 Joint on a spit being rotated by the dog in the wheel. The tray below the joint is to catch the fat and the long handled ladle is to baste the joint. Based on a drawing by Rowlandson, 1798, in the Rural History Centre, Reading.

"PORK. The meat of pigs cut, or spayed, when young, is the best. That of a boar, though young, or of a hog , cut at full growth, the flesh will be hard, tough, reddish, and of a rank smell; the fat skinny and hard, the skin very thick and tough, and, being pinched up, it will immediately fall again. If it be young, in pinching the lean between your fingers, it will break; and, if you nip the skin between your nails, it will be dented. But, if the fat be soft and pulpy, like lard, if the lean be tough, and the fat flabby and spongy, and the skin so hard, that you cannot nip it with your nails, it is old. If there are little kernels in the fat, like hail shot, the pork is measly and unwholesome, and butchers are punishable for selling it. The freshness of pork may be known by putting the finger under the bone, and smelling it. The flesh of stale pork, also, is sweaty and clammy; that of fresh killed is cool and smooth. Pork fed at still-houses is not good for curing, the fat being spongy. Dairy fed pork is best."[5]

Although there is no indication of the numbers of sucking pigs marketed in the 19th century there are enough recorded praises of this luxury which would indicate that the consumption of sucking pigs was not uncommon. These praises include one of Charles Lamb's 'Essays of Ellia' which includes "a kind of animal manner, or rather, fat and lean so blended and running into each other, that both together make but one ambrosian result". According to Youatt "Those intended to be killed for sucking pigs should not be above four weeks old; most persons kill them for this purpose on the twenty first or twenty second day" (Youatt, 1847).

THE SUBLIME SOCIETY OF BEEFSTEAKS

This Society was founded in 1735 by Henry Rich, the harlequin and machinist (General Manager) of the Covent Garden Theatre. The Society was restricted to 24 brethren and its objectives, procedures and customs were archaic and enforced with rigidity. The Society motto was "Beef and Liberty" and there were numerous connections between eating beef and patriotism and being British (Fig 16.13).

The following is the first verse of the Song of the Day which was sung by the brethren at their meal of beefsteak which exemplifies the objectives of the Society:

"No more shall fame expand her wings
To sound of Heroes, States and Kings
A nobler fight the Goddess takes
To praise our British Beef in steaks
A joyful theme for Britons free
Happy in Beef and Liberty"

Many members of the Society were of the aristocracy including at one time George IV and his brothers the Dukes of York and Sussex. Membership was not confined to the aristocracy; anyone could become brethren as long as they fulfilled two conditions, viz. they were rich and were entertaining companions at dinner.

[5] Note: The term still-house probably refers to distilleries which kept pigs to feed them on the grain left after fermentation.

Fig 16.13 Dining Room of the Sublime Society of Beefsteaks.

One can be excused from concluding that the fundamental objective was the over indulgence in eating good quality beefsteaks washed down with lavish amounts of porter, port and whisky. The beefsteaks were cooked on a large gridiron and served on hot pewter plates with vegetables, baked potatoes, Spanish onions, cold and fried beetroot and chopped eschalot.

The sublime Society of Beefsteaks came to an end in 1867 (Swatland, 1998).

Chapter 17

Meat Preservation

INTRODUCTION

The need to conserve meat or to transport meat has been a major factor in the quest for methods of meat preservation. The development of methods of meat preservation has resulted from this need, coupled with the contemporary level of technology. In the 19th century the rapid rise in urban populations in Europe and North America led to a pressing requirement for effective means of meat preservation for the purpose of storage and especially for meat transportation, not only across land but also across the seas. In the latter part of the 19th century the dead meat trade had increased considerably with the consequence of carcase meat being transported over greater distances and taking longer to reach the meat markets and butchers' shops. This meant that ways to extend the storage life of meat were more important than previously.

The hunter gatherers of Palaeolithic times had very little facility for keeping the surplus meat from their kills. Suspending meat in trees as leopards do would have been a useful procedure for early man as the meat would have been out of the reach of most of the scavengers. The effect of air circulating around the meat would have dried the exposed surfaces of the muscles arresting bacterial decomposition thus keeping the meat in an edible state for several days. During the ice ages the people living on the edge of the glaciers had access to natural refrigeration, although making practical use of it would have presented many problems.

PAST METHODS OF KEEPING MEAT ALTERNATIVE TO SALTING

A cookery book and food guide from Ancient Rome, '*Apicius*', prescribes two methods of preserving meat other than salting (UT CARNES SINE SALE QUOVIS TEMPORE RECENTES SINT). The first method was to cover fresh meat with honey and suspend it in a vessel. According to the book it would keep for a long period in the winter but only a few days in the summer. The second method was for cooked pork or beef and required that the meat was placed in a pickle of mustard, vinegar, salt and honey with the pickle completely covering the meat (Vehling, 1977).

'*The Experienced Butcher*' listed a number of methods other than salting for keeping meat, most of which may seem a little odd or unpalatable today but they must be considered against the options available at the beginning of the 19th century being very limited:

One of the methods was to wrap the meat in a clean linen cloth and bury it in a box filled with dry sand, "... it will remain sweet for three weeks, if deposited in an airy, dry, and cool chamber".

A German method of preservation for veal and lamb was the immersion of a joint in skimmed milk. "In warm weather the milk should be changed twice the first day, and once in twenty-four hours afterwards. Thus, the meat may be kept in a sweet state for several weeks; but it ought to be washed in spring water before it is dressed."

A less drastic method given for keeping a joint of meat "for several days, even in summer", was "by wrapping it in a clean linen cloth, previously moistened with good vinegar, placing it in an earthen pan or hanging it up, and changing the cloth, or wringing it out afresh in vinegar, once or twice a day ..."

Where it was feared that meat would not keep until the day required it was recommended that it be parboiled.

HOW TO RECOVER TAINTED OR PUTRID MEAT

According to '*Apicius*' the method of dealing with strong smelling birds, or birds with a goatish smell, was to make a blend of pepper, lovage, thyme, dry mint, sage, dates, honey, vinegar, wine, broth, reduced must and mustard which was then heated and added to the roasting pan, the bird being basted during cooking. A strong flavoured fish sauce called garum was produced in ancient Rome from a variety of fish, particularly mackerel, using fish livers and intestines which were left to ferment in the sun, placed in wooden vats with salt added and liquid that ran off was collected as the sauce (liquamen). This sauce was used for meat or poultry that was developing a putrid odour as the sauce was strongly flavoured enough to counteract the taint of the meat

The following advice was given by '*The Experienced Butcher*' on ways of removing the taint and destroying the smell and effects of putrid meat:

> "Put the meat, if intended for making soup, into a saucepan of water, scum it when it boils; and then throw into the saucepan a burning coal, very compact and free from smoke. Leave it there for two or three minutes, and it will have contracted all the smell of the meat and soup (Fig 17.1)."

Fig 17.1 A Hot Coal put into a simmering pot of tainted meat.

"Charcoal powder is a very powerful antiseptic, and meat may be preserved, or rendered much more palatable, even when considerably tainted, by covering with charcoal powder, ..."

An example was given:

"... of a gentleman, who invited a party to dine with him on a haunch of venison. But when the day came on which it was to be dressed, it was so putrid, he provided something in its place, and when the company came, made his apology for there being no venison. One of the party begged, notwithstanding, that he might have it. The venison was sent to his house, and at the end of the evening, when the party broke up, he invited all to dine with him the next day. The invitation was accepted, and when the company met, and sat down to dinner, a very fine haunch of venison was on the table, and no unpleasant smell. All partook of it and pronounced it excellent; When the host said it was the same his friend had forborne to dress the former day ... Impossible ... what had he done to it? Covered it with charcoal powder."

"Such are the powers of this antiseptic. It is well known, that charcoal powder is now used to clean the teeth, as a sweetener of the breath, and applied to offensive wounds to purify them."

KNOWLEDGE RELATING TO THE PRESERVATION OF MEAT IN THE 18TH AND EARLY 19TH CENTURIES

Butchers and others responsible for the care of meat have been aware for many centuries of the main environmental conditions that influence the storage life of meat. This empirically based knowledge is clearly shown in the section 'On Keeping Meat' in '*The Experienced Butcher*':

"Every animal body, when deprived of life, suffers a gradual dissolution, or decomposition, commonly called putrefaction. ..... The circumstances under which putrefaction goes on most rapidly, are, heat, a little moisture, and confined air. The colour of the animal matter first becomes pale; its consistence, or hardness, becomes less; its texture becomes looser; and gives out a faint and disagreeable smell. The colour at this time changes to blue and green, the parts become more and more softened, the smell becomes very offensive and fetid, and the colour of an obscure brown. The fibres now yield, the texture is more resolved, the putrid and nauseous smell is mixed with a smell of more penetrating kind; after this, the mass becomes of still less and less consistence, and the smell becomes more faint and nauseous, and the effluvia, or vapour, arising from it, exceedingly active and hurtful. ... As the causes of putrefaction seem to be heat, moisture, and confined air, the absence of these will retard, if not altogether prevent it."

It is obvious that there was an appreciation of the problems of preserving meat at the beginning of the 19th century but it was not until the work of Pasteur in the latter part of the century, that the role of bacteria in causing putrefaction was established. This understanding of the problem paved the way for the development of technology to provide solutions.

ADVICE ON THE STORAGE LIFE OF MEAT IN THE 18TH AND EARLY 19TH CENTURIES

With regard to its stated causes of putrefaction, '*The Experienced Butcher*' continues with this advice to the butcher:

> "It is on the knowledge of these facts that butchers' shops, larders, pantries, and safes should be constructed. They should be sheltered from the sun, and otherwise removed from heat, be dry, and, if possible, have a current of dry, cool air through them. With this view, it would be advisable to have windows, or openings, on all sides, which might be closed, or opened, as might seem good, according to the way from which the wind blows, the time of day, or the season of the year."

If windows on both sides were not possible the advice was for the construction of a metal or wooden duct to run across the top of the shop to create a draught. '*The Experienced Butcher*' continues:

> "His shop should be kept, too, with the greatest attention to cleanliness, both, as a pure smell will be least attractive to flies, and best to keep the meat from tainting. It will be better, also, if the walls of the shop are, from time to time, washed with hot lime, and the dressers, hooks, scales, steelyards, block, tray, instruments, skewers, &c. all kept scrupulously clean. It is advisable for butchers to have canvass blinds, or awnings, over the windows of their shops, if at all visited by the sun in the summer; and if these, in very hot weather, were, from time to time, watered from above by a watering pot, the evaporation would produce cold, and tend to keep the shop much cooler."

It was advised that meat safes were open on two sides and positioned according to the wind for a draught of air to pass through and that these openings were covered with 'fly-wire'. It was also suggested that smaller safes could be hauled by pulley into the shady part of a tree (Fig 17.2).

'*The Experienced Butcher*' lists various cuts, giving the length of time a butcher can expect to keep them in this pre-refrigeration period with advice on improving the storage life of these cuts:

> "The best meat for keeping is mutton, and the best joint of that a leg, which, with care, if the weather be only moderately hot, in summer, will keep about a week. In winter, if the weather be open, a fortnight. A shoulder is the next best joint. The scrag end of a neck keeps the worst, and, in warm weather, will not keep above two days: if very warm is bad the second day. The kernel (lymph node) in the fat on the thick part of the leg should be taken out by the butcher, for it taints first there. The chine

(vertebrae) and rib bones should be wiped every day; and the bloody part of the neck should be cut off to preserve it. The brisket changes first in the breast; and, if it be kept, it is best to rub it with a little salt, should the weather be hot. The pipe that runs along the bone of the inside of a chine of mutton (aorta), should be taken away; and, if to be kept a great time, the part close round the tail, should be rubbed with salt, after first cutting out the kernel. Every kernel, of all sorts of meat, if not taken out by the butcher, should be taken out by the cook as soon as brought in: then wiped dry. Mutton for boiling will not look of good colour if it has hung too long."

Fig 17.2 Meat Safe hauled up into the branches of a tree to get the benefit of the coolness of the tree and a good circulation of air.

"In beef, the ribs will keep best, and, with care, will keep five or six days in summer, and in winter ten. The middle of the loin is the next best, and the rump the next. The round will not keep long, unless salted. The brisket is worst, and will not keep longer than three days in summer, and a week in winter. The butcher should take out the kernel in the neck pieces, where the shoulder clod is taken off (prescapula lymph node), two from each round of beef; one in the middle which is called the pope's-eye (popliteal lymph node); the other from the flap: there is also one in the thick flank, in the middle of the fat (subiliac lymph node). If these are not taken out, especially in the summer, salt will be of no use in keeping the meat sweet. There is another kernel between the rump and the edge-bone (ischiatic lymph node). When these are taken out, the beef intended for roasting should be slightly sprinkled with salt."

"Lamb is next in order for keeping, though it is considered best to eat it soon, or even the day it is killed. If it is not very young, a leg will keep three or four days in summer. Veal and pork are about the same. A leg will keep three or four days in summer, and a week in winter. Scrag end of neck will not keep above a day in summer, and three or four days in winter. The first part that turns bad of a leg of veal, is where the udder is skewered back."

THE PROBLEM OF FLIES

Butchers' shops have always been beset with the problem of flies in the summer, which were considered by '*The Experienced Butcher*' as the butchers' greatest enemy. It describes four sorts that will 'blow meat' and states that:

> "If the meat be all bruised, the flies will take that part first; they also take the kernels, which should always be taken out. Where flies have blown the meat, the part should be taken out, and some pepper put upon the place. ... Butchers frequently keep a fly-flap in their shops, made of a piece of thick flat leather about two inches in diameter, tied to the end of a stick about a foot long, with which to flap away, or kill the flies; but, as it frequently crushes the flies upon the meat, it is not altogether a good way of getting rid of them. They might be caught with greater advantage in bottles, ..." (Fig 17.3, Fig 17.4, Fig 17.5).

It then suggests that bottles be half filled with grounds of wine or beer mixed with sweepings of sugar, honey, or grounds of treacle.

Fig 17.3 Fly Trap. Flies entered from the bottom and were unable to get out.

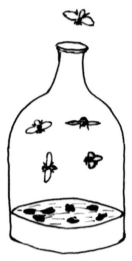

Fig 17.4 Fly Trap. Flies were attracted by the sweetened fluid and once in the bottle were more likely to finish up in the fluid rather than escape.

Fig 17.5 Fly Flap. Butchers were advised not to kill flies on the meat.

LIVE ANIMALS AS MEAT RESERVES AND AS A MEANS OF TRANSPORTING MEAT

A standard way of conserving meat from earliest times was to keep the animals alive until needed. The problem in the winter months was the shortage of winter feed. This situation was considerably improved by the introduction of turnip feeding in the 18th century. The establishment of the medieval deer parks after the Norman conquest was to provide a reserve of meat for the castles and manorial establishments. They were not parks as we know them today but enclosed areas of land. To retain the animals, especially the deer, it was usual to dig a ditch around the park, piling the earth from the ditch to create a bank outside the ditch and then place a fence or wall on the top of the bank. These parks contained cattle as well as deer and were an important source of fresh meat during the winter months. As all deer belonged to the crown the local lords needed a licence from the King to keep deer in their parks for their own meat supply. The parks were a source of meat for great feasts at religious festivals. An order went out from Henry III to Robert de Maris, custodian of the King's park at Moulton, to take 20 does and deliver them to the Sheriff of Northampton who was to take them to Westminster for the feast of St. Edward.

Herds of cattle were of logistical value to armies, providing milk and meat for the troops as well as leather and tallow. Problems could arise with an army 'on the march' if adequate grazing was not available, which would mean acquiring fodder to feed the animals. Droving live animals across the country was the only practical way to supply the large towns and cities with adequate quantities of meat before the advent of refrigeration and of bulk transportation over long distances (e.g. by rail). Until the 18th century few reasonable roads existed and most travelling was along tracts which were not generally suitable for wheeled vehicles. The drove roads where broad tracts of the countryside used by the cattle and sheep drovers. There was a regular trade in cattle and sheep from Wales to England at least from the time of the Norman conquest. Welsh cattle were bought up and driven to Southampton to supply the army during the 100 years war (1337-1453). The droving of Scottish cattle into England built up during the 17th century with an estimated 15,000 animals per annum crossing the border in the mid 1600s rising to 100,000 by the end of the 18th century.

The first shipments of meat from abroad were in the form of live animals. There had been the importation of cattle from Ireland over the years but with the freeing of trade in 1842, imports of cattle, sheep and pigs from Europe began. The trade in meat animals from North America began in the 1870s. The importation of live animals declined after refrigerated shipments were successfully established, bringing chilled and frozen meat to Britain at a lower cost than shipping live animals. Some shipments of livestock continued, particularly cattle from North America, because the premium in the price paid for fresh killed meat compensated for the higher shipping costs. The live cattle shipments from Ireland continued well into the 20th century before giving way to the shipment of dressed carcases.

PRESERVATIVES USED FOR MEAT

The following are a range of preservatives recommended in '*The Experienced Butcher*' 1816:

> Chamomile flowers, Virginian snake-root, pepper, ginger, saffron, contraycrva root and galls were all rated as being twelve times more antiseptic than sea salt.

Infusions of mint, angelica, ground ivy, green tea, red roses, common wormwood, mustard, horseradish and decoctions of poppy heads were also claimed to be more effective than sea salt.

Decoctions of wheat, barley and other grains, checked putrefaction by becoming sour.

A patent was granted to a Mr John Donaldson in 1793 for a preservative consisting of wheat or barley meal mixed with a solution of common gum and baked in a moderate oven; this mixture was then ground into a powder which could be used to cover meat to keep it "free from corruption, for any length of time".

Saffron Hill, close to Smithfield Market, was given its name because of the large numbers of autumn flowering crocuses grown there from which saffron is produced. This production of saffron probably started in the 14th century and although saffron is effective as a preservative its reputation was mainly as a means of masking tainted meat.

Chemical preservatives were used for preserving meat until the 20th century when most of them were banned. Sir John Pringle, physician to King George III and president of the Royal Society, carried out some experiments in the 18th century to determine the effect of certain substances to promote or prevent putrefaction. He established that one drachm (one eighth of an ounce) of sea salt in two ounces of water retarded putrefaction of two drachms of beef for over 30 hours, compared with two drachms of beef in water without salt putrefying in 14 hours; both samples were held at 90° Fahrenheit. Sir John used this level of salt as his standard against which he compared other substances. Alum, which was used to preserve meat, was rated as 30 times more effective than sea salt by Sir John. Borax was rated by Sir John as twelve times more effective than sea salt.

Borax and boric acid were used extensively as preservatives in meat products up until the first part of the 20th century. Recipes for brines generally included dry antiseptic (preservative) which consisted of boric acid or borax or a mixture of the two, e.g. recipe for making a 20 gallon brine for pickling meat (Leighton & Douglas 1910):

    55lb of salt
    5lb of saltpetre
    5lb of sugar
    5lb of dry antiseptic

Sausage recipes in the 19th and early 20th century often included preservative in the form of dry antiseptic (borax/boric acid) usually between 0.4% - 0.5% of the finished sausages. In some cases the preservative recommended was bi-sulphite of lime at the rate of one wine glass full to about 40 lb of sausages. Bi-sulphite of lime was also recommended for use on fresh meat and bacon for sponging over the surfaces. The active ingredient of bi-sulphite of lime is sulphurous acid, the same as the active ingredient of sulphur dioxide.

In the closing years of the 19th century there was considerable debate regarding the effect of borax and boric acid on consumers. A number of European countries had banned their use as food preservatives. In the UK, the Sale of Food and Drugs Act, 1875, section 3 states "No person shall mix, colour, stain or powder ... any article of food with any ingredient or material so as to render the article injurious to health ..." (first offence - maximum fine £50; subsequent offences - up to six months imprisonment with hard labour). This differed from the 1872 Act which prohibited the use of any substance that in itself was injurious to health. These acts resulted in some of the substances used as preservatives being banned but borax and boracic acid continued to be used on the grounds that they did not render food injurious to health and it was argued that these preservatives protected the consumer from the dangers of ptomaine poisoning and other dangers from the consumption of food that had undergone a degree of decomposition. A Royal Commission was appointed to investigate the use of preservatives in 1899 and their report contained the following statement:

> "After very carefully weighing the evidence, we have come to the conclusion that, as regards the trade of fresh and cured meat, fish, butter, margarine and other food substances, in the consumption of which but small quantities of the antiseptic are taken into the system, there exists no sufficient reason for interfering to prevent the use of boron preservatives."

The use of borax and boric acid as a preservative in meat products continued until January 1927 when the Public Health (Preservatives Etc., in Food) Regulations 1925 came into force.

DRYING AND SALTING MEAT

The two oldest methods of preserving meat still in use are drying and salting. Cured and dried meats were being eaten before 1000 BC; in Egypt, fish was being dried and salted for export to Syria and small birds were pickled in brine. In many cases preservation was due to a combination of both salting and drying.

The usual method for drying meat was to cut the meat into strips, which were then hung to dry in the sun; a method used by the North American Indians to produce pemmican. Sun-dried meat was produced in South America. In Uruguay it was known as 'jerked beef' or 'tasajo' and in Brazil and Chile as 'Charque'. Biltong produced in South Africa was meat lightly salted after cutting into strips and then sun-dried (Lawrie, 1998). An alternative to sun-drying methods was drying strips of meat over a wood fire which imparted the smoked flavour into the meat. Some cured products such as hams were hung in the kitchens to be dried by the fire. Where cured products such as bacon were smoked after curing, the surface drying resulting from the smoking would have further increased their storage life and in addition the smoke would have contained substances such as phenols that had bactericidal properties.

Salting or curing meat was the most widely used method of preservation before the advent of mechanical refrigeration. Salt has always been an important commodity, in general because it has a marked effect in improving the palatability of food, especially those foods that are bland to the taste. The use of salt for its other function, the preservation of meat, increased considerably from the ancient civilisations through to the 19th century. Roman soldiers received a regular salarium or salt ration from which we have the word 'salary'. Salt along with spices was one of the major trading commodities of the early merchants. The Venetian merchants built up much of their trading supremacy in the 14th and 15th centuries trading in salt. The medieval trade in Britain was conducted by salters. The London Guild of Salters is an ancient guild, being one of the 'twelve great companies'. Salt was obtained by evaporating sea water or the water from brine pools. The other source was rock salt from the salt deposits found in some areas. There were also importations of salt from the Continent, especially from the La Rochelle area in France. Cheshire has been a major centre for the production of salt, dating back to the Roman occupation. This salt was obtained by boiling brine from the brine pits in the area. The discovery of rock salt near Northwich, Cheshire, in 1670 increased the importance of this area as a source of salt supplies in Britain. Pack horses laden with salt would journey along the 'salt ways' which were the regular routes taken by the salters to the towns and cities or other centres where there was a demand. In 1338, Edward III bought 100 oxen to feed his army plus 10 quarters of salt to preserve the meat (Watson, 1963).

Salting meat was one of the main methods of laying in stores for the winter. Pork became the most popular meat for curing and the term 'bacon' has been used to refer to cured pork for centuries.

Shakespeare, in Henry IV Part I, refers to two carriers in a Rochester inn yard having "a gammon of bacon and two razes of ginger to be delivered as far as Charing-cross". John Pynkard was punished in 1517 for having sold four flitches of stinking bacon, by having to ride upon his mare from Newgate to Leadenhall with two of the flitches fastened on him with a notice on his head which read, "For puttyng to sale of mesell of stynkying bacon" (Jones, 1976).

The Autumn kill of animals and the salting of their flesh was a standard practice in the temperate areas through the medieval period until the 19th century. A medieval book of occupations throughout the year has an illustration for 'November' showing the slaughter of cattle and similarly a 17th century almanac's illustration for November shows the slaughtering of pigs and cattle (Wilson, 1991). Hanging bacon and hams in close proximity to the fire after salting was a common practice, drying the surface and increasing the keeping quality. An inventory taken on 4th June 1639 of the goods and chattels of John Totty, husbandman, (deceased) of Caldey in the County of Chester included two flitches of bacon valued at 13 shillings. This confirms the fact that bacon and hams were stored throughout the year, including the summer months. While the aristocracy could supplement their winter diet with fresh meat from their parks and dovecotes, the poor would have little in the way of meat except for the occasional piece of bacon or dry sausage.

The method of storing meat by chopping it fairly fine, salting and then filling into cleaned intestines was practised in the early civilisations. Ancient Greek writers referred to salami and it is thought that the name salami is from the Greek city Salamis which was destroyed in 449 BC. The word sausage is from the latin salsus meaning salted (i.e.salted meat).

By the time of ancient Rome the curing of hams was well established with Southern Gaul being noted for its high quality hams which were exported to other parts of the Roman Empire. Many of the traditional hams began as a means of conserving meat for the winter months. The reasons for curing to be concentrated in the autumn were two-fold: firstly there were more plentiful supplies of suitable livestock that had fed well during the summer: secondly the temperature during late October and November was more appropriate than the earlier months. The ideal temperature for curing is 40°-50°F (4.4°-10°C); at lower temperatures the curing process is much slower and at higher temperatures spoilage of the meat will occur before curing is complete. York hams and Bradenham hams take five to six months to cure and mature, and can be held in cool non-refrigerated store rooms for several weeks and still be in a perfectly good condition. Traditional hams were generally dry salt cured. Salted meat normally had an unappetising grey colour but some farmers using brines for curing made from well water which contained nitrites; the effect of these nitrites was to give the meat the attractive pink colour associated with modern bacon. Curing recipes from the Middle Ages onwards include saltpetre or petresalt added to brines and dry curing mixtures so that the nitrate was reduced to nitrite by bacterial action, thereby producing the pink colour of the meat.

Apart from the benefits of the improved colour, nitrite is itself a preservative, inhibiting the growth of many bacteria. Sugar was also added to some of the curing recipes. The properties of sugar as a preservative are contained in '*The Experienced Butcher*':

> "Sugar is one of the most effectual means of preventing putrefaction, which arises from its great tendency to run into what is called the vinous fermentation, or the fermentation which wine undergoes. Hence sugar is used with salt in curing hams."

Among the substances tested by Sir John Pringle in the 18th century for its preservative effect compared with sea salt was sal-gem or rock salt which he rated slightly higher than sea salt. He rated nitre or saltpetre at more than four times sea salt as a preservative.

Bacon had throughout the medieval period been an important reserve of meat, especially for the winter months. It had been very much a local product with farmers, cottagers, etc., who prepared and cured their own bacon and hung it in the chimneys or in the kitchens in a position where it would be dried by the fire and remain hanging in the chimney until needed. Gilbert White, in his '*Natural History of Selborne*' (1789) writes of the notion of some people that bats came down the chimney during the night and gnawed the bacon. During the latter part of the 1700s the growth of the industrial towns resulting from the Industrial Revolution caused a considerable increase in the demand for bacon and pickled pork, especially among the poorer classes. This galvanised the entrepreneurial farmers and other business men into organising the production of bacon and pickled pork on a large scale and shipping it to the town markets. One such entrepreneur was Robert Henderson, a farmer of Dumfriesshire. He began by curing as many as 500 carcases and then distributing the flitches and hams around the farmhouses and cottages in the area where they would be hung in the kitchens to dry and remain until Henderson had orders to fulfil. An account of this was given by Robert Henderson in 'A Treatise on the Breeding of Swine and the Curing of Bacon', 1814:

> "I practised for many years the custom of carting my flitches and hams through the country, to farmhouses, and used to hang them in their chimneys and other parts of the house to dry, some seasons to the amount of five hundred carcases. This plan I soon found was attended with a number of inconveniences, as I had to take along with the bacon pieces of timber to fix up in the different houses, for the purpose of hanging the flitches and hams. For several days after they were hung up, they poured down salt and brine upon the women's caps, and now and then a ham would fall down and break a spinning-wheel or knock down some of the children, which obliged me to purchase a few ribbons, tobacco, &c., to make up peace. But there was a still greater disadvantage attending this mode: the bacon was obliged to hang until an order came for it to be sent off, which being at the end of two or three months and often longer, the meat was over-dried in most places, and consequently lost a good deal of weight."

Because of the difficulties and work involved in this distribution and subsequent collection of the bacon and hams, Henderson built himself a smoke-house so that he could dry the bacon and hams over smouldering sawdust as and when required to meet orders. It would seem that smouldering sawdust was used initially to dry the bacon and hams because of the low controlled heat that was not possible with wood fires. It was soon understood that different types of sawdust imparted different flavours to the bacon or ham. According to Henderson, Dumfriesshire had become a major supplier of bacon and ham to the London market by the end of the 1700s. In 1760 there were few pigs in the county but numbers increased markedly by 1770. Likewise there were very few bacon curers in 1770 but by the end of the century the curing of fliches and hams had become a major industry which was mainly concentrated in the Annandale area. This industry was supported by numerous jobbers (dealers) attending markets over a wide area and visiting farms where pigs were bred, to obtain large numbers of shots (6 - 8 month old pigs) for feeding on to about 12 - 15 months on Dumfriesshire farms.

Fig 17.6 Pickle Pump with a circular wooden pickle tank, fitted with a large copper air vessel and gauge. Capacity 40 gallons (Douglas, 1905).

Several companies in Inverness and Cromartie were engaged in the supply of pickled pork to London. The pork was cut into pieces and packed into kits (wooden tubs which held 1 - 2 cwt) and covered with a brine (Henderson, 1814).

In England the organisation of a bacon industry was taking place. In the 1700s Welsh pigs were being driven to Wiltshire for fattening and finishing and many of these would have been turned into bacon. Edward Lysle in his *'Observations on Husbandry'*, 1705, states that bacon curing was prevalent in Wiltshire but not as an organised industry. This changed with an increase in curing and a more organised industry towards the end of the 1700s. In 1770 C. & T. Harris built a bacon factory at Calne, Wiltshire. They established the style of preparation of sides of bacon and the method of curing the Wiltshire side, which became a world-wide standard.

The bulk of the meat used to provision ships was heavily salted and often packed in barrels. The nature of the old wooden ships meant that everywhere on board was damp and humid so it would not have been feasible to carry the dried flitches of bacon. The Royal Navy had its own slaughterhouse in its victualling yard at Deptford from the mid 17th century and by 1800 the victualling yards at Chatham, Dover, Plymouth and Portsmouth also had slaughterhouses. After slaughtering and dressing the animals (cattle and pigs) the meat was salted and packed into barrels ready to supply the ships. During the 18th and 19th centuries the amount of salt meat required by the Royal Navy, especially in times of war, was considerable. The ration for ordinary seamen in 1808 was 6 lb of salt meat per week.

A piece of equipment called the 'Auto-cure' was demonstrated at the 1867 Paris Exhibition. It consisted of a cylinder about two metres in diameter. Meat for pickling was laid onto low trucks to enable the pieces of meat to be kept from touching and then the trucks were pushed into the cylinder. The cylinder was then closed and made air-tight and the air pumped out producing a vacuum, which was intended to open up the meat tissues. Brine was then pumped into the cylinder and the pressure raised to 120 lb per square inch to force the brine into the meat. Meat was perfectly pickled after five hours.(Schwartz, 1901)

Towards the end of the 19th century a Danish zoologist, Aug. Fjelstroop, invented a new method of pickling carcases. The method was to take the carcase of a well-bled animal and inject brine into the arteries 'from the heart outwards' (i.e. arterial pumping) (Schwartz, 1901). Littlejohn in his book "*Meat and Its Inspection*" states that Madagascar was the first country to carry out arterial pumping of a carcase for curing. The method was to insert a canular into the aorta of a pig after slaughter and scalding and to pump the brine through the arterial network into the tissues. By the middle of the 19th century pumping brine into the meat using a hollow needle with perforations along its side was widely adopted as part of the curing process.

Fig 17.7 Chill Room of an Irish bacon factory. It is evident from the picture that the average fatness of bacon was much higher than would be accepted today (Douglas, 1905).

During the latter half of the 19th century, bacon factories were establised that began to dominate the bacon curing industry. The bacon industries of Ireland and Denmark were established at this time and set up a thriving export market to England. The first Danish bacon shipped to Britain was six bales of green sides in 1847. Henry Denny developed a new method of bacon curing which resulted in the bacon from his factories at Waterford and Limerick being very popular in London.

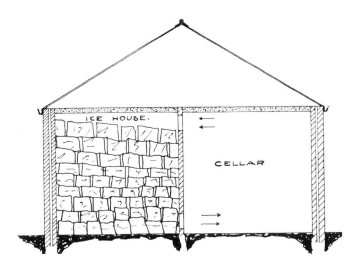

Fig 17.8 Danish Bacon Curing-Cellar cooled by blocks of ice (Leighton & Douglas, 1910).

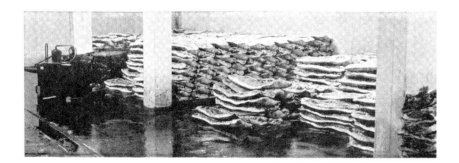

Fig 17.9 Curing Cellar in the bacon factory in Roscrea. Following the injection of brine and immersion in the brine tank for the required time, the sides of bacon were placed in the curing cellar for a few days to mature. The maturing process resulted in the cure diffusing evenly through the meat. The temperature of the curing cellar was maintained at about 41°F (5°C) (Leighton & Douglas, 1910).

CANNING

The principle of canning is the heat sterilisation of food and sealing it in air tight containers. By the 17th and 18th centuries potted meats or brawns were being produced, which apart from their culinary attraction had the advantage of keeping in good condition for a period of weeks. The basis of their extended keeping quality was that the cooked meat, therefore being sterilised, was then packed into a glass or earthenware jar and sealed in with a layer of melted clarified fat or butter. This seal of fat prevented air contact with the meat and it would have been well known that once the fat seal was broken the potted meat or brawn needed to be consumed within a short period. A jar of potted meat was regarded at the time as an ideal addition to the food carried on a long journey. There is a recipe in *"The Art of Cookery Made Plain and Easy"* by Hannah Glasse,

1747, for potted venison, recommending that it would keep for several weeks and another recipe in *"The Compleat Cook"* by Rebecca Price, 1681, for brawn, with the claim that it could keep for two or three months. Rendering and clarifying fat (including butter) was well known as a method of keeping fat for extended periods reducing the chance of rancidity (oxidation).

Preservation of fruit and vegetables, apart from drying, was by placing them in glass or earthenware jars and then sealing the jars to make them airtight (i.e. the principle of fruit bottling). Earthenware jars specifically for the purpose were made with close fitting lids which were then sealed by running melted wax in the narrow gap between the rim of the jar and the lid.

The French chef Nicolas Appert, at the end of the 18th century, used the then current knowledge of preserving potted meats or paté and the methods of preserving fruit and vegetables to develop the techniques that led to canning. Although the containers he used were glass jars, the principle was heat sterilisation of the food in the container, which caused the expulsion of all the air, followed by sealing the container. The cooling of the food caused a vacuum in the container. The same principle applies in canning today. Meat, vegetables and fruit processed by Appert's method were tried out by the French Navy in 1806; this proved very successful.

Fig 17.10 Labelling Department in a canned meat export factory in Queensland, Australia (Leighton & Douglas, 1910).

The early British pioneers of canning were John Hall and Brian Donkin who used iron containers instead of glass. The British Navy began using canned foods from 1810 and Arctic explorers found them valuable. In 1839 cans made of thin steel were used but problems arose due to rusting and the reaction between the metal and the contents. These problems were overcome by covering the steel with a thin layer of tin-plate; hence the tin can which gave rise to the products being called either tinned food (tinned meat) or canned food (canned meat). Mr Goldner, a Hungarian Jew, contracted to supply the British navy with canned meat from his canning plant in Britain but the high cost of local livestock persuaded him to set up a canning plant in Galatz on the Danube in 1842. Meat produced from the large herds of cattle that grazed the plains of Moldavia was well in excess of the needs of the local markets. The price of the hides and horns exported to Constantinople

Fig 17.11 Soldering Cans in a canned meat export factory (Leighton & Douglas, 1910).

covered the value of the animals, leaving Mr Goldner with low cost raw materials for his canning operation. Mr Goldner continued to supply the British Navy with canned meat from this factory until 1846 when the contents of some of the cans from consignments were found to contain rotten meat, or in some cases offals instead of carcase meat; this led to a scandal and the cancellation of the contract (Perren, 1978). Canning, as with curing, began as a means of preserving or transporting meat over long distances but there came the development of a range of specialised canned products such as corned beef and luncheon meat, which found a market as a specialist product.

REFRIGERATION

The value of low temperature for the preservation of meat has long been appreciated. Meat remaining in good condition for longer periods in colder weather is a known fact that is stated or implied in recommendations for storing meat, contained in various documents from antiquity, and similarly is implied in the statutes allowing more time to sell meat in winter than in summer.

The following is an account given in '*The Experienced Butcher*':

"What is called the freezing temperature, or that state of the air at which frost begins, namely, at 32 degrees on the scale of Fahrenheit's thermometer, it is a complete preservative from putrefaction, as long as the animal substance is exposed to it. Hence the common practice of keeping meat in snow, in the frozen climates of the North; and of packing fish in ice, and sending them in that state from Scotland to the London market. There is annually at St Petersburg, what is called the Winter or Frozen Market, for the sale of frozen provisions. In a vast open square, the bodies of many thousand animals are seen on all sides, piled in heaps like pyramids: oxen, sheep, hogs, fowls, butter, eggs, fish, all stiffened into granite (Fig 17.12). The fish are attractively beautiful, possessing the vividness of their living colour, with the transparent clearness of wax imitations. Most of the larger sort of beasts being skinned, and classed according to their species: groups of many hundreds are seen piled upon their hind legs, one against another, as if each were making an effort to climb over the back of his neighbour. ... Their hardness, too, is so extreme, that the natives chop them up for the purchasers like wood. ... In consequence of the multitude of these commodities, and the short period allowed to the existence of the market, they are cheaper than any other period of the year; and are, therefore, bought in large quantities, to be laid up as winter stock. When deposited in cellars, they keep for a length of time."

Fig 17.12 Open-air Christmas Frozen Meat Market in Russia. The description given by '*The Experienced Butcher*' of the St Petersburg Market of about 1800 is virtually identical to the picture (Leighton & Douglas, 1910).

This was a description of the Winter Market in St Petersburg, Russia, about 1800 but this Frozen Market had been in existence long before this time. Sir Humphry Davy's '*Elements of Agricultural Chemistry*' published at the beginning of the 19th century states:

"The antiputrescent quality of cold climates is fully illustrated in the instances of the rhinoceros and mammoth lately found, in Siberia, entire beneath the frozen soil, in which they must probably have existed from the time of the deluge."

The death of Francis Bacon was said to be the result of contracting pneumonia while stuffing a chicken with snow to preserve it.

Apart from the exploitation of low climatic temperatures in the colder regions, ice has been used for cooling food stores for centuries. As long ago as 600 BC the Chinese were collecting large quantities of ice from frozen rivers in the winter and storing it in underground chambers. This ice was then used during the summer. Also in Europe natural ice was often collected from rivers and lakes in the winter and stored for use in the summer. The ice put into the ice house was usually in pieces and in some cases snow was included, but as the bulk increased it compacted into a solid mass. The storage of the ice was in a large bulk which because of its mass, coupled with the thermal requirement of latent heat, was very slow to melt. This ice was stored in caverns or heavily thatched buildings to insulate it from the summer heat.

Mansions and the large houses of the wealthy were being equipped with icehouses increasingly in the late 18th century and 19th century. The incentive to build icehouses was primarily for the luxury of having ice for cooling drinks in the summer or for making ice cream, sorbets, etc. The fashion for having icehouses probably resulted from the upper classes going on the grand tour. The basic design of these country house icehouses was a conical shaped ice cellar built underground with an insulated top, usually conically shaped, and an entrance passage with at least two doors to prevent too much ingress of warm air (Fig 17.13). The capacity of these ice-wells was, in some cases, more than 30 tons but was usually between 15 and 25 tons (Buxbaum, 1992). William Cobbett published in 1822 instructions aimed at the small farmer for constructing an icehouse using a timber frame, straw walls and roof. The walls were suggested to be four feet thick and the roof a straw thatch also four feet thick (Cobbett, 1822).

Early in the 19th century there was the realisation of the potential of icehouses for keeping food fresh, either by storing food in the icehouse or using ice to pack around food. An early use of ice in this respect was to keep fish fresh. Salmon transported from Scotland in the early 19th century was kept in a fresh condition by being packed in ice. In 1819 John Papworth, an architect, stated;

> "The icehouse forms an excellent larder for the preservation of every kind of food liable to be injured by heat in the summer; thus fish, game, poultry, butter, etc., may be kept for a considerable time, indeed in London they are used for such purposes who deal largely in either fish or venison; and for the table, where coolness is desirable, the use of ice in the summer is a great luxury."(Buxbaum, 1992)

A drawing by J. E. L. Calger, 1967, of an ice-well in the Royal Military Repository Grounds at Woolwich shows a room used as a cold store connected to the entrance to the ice-well (Fig 17.14). Often boards were placed on the ice in the ice-well and food stored on these boards or meat, game or poultry was hung above the ice.

The supply of natural ice became a big business during the 19th century in the USA with millions of tons of ice being collected in the winter and stored in insulated buildings. In view of the demand for ice for refrigeration, the Wenham Lake Ice Company of America began shipping consignments of natural ice to Britain during the 1840s. It was soon discovered that natural ice could be obtained at a lower cost from Norway. Shipments of natural ice to Britain increased during the latter part of the 19th century, mainly from Scandinavia; the total imported in 1865 was 38,605 tons which rose to a peak of half a million tons in 1889. Thereafter the imports declined. The demand for ice was a major incentive for the development of ice making machines to supplant natural ice for refrigeration.

Ice was commonly used for cooling the bacon curing-cellars to avoid spoilage of the meat during curing in the warmer months of the year. (Although called cellars they were often buildings above the ground.) The Swedish and Danish curing-cellars had the benefit of a more readily available supply of natural ice. They generally consisted of two large rooms of equal size; one filled with ice and the adjacent room for curing bacon. Grills were fitted in the partition wall to facilitate the flow of cold air from the ice. Large stacks of ice, covered with sawdust for insulation, were held in the yards of the bacon factories to replenish the ice in the curing-cellars.

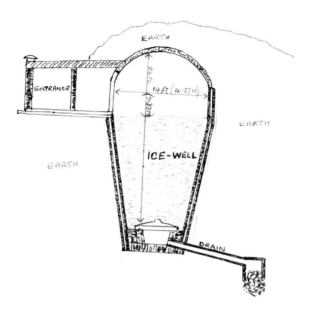

Fig 17.13 A Drawing showing the cross-section of a typical ice-well based on one at Chistlehurst, Kent (Calger, 1966).

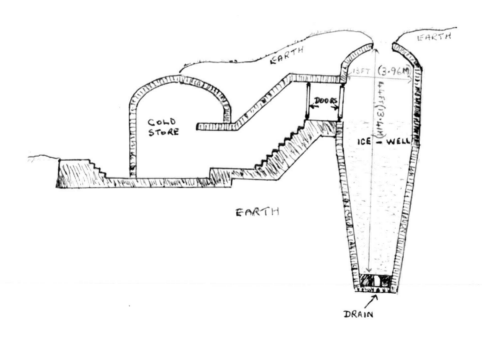

Fig 17.14 Cross-section drawing of an ice-well and cold store (or ice-house) in the Royal Military Repository Grounds, Woolwich (Calger, 1967).

Ice was used to maintain a chill temperature throughout the voyage of the first shipments of chilled meat from North America to Britain. The problem with the use of ice for refrigeration was the bulk required, and the space it occupied could equal the storage space for meat; a disadvantage, especially with regard to shipping. The first cold stores for retail butchers were cooled by ice and began to appear in butchers' shops in the latter part of the 19th century (Fig 17.15). They were similar to the modern butcher's cold store, although generally smaller, with a separate compartment high up on one side of the chamber to contain the ice. There were pipes to drain the water from the melting ice, usually into a pail. Very often the cold store was built into a cellar beneath the shop, with a pulley to bring the meat up through a trap door. Regular deliveries of ice were made to butchers' shops to enable chill temperatures to be maintained. The temperature range of ice chilled cold rooms was about 40°-44°F (4.4°-6.7°C).

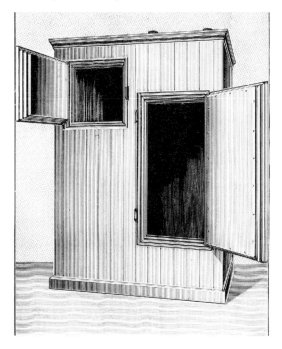

Fig 17.15 Retail Butcher's Cold Chamber or ice box. Ice was placed in a wrought iron and galvanised cage through the small door on the left. As the ice melted it was collected in a drip tray and run off by a trapped pipe to an outside drain (Douglas, 1905).

There was a practice of adding salt to ice to lower the temperature. When an ice-well was being filled a brine was sometimes sprinkled over the ice. Brands Encyclopaedia, 1847, contained a recipe for a freezing mixture consisting of five parts ammonium chloride and five parts potassium nitrate disolved in sixteen parts water which would result in a fall in temperature from 50°F (10°C) to 10°F (-12.2°C). In 1755 William Cullen demonstrated at Glasgow University the process of lowering the temperature by evaporating liquids (Ibid).

An 18th century set of recipes contains one for making ice. The method is to half fill a metal vase with water and gently add an equal amount of ether. By pumping out the air from the flask the ether will evaporate turning the water into ice (Bloom).

The substantial rise in the use of ice for refrigeration in the first half of 19th century resulted in the trade for natural ice becoming big business. This created a considerable incentive for the scientists and engineers to invent a machine that would freeze water so that ice could be continuously produced. Such a machine would eliminate the need for long term storage and transporting the ice over long distances from glaciers to the towns and cities. Once the inventors had achieved their goal and ice making machines became a reality, it was a short step to utilising these machines for direct use in refrigeration (Fig 17.16).

Fig 17.16 Refrigeration Installation for a butcher. Note the extensive equipment necessary for refrigerating a small chamber and the ice covered pipe running from the compressor to the top of the cold chamber. There were very few mechanical cold stores in retail butchers' establishments before the first world war (Douglas, 1905).

It is clear that before the advent of mechanical refrigeration people engaged in the meat trade were well aware of the value of low temperatures for improving the storage life of meat and the importance of freezing for long term storage of meat. It follows therefore that the pioneers of mechanical refrigeration understood the end result that they were trying to achieve. To accomplish this they had to develop a technology for lowering temperatures in a meat store. The changes in the 19th century affecting populations and wealth, largely the result of the industrial revolution, provided the need (and the promise of rich rewards) for improved methods for storing and transporting meat. The state of science and technology by this time made it possible for the pioneers of mechanical refrigeration to succeed.

The work of Antoine Lavoisier and Michael Faraday on the liquefaction of gasses was the basis of experiments that led to mechanical refrigeration. The first patent for refrigeration was taken out in 1819 by Salmon & Warrell and 137 patents for refrigeration had been registered by 1876. In 1834 Joseph Perkins took out an English patent that embodied the principles of the refrigeration compressor. In France in the 1850s, M Carré produced refrigeration equipment, first using ether, and then ammonia which proved successful; he patented the Carré Julien refrigeration system. James Harrison of Australia and Professor Twining of Ohio both built machines for making ice and were producing it commercially by 1855. Thomas Mort and Eugene Nicolle developed refrigeration equipment and established the first meat freezing works in Australia in 1861. The highly successful refrigeration equipment that led to the first shipments of frozen meat from Australia and New Zealand was developed by the brothers Henry and James Bell in collaboration with Mr J. J. Coleman. Bell-Coleman refrigeration equipment, a cold air system, was fitted into the Strathleven in 1879, which carried the first successful shipment of Australian frozen meat to London.

Fig 17.17 Refrigeration Installation in a bacon factory (Douglas, 1905).

The power for the first mechanical refrigeration plants was supplied by steam engines; usually the refrigeration equipment was belt driven by the steam engine (Fig 17.17). This fact, coupled with the size of operation that the early pioneers were attempting, meant that the equipment tended to be on a large scale. As with all new technologies, there were several types or systems developed as follows:

COLD-AIR SYSTEM. One of the first methods developed was the cold-air system whereby air was compressed and then cooled while in the compression chamber by water passing around the outside of the chamber (Fig 17.18). This compressed air was then ducted to the cold store where on release expanded, with the result that when the air was back to atmospheric pressure it had a much lower temperature, therefore cooling the store.

Fig 17.18 Hall's Cold Air Machine built 1886.

VACUUM SYSTEM. The refrigerants in this system were substances that were liquids at ambient temperature and normal atmospheric pressure e.g. water. The liquid was in an evaporator where the pressure was lowered by sucking out the air with a vacuum pump. At a given low pressure the liquid was forced to evaporate, absorbing the latent heat of evaporation from the air surrounding the evaporator, which was generally the cold store. This vapour was then drawn through a pipe to a condenser, which was outside the cold store, where it turned back into a liquid as the pressure returned to normal, thus releasing heat to the surrounding atmosphere. Although this system worked it was soon found to be less practical than other systems.

AMMONIA ABSORPTION SYSTEM. This system used ammonia dissolved in water which passed into a boiler where the heat was sufficient to drive off the ammonia as a gas. This gas passed to a condenser which was cooled by water and the effect of this cooling, combined with the pressure of the ammonia gas, caused the ammonia to condense into a liquid. The liquid ammonia then passed through a valve into an evaporating coil where the pressure was lower, resulting in the ammonia vaporising and absorbing heat. The heat absorbed was from the cold store. The gaseous ammonia then passed to the absorber which contained water. Because of the great affinity that water has for absorbing ammonia it had a suction effect on the gas from the evaporating coil causing a partial vacuum i.e. lower pressure.

COMPRESSION SYSTEM. This was the most successful of all and is the principle of all modern refrigeration systems. The system used refrigerant gasses which had the essential property of being a gas at ambient temperature and atmospheric pressure but which would liquefy under higher pressure (Fig 17.19). Suitable gasses were carbon-dioxide, sulphur-dioxide and ammonia. Of these, ammonia proved to be the most practical. The function of the system was a cycle commencing with the compressor increasing the pressure of the gas in the condenser coil. Under pressure the gas condensed into a liquid and the heat generated was removed by passing air or water over the condenser coil. A pressure release valve would then open to release the liquid through a pipe into an evaporator coil. As the liquid refrigerant was no longer under pressure it evaporated absorbing the latent heat of evaporation which was generally the heat from the cold store. This gas then passed to the compressor to complete the cycle.

Most of the refrigeration installations in the 19th century had indirect means for cooling the cold stores. In some cases air was cooled by the evaporator coil of the refrigerating plant and then passed through ducts to the cold stores. The most common method was to have the evaporator coil in a tank containing brine and the cooled brine was circulated by pipes to a series of pipes arranged along the wall or across the ceiling of the cold store. The circulation of the brine would function in the reverse way to a central heating system, with the cold heavier brine gravitating to the lowest pipes in the cold store and as the brine absorbed heat from the store it expanded and flowed upwards to the tank containing the condenser. A number of the installations had pumps to circulate the brine but the design of the systems were all related to the natural brine flow. Many of the cold store buildings had the refrigeration equipment sited on the roof to facilitate the natural flow of the brine. Brine circulating systems were commonly in use on ships. Calcium chloride brines were found to be more efficient than sodium chloride (common salt) brines because of a lower freezing point; 25% sodium chloride brine has a freezing point of 0°F (-17.7°C) whereas 25% calcium chloride brine's freezing point is -21.8°F (-29.9°C).

Fig 17.19 Hall's CO$_2$ Compressor.

Some seemingly strange insulating materials were used in the early pioneering days of refrigeration. For the first attempt to ship frozen meat from Australia in the sailing ship *Northam* the holds were insulated with 15 inches (38 centimetres) of tallow; tallow being in plentiful supply in Australia at the time. Sawdust was commonly used in the early days but it was found not to be very suitable, therefore other materials were tried. Cow hair that had been cleaned with acid, then washed and dried, proved to be a good insulator. Charcoal was sometimes used but had disadvantages as it was difficult to pack. By the end of the 19th century silicate cotton and cork were found to be the most useful insulating materials.

The successful development of mechanical refrigeration substantially changed the nature and organisation of the meat industry.

J & E HALL OF DARTFORD, KENT

J & E Hall was a prominent manufacturer of marine refrigeration equipment. Their development of refrigeration technology would seem to reflect the general development of the technology. Their first commercial refrigerating machine was a cold-air machine based on the cold-air machine patented by Paul Griffard in 1873. Halls were producing commercial cold-air machines through the 1880s, installing them in many meat carrying ships.

It became apparent that the compression system was much more efficient than the cold-air system because the compression system exploited the latent heat value of evaporation. Halls chose the CO$_2$ compression system which they introduced into their commercial range in 1887 which they installed into a cold store in Smithfield in 1889. The first vessel in which Halls installed a CO$_2$ compression system was the '*Highland Chief*' in 1890.

The choice of CO_2 by Halls was based on the fact that it was non-toxic but there was concern over the use of the compression gases including CO_2. A ruling by the Board of Trade required that machines using ammonia or other poisonous gases should be housed away from the engine room and passenger accommodation on ships. These problems were overcome by using the brine circulating systems. There was the added advantage with the brine circulating system that the pipes carrying the high pressure side of the compression system would only have a short run to the brine cooling tank instead of a long run to the cold store rooms.

Halls introduced ammonia refrigerating plant into their range in 1910 (Fig 17.20). In the early days of mechanical refrigeration the high cost of installations put them beyond the retail butcher. There was also the problem of need for heavy compressors to meet the pressure requirements of the ammonia or CO_2 systems (Miller, 1985).

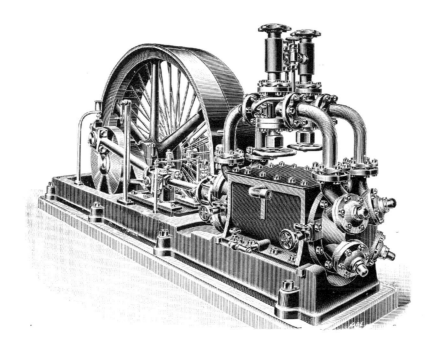

Fig 17.20 Horizontal Belt Driven Ammonia Compressor.

Chapter 18

The End of Smithfield Livestock Market and Long Distance Droving

THE CHAOS OF THE SMITHFIELD LIVESTOCK MARKET BEFORE ITS CLOSURE

Towards the end of the droving era the livestock market at Smithfield was closed. The numbers of animals entering the market at the beginning of the 19th century had increased, accentuating the problems of a livestock market in the centre of a heavily populated metropolis. Mr A.B.Robertson stated in the East London Papers (IV, No.2) that between 1734 and 1794 the numbers of animals entering Smithfield each year rose from 76,210 cattle and 514,700 sheep to 109,064 cattle and 717,990 sheep. By 1845, these numbers had risen to 222,822 cattle and 1,539,660 sheep, averaging 4,285 cattle and 29,600 sheep per week, which were marketed on Mondays and Fridays along with pigs and horses (Fig 18.1) (Thornbury 1987).

Fig 18.1 Smithfield Market Monday 11th, December 1843, before the live cattle market was moved to Islington in 1855. The numbers of well-finished long horn cattle indicate the nature of the Christmas meat trade in the middle of the 19th Century.

The way the market was perceived by the citizens of London was expressed by an article in the City Press:

> "Smithfield Market, on a rainy morning in November... was a site to be remembered by any who ventured through it. It might be called a feat of clever agility to get across Smithfield, on such a greasy muddy day, without slipping down, or being knocked over by one of the poor frightened and half-mad cattle toiling through it. The noise was deafening. The bellowing and lowing of cattle, bleating of sheep, squeaking of pigs, the shouts of the drovers and often the shrieks of some unfortunate female who had got amongst the unruly, frightened cattle could not be forgotten. The long, narrow lanes of pavement that crossed the wider part of the market, opposite the hospital, were always lined with cattle, as close together as they could stand, their heads tied to the rails on either side of the scanty pathway, when the long horns of the Spanish breeds, sticking across towards the other side, made it far from a pleasant experience for a nervous man to venture along one of these narrow lanes, albeit it was the nearest and most direct way across the open market. If it was foggy, then the glaring lights of the drover-boys' torches added to the wild confusion, whilst it did not dispel much of the gloom."

The residents of the Smithfield area also suffered from the animals being driven through the adjoining streets leading to the market the night before and through to the early hours of the morning of a market day. There would be the continuous noise of the animals accompanied by the shouts of the drovers and the barking of their dogs. Any citizen venturing out was in danger of being knocked down and gored or trampled on by some of the numerous beasts, many in a state of near panic, being hustled through the darkened streets. When residents emerged from their houses in the morning they would have to pick their way through streets covered with the dung left by the passing animals. The very unpleasant conditions caused by the Smithfield Market were made worse by the associated trades established in premises around Smithfield, such as the gut scrapers, bone boilers and fat renderers, tripe dressers, etc.

A document signed by 177 farmers and graziers, 99 salesmen and butchers and 30 inhabitants of Smithfield was presented to the Privy Council in 1809 which alleged:

> "That the ancient market place at Smithfield is much too small to contain the live cattle necessary for the supply of the immensely increased and increasing population of the metropolis and its environs; - That the cattle often bruise and lame, and sometimes trample upon and kill each other, by being confined for hours together in a crowded state in the market; and some of them are maimed and or bruised in a shocking manner by the waggons, carts, or drays driven through Smithfield during market hours; - That the buyers cannot go between or among the beasts in their very crowded state at market, to examine them, without danger of sustaining serious bodily injury."(Perren, 1978)

The conditions for stock in Smithfield Market resulted in much economic loss due to the damage and deterioration of the animals. A report in the Journal of Agriculture for July 1852 estimated the annual loss at £500,000 which was a considerable proportion of the total value of the stock sold. It was reckoned by people in the trade that a grazier who sent cattle to Smithfield would not be able to recognise them four days later (*Ibid*). Apart from the effect of the cramped conditions and lack of facilities at Smithfield, much of the damage and deterioration of stock was blamed on the Smithfield Drovers who were hired to drive the animals, usually short distances, into the market or from the market to the slaughterhouses. There were many complaints by the farmers and graziers, salesmen and butchers of the cruelty and abuse of the animals and lack of proper care by the Smithfield Drovers (see extracts from '*The Experienced Butcher*'). The Smithfield drovers were licensed by the Corporation of the City of London.

A number of efforts were made from the beginning of the 19th century to get the livestock market moved to Islington without success. The building of a market at Ball's Pond, Islington was started in 1833 by John Perkins. There was considerable opposition by the Corporation and other interests in the City but in spite of this John Perkin's livestock market opened in 1836. Most of the livestock was still going into Smithfield, so that the lack of support for the new market forced it to close shortly after it had opened.

The position of Smithfield had become so bad that a Royal Commission was set up in 1849 which recommended that the market be removed but the City of London Corporation rejected these findings, mainly due to the fact that they would lose the income from the market. Three years later in 1852, the Commissioners succeeded and the Smithfield Removal Act was passed which provided for the livestock market to be relocated at Copenhagen Fields in Islington. The new livestock market was called the Metropolitan Cattle Market and was opened on the 13th June 1855 by Prince Albert. The market flourished through the rest of the 19th century but declined during the 20th century and was closed at the end of 1963. Along side the livestock market there became established a general market called the Caledonian Market which was renowned for the bargains that could be obtained and a place where the unscrupulous disposed of stolen property.

THE LONDON MEAT MARKETS PRIOR TO SMITHFIELD MEAT MARKET

At the beginning of the 19th century, there were 15 meat markets in London. Honey Lane market built after the great fire of London was closed in 1835 and the site taken for the City of London School. The main meat markets were Newgate and Leadenhall where there was a considerable amount of wholesale meat trading which had expanded in these markets from the end of the 18th century (Fig 18.2, Fig 18.3). The growth of wholesale meat trading was due to the number of small butchers who had set up their shops and stalls in the growing metropolis and the surrounding areas but who had insufficient capital to buy live animals or the facilities to slaughter them. A number of established butchers took on the role of meat wholesalers, supplying these small butchers with carcase meat and offals. The trading pattern remained unchanged for the butchers in the rural areas and in the small country towns. These butchers having been established for many years, often for many generations, bought their animals from the local market or from local farmers. Many of the country butchers grazed their own animals, often bought as stores from the market, until they were ready for slaughter.

Leadenhall Market at the beginning of the 19th century was described as having three courts, the first of which was called the Beef Market, consisting of numerous butchers' stalls. A nuisance

Fig 18.2 Newgate Market before the opening of the Central Meat Markets (Smithfield) in 1868.

Fig 18.3 Newgate Market showing the inside of the market hall, 1860.

Fig 18.4 Leadenhall Poultry Market, 1873.

complained of here, which occurred in many of the meat markets, was the practice of butchers bringing into the market hides and skins and depositing them on the footpaths and streets. A significant proportion of the supply of meat for Newgate and Leadenhall markets in the early part of the 19th century was from animals slaughtered outside the city and brought into the markets by horse-drawn vehicles. Recommendations in '*The Experienced Butcher*' for carrying this meat were:

> "Meat which is carried into market by butchers from the country should be cleanly and carefully packed, as well to preserve it from dust and dirt, as to defend it from the frost in winter. The flats and peds in which they are put should be kept constantly cleaned, as well as the cloths, and there should be fresh cloths to lay the meat upon at market."

The increasing demand for meat in London and therefore the amount of meat passing through the meat markets, expanded considerably in the first half of the 19th century. The largest of the meat markets was Newgate, which was totally inadequate in terms of size and access to cater with the volume of trade. At the end of the Napoleonic war (1815) there were 13 meat salesmen in Newgate Market and by 1849, this number had risen to 200. A report on Newgate and Leadenhall markets by Joseph Fletcher in 1847 described them as "disgraceful to any large city of present day". Because of the inadequacy of the selling space, the slaughtering was carried out in cellars below the market, which were dark and generally in a filthy condition. Large numbers of animals were crowded into small spaces awaiting slaughter and in some of these cellars there was no provision of water, making cleaning virtually impossible. The crowded conditions made it very difficult for the butchers to slaughter, skin and eviscerate the animals, resulting in a detrimental effect on the dressed carcases (Perren, 1978).

A further investigation of Newgate Market by Joseph Gamgee in 1857 indicated that no improvement had taken place, by his following description:

> "... its smallness altogether unfits it for the enormous business of the day; while the vast number of its dark little shops, or rather holes, offers great facility to the hiding (of) bad meat, which during the day is perfectly visible and when brought out under a gas illumination on Saturday night does not show its true colours, and finds purchasers in poor and hard working population."(Perren, 1978)

The situation in Newgate and Leadenhall Markets was further exacerbated by the restrictions of cattle movements in 1866 due to cattle plague (rinderpest). Live cattle were not allowed to be brought into London, therefore supplies of beef were brought in as carcase meat, increasing the pressure on the meat markets. The amount of meat passing through Newgate in 1866 was estimated at 4,450 tons per week which was double that handled the previous year. In an attempt to meet demands, the Newgate traders employed agents in various parts of the country to buy carcase meat and send it by rail to the market. Part of the shortage of beef carcase meat from Britain was made up by imports of cattle from the Continent. Such was the congestion caused by the increase of market traffic that Newgate Street was closed to general traffic until late afternoon so that it was clear for the railway company's waggons (horse-drawn) to get through. In many cases meat remained on these waggons for several hours as there was no room in the market shops until the buyers had removed the meat sold earlier (Perren, 1978).

THE ESTABLISHMENT OF THE CENTRAL MEAT MARKETS, SMITHFIELD

In 1860, an Act of Parliament was passed enabling the Corporation of the City of London to close Newgate market and erect a new building to house the Central Meat Markets (Smithfield Meat Market). The Market was opened on 24th November 1868 and extended by the addition of the Poultry Market in 1873. Further extensions were made by additional buildings continuing from the Poultry Market to Farringdon Street in 1879 and 1899. These latter buildings were called the General Market, intended for fish, fruit, flowers and vegetables but because of the proximity of Billingsgate to the east and Covent Garden to the west, this intention did not materialise. The General Market is commonly known as 'The Village'.

The Smithfield meat market was built during a period of rapid growth of the railways (Fig 18.5). This resulted in the market being constructed with extensive space underneath for railway sidings, with the market shops and road access at ground level. This enabled carcases to be brought by rail from different parts of the country directly into the market where meat could be offloaded in these underground sidings and moved by lift into the selling area above (Fig 18.6). The approach to the railway sidings from the road was by the Rotunda situated in West Smithfield. These sidings have now been converted into a car park. In the first year of trading (1868), 120,000 tons of meat passed through the new Smithfield Meat Market, which increased to 175,000 tons by 1876.

Fig 18.5 Smithfield Meat Market (Central Meat Market) showing West Smithfield and the Rotunda which is the approach to the Railway Goods Station. Horse and cart was the main means of transporting meat from railway to market and market to butchers' shops until the coming of the motor vehicle (Critchell & Raymond, 1912).

Fig 18.6 View of the South Central Avenue inside the Smithfield Meat Market (Critchell & Raymond, 1912).

METHODS OF TRADING IN THE MARKETS

Those trading in meat in London in the early 1800s, according to the author of '*The Experienced Butcher*', fell into three categories, cow-jobbers, carcase butchers and retail butchers, and these were:

> "... cow-jobbers or salesmen who buy and sell cattle acting between the butchers and the breeders or feeders, ... carcass butchers who kill meat in great quantities, and sell it to another sort, called retail butchers, dispersed in villages, and towns near the city. ... Something like this obtains also in Paris."('*The Experienced Butcher*' 1816)[1]

The method for selling animals in the fairs and markets throughout the country was usually by a straightforward transaction between seller and buyer. It was not until the early part of the 19th century that auctioneers began to conduct auction sales of livestock .

Most of the selling in the Smithfield livestock market before its closure in 1855 was conducted by commission salesmen. It would not have been wise or expedient for farmers or graziers to come to the market themselves to sell their animals because of their lack of knowledge of the market and the amount of time they would need to spend accompanying and selling a few animals. The market salesmen would, in many cases, have arranged the collection of animals from the farms and the droving to market. A number of salesmen employed their own drovers. The salesmen knew most of the regular buyers (retail and wholesale butchers, dealers and contractors) and the type of animals they would buy. They were also well aware of market prices and generally had a good idea of probable market trends, and were therefore able to get a good deal for the farmer. The commission salesmen operated on fixed rates regardless of the prices realised for stock sold. In 1850 these rates were four shillings for cattle and six to eight pence for sheep. As a protection against underhand dealings by salesmen, there was a law that forbade salesmen in London from buying animals for themselves, but there are doubts on how well this law was enforced. The same system continued in the Metropolitan Cattle Market (Perren, 1978).

Jobbers also operated in the Smithfield livestock market. As distinct from salesmen, jobbers bought animals which they went on to sell with the object of making a profit. The jobbers visited a number of farms, buying stock which they would then sell in Smithfield. Jobbers also travelled to the livestock markets around London, such as Romford, Southall and Barnet, hoping to buy stock at a price that would enable them to sell at a profit in Smithfield (Ibid).

The collection of money and its remittance to the farmers and graziers for stock sold at Smithfield was mostly carried out by the 'money-takers'. Within the Smithfield area seven firms carried out this function. The salesmen would sell the animals from one farmer to a number of buyers and would pass on to the money-taker all the details of the buyers, the amounts and the name of the farmer. The buyers would then pay bills they owed for the animals they had bought at the money-taker's office. The money-taker would transfer the amounts to the farmer's bank, having deducted his commission. The volume of business that money-takers conducted was quite large; one money-taker in 1847 estimated that between £30,000 and £40,000 was handled by the firm each week. In many cases, apart from their market activities, money-takers also carried on the business of banking (Ibid).

---

[1] Note: Villages mentioned above were such as Battersea, Chiswick, Hampstead and Fulham.

SHARP PRACTICE BY SMITHFIELD SALESMEN

There was a report of a Court Case in the '*Edinburgh Advertiser*' June 13th 1800, relating to sharp practice by a Smithfield salesman. The plaintiff, Mr Dent, was represented by Mr Garrow, who stated to the Jury:

> "that the plaintiff's object in this action was not so much the money, as to correct a great and growing evil which has long existed, and still continues; he meant the exorbitant, and he thought he might add too, the scandalous price of butcher's meat. The plaintiff had sent 3 rams, 8 ewes and 62 lambs, to Smithfield Market, to be sold by the defendant, who was to receive the customary percentage for his trouble. From the selling prices of mutton and lamb at that time, which was in June 1799; and from the condition of his sheep, the plaintiff expected £4 a head for his rams, and they were sold for a guinea and half; 25s a head for his lambs, which were sold for 8s. Mr Garrow attributed the present high price of butcher's meat to the iniquitous practice of forestalling, which, he said, was grown to a dreadful height, and was, he feared, much increased by the salesmen, or middlemen, as they are called, purchasing great numbers of different cattle on their own account, and then selling them in large lots to the monied men. He himself, or one of the Jury, could not buy sheep at Smithfield; they were not intitled to the privileges of Smithfield Market, and cannot buy because they want but a few. A great man who steps out of his carriage in Cow-lane, pops on a great-coat, and wants 400, can have them in a moment. Thus only the very rich jobbers, and carcase butchers, get the best part of the cattle into their hands, and will not sell to the little butcher who retails it to the public, but at their own extravagant prices, and thus the public is forced to pay the shameful price they do for butcher's meat."

Mr Ersaine for the defendant, Mr House, claimed that the sheep and lambs were sold at the very highest prices given in the course of that day and produced a witness who declared he would not have bidden more than 6s a head for them; that they were in such a miserable state, that they were good for nothing but to study anatomy.

Lord Kenyon said that a great deal of mischief and injury arising to the public from the present enormous price of provisions was owing to the scandalous custom of forestalling. The Act of Parliament against forestalling had existed from the time of Edward I until a few years earlier. He said he was sorry the Act had been repealed. He considered the statement by Adam Smith in his 'Wealth of Nations' that "there were no more danger from forestalling than from witchcraft." On the basis that man was bound only by his contract, Lord Kenyon directed that the Jury could not do otherwise than find for the defendant.

TRADING IN THE MEAT MARKETS

In the Newgate and Leadenhall Markets carcase meat from animals slaughtered outside of London was sent in to be sold on commission by the meat salesmen. There were also sales by the carcase butchers or wholesalers who were selling meat from animals they had slaughtered. They either purchased live animals which they slaughtered or bought their meat as carcases. Apart from the retail butchers, the meat salesmen and wholesalers would have sold meat to the London hotels and eating houses. These were the methods of trading that continued in the Central Meat Markets.

Farmers in the grazing and feeding areas usually sold their animals in the small local markets and sometimes direct to the local butchers or dealers; the farmers receiving less for their stock than could be obtained in the main provincial markets. This would suit the farmer because he avoided the cost of getting the animals to a main market, which could take a whole day even if it only involved a small number of cattle or sheep. Dealers travelled around the local markets buying up livestock or buying directly from the farmers for the purpose of taking this stock to a main market, profiting from the higher prices they could expect to make in those markets. Some of the stock from these main markets (i.e. Norwich, Northampton, Leicester) was bought by dealers to be sent on to London. In the livestock markets in the 19th century there was a practice aimed at deception over sale prices, which was most prevalent in Ireland and Scotland. This practice involved a sale taking place in the market at above the current price and afterwards the seller would pay back to the buyer a pre-agreed sum, usually between 5% and 15%. The practice throughout Britain, which was much the same, was that of 'luck money'. 'Luck money' was a pre-agreed sum per head paid by the seller back to the buyer after the sale was completed. In 1860, for most markets in England, the standard for 'luck money' was a shilling per head for cattle and a shilling per score for sheep. From the seller's point of view, these practices might bolster the future market prices, and he could at least boast of his astuteness as a livestock seller. From the buyer's view point, especially if he was a dealer, this would enable him to use the evidence of the sale for getting a better price when he was 'selling on'. If the dealer was buying on commission, he would claim the full price of the sale plus his commission, having pocketed the 'luck money' (Perren, 1978).

TOWN DAIRIES; CULL COWS FOR THE MEAT MARKET

Through the 18th century and the first half of the 19th century, there was a considerable growth in dairies in or close to large towns and cities in order to supply the inhabitants with fresh milk and cream. The meat trade benefited from these town dairies in a number of ways. Firstly there were the cull cows which were fattened for the meat trade and were close to the town markets and slaughterhouses, cutting out the need for long distance droving. Then there was the supply of calves for the veal trade. Additionally, in a number of cases, the larger dairies also had piggeries to produce dairy fed pork. In London, a significant proportion of the dairying was in the area extending from Islington to the line of Tottenham Court Road in the west where, in 1800 approximately half of the capital's seven thousand dairy cows could be found. In Tudor times, Islington was known as 'Cow Town' and had supplied cooks with "creame for theyr custards not frothed nor thykened with floour" (Hetherington, 1987).

In 1800 dairying in Islington was dominated by two farms, one owned by Samuel Rhodes and the other by Daniel Sebbon. The Sebbon farm passed to Sebbon's stepson Richard Laycock in 1818 who developed it into a large, flourishing, well organised business. It is interesting to note that Richard Laycock's grandfather, Charles Laycock, had established a goose farm in Islington at the junction of New Road and St John Street, gaining the reputation of 'one of the greatest goose feeders in the kingdom'. Above the gateway, which was the main entrance to the dairy, was the sign 'Laycock's Dairy and Cattle Layers'. Past the coach house and stables, with adjoining saddle and harness room, there was a main avenue running west through the centre of the property. The buildings lining this main avenue were the administration block, the measuring room (for regulating the milk and cream for delivery to customers), the creameries, and the fattening house for the cows that had ceased to yield an adequate amount of milk (these cows being fattened for Smithfield) (Hetherington, 1987). The average yield of these cows was two gallons per day. The Shorthorn, or Holderness, cows were the usual preference for the town dairies and in the 1830s were generally sold to the butcher after fattening for more than the dairyman paid originally. This good price for the fattened cows gave rise to some town dairymen adopting the policy of milking the cows for one lactation fattening them and buying in replacement cows. This was not the case with Mr Laycock who preferred to keep his best cows and put them to the bull for further lactations (Youatt, 1834).

The Laycock establishment included piggeries for producing the popular dairy fed pork and a slaughterhouse nearby for the slaughter of these pigs. Part of this commercial empire included the 'Hope Inn' in Cowcross Street and the 'Porter Block' in St. John Street. These City of London inns brewed ale, and the residual grain from this brewing was used to feed the cattle. In the 1820s, Laycock built layers (accommodation) for 2000 cattle and pens for 5000 sheep, which were for holding animals for two or three days ready for the final short journey into Smithfield Market. These animals came mainly from the Midlands and the Eastern counties, many of the cattle being the black Scottish cattle that had been fattened in these areas (Hetherington, 1987). Apart from charging a shilling a night per head for the cattle, Mr Laycock claimed the milk of any cows as his perquisite (Youatt, 1834).

This type of dairy operation, though mostly less extensive, would have existed in, or in close proximity to, many other cities and towns of Britain during this period.

TOWN MADE PORK

The medieval practice of herding pigs in the forests and woodlands to feed themselves was being replaced during the 17th and 18th centuries by housing and feeding them in sties. In many parts of the country, villagers would keep one or two pigs in a sty at the back of their cottage, hence the term 'cottage pig' became common. This practice spread to the towns where the pigs consumed the waste collected by the householders and provided them with some extra income.

'Town made pork' was another source of meat supply locally within London coming from pigs kept in back yards by people living in the suburbs. This pig keeping was mainly carried on by the Irish population which had settled in London, in the Kensington and Shepherd's Bush areas. The cottage pig had been commonplace for these people in the villages of Ireland and they continued the practice of pig keeping in London. In the mid 19th century, Shepherd's Bush was known as 'the pigsty of the metropolis' (Perren, 1978).

Urban pig keeping was common in Manchester and Salford in the late 18th and early 19th centuries. The population of Manchester and Salford had a dramatic increase from 29,151 in 1773 to 257,265 in 1871 due mainly to the growth of the cotton industry. The immigration was mainly of working classes, most coming from the surrounding rural areas and, in the 19th century from Ireland.

The keeping of one or two pigs by a working class family would have contributed considerably to their meagre living when the pigs were ready for slaughter. Pigs escaping and causing damage and disturbances were a constant problem.

By the 1860s the towns were increasingly congested and the need for improving hygiene conditions became more apparent and the Urban Authority prohibited the practice of pig keeping in the backyards or even in the houses of the town. Keeping pigs in the urban areas would have been common practice for many of the towns at this time but the problem would have been less acute in the smaller, less congested, country towns (Scola, 1992).

Brewers, distillers and cider makers in the towns often kept pigs, feeding them on the grains, apple, etc., left after fermentation. In this way they obtained an extra source of income by the sale of these pigs to the local butchers. Reports indicate that while these pigs were being reared they were well contented, being in an alcoholic stupor for much of the time.

THE PEAK OF DROVING

There was an increase in the droves of cattle from about 40,000 per year middle of the 18th century to 100,000 by the end of the century according to a Scottish statistician (Haldane, 1968).

The stimulus for the droving trade was the growth of the great conurbations, especially London. Many of the inhabitants were attracted by the growing industries in these areas or were forced there by displacement from the rural areas. A significant proportion of the population of these cities were the middle classes, consisting of those members of the community who had become relatively wealthy through trade or industry. These middle-class households would have had a potential for consuming large quantities of meat. The markets supplying meat to these conurbations needed a large, constant supply of animals that was not always met by the surrounding districts.

THE FINANCIAL RESPONSIBILITY OF DROVERS

Due to the trust placed by the farmers on the drovers to pay for their animals at the end of the drove, an act of 1706 did not allow a drover to be declared bankrupt; therefore drovers could not escape the legal commitment for their debts by declaring themselves bankrupt. The price paid for cattle in Scotland and Wales by the drovers was about £3 to £6 at the end of the 18th century but it more than doubled during the Napoleonic wars. After the defeat of the French in 1815, prices of livestock and other rural products slumped (Bonser, 1970).

From the middle of the 18th century, Lowland areas of Scotland were converting to more efficient forms of agriculture. The Lowland farmers were fattening and finishing good quality cattle to supply a growing demand by the Scottish towns in the South. Although the per capita consumption of meat in the urban areas was not high, population increases were responsible for raising demand (i.e. the population of Glasgow had risen from 12,000 to 84,000 during the 18th century (Haldane, 1968).

The main, and by far the largest, of the fairs or trysts for the sale of Scottish cattle and sheep were the Falkirk Trysts which were held three times a year; August, September and October. Cattle and sheep brought by drovers to the Falkirk Tryst came from different areas of Scotland, having been obtained direct from the farmers, landowners, etc. or from other trysts or markets. Falkirk, being midway between Glasgow and Edinburgh, was ideally situated for the commencement of droves into England. The drovers could either take the route to Carlisle, through Cumberland and Lancashire travelling west of the Pennines, or down to Northumberland, through Yorkshire on the east of the Pennines. By 1800 it was estimated that 80,000 cattle per year were sold at the Falkirk trysts (Bonser, 1970).

THE SUPPORT SERVICES TO THE DROVERS

Droves of cattle usually numbered between 200 to 1000. Exceptionally, some herds were well in excess of a 1000. Less than 200 would not be very profitable. The sheep flocks from Wales could number 1500 to 2000. While the hills of Wales and the Highlands of Scotland were breeding grounds for hardy stock, their pastures were too sparse for fattening these animals, so the droving trade developed on the basis of cattle and sheep being moved to richer pastures within easy distance of the great markets. Cattle in Sutherland needed feeding to put on weight from an average of 350lbs (159kg) to 450-550lbs (204-250kg) to get them into travelling condition; these were usually four year old stots (steers) (Youatt, 1834). A large proportion of the droving was from Wales or Scotland and the North of England to the pastures of Norfolk, Suffolk or the Home Counties. These animals when fattened would make their final journey to Smithfield Market. (Bonser, 1970).

In preparation for the journey, cattle would be shod. Shoeing oxen used for the plough or cart was a common practice (Fig 18.7). The shoes were light crescent shaped pieces of metal called "cues" or "kews", two for each foot, to allow the spread of the cloven hoof, although sometimes only the outer (lateral) hoof was shod (Fig 18.8). To shoe these animals, they were thrown on their sides because cattle are unable to stand with one foot adequately raised as a horse for shoeing (Fig 18.9). While the animals were on their sides, their feet were trimmed and the shoes nailed on (Bonser, 1970).

A drove usually covered about 14 to 16 miles in a day (travelling about two miles an hour). From Wales a drove could take 20 to 25 days to get to its destination near London; from Devon the journey would take 9 to 12 days and from Scotland the drove would last several weeks. In some cases it took as long as four weeks for the Scottish droves to reach the border. The drovers were mounted on horses or ponies and one often went on ahead to arrange for a field in which the herd could spend the night, with enough grass to satisfy the animals' needs. Farmers along the route of the drove roads kept fields aside especially for the use of the drovers for a charge which might be halfpenny per head of cattle; many still bear the name Halfpenny Field. At times when grass was not available the drovers would have to buy hay or other feed for their animals, which increased costs. The men would spend the night in an inn, or in some cases in a barn (Bonser, 1970).

Apart from the cost of feed for the stock on a drove, the other major cost was the wages for the drivers and their expenses. Other costs included the shoeing of cattle, tolls at the toll gates or crossing bridges, cost of ferrying across rivers, market dues, etc. The Scottish drovers at the beginning of the 18th century received wages of about 1s per day, which rose to between 3s and 4s per day by the 19th century. From this they had to pay for their own food and lodging and had no allowance for the return journey. Scottish drovers carried their own provisions in the form of

Fig 18.7 The trevis was a structure used for shoeing oxen. The use of the trevis was recommended by Robert Bakewell and William Youatt, as the alternative to throwing the oxen and shoeing it when it was down, which was dangerous for both the oxen and the men. The trevis was more commonly used for draught oxen and the cattle for droving were generally shod by throwing as they were much lighter in weight. The trevis shown above is one photographed in France that has been preserved and renovated.

Fig 18.8 This illustrates the way the trevis was used.

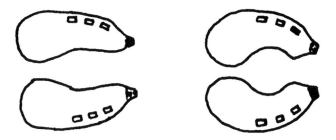

Fig 18.9 A drawing of a half-set of ox shoes. Each foot required two shoes; one for each toe (Youatt, 1834).

leather bags filled with oatmeal, rams horns filled with whisky and some onions. They would mix the oat meal with cold water to make a form of porridge and sometimes they would bleed one of the cattle and mix the blood with oatmeal and onion to produce a type of black pudding. This frugal fare was occasionally supplemented by a meal at an inn where they stopped with the drove for the night (Bonser, 1970).

Pigs were also driven to London from as far as Wales and the West Country but not in the same numbers as cattle or sheep. Drovers needed a great deal of skill and patience for driving herds of pigs these great distances. Progress was slow with a rate of about six to ten miles per day. Pigs were less suited than cattle and sheep to cross the open country and therefore needed to follow the roads or well-beaten tracks; also pigs could not swim across rivers (Bonser, 1970).

The droving of geese to the markets and fairs goes well back into history. Pliny writes about flocks of geese being driven all the way from Gaul to Rome. Geese were highly suited to droving as they tended to keep together in a main body and provided there was no sudden disturbance to scatter them they would move steadily forward in this way stopping occasionally for short rests. The geese would feed from the grass at the roadside while the drove was on the move. Large numbers of geese would be driven each year from East Anglia to the Nottingham Goose Fair. During the 18th century, turkey flocks as well as geese flocks were seen on the move from East Anglia making their way to London, many of them destined for Leadenhall Market or the east part of Cheapside which is called Poultry; this being the part of London where the poulterers plied their trade. Some of the droves of geese and turkeys would have consisted of several hundred birds (Bonser, 1970).

At the end of the 18th and beginning of the 19th century, some of the Scottish cattle being driven south would have been acquired by the graziers around the north country towns and ports, to fatten for the supply of the local populations. A large number of the cattle from these Scottish droves went to the Eastern counties for fattening on the pastures of Lincolnshire, Norfolk and Suffolk but more commonly, they would have been kept in yards or stalls and fed on root crops. Many of the Welsh cattle (known as Welsh runts due to their small size) went to the graziers of the Midlands to fatten on the Warickshire, Leicestershire and Northamptonshire pastures. As the numbers of Irish stores increased, they tended to replace the Welsh cattle in these counties. The Welsh droves that went farther east supplied the graziers of Essex, Kent and Sussex with store cattle to fatten for the London market. By this time Birmingham and the other Midland Industrial centres were competing with London for the beef produced in the Midlands. The numbers of animals constituting the droves rose during the early part of the 19th century reaching a peak in 1835.

THE END OF THE DROVING ERA

Droving became more difficult at the beginning of the 19th century with further land enclosures reducing the amount of open land over which the droves could pass. This open land had provided many droves with some free grazing. Droves were forced to follow narrow tracts or the turnpikes; the latter raising the cost of droving because of the tolls. Shipping livestock by coastal vessels from Scotland built up as an option in the 1830s. Coasters carried animals from the East Coast Scottish ports to London cutting down the time and cost to get these animals to the London market. It also enabled animals finished in East Scotland to be shipped to London which was not practical by droving.

There was some use made of canals for transporting livestock but it did not seem to be very extensive. A report in the '*Northampton Mercury*' of 1806 is as follows:

> "On the evening of Thursday, upwards of 100 live, fat sheep arrived in a boat, fitted
> up for the purpose, at Mr Horner's Paddington Wharf, from Braunston, in this county
> (a distance of 95 miles). This being the first attempt of its kind, since the opening of
> the canal."

The boat was fitted with two decks, one above the other, divided into pens. There was also the movement of Irish pigs from Liverpool to Manchester by canal. (see chapter 19).

The Liverpool and Manchester railway opened in 1830 and began carrying livestock in the early days of its existence. As the railway network built up throughout the country it was increasingly used to transport livestock, particularly for the longer distances. Droving was still preferred for shorter distances as was the case with the movement of Irish cattle and sheep from Liverpool to Manchester.

The railways progressively replaced the drovers for the movement of livestock. There was additional competition in the transport of livestock by the railways in that railways proved a practical method of transporting carcases and primal cuts of meat. This enabled animals to be slaughtered and dressed close to the area where they were fattened. By the 1840s and 1850s the railways were bringing the final demise of droving.

Chapter 19

Shipping Live Animals for Slaughter

THE NEED TO SUPPLEMENT HOME PRODUCTION WITH IMPORTS

The vagaries of the British climate resulted in failures of harvests in some years and occasional low stock numbers available for slaughter, causing severe food shortages, which in some cases led to riots. In 1879 grain was imported from the USA, which for the first time freed the population from dependence on the British harvest. Imports of cattle and sheep from the Continent and later in the 19th century from the USA and Canada, offset the shortage of home-produced slaughter stock.

In 1801 the population of Great Britain was estimated at 10,501,000 of which nearly one million lived in London. By the middle of the 19th century (1851) it had risen to an estimated 20,817,000 and by 1901 the population of the country was up to 37,000,000. Most of the increased population was concentrated in the cities and the great industrial conurbations. This increase resulted in a growing demand for meat that outstripped the home producers' ability to supply.

Shipping animals by sea has been a common feature throughout history, mainly for breeding stock. By the early 1600s store cattle were being shipped from Ireland and cattle from the Scottish Islands had to be carried by boat to the markets on the mainland. The ban on Irish cattle imposed in 1666 restricted the trade, although some illegal importations occurred. '*A Large Description of Galloway*' by the Rev. Andrew Symson published in 1682 gives an account of some Scottish cattle sent to England by Sir David Dumbar of Baldone which were mistaken for illegal Irish imports with a very unfortunate outcome:

> "Those of his own breed are very large, yea, so large, that in August, 1682, nine and fifty of that sort were seized upon in England for Irish cattell, and because the person to whom they were entrusted had not witnesses there ready at the time to swear that they were seen calved in Scotland, (although he offered to depone that he lived within a mile of the park where they were calved and reared,) they were, by sentence of Sir J. L_____ and some others, knocked on the head and killed: a very hard measure, and an act unworthy of persons of that quality and station."(Youatt, 1834)

Acts of parliament of 1765 and 1776 allowed the free import of cattle and sheep from Ireland which paved the way for an extensive trade in store cattle that was to continue until well after the Second World War. In 1776, at the Ballinasloe Fair in Ireland, 67,512 sheep and 14,110 cattle were presented for sale, many of which were bought up for export to the British mainland (Trow-Smith 1959). In the latter part of the 18th century and the early part of the 19th century the Irish cattle were shipped to the west coast of Britain, many going to Scotland whence they would join the

Scottish cattle droves down to England. A large proportion of the Irish cattle at this time was purchased for victualling the army and navy as salt beef; for this purpose a fairly mediocre quality was acceptable (Perren, 1978).

SHIPMENTS BY COASTERS FROM SCOTLAND TO LONDON

Shipment of cattle by sea from Scotland to England was apparently well established in the 17th century in that an act of the Scottish Parliament in 1663 provided for the exemption from customs dues for cattle exported by sea. The early 19th century saw the first of the steamships, which were sailing ships with steam engines fitted. By the 1830s, there were regular steamship services shipping cattle from the east and west coasts of Scotland to London and other English ports. The effect of these steamship services on the Scottish livestock trade was very significant because it cut down the time and cost of getting the cattle to their destination, compared with droving, added to which the Scottish producers were able to send finished cattle. Fat beasts, apart from being less suitable to make the journey by foot compared with lean cattle, would also have lost a great deal of weight on the drove. This gave the farmers of the Eastern counties of Scotland (particularly in Aberdeenshire) the benefit of utilising the good beef finishing potential of the area, therefore obtaining a much better profit from the London market. For the year from 31 May 1836 to 31 May 1837 there were 9,606 cattle, 6,613 sheep, 7,569 lambs and 2,162 pigs shipped from Inverness, Aberdeen, Dundee and Leith, most of which were destined for London (Perren, 1978).

IRISH CATTLE TRADE

During the Napoleonic war large numbers of Irish cattle were slaughtered in Cork to supply the British Navy, to the extent that it was estimated more than half the number of Irish cattle sold went for this purpose. As the Napoleonic Wars drew to their end more Irish cattle were available for shipment to England. In 1812, 79,285 oxen and cows were shipped to England, which according to Youatt was equal to 12½% of beef consumed in England. The number of cattle for the Irish trade showed a slight decline until 1825 when the total fell to 63,524(Youatt, 1834). Up until the 1830s, the cattle shipments from Ireland were predominantly lean stores shipped to Scotland for onward droving to England. The poor quality beasts were supplied to the contractors for victualling the army and navy. The steamship packets were taking over the shipment of the Irish cattle by 1830 and as the quicker and more reliable sailings resulted in the animals arriving more regularly and in better condition, the effect was to increase the demand for better quality finished cattle. By the 1850s there were 195,000 head of cattle shipped annually to Britain from Ireland, this figure rising to over 600,000 by the late 1870s and at the end of the 19th century there were about 280,000 fat cattle ready for slaughter and 418,000 Irish store cattle arriving each year (O'Donovan, 1940). The trade in finished Irish cattle became well established, with shipments going to the western ports, ranging from Glasgow to Bristol, the major receiving port being Liverpool. Slaughtering took place in slaughterhouses close to the ports. This trade carried on well into the 20th century with the slaughtering of Irish cattle at Birkenhead being a regular feature of the 1950s and 1960s, with a separate quote on the Smithfield price list for Birkenhead killed Irish cattle. The main Irish port engaged in the export of cattle was Dublin, with a lesser role played by the ports of Belfast, Cork, Londonderry and Waterford.

As the Irish livestock supplies increased after the Napolionic War, meat of Irish origin became a major part of the supply for Manchester and Salford. To suit the Irish trade representations were made to get the market day changed at the Cross Lane Salford market to Tuesday, which succeeded in 1861. The affect of a Tuesday market day had the advantage of enabling the Irish dealers to attend the market and get back for the Thursday markets in Ireland.

The opening of the Liverpool to Manchester railway in 1830 envisaged carrying much of the Irish livestock from Liverpool to Manchester (Fig 19.1). With regard to pigs, by the mid 1830s the numbers of Irish pigs transported was divided between the canal and the railway. By the 1840s the number of Irish pigs transported by the railway from Liverpool to Manchester rose to about 80,000 per annum.

The choice of moving the Irish pigs by rail was because pigs lose weight when driven such distances. In the case of sheep and cattle the distance did not affect the weight significantly. Droving cattle from Liverpool to Manchester would have taken two days. Droving sheep and cattle over this short distance was the preferred option; cost may have been a factor. When Irish cattle were being shipped to Holyhead and Morecombe in the 1860s, the railway network had increased to enable the cattle to be transported to Manchester by railway (Scola, 1992).

FAT CATTLE SHIPPED BY RAIL FROM SCOTLAND

By the 1780s the farmers in the southern counties of Scotland had adopted the method of feeding stock on root crops in the winter and at first the markets of Glasgow, Edinburgh and Morpeth were able to absorb the finished animals produced. It was not long before the spread of these improvements in cattle feeding resulted in the numbers of fat cattle coming onto the market in Scotland exceeding the demand. There was a period when these excess fat cattle were driven to England, even as far as London, resulting in a considerable loss of weight and deterioration in condition. The advent of the railways ended this unsatisfactory situation. The railways were somewhat later than the steamships in taking on the role of shipping livestock but by 1850 the movement of livestock by rail was becoming common. By the 1850s, the railway network extended over much of the country and there was a direct link between Aberdeen and London. Aberdeen became the centre for Scotch beef and the London demand for quality Scotch beef was to grow and be sustained up to the present day.

An effect of the railways was to give more flexibility to the dealers and livestock buyers. Southall in Middlesex, being close to London and on the main west route into London, had become a dispersal market during the droving era. Local farmers made money by buying cattle when too many arrived at the market together (resulting in a low price) and selling when the market recovered. Alternatively, the farmers could charge high rates for their grazing to drovers or dealers with cattle waiting for the next market. The coming of the Great Western Railway resulted in dealers being able to move excess stock to another market on the same day. Not only did the railway remove this economic advantage for the local farmers but because the railways were able to bring large numbers of sheep and cattle into the market on the day, the prices were averagely lower, resulting in the Middlesex farmers getting an overall lower return for their livestock.

The railways carried large numbers of Irish cattle from Liverpool from the 1860s. Irish store cattle were taken to the feeding areas of East Anglia and to the graziers of Hereford and the Midlands. The Irish fat cattle were carried to the London and Birmingham markets. Welsh store cattle were collected at Shrewsbury and from there went by rail to the Midland graziers. The Metropolitan Cattle Market at Islington became a distribution centre as well as the market for London. By 1865, an average of 5500 cattle were passing through the market each week and of this number about 20% were sent by rail to Birmingham and towns on the south coast. Large numbers of Irish pigs shipped into Liverpool were taken by rail to Manchester.

Fig 19.1 The beginning of the transportation of live animals on the railways. This drawing depicts cattle and pigs carried on the Liverpool to Manchester Railway in 1831.

SEASONAL NATURE OF SUPPLIES

There was a seasonal nature in the supply of beef cattle for the London markets in the 1830s. The major part of the supply for the early summer through to December and the Christmas trade came from the graziers of the Home Counties and the Midlands. For winter and early spring, the supplies were mainly from the stall fed cattle from the counties of eastern England, with a small number of animals coming by sea from Galloway and the counties of east Scotland (Youatt, 1834). In the early part of the 19th century supplies of mutton were available all the year round but varied in that they were plentiful from June through to the end of the year but in short supply through the winter and early spring. Lamb was most plentiful from April to June and veal from February to July (Perren, 1978).

The pattern of beef cattle supplies to the Metropolitan Cattle Market after its opening in 1855 can be seen from the following list given in the '*Journal of the Royal Agricultural Society of England*' under the title 'Statistics of Livestock and Dead Meat for Consumption in the Metropolis' by R.Herbert.

Cattle sold in the Metropolitan Cattle Market 1858:

    From Northern Counties, Jan.-Jun. 4,000
    (including the North Midlands) Jul.-Dec. 66,260

    From Eastern Counties, Jan.-Jun. 66,890
        Jul.-Dec. 6,970

Other Counties of England Jan.-Jun. 14,560
  Jul.-Dec. 13,830

Scotland, Jan.-Jun. 8,456
  Jul.-Dec. 2,674

Ireland, Jan.-Jun. 4,820
  Jul.-Dec. 13,760   (Herbert 1859-1863)

IMPORTATION OF EUROPEAN LIVESTOCK

Before 1842 restrictions resulted in the importation of livestock for slaughter being virtually non-existent. Freeing of the trade by the free trade budgets of Sir Robert Peel in 1842 paved the way for the considerable development in the international trade in livestock and meat. Britain was to become the focus of the international meat trade in the latter half of the nineteenth century. The reasons given for the need to import foreign meat were the increasing population of Britain coupled with a rise in the per capita consumption of meat and the inability of the farmers to meet this extra demand. A major constraint on the production of more cattle and sheep was the considerable rise in the amount of fodder and feed grain required to feed the increased number of horses employed on the farms and the vast number used for transport in the towns and industrial establishments (e.g. pit ponies, large numbers of horses employed by carriers, including the railway companies). The number of horses in 1811 was 1,287,000 rising to 2,112,000 by 1871. The century before had seen much of the draught work on the farms done by oxen, which were slaughtered for meat at the end of their working life. The market for horse flesh in the mid 19th century was very limited. There were some attempts to encourage the eating of horse meat with little success (Perren 1978).

The level of imports began modestly with 4,264 cattle, 644 sheep and 410 pigs in 1842 rising to peeks of over 1,000,000 sheep per year in the 1880s and 500,000 cattle per year in the 1890s. Until the 1870s, all the imports of meat animals were from Europe. During the 1870s imports of cattle and sheep from the USA and Canada commenced and were to replace the European imports by the close of the 19th century. The reader is reminded that whenever the term foreign is used it does not include Irish livestock or meat imports.

The imports of livestock from Europe entered mainly through the London and the East coast ports of Newcastle, Hartlepool, Hull, Lowestoft and Harwich. The British market attracted supplies from all over Europe and could be grouped as follows:

- Spain and Portugal
- France and Belgium
- Holland
- Denmark, Norway, Sweden and Iceland
- Germany.

A number of the railway companies invested in steamships to take full advantage of the transport opportunities. The Lowestoft Harbour and Railway Company formed the Northern Steam Packet Company to ship Danish cattle into Lowestoft and then by rail to the London Market; this being the shortest route, the cattle arrived in less time and in better condition than if the full sea journey into London was used. Denmark and Holland developed their beef production to take advantage of the British market and soon gained the reputation of supplying the best imported beef cattle. On the other hand, cattle coming from northern France were mainly very old cows or draught oxen, poorly fleshed and carrying little fat. The Spanish cattle, although having a better shape than the French cattle, did not kill out very well, producing poor carcases. The German sheep generally were considered of poor quality. The carcase weights of imported cattle were very low compared with the home produced animals but were to increase in subsequent years due to the influence of the British market. In the 1840s, carcases from imported European cattle were not more than 480 lb whereas British cattle were producing carcases of around 700 lb. By 1859 the carcase weights of the imported cattle were up to an average of 584 lb.

CONTROLS UNDER THE CONTAGIOUS DISEASES OF ANIMALS ACT

From the time that the importation of foreign livestock opened up in 1842, until the 1860s, it was a free trade with virtually no restrictions or control. Apart from the main east coast ports, animals were being landed at odd places all along the coast. The inevitable result was the introduction of diseases to the British livestock, removing the hitherto protection afforded by Britain's island situation. In 1848, a cargo of German sheep brought sheep pox into the country, which resulted in an Act that gave Port Authorities the power to inspect animals entering the country and the authorisation to destroy any suffering from disease. In 1865, the *S.S. Tonning* arrived in Hull from the Baltic port of Revel to discharge its cargo of cattle and sheep. A number of the cattle were affected with rinderpest which led to a disastrous epidemic of cattle plague, resulting in the death of a very large proportion of the British cattle herd; the losses were about a quarter of a million cattle (Perren, 1978)

The effect of this cattle plague epidemic was to force the government of the day to take some action to control the importation of livestock. The Cattle Diseases Prevention Act 1866 restricted the number of ports at which cattle could be landed and required that they be slaughtered at the port. Later, exceptions were made allowing cattle to be moved from the Port of London and from some other ports, to the London market. In 1867 an order was made requiring that these animals be detained at the port for 12 hours for inspection before being moved. Sheep were subjected to the same restrictions from 1868 because of the danger of sheep pox. There was considerable opposition to the introduction of these restrictions on the grounds of interfering with free trade, causing a rise in prices, which had an adverse effect on the availability of cheap meat for the poor people.

The importation of livestock from countries clear of disease was eased by a system of scheduling countries under the Contagious Diseases (Animals) Act, 1869. Countries where certain diseases were endemic, or where outbreaks of certain diseases occurred, would be scheduled countries and any imports of livestock coming from these countries could only be landed at specified ports and had to be slaughtered at those ports. Animals from non-scheduled countries could then enter the country through a larger number of ports and could be moved alive to the markets in different parts of the country. The importers of livestock from scheduled countries were at a commercial disadvantage in having to sell their animals at the foreign animal markets set up at the ports. This resulted in lower prices than would have been the case if the animals had been taken to other markets where the buyers were more numerous (e.g. Metropolitan Cattle Market). There was the added disadvantage in that the animals had to be slaughtered within ten days of landing; therefore if the market was over supplied the importers could not keep the animals alive with the prospect of the market improving and better prices being obtained some weeks later.

The restrictions on animals from scheduled countries led to the building of the Foreign Animals Market at Deptford, London, which was opened in 1872. Apart from the market and holding pens there was also a slaughterhouse. The nearby tanneries at Bermondsey were an outlet for the hides and skins. There had been tanneries and a leather industry at Bermondsey since the early Middle Ages. It became apparent that there was a need for cold storage for the carcases of the animals slaughtered at Deptford. This led to the construction in 1889 of a chill room with a capacity for 450 sides of beef, followed in 1891 by the provision of a second chill room for 350 sides of beef. In April 1897 there was a further increase in the cold store capacity with the opening of a large chill store for 1600 sides of beef (Leighton & Douglas, 1910).

By 1870 the trade in livestock from Europe was well established. Most of the shipping engaged in the trade was British owned. Ships varied in size with the average cargo being 400 cattle. The number of animals that could be carried depended on their size and type. Ships could carry more Dutch cattle than the long rangy German animals or the longhorn Spanish cattle. Journey times to London ranged from one day from Rotterdam to four days from Oporto. Most of the cattle imported in the late 1860s were shipped through the ports of Hamburg and Rotterdam. These ports at this time were connected by a railway network to central Europe and much of east Europe so that the imported animals could be coming from as far afield as Poland and Hungary. This close relationship of the countries of Europe and the free movement of animals across borders made them vulnerable to the spread of disease and by the end of the 1870s most of the countries of Europe, apart from Scandinavia, had become scheduled countries under the Contagious Diseases Act, resulting in the restrictions being placed on imports of their livestock. Adding to the disease problems of rinderpest and sheep pox on the Continent, there were also the outbreaks of contagious bovine pleural-pneumonia and foot and mouth disease (Perren, 1978).

Denmark began the 1870s as an exporter of grain and livestock but as the price of grain fell during the 1870s, Denmark switched to feeding grain to stock to gain a better return. By 1880 Denmark's major exports were livestock, meat and dairy products and the country had become an importer of grain. Where there was a large and constant export of livestock from a centre such as Rotterdam or Hamburg, the trade was handled by dealers/exporters who bore all the costs and made all the arrangements up to the point where the livestock was sold in the markets in Britain. Where the supply was more seasonal, such as Scandinavia, the farmers themselves carried the financial risk. Farmers of the Duchies of Schleswig and of Holstein would ship their cattle through the port of Tonning. The shipping company's agent would organise things in such a way that he would contact a number of farmers with sufficient cattle to fill one ship and arrange that the farmers turn up with their cattle on the day the ship docked. Each farmer would consign his animals to an English salesman who would meet the ship to take charge of the animals and sell them, forwarding the money to the farmer after deducting his commission (Perren, 1978).

As the bulk of the imported livestock entered London, this attracted dealers from other parts of the country. The European sheep being lighter than the home produced animals, they were more suitable for the trade in Manchester, the Midlands and Wales. Although these dealers preferred to send the sheep alive to their destinations, after the Contagious Diseases (Animals) Act 1869, they purchased the sheep in the Deptford Foreign Animals Market, had them slaughtered at Deptford and their carcases sent by rail (Perren, 1978).

IMPORTATION OF NORTH AMERICAN LIVESTOCK

The first shipments of cattle from the USA were in 1868 into Glasgow and London. These were small experimental shipments which were followed by further small consignments in 1873 and 1874 from the USA and Canada. The trade got under way in 1875 with the result that the North American trade in livestock was to take over from Europe. After the civil war, the cattle industry in the USA expanded using good quality Hereford, Shorthorn and Aberdeen Angus stock from Britain. The same was happening in Canada. Apart from the good grasslands in the USA, the Americans were exploiting the value of Indian corn or maize as a feed crop. Maize was not only used for finishing cattle but also as a basis for building up a very large pork industry.

The quality of the North American cattle was above that of the animals imported from Europe, therefore commanding a higher price and being in greater demand, especially in London. The rising demand for meat in Europe reduced the number of livestock that were surplus for export. In some cases countries, such as France, became importers of livestock, therefore competing for the animals that were available from other European countries. France had exported 21,800 sheep to Britain in 1872 but by the 1880s was importing 600,000 sheep per year, partly from her Algerian colony and partly from other European countries. The other cause of the decline in the European imports into Britain was the restriction under the Contagious Diseases (Animals) Act. By 1890 the only cattle imports allowed from Europe were from Holland, Denmark, Norway and Sweden and by the end of the decade there were no more European cattle imports. European sheep imports continued until 1908. The effect of these factors resulted in the North American imports replacing those from Europe (Fig 19.2).

Most of the North American livestock entered through the ports of London, Liverpool and Glasgow with Liverpool taking the largest share. These ports were ideally suited as they were both centres of large populations and had good rail connections with the rest of the country. At the commencement of the North American trade there were no restrictions on the animals imported as there was little evidence of disease on the other side of the Atlantic. It was not long before contagious bovine pleural-pneumonia was discovered in a shipment of cattle from the USA, resulting in the restrictions being placed on the livestock imports from the USA under the Contagious Diseases (Animals) Act 1878. The movement of Canadian cattle remained free until 1893 when they too came under the restrictions after contagious pleuro-pneumonia was discovered in a consignment of cattle from Montreal in 1892 (Perren, 1978).

The restrictions on the USA livestock required their slaughter at the port of entry which limited the number of ports that were suitable to handle the imported livestock from North America. The livestock imported into London were landed at Deptford at the Foreign Cattle Market which was built by the Corporation of London alongside the Royal Victoria Victualling Yard covering 30 acres and was opened on the 1ˢᵗ January 1872. By 1900 there were twelve lairages capable of

Fig 19.2 Cut-away drawing of a Cattle Ship. The top layer of cattle were housed in shedding built on the deck (Plimsoll, 1890).

accommodating 5,000 cattle and 22,000 sheep and 66 slaughterhouses attached to the market. As there was not sufficient draught for the ocean going ships alongside the landing jetties, the animals had to be transhipped using two smaller vessels supplied by the Corporation of London. In view of the importance attached to restricting the entry of animal diseases into the country, inspectors of the Board of Agriculture examined every animal slaughtered at Deptford and with any animal found to be diseased, its carcase and organs were consigned to the digester. Chill rooms were erected at Deptford in 1888 and extended in 1892. About two thousand people were employed in and around the market with a large number of women employed in the offal sheds, cleaning the offals and gut scraping. They were referred to locally as the 'Gut Girls'. The Foreign Cattle Market closed in 1913 with a significant affect on the local employment and economy (Leighton & Douglas, 1910; Steele, 1993).

Liverpool had for many years been the main port for landing Irish cattle imports. The earliest landing of Canadian cattle was 1876 at Birkenhead at the Woodside Landing Stage. As the imported livestock numbers increased extensive lairage sheds were built alongside the Woodside Landing Stage and further sheds alongside the Wallasey and Alfred docks. With the requirement to slaughter imported animals at the port of entry, extensive slaughtering facilities and cold stores were built. Cattle were mainly dealt with at Woodside and sheep at Wallasey. Although there was the decline in the use of the foreign livestock facilities as the North American trade declined, the Irish cattle trade continued through Birkenhead well into the 20th century.

In Scotland the main port for livestock imports was Glasgow. The Foreign Animals' Wharf was built by the Corporation in 1879. Further buildings were erected in 1886 and 1893 providing a covered lairage having three floors. There were slaughtering facilities to meet the legal requirements at the port of entry.

In view of the good quality of the American meat slaughtered at the ports, there was a good demand for it in many parts of the country. Most of the American beef from animals slaughtered at Deptford that went to the Northern and Midlands markets would have been handled by the London carcase butchers (slaughterers/meat wholesalers). Chilled meat was being shipped from the USA at the same time as the livestock trade was flourishing. It cost a great deal less to ship a carcase of beef compared with a live beast. Although with live cattle there was no cost of refrigeration involved, there was the additional cost of feeding and attention during the voyage. By shipping chilled carcases, little more than half the weight of the live animal was carried. The cost of shipping cattle from the USA in 1877 was £7 per head plus £1-10s for attendance on the voyage, giving a total of £8-10s, compared with the cost of £1-10s for a chilled beef carcase. In spite of this, the higher price obtained for the carcases of animals slaughtered at the British ports more than compensated for these extra shipping costs. As the North American trade expanded and the European trade declined Liverpool became the major livestock port, exceeding the number of animals landed at London, much to the dismay of the traders and authorities at Deptford (Perren, 1978).

Because of the good quality and bright appearance of American beef slaughtered at Deptford and Birkenhead there were numerous complaints of butchers selling this beef as English or Scotch. Various bodies, particularly those representing farmers, were pressing for legislation requiring the marking or labelling of foreign meat. The Merchandise Marks Act 1887 made it an offence to apply a false description to anything offered for sale. It therefore became an offence to label imported meat as English or Scotch.

FOREIGN LIVESTOCK IMPORTS
5-Year averages for 1842 - 1904 and yearly figures for 1905 – 1913 (Perren 1978)

CATTLE

	Europe	N. America	Total
1842-1844	3,558		3,558
1845-1849	50,756		50,756
1850-1854	97,127		97,127
1855-1859	89,695		89,695
1860-1864	138,437		138,437
1865-1869	211,150	*(88)	211,150
1870-1874	203,554	338	203,892
1875-1879	204,245	41,293	245,538
1880-1884	220,064	167,956	388,020
1885-1889	155,831	226,217	382,048
1890-1894	43,558	443,276	486,834
1895-1899	31	460,760	460,791
1900-1904		481,497	481,497
1905		563,620	563,620
1906		559,575	559,575
1907		470,213	470,213
1908		381,786	381,786
1909		319,032	319,032
1910		217,078	217,078
1911		198,056	198,056
1912		46,787	46,787
1913		11,848	11,848

SHEEP

	Europe	N. America	Total
1842-1844	1,226		1,226
1845-1849	102,630		102,630
1850-1854	203,650		203,650
1855-1859	185,594		185,594
1860-1864	371,929		371,929
1865-1869	659,153		659,153
1870-1874	801,367		801,367
1875-1879	887,035	75,718	962,753
1880-1884	879,677	132,686	1,012,363
1885-1889	817,285	61,799	879,084
1890-1894	145,896	88,927	234,823
1895-1899	44,879	328,531	373,410
1900-1904	14,163	292,463	306,626
1905	4,749	178,335	183,084
1906	4,879	98,480	103,359
1907	2,532	103069	105,601
1908	2,515	76,385	78,900
1909		8,131	8,131
1910		427	427
1911		47,673	47,673
1912		15,430	15,430
1913		501	501

PIGS

	Europe	N. America	Total
1842-1844	352		352
1845-1849	2,292		2,292
1850-1854	11,449		11,449
1855-1859	11,083		11,083
1860-1864	37,084		37,084
1865-1869	72,248		72,248
1870-1874	78,714	*(82)	78,714
1875-1879	41,027	7,781	48,808
1880-1884	28,308	4,967	33,275
1885-1889	21,908	64	21,972
1890-1894	703	1,005	1,708
1895-1899	0	154	154

Trial shipments *.

The following prices quoted on the Central Meat Markets (Smithfield) were given in the Meat Trades Journal dated April 1888 (the prices are in shillings and pence per 8lb stone):

Beef;

Scotch sides 3/10 - 4/2
English sides 3/8 - 4/-
Deptford killed USA sides 3/9 - 3/11
Liverpool killed USA sides 3/9 - 3/10
Chilled USA hindquarters 3/8 - 4/-
Chilled USA forequarters 2/6 - 2/9

Mutton;

Scotch 4/6 - 5/-
English 4/6 - 5/-
German 4/9 - 4/10
New Zealand 2/6 - 2/8
Sidney 2/6
Lambs; English 6/8 - 7/-
German 5/4 - 6/-
New Zealand 3/4 - 4/2
Pork; English 3/4 - 4/-
Dutch 3/2 - 3/6

During the last decade of the 19th century the US exporters of cattle were finding the margins narrowing and the trade becoming more hazardous. It needed a price difference of 3d to 3½d between the Chicago price and the price obtainable at Deptford or Birkenhead. Exporters had to engage shipping space in advance so that if the price difference narrowed they either shipped cattle at a loss or they would lose the cost of the shipping space. In the last few months of 1892 and the early part of 1893 most US exporters lost money. A major factor in the reduction of the margin between the Chicago prices and British prices was the growing demand for beef in the USA. These were early signs of the demise of the transatlantic livestock trade which had a tentative revival in the 1920s but was soon to end totally.

By the 1890s only seven ports had suitable quarantine and slaughtering facilities to qualify for receiving foreign livestock; these being London, Liverpool, Manchester, Glasgow, Bristol, Hull and Newcastle. All of these, except Newcastle, had made provision for cold stores for the storage of any carcases not dispatched on the day of slaughter (Perren, 1978).

Shipments of live cattle and sheep from Argentina were started in 1889. The numbers were not very significant during the period to 1894 but then increased to average 70,756 head of cattle per annum for the years 1895-1899. From 1900 there was a complete ban on livestock imports from Argentina and Uruguay because of foot and mouth disease. This ban was lifted during 1903 but only for a short period and then reimposed permanently.

CRUELTY TO LIVESTOCK BY SOME SHIPPERS

There were objectors to this transatlantic trade in livestock on the grounds of cruelty. A book entitled '*Cattle Ships*' by Samuel Plimsoll published in London in 1890 was for the sole purpose of getting the trade banned or more strictly regulated (Fig 19.3). Apart from cruelty to the animals carried on these ships the book also expounded the danger that the seamen faced when these ships were grossly overloaded and therefore liable to capsize. Under the terms of insurance for the animals carried, all attempts had to be made to get the animals to port alive and insurance companies would only pay on animals that had died of natural causes or the result of an accident. This prevented those in charge of animals at sea from putting any beast out of its misery that was suffering from disease or injury (Plimsoll, 1890).

Fig 19.3 A drawing of cattle penned in a Cattle Ship. The animals were penned facing alternate directions to get more animals on the deck (Plimsoll, 1890).

Overloading the cattle ships was practised by unscrupulous ship owners to make more money on the freight charges. The effect of overloading resulted in very bad conditions for the cattle and also led to the instability of the ships. Animals were packed in so close that they could not lie down. When one of these ships encountered heavy seas the animals were thrown heavily against each other and the deck structures, causing much bruising, broken bones and goring from the animals' horns. Sometimes a number of animals broke loose when the ship was pitching in heavy seas resulting in mayhem and considerable injury to a large number of animals. If a ship ran into storm conditions (a common occurrence in the North Atlantic) there would be a need to batten down the hatches, resulting in inadequate ventilation for the large number of animals down in the main decks. When the hatches were opened, it was often the case of finding that a number of animals were dead as a result of suffocation. 'Cattle Ships' relates the case when 200 cattle on one ship were lost in this way (Plimsoll, 1890).

To increase the space for cattle on some ships, temporary wooden structures were built on the upper deck of the ship as accommodation for extra cattle. These structures would cover the whole deck necessitating the deck hands to walk on boarding covering part of this cattle shed. This raised the working deck level above the bulwarks, making it dangerous for men working on the deck. The steamship *Erin* of the National Steamship Company, so fitted on her upper deck, sailed from New York on 28th December 1889 bound for London, carrying 527 cattle and with a crew of 74 men.

The loading was 275 on the main deck and 252 in the temporary shed on the upper deck, which was 52 more than the maximum permitted by the insurance company. The *Erin* never reached London. It was obvious that she capsized in heavy seas being top-heavy due to the weight of cattle on her top deck (Plimsoll, 1890).

The livestock exporters were proud of their expertise in selecting good stock to suit the salesmen and carcase butchers of Deptford, Birkenhead and Glasgow so they would not have been happy with the actions of some ship owners. Likewise, the butchers in Britain had the unenviable task of trying to do their best to produce saleable carcases from the animals that had suffered badly; especially as they knew they had been in prime condition about two weeks previously. One could have hardly expected any compassion by the guilty ship owners for the animals carried in their ships, taking into consideration the way they treated their seamen. When the *Erin* had been overdue for some time, some wives of the seamen on board were in very difficult financial circumstances, especially as most of them had young children. These women went to the offices of the National Steamship Company in Leadenhall Street, London, to ask for a few shillings against the wages owing to their husbands. The company's attitude was that they could do nothing until the *Erin* was posted missing. When the company did finally pay the wages to the lost seamen's wives, they only paid what was calculated due to the date that the ship was last seen, 30th December, although it was fairly certain that the vessel was lost in a gale between the 6th and 8th of January, 1890.

Although there was less publicity regarding the conditions for the Irish livestock shipped to England and Scotland, there were many complaints in the 1870s of cruelty, due to overcrowding on the ships and the treatment by the drovers when loading animals onto the ships. There were cases of severe brutality by the drovers in their endeavours to get the cattle on the ships into the cramped space available. Much of this ill-treatment would have been avoided if the shipping company had employed full time, experienced or trained drovers instead of their normal practice of engaging casual workers. In many cases the animals were not fed and watered, either at the port or on board the cattle boat and the overcrowding resulted in poor ventilation. These conditions led to a great deal of bruising and broken bones among the cattle and a considerable damage to the animals from each other's horns. Complaints about these matters were made by the dealers at Liverpool and the other ports. These complaints were later supported by the Veterinary Inspectors of the Privy Council when involved at the ports inspecting animals under the Contagious Diseases Act (Perren, 1978).

The owners of the ships were often railway companies who in the main were responsible for this inhumane treatment of the Irish cattle. They would employ agents in Ireland who were very active obtaining business and overfilling the cattle boats. This suited the owners as they were getting more in freight charges. It was often the case that a beast which would have been worth £15 was sold for as little as £12 because of the severe damage from horns. In the early 1860s, London buyers would make the journey to Liverpool to buy Irish cattle but the condition of the animals due to bruising and horn damage got so bad that they no longer matched the quality required on the London market. The dealers handling the Irish cattle could now only find outlets among the butchers of Liverpool and Manchester at lower prices (Perren, 1978).

Conditions for animals in the cattle ships improved by the 1890s due to the introduction of regulations, plus the pressure on the shipping companies from the trade which was losing money. Regulations were imposed against the upper deck loading of cattle and the general overloading of ships. There was a considerable reduction in the mortalities for cattle shipped across the Atlantic;

the figure for cattle deaths for 1892 was 0.6% of the total number of cattle carried. There were also improvements for the animals shipped from Ireland but the Irish livestock trade was less well regulated than the North Atlantic trade as it was part of the domestic trade of the United Kingdom.

Although there were few complaints against the railways carrying livestock, when the stock was carried on long journeys they were not fed and watered. The journey from Aberdeen to London took 36 hours, which was judged far too long without feeding and watering, especially as the animals had probably come straight from market for loading onto the railway waggons. It was suggested that for this journey they should be fed and watered at either Newcastle or Carlisle, depending on the route taken. Others involved in the trade were of the opinion that if the animals were fed and watered before the start and at the end of the journey they would not suffer unduly. The railway companies argued that if the animals were watered some would lie down with the risk of being trampled on by others (Perren, 1978).

Chapter 20

Trade in Carcase Meat

INTRODUCTION

For many centuries the trade in livestock for slaughter was local in nature, the farmer selling to the local butcher who slaughtered the animals and sold the meat from the same premises. There may have been instances where meat was taken from the place of slaughter to a nearby market and usually the transport of meat would only have been over short distances. Armies on the march were accompanied by herds of cattle and flocks of sheep to supply them with meat.

VICTUALLING SHIPS OF THE BRITISH NAVY

Although ships also carried livestock as a food supply, salt meat was the main source of meat for the early mariners. The usual practice was to salt the meat and pack it in barrels for transportation and storage. Salt beef and pork for the Navy during the 17th century was mainly supplied by contractors, the season for salting being from September to March. The cattle were supplied mostly from Scotland, Wales and North West England; the pigs from the Midlands, Herefordshire and Hampshire. According to the records for the administration of the Navy, 7,500,000 lb of beef and pork were supplied to the Navy in 1663, with some of the livestock being slaughtered at the Navy's own slaughterhouse at Deptford.

The supply system became so unsatisfactory because of abuses during the war against France (1689-1697) that responsibility for the supplies for the Navy was taken over by the Commissioners of Victualling. They bought the meat and had facilities for salting and storing at the Victualling Office at Tower Hill with its cutting house and pickling sheds. Supplies were sent from Tower Hill to the victualling ports; London, Dover, Portsmouth, Plymouth, Dublin and Liverpool. A well-known Secretary to the Admiralty with responsibilities for victualling, was the diarist, Samuel Pepys. The Napoleonic Wars resulted in a considerable increase in the Navy's requirement for meat which, along with the requirement for the Army, helped to raise the price of livestock. At this time large numbers of Irish cattle were used for the provision of salt beef to the Army and Navy. In 1805 an estimated 16,000 cattle were slaughtered to supply the victualling stores at Chatham, Deptford, Dover, Plymouth and Portsmouth. The victualling yards at Chatham, Deptford, Dover and Plymouth had buildings for slaughtering livestock. The meat from the animals slaughtered was salted and packed into barrels in these yards. The allowance of meat for the ordinary seaman was 4 lb of beef and 2 lb of pork per week (1808) (Bonser, 1970). The warship "*Duke of Wellington*", a screw driven war steamer with 131 guns that towered over the Baltic fleet in 1854 required stores of 20 tons (20,321 kg) of salt beef in 8 lb pieces and 20 tons (20,321 kg) of salt pork in 4 lb pieces for the ship to be ready for active service. This gives some idea of the vast amount of salt meat the Navy required during the 19th century especially in times of war (Dodd 1856).

Ships sailing from Scottish ports in the 17th and early 18th century preferred to put into an English or Irish port for their provisions of salt meat in view of the poor quality of salt beef that was produced in Scotland. The poor quality of the meat was due to the cattle presented for slaughter being thin and unfinished so that the very lean meat, when salted, was hard and unpalatable. Added to this was the fact that the only salt produced in Scotland was from sea water and this salt was unsuitable for curing as it imparted an unpleasant flavour. William Mackintosh, advocating the enclosure of land, used the argument that it would enable Scottish cattle to be finished so that the meat would be suitable after salting for the provision of merchant and navy ships. There were many complaints during the 18th century with regard to Scottish Salt Laws in that they restricted the availability of imported salt for curing, which constrained the meat industry and also the fish industry (Haldane, 1968).

SHIPMENTS OF SALTED MEAT AND BACON

Salt meat was shipped for domestic trade but the demand was generally poor. (This heavily salted meat, usually shipped in barrels, should not be confused with bacon and hams which were not so heavily salted and more palatable.) In the 1830s, the early days of steamships carrying cattle from Aberdeen to London, some shipments of carcase meat were carried in addition to the cattle. As it was a new type of venture, a number of the individuals who got involved in the trade lacked the knowledge of meat and the London market requirements. Some of the meat sent was from unfinished animals or was salted for preservation in the hot weather. For this type of meat it was difficult to find buyers on the London market.

After the freeing of the trade for foreign meat, meat imports in the form of salted and cured meat started to arrive from the USA. Some of this import came as pickled pork, the pork being immersed in brine and contained in barrels; 200 lb of meat packed into each barrel. The alternative was pork packed between layers of salt in wooden boxes. By the time this meat reached London or Liverpool, the pork was cured (i.e. bacon). The product had disadvantages on the British market in that the pork was from maize fed pigs from the US Middle West and was therefore over-fat and the period of curing had made the bacon over salty; a combination unattractive to British consumers. Due to the American Civil War, the Southern States were not available as a market for pigmeat from the North, resulting in much of this meat being diverted to Britain in the 1860s. Quantities of American bacon were re-exported from Liverpool to Ireland where, in spite of its saltiness and greasiness, it was taken up because of its low price by the many Irish people on very low incomes. The Liverpool wholesalers would ship in the high quality Irish bacon which commanded a high price on the English market (Perren, 1978). By the 1890s the USA was shipping to Britain an average annual total of 12,407 tons of salt beef (Leighton & Douglas, 1910).

Imports of salt beef and pork (including bacon and ham) came from the Continent, rising from about 4,000 tons in 1842 to an estimated 24,000 tons per annum in the 1860s. The first Danish bacon to be exported to Britain was in 1847 when 6 bales of green sides were shipped to London on board the steamship *Rattler*.[1] The major European exporter of pork meat to Britain was Germany; the German bacon trade being based largely on pigs from Shleswig-Holstein and Jutland, with curing taking place in Hamburg. Germany became noted for its lean 'Hambro' bacon in the 1880s. The first Danish co-operative factory 'Horsens' started exporting bales of bacon in 1887 and from that year Denmark took the role of the leading foreign bacon supplier to Britain. In Ireland, Henry Denny had established new methods of bacon production and was turning out good quality bacon from his factories at Waterford and Limerick for shipping to Liverpool and London. Denny's dry salted 'Star' bacon was very popular in London. In the latter part of the 19th century, the quality of Irish bacon was such that it commanded a price premium over Danish bacon. Henry Denny acquired control of the business of I.D.Koopmann, a Danish bacon producer, and introduced his own curing techniques to the Danish industry (Hogan 1978). In the latter half of the 19th century bacon became a major part of the diet of the working classes of the large towns and cities.

COUNTRY KILLED MEAT TRANSPORTED TO TOWN MARKETS

Although the general rule up until the 19th century was to slaughter meat animals in close proximity to where the meat would be sold, there were the occasions when carcase meat was transported over relatively short distances. At the beginning of the 19th century, animals were being slaughtered in the country and their carcases transported, usually on horse-drawn vehicles, to markets in the towns. '*The Experienced Butcher*', 1816, writes of country slaughtered meat which was carried into the flesh markets of London and advises on the care to be taken with the meat:

> "should be cleanly and carefully packed, as well as to preserve it from dust and dirt, as to defend it from heat in summer, and frost in winter. The flats and peds in which they are put should be constantly cleaned, as well as the cloths, and there should be fresh cloths to lay the meat upon at market. Flannel, or woollen-cloth, is frequently used to defend bodies from the warm air of summer, as well as the cold air of winter; and it might be worthy of trial, whether woollen might not be used to advantage by butchers for this purpose. Cloth, however, must, at any rate , be put next to the meat, and the woollen kept particularly clean. When butchers send calves to London in winter, they sometimes wet the cloths, especially if the meat be not very white, as they think it makes it whiter, and prevents it losing weight."

Slaughtering livestock outside London and transporting it into Leadenhall and Newgate markets in the early 1800s seemed to be fairly common, probably resulting from the rapid rise in the amount of meat required in the metropolis exceeding the slaughtering capacity in town. Estimates given to George Dodd by Mr Giblet, a meat trader of Newgate Market in the 1850s, was that three quarters of the meat coming on to the London markets was country killed (Dodd, 1856). The term 'country killed' for meat was apparently in common use in the early 1800s which would have led to the

---

[1] Note: Until the 1970s, the usual way to transport bacon was as bales consisting of four sides, meat surface against meat surface, wrapped in a large square of hessian; in the early days, canvas may have been used for wrapping. Today, most bacon is shipped in containers.

opposite, 'town killed' which carried the implication that the carcase was fresher, the animal having been slaughtered in a town slaughterhouse. The term 'town killed', abbreviated to TK, became commonly used in Smithfield meat market even when the Islington Slaughterhouse closed after the Second World War, ending the main town slaughterings, by which time TK was applied, or misapplied, to all English meat.

CARCASE MEAT CARRIED BY THE RAILWAYS

With the advent of the railways and steamships, the carriage of carcases from more distant parts of Britain took place, with sides and quarters of beef travelling from as far as Aberdeen to London. It became more practical to slaughter the cattle in Scotland and send carcases by rail to London and by 1855 this was how the bulk of beef from Aberdeen was being sent. This helped to build the reputation for the quality of Scotch beef because this journey would have given the meat at least three days to mature or age, and being non-refrigerated, the ageing process would have been most effective. In 1856 George Dodd wrote:

> "There has been an increasing tendency in recent years to send up to London country-killed meat; but nothing less than swiftness of conveyance could render such a system practicable. The meat must be fresh to command a good position in the market; and taint arising from the long continuance of a journey would exercise a most injurious influence on the price obtained." (Dodd, 1856).

Throughout the 19th century horse-drawn transport was the main means of moving goods (Fig 20.1, Fig 20.2, Fig 20.3). With the coming of railways the horse and cart was still the transport for shorter distances, including goods carried to and from the railway sidings. During transportation sides of beef were usually laid, outside down, on clean straw on a horse drawn lorry (long flat wagon). Sometimes sides were loaded onto wagons, with sides laid with their backs on straw and perched-up so that the shins and briskets were projecting upwards. In this way a larger number of sides could be carried without stacking sides on top of each other. Mutton and lamb carcases were carried hanging from an overhead structure, when possible.[2]

---

[2] Note: The carriage of unrefrigerated carcases for lengthy periods of time continued well into the 20th century. In the 1950s and 1960s it was usual for the journey to start with the loading of carcases on unrefrigerated vehicles in the morning of the first day to travel to Smithfield and be pitched onto the market (i.e. unloaded from the vehicles and hung on the rails in the market shops) during the night for sale the following morning. While in Smithfield the carcases would not be refrigerated and after they were sold they would generally be loaded into unrefrigerated vehicles again, to be moved to their final destination where the carcases would then be placed into refrigeration, probably late on the second day. The reader will need to appreciate that healthy animals slaughtered in an unstressed state will have sterile tissues throughout the body. Therefore, the main cause of spoilage, i.e. bacterial decomposition (putrefaction), will only occur on those surfaces of the meat exposed to contamination, i.e. cut surfaces. Fat is much less vulnerable to spoilage than muscle and a good covering of fat on the outside of the carcase protects the muscle underneath. A whole side of beef or a carcase of mutton has little exposed muscle and, providing there is a good flow of air, there is surface drying of cut surfaces which retards bacterial growth. The most vulnerable area of a carcase is the neck with exposed muscle smeared with blood from bleeding the animal; bacterial growth in this area can give rise to strong putrefactive odours.

Fig 20.1 Horses and carts were the principal means of transporting carcases to and from the market. Many of the carts were fitted to carry the carcases hanging from beams across the top which assured the carcases arriving in the best condition (Plimsoll, 1890).

Fig 20.2 A cart loaded with frozen Australian mutton (Plimsoll, 1890).

Fig 20.3 Horses and carts lined up at Smithfield Market ready for unloading meat (Plimsoll, 1890).

Although the London trade in 'country killed' meat increased markedly up to the mid 1850s, there was little further increase until the late 1860s. The highly congested state of Leadenhall and Newgate markets would not have encouraged expansion of this trade but the opening of the Central Meat Markets in 1868 brought about a change in the situation. It was reported in the Journal of the Royal Agricultural Society by Robert Herbert in 1859 that the annual totals of 'country killed' meat received in the markets of Leadenhall and Newgate were; 22,000 beef carcases, 98,700 mutton carcases, 34,500 lamb carcases, 3,250 veal carcases and 227,200 pork carcases. Some 90,000 of the pig carcases in this report had come to London from the West, mainly from pigs imported from Ireland, and slaughtered at the ports for onward carriage as carcases.

Some centres in the livestock areas, such as Aberdeen, Edinburgh and Leeds, had organised their meat industry to slaughter animals and send the carcases to other parts, although the destination was invariably London (Fig 20.4). One of the major factors governing a town's ability to slaughter animals locally and send the carcases to London (apart from a good rail service), was the establishment of local industries to handle the by-products; i.e. the various offals, especially the hides, fleeces, tripes, feet, heads and tallow. The town of Leeds in 1861 had a well-organised meat industry employing a large number of its 200,000 population. There was a very good market, six or seven large slaughterhouses and a large tanning industry. Tanning provided the raw material for the extensive leather industry in Leeds. There was an ample outlet for fleeces to the towns of the West Riding woollen industry which were close to Leeds. The large working class population of Leeds provided a ready market for the large quantity of edible offals coming out of the slaughterhouses (Perren, 1978).

Fig 20.4 Sides of Beef arriving at the railway siding from the slaughterhouses in Aberdeen loaded on flat horse-drawn wagons (lorries). Their destination was Smithfield Market (Leighton & Douglas, 1910).

The advantages of using the railroad for the transport of carcases soon became apparent to the meat packers in the USA. Due to the much greater distances there was a necessity for the early development of refrigerated rail cars. In the 1860s, insulated rail cars with meat packed on ice were used but air circulation was lacking resulting in some of the meat arriving in poor condition. Improved refrigerated cars followed with the Swift-Chase car coming into service in 1879. This gave the advantage to meat packers shipping carcases from Chicago and the Midwest to the East Coast.

Apart from the fact that the transportation of livestock by rail was much quicker there was the added fact that carcases could be carried rather than the live animal with all the associated savings.

The devastating affect of the cattle plague resulted in the setting up of a Royal Commission which looked at the current situation with regard to the trade in meat and live cattle. The Cattle Diseases Prevention Act 1866 at first prohibited the movement of cattle by rail but was later amended to restricting the movement of cattle except under licence. The complete ban on the movement of cattle in 1866 caused considerable disruption to the meat trade and hastened changes to the carcase meat trade. The amount of 'country killed' beef entering the large towns increased dramatically. There was tremendous pressure on the London flesh markets resulting in chaotic conditions in those markets, but the situation was generally worse outside London because in many cases there were not the facilities or the organisation to handle bulk carcase meat. London had the advantage of shipping in foreign cattle, although these had to be slaughtered at the port. The restrictions on movement of animals imposed by the Cattle Diseases Prevention Act 1866 and the later Contagious Diseases (Animals) Act (1869) caused an increase in the transportation of carcase meat. The requirements to slaughter foreign livestock at the port of entry added further to the amount of meat transported by rail. In 1867 the Great Northern Railway alone carried 22,065 tons of meat to London. This increase in freight business for the railways caused them to improve their handling and carriage of carcase meat. In the 1860s most of the meat was packed into large hampers for the rail journey; 10 to 15 lambs, or 4 quarters of beef to a hamper (a total of between 500 lb and 800 lb in weight). The quarters of beef did not travel too well in the hampers and damage occurred in the loading and unloading. Special railway wagons were later constructed that carried whole sides of beef suspended from the roof, which not only reduced damage but also permitted a flow of air between the sides.

The building of the new Central Meat Markets at Smithfield (1868) along with the restrictions on livestock movements, were major factors in the London meat trade switching to a predominantly 'dead meat' trade. Carcase meat was so readily available from Smithfield that many of the London retail butchers who had small slaughterhouses at the back of their shops ceased to use them. With the expansion of the carcase meat trade in the latter half of the 19th century, there were occasions when trade on Smithfield was poor or too much meat had arrived at the market: this caused prices to slump and salesmen had to take what price they could get to clear the meat at the end of the day, frequently resulting in a financial loss. The same applied to meat markets that were being established in other large towns. Often the meat was sold on commission; therefore it was the person sending the meat to market who suffered the loss. The livestock trade had an advantage in that animals could be held over when the prices slumped, with the hope of a recovery of the price by the next market day. The size of Smithfield market, the scope of its trade potential and the vast turnover of meat per day meant that there was a better chance of obtaining an economic price for a consignment of meat than if it were sent to one of the provincial centres.

INTERNATIONAL MEAT TRADE

With the advent of the steamship there came the potential for the export of carcase meat from Ireland to the west coast ports of England by the 1830s. According to Youatt:

> "The perfect establishment of steam navigation, while it affords facilities for the transport of live-stock, yields still greater ones for the carriage of the carcase; and cattle may now be slaughtered in the evening at any of the ports on the eastern coast of Ireland, and sent to Liverpool, and, by means of the railway, even to Manchester, in time for the morrow's market."

There were some imports of fresh meat from Europe during the mid 19th century, but this was mainly confined to the short direct voyages such as Hamburg (48 hr) and then only during winter months. For the year 1864, records showed that 2,198 tons of beef and 1,931 tons of pork were imported.

The early Age of Merchantilism exploited extensively the luxury imports, spices, silks, precious stones and metals, from the Indian Sub Continent, East Asia, East Indies and West Indies. At the beginning of the 19th century the vast plains and grasslands of North America, South America, Australia and New Zealand were still untapped in respect of their massive potential for the production of cereals and livestock.

During the American Civil War the cattle numbers declined except in Texas where the cattle were breeding freely on the open range. There were many wild unclaimed maverick cattle in Southwest Texas and in the words of J. Frank Dobie "all it took to make a cowman an owner was a rope, and the nerve to use it, and a branding iron". The livestock numbers in the USA expanded rapidly after the Civil War giving rise to the establishment of the large Meat Packers (Skaggs, 1986).

The Argentine livestock industry started to establish in the early years of the 19th century but it was not until the latter years of the 1800s when outlets for their meat materialised that numbers escalated. The following are the results of some censuses of livestock:

	Cattle	*Sheep*
1875	13,337,862	57,501,261
1888	21,963,930	66,701,097
1895	21,701,526	74,379,562
1908	29,116,625	67,211,754

(Bicknell, 1903)

At the beginning of the 19th century, Australia and New Zealand were in the early stages of colonisation. It can be seen from the following censuses that the numbers of livestock increased to meet the export potential:

Australia	Population	Cattle	Sheep
1851	403,889	1,894,834	15,993,954
1861	1,153,973	3,846,554	20,135,286
1871	1,668,377	4,277,228	40,072,955
1881	2,252,617	8,010,991	65,078,341
New Zealand	Population	Cattle	Sheep
1851	26,707	68,000	233,043
1861	99,021	193,285	2,761,383
1871	256,393	436,592	9,700,629
1881	489,933	698,637	12,985,085

(Critchell & Raymond, 1912)

The case of the USA was different in that, while it was successfully exploiting its vast agrarian potential, it was also going through its own industrial revolution after the Civil War. As a result it was consuming a large proportion of its increased animal products to the extent that it became a net importer of beef by 1913 (Skaggs, 1986).

The latter part of the 19th century in both Britain and America was the heyday of the entrepreneur. Individuals could see all around them real or imaginary opportunities for making fortunes. There was a growth of the meat packing house in the post civil war period to exploit the expansion of livestock production. The men who led the post civil war meat packing expansion were T.C. Eastman, Gustavus Swift and Philip Armour. They were to dominate the USA meat industry and became heavily involved in the South American and British meat trade.

The American packing house concept originated in the 17th century when the New England colonists were salting meat, especially pork, and packed it into barrels or boxes. This salted meat was used for victualling the ships using the East Coast ports and was also used to supply the West Indies settlements which failed to get meat supplies from Britain during the British Civil War. (Hinman & Harris, 1939).

The function of the American Meat Packer was to dress and prepare carcases and ship them to the markets. In most cases, they also took on the function of slaughtering. Before the advent of the refrigerated rail cars, meat packing was mainly cured pork and was centred in Cincinnati but as the beef trade expanded, Chicago became the national centre for the livestock industry.

The US meatpackers' main markets were the rapidly developing towns of the East Coast and beyond that meat exports. The initial shipments of carcase meat to Britain were from the US meatpackers.

CHILLED MEAT IMPORTS

The first cargo of chilled beef was shipped from New York by T.C.Eastman in October 1875 to

John Bell and Sons of Glasgow. The success of the shipment led to Eastman fitting three steamship lines as cold store ships; the Anchor, White Star and Williams & Gueton. Eastman's Ltd of London was set up to distribute the USA chilled meat which was being shipped at 4,000 carcases per week (Skaggs, 1986). As is usual with new areas of commercial activity, a number of business men became heavily involved in the trade and the market was over supplied, resulting in a fall in the prices of chilled beef on the British market; this resulted in a number of bankruptcies. There were sections of the meat trade that were opposed to the importation of chilled beef, particularly those connected with the live cattle trade or the home trade and they criticised imported chilled beef as being of poor eating quality (Perren, 1978). Regardless of this, the imported chilled beef trade was to expand and become a major sector of the meat trade.

As the chilled beef trade expanded, Liverpool became the main British port for landing the meat, with some of the cargoes going to Southampton, Bristol and Glasgow. The condition of the meat when landed was good enough for onward shipment by rail to London. The railway wagons used had holes for ventilation cut in front of the van to create an air flow around the quarters of beef but unfortunately some of the quarters arrived with a covering of soot or coal dust. The chilling of the meat during the voyage for the initial shipments was mostly effected by large quantities of ice taken on board the ships. In some cases the ice was used to chill water in tanks and the water was then pumped through pipes running round the hold containing the meat. An alternative method was for air from fans to pass over quantities of ice into the chill storage hold. These ice chilling systems were able to maintain a temperature of between 1°C and 3°C in the chill storage holds. With the introduction of mechanical refrigeration into the ships, apart from the improvement of efficiency, there was considerable saving of cargo space that had previously been taken up by the large quantities of ice.

The chilled beef from the first shipments into Liverpool, being something new, attracted the consumers. The first butchers' shops stocking the meat in Liverpool were inundated with customers and were quickly sold out of this chilled meat. In the early days of the trade there was very little cold storage space available in Britain so it was important to move the meat to the traders and butchers as quickly as possible. If the markets became overstocked with chilled meat the salesmen would be forced to take any price offered as they could not hold on to the meat, especially if more chilled beef was due. In some cases the unloading of meat from a ship could be delayed so that the meat could remain in the chill stores on board ship for an extra day or two, but the need to turn round the ships restricted the use of this option. Agents for the shippers of chilled beef were very active while a consignment was still on the high seas, trying to place the meat with traders. It was not long before large cold stores were built at the docks and markets, especially with the commencement of the frozen meat trade creating an additional need for these stores. This eased the pressures on those conducting the chilled beef trade. The 1880s saw the pattern established for the US chilled beef trade which was concentrated mainly on London and Liverpool.

The following table shows the average annual totals of beef imports for each of the five-year periods 1875 to 1908. The USA beef was mostly chilled whereas the Argentine, Australian and New Zealand beef was frozen (Leighton & Douglas, 1910). The first chilled beef from Argentina was in 1900.

Periods Ave. per annum	USA Tons	Argentina Tons	Australia Tons	New Zealand Tons
1874 only	55			
1875-1879	16,333			
1880-1884	34,615	25	107	
		(1884 only)	Australia +NZ 1883/84	
1885-1889	43,208	203	437	1,438
1890-1894	86,581	724	6,325	2,753
1895-1899	110,246	4,168	26,825	3,457
1900-1904	134,278	49,354	8,772	11.109
1905	111,610	129,008	951	7,267
1906	121,332	139,796	1,723	11,829
1907	120,880	134,578	6,302	19,565
1908	71,607	197,515	5,629	17,394

(Leighton & Douglas, 1910)

THE SURPLUS LIVESTOCK IN THE SOUTHERN HEMISPHERE PROVIDING MARKETING OPPORTUNITIES

With the build up of large sheep flocks and cattle herds in Australia, New Zealand and Argentina, the level of livestock production in these countries soon exceeded the meat demand of the local populations and the only export from the surplus animals was hides, skins, wool and tallow; the meat was wasted. The growing demand for meat in Britain was outstripping home production creating a very large and lucrative potential market. It soon became apparent to many of the entrepreneurs of the time that there were fortunes to be made by anyone who could solve the problem of shipping the very cheap surplus meat from Australia, New Zealand and Argentina half way round the world to Britain. The shipment of live animals was not practical due to the distances involved, although some Argentine cattle and sheep were shipped in the last decade of the 19th century. The incentive to find an answer to the long distance shipping of meat was a major reason for the 139 patents for mechanical refrigeration that were taken out between 1819 and 1876. These were apart from the various non-mechanical methods of refrigeration patented. The Society of Arts offered a prize of £70 and a medal in 1863 for the first person to provide a practical means of importing fresh meat from Australia and New Zealand.[3]

One method of utilising the surplus beef from Uruguay was by producing a concentrated extract of meat. This was made possible through a system invented by Baron Justus von Liebig; he published the details of the process in 1847. In the 1860s plants were built in Uruguay to produce the beef extract which was then exported to Europe. In 1865 Robert Tooth set up a plant in New South Wales, Australia, to produce meat extract and started exporting to Britain in the following year.

---

[3] Note: The reader needs to bear in mind that Australia and New Zealand were British Colonies, therefore there was a great deal of incentive and facility for Britain and British businesses to become involved in commercial developments in those countries.

Meat canning was seen as a method of preserving the Southern Hemisphere's surplus meat to enable it to be shipped to Europe. In 1847 William and Henry Dangar established a meat canning factory in New South Wales and exported large quantities of canned beef, mutton, tongues, soup and bouillon to London. The gold rush in Australia in the 1850s caused a sharp rise in the price of cattle which put the Dangar plant out of business. When the cattle trade settled down again a number of canning factories were established and by 1870 the annual export of Australian canned meat to Britain was up to 1,000 tons. Canning factories sprang up in North and South America with Chicago becoming a major centre for meat canning in the USA. Imports of canned meat into Britain built up in the mid 19th century. Canned meat was very popular in the industrial towns of the Midlands and North of England.

FROZEN MEAT TRADE

The development of mechanical refrigeration paved the way for the international frozen meat trade. The first attempt at shipping frozen meat was from Australia to London by James Harrison in 1873. He had been successful with a machine for making ice and used the same type of machine to freeze 20 tons of beef and mutton in tank-like chambers on board the *S.S.Norfolk*. The ship sailed from Australia in July 1873 but on its arrival in London in October, the meat was found to have deteriorated to a point rendering it unfit for consumption. Thomas Mort, an emigrant to Australia from Bolton, Lancashire, who had been successful in a number of business enterprises, met a French engineer, Eugene Nicolle, and they worked together to develop equipment for freezing meat. This equipment was for the world's first freezing works built at Darling Harbour, Sydney, in 1861. Mort chartered a sailing ship, the *Northam*, which was fitted with ammonia refrigerating equipment similar to that used in the freezing works. The equipment reduced the temperature of brine held in tanks which was then pumped through a series of pipes running round the hold in which frozen meat would be held. The holds for the meat were insulated with 15 inches (38 centimetres) of tallow. Mort loaded this ship with a cargo of frozen meat bound for London, but unfortunately the brine pipes which were vulnerable to the movement of the ship, started leaking before the ship sailed and the cargo had to be discharged, resulting in this attempt at exporting frozen meat ending in failure (Hammett & Nevell, 1929). There were occasions when leaks from the brine pipes contaminated some of the carcases causing brine stains that needed trimming.

The first success in shipping frozen meat to Europe was in 1877 when the *Frigorifique,* fitted with a Charles Tellier vapour compression machine using methyl ether, sailed from Buenos Aires with a cargo of frozen Argentine meat bound for Rouen, France. On arrival the meat varied in condition with some of the cargo in an unfit state. Another Frenchman, M. Carré, fitted his patented ammonia refrigeration equipment into the steamship *Paraguay* and in 1878 shipped 5,500 frozen mutton carcases from South America to France, which arrived in good condition. Although this enterprise was successful it did not seem to arouse much enthusiasm in France so the project was dropped (Miller, 1985).

The brothers, Henry and James Bell of Glasgow, became interested in mechanical refrigeration with a view to using it in ships. One of the brothers was an agent for T.C.Eastman, the shipper of the first chilled meat from North America. The Bell brothers consulted Lord Kelvin (Professor at Glasgow University) who had carried out research in fundamental thermodynamics and produced the absolute temperature scale - the Kelvin scale. The Bells then worked with Mr J.J.Coleman which led eventually to the patenting of the Bell-Coleman refrigeration equipment in 1877. In 1879 Bell-Coleman refrigeration was fitted aboard one of the Anchor Line ships for the North American trade. Also in that year, the *Strathleven*, a sailing ship of 2,436 tons with an auxiliary steam engine, was fitted in Glasgow with Bell-Coleman refrigeration. The *Strathleven* carried a 40-ton cargo of Australian frozen beef, mutton and lamb, the animals having been slaughtered ashore and their carcases frozen on the ship. The *Strathleven* arrived at the Port of London on the 2nd February 1880. The meat was in good condition and was quickly taken up by butchers on Smithfield market (Gerrard, 1956). The *Daily Telegraph* gave a report on the meat: "It has been tested by ordinary methods of cooking and found to be in such good condition that neither by its appearance in the butchers' shops, nor by any peculiarity of flavour when cooked for the table could it be distinguished from fresh killed meat." A carcase of lamb from the consignment was presented to Queen Victoria. Thomas Mort, the pioneer of frozen meat shipments, died at Bodalla, New South Wales in 1878 and was therefore unable to witness the ultimate fulfilment of his vision.

The New Zealand frozen meat trade began in 1882 with the sailing ship *Dunedin* (1,320 tons) being fitted with Bell-Coleman refrigerating plant (Fig 20.5). A number of carcases from selected sheep were frozen on board the ship but unfortunately there was a mechanical break down in the engine driving the refrigerating plant resulting in the frozen carcases having to be unloaded. These carcases were sold locally, thus the New Zealanders themselves were the first consumers of frozen New Zealand mutton. When repairs had been made to the engine, further animals were selected and slaughtered and their carcases taken aboard and frozen. The cargo consisted of over 5,000 carcases of mutton and lamb and some pork. The *Dunedin* sailed from New Zealand on the 15th February 1882 arriving in London on the 24th May 1882. The consignment was well received on Smithfield Market, the meat being in very good condition.

Fig 20.5 The *Dunedin* brought the first shipment of frozen meat to Britain from New Zealand in 1882. In the centre of the ship is the chimney of the steam engine driving the refrigerating equipment. On the right is a picture of Captain Whitson, captain of the Dunedin on its historic voyage.

The large number of sheep on the Falkland Islands inspired shipment of frozen mutton in 1886 totalling 30,000 carcases, the largest shipment at the time. The Ship, *S.S. Selembria* was fitted with a J. & E. Hall's cold air machine. In addition to the ship's crew there was a team of butchers to slaughter and dress the animals and stevedores to stow the cargo (Miller, 1985).

The following are the accounts of the first New Zealand frozen meat consignment:

No.	Weight (lb)	Where sold	Per lb	£ s d
Sheep				
3,136	244,073	London	6.56d	6,675 9 7
373	29,415	Glasgow	6.54d	801 13 6
8	477	to Captain	6.00d	11 18 6
3		to Manager		6 7 9
1		Condemned		
Lamb				
425	16,846	London	6.45d	453 0 11
24	950	Glasgow	7.60d	30 1 1
Pigs				
22	1,164			31 2 11

Expenses for the Shipment

	£ s d
Calico for bags	91 8 9
Holding meat in Dunedin after arrival	43 11 9
Freight on 296,477lbs	2,779 9 5
Insurance on £7,500	414 13 9
Supervision during discharge etc.	29 13 6
Dock Co. a/c for discharging	78 5 7
Carriage to Smithfield	65 10 0
Onward carriage to Glasgow	51 4 3
Commission, Bank Charges etc.	239 5 4
Total	3,793 2 4

(Hammett & Nevell 1929).

The first exports of frozen meat from South America to Britain were by the River Plate Fresh Meat Company Ltd. in 1883 consisting of a cargo of 7,500 frozen sheep carcases. The company was set up in 1862 by an English businessman, Mr George Drabble, who was at the time involved in South American banking and railways. There were some shipments of frozen mutton and lamb from the Falkland Islands between 1886 and 1895, averaging between 10,000 and 20,000 carcases in each year, with a peak of 45,552 carcases in 1887.

By 1888 there were 57 ships engaged in the frozen meat trade, the combined capacity being close to a million mutton carcases. The number of ships increased to 143 by 1889, with a total capacity for carrying over 6.5 million mutton carcases, which capacity was not fully utilised. The combined capacity of the 30 vessels carrying the South American meat was utilised to about 80%

whereas it was only about 40% for those on the Australasian run. The *Dunedin* was sadly to end her part in the trade in 1890, after completing nine voyages carrying New Zealand mutton and lamb to Britain. A wager was made between the *Dunedin* and three other ships engaged in the New Zealand frozen meat trade to establish which vessel could make the fastest time to London. The *Dunedin* sailed in March 1890 from the port of Oamaru in the South Island, carrying a cargo of frozen meat and wool with a crew of 34. The captain, a Mr Roberts, had his young daughter with him. The *Dunedin* was last seen heading for the Cape Horn which was the last sighting of her as she was lost on this voyage. Tragedy also overtook the *Malborough*, another of the ships in this ill-fated race; its wreck was discovered near Tierra del Fuego on the southern tip of South America in 1911. Skeletons of the crew were found on the deck with rusty pistols at their sides (Harrison, 1963).

The first successful frozen meat shipments paved the way for the extensive development of the frozen meat trade in the last two decades of the 19th century. The resultant structure consisted of:

- Collection points for livestock, slaughterhouses and freezing works in Australasia and South America.
- Refrigerated ocean going freighters.
- Cold stores at the docks and main meat trading centres in Britain (e.g. London, Liverpool, Birmingham, Glasgow).
- A distribution network of agents and wholesalers organised to handle frozen meat.

THE AUSTALASIAN TRADE

The Australian and New Zealand end of the trade was closely connected to the producers, with a number of farmers owning or having a financial interest in freezing plants. In many cases the farmers worked directly with particular freezing plants, enabling good co-ordination between the producers, freezing works and shippers. Some farmers would remain owners of a consignment that was shipped until it was sold by an agent in Britain. The New Zealand trade developed to a greater extent than the Australian trade in the 1880s and 1890s. New Zealand had (and still has) the benefit of a consistent climate with a good rainfall, which is most conducive to good grass growth and a long grazing period. This resulted in the New Zealand farmers being able to supply their freezing works with consistent numbers of sheep of a good quality. The quality of the sheep was also aided by the type of New Zealand breeding stock which was of a better meat type animal than either the Australian or South American stock. The New Zealand sheep flocks started with imports of Merinos from Australia. Merino ewes were crossed with Leicester and Lincoln rams to produce the Corriedale, which was much better for mutton and fat lamb production than the pure Merino. With an eye to the developing mutton and lamb export trade, the New Zealand farmers imported Romney Marsh sheep for a further improvement of the meat quality of their animals. The development of the Australian frozen mutton trade suffered from periods of prolonged droughts which decimated the sheep flocks, leaving the export freezing works without supplies for long periods while flock numbers were recovering. There was the added fact that the Australian sheep farmers in a number of areas were more dedicated to the wool trade than the carcase trade.

Merino sheep produce the best wool if reared in warm dry climates on marginal land, resulting in an excellent fleece and a poor carcase. The sheep stock in Argentina in 1880 was not very good for the production of mutton carcases as it consisted mainly of Spanish Merino or Rambouillet, which were wool breeds. The Argentine farmers also imported the Romney Marsh breed to improve their stock. An average of the prices quoted on Smithfield in 1888 for frozen meat was; New Zealand mutton - 4½d per lb, New Zealand lamb - 6¾d per lb, Australian mutton - 4d per lb, Argentine mutton - 3¾d per lb.

Freezing works were soon established throughout the North and South Islands of New Zealand, there being 25 freezing works by 1899. A number of these freezing works were quite small but were commercially viable in the initial stages of the trade because of the good price that New Zealand mutton and lamb was making on the British market. In the 1890s the prices of frozen mutton in the British market fell, putting pressure on the New Zealand exporters to increase their efficiency and reduce costs in order to compensate for the lower profit margins on the mutton consignments. There were occasions when several consignments of frozen meat arrived within a short space of time and the shortage of cold storage in Britain meant that the meat could not be held back from the market, resulting in an oversupply and a fall in price. A conference of producers was arranged in October 1887 for the purpose of considering combined action to manage the market and maintain reasonable levels of price. There was no agreement. Conferences were held again in 1893 and 1898 but still without agreement due largely to the many individuals involved in the trade and the divergence of interests in many cases (Perren, 1978). One area that came to the fore in producing good quality New Zealand lamb was Canterbury in the South Island. The name Canterbury lamb soon became well known to butchers and consumers as a good quality product and to some extent the term Canterbury lamb became synonymous with New Zealand lamb.

Fig 20.6 The New Zealand Shipping Co's S.S. *Remuera* which was carrying frozen meat cargoes from the early 1880s.

As in New Zealand, the Australian freezing works, which numbered 17 in 1899, were distributed over a wide geographical area situated in the four chief livestock producing states (which at that time were separate British colonies); Queensland, New South Wales, Victoria and South Australia.

In some cases it necessitated a ship calling in at more than one port to collect enough meat to make up a full cargo; this added to the shipping cost.

THE ARGENTINIAN TRADE

The meat export trade in Argentina was carried on by five firms in 1885, reducing to only three by 1890, which meant that the exporters could influence a good deal more control over the trade than was possible by the New Zealand or Australian operators. There was a further advantage for the Argentine trade in that all the meat freezing plants in Argentina were built along the River Plate and were therefore less geographically dispersed than those in Australasia. Of the three successful exporting companies two were British (The River Plate Fresh Meat Company formed by George Drabble in 1882 and Nelson's River Plate Meat Company which was a subsidiary of James Nelson and Sons - cattle salesmen and meat traders of London, Manchester and Dublin). The remaining firm was Argentinian owned, the Compania Sansinena de Carnes Congeladas, which was more commonly known in Britain as the Sansinena Company. The Sansinena Company was concerned about the marketing side of its organisation and opened an office in Liverpool in 1887 and another in London in 1888. As there were only three exporters to buy livestock from the Argentinian ranchers, there was no active competition and therefore prices were kept at a low level, which maintained a high profit for the meat companies (Perren, 1978).

Fig 20.7 The Argentine Cargo Line S.S. *El Argentino*. Shipments of frozen meat from Argentina started in 1883.

TOTAL IMPORTS OF FROZEN MUTTON

The table overleaf shows the average annual totals of frozen mutton imported; 1882 - 1908.

The seasonal pattern of production, particularly for mutton and lamb, soon established an affect on the frozen meat trade. These supplies coming from the southern hemisphere had the advantage that their seasonal calendar for lambing and the optimum finishing of animals for slaughter were opposite to that in Britain. Killing new season lambs commenced in November in New Zealand's North Island and a month later in the South Island and continued for about six months. The Australian lambing was ahead of that in New Zealand, enabling the Australian exporters to get new season

Periods Ave. per annum	Argentine Tons	Australia Tons	New Zealand Tons
1882-1884	1,095	2,112	5,306
1885-1889	12,946	2,203	20,933
1890-1894	24,439	12,445	43,205
1895-1899	46,731	31,259	63,428
1900-1904	66,471	15,881	82,728
1905	73,127	25,271	76,249
1906	71,655	30,844	87,409
1907	70,115	42,911	100,254
1908	77,837	31,802	86,880

(Leighton & Douglas 1910)

Antipodean lamb onto the British market first. Home-killed mutton was in short supply on the British markets during the winter and early spring and home-produced lamb was not readily available until late April or May. This provided the shippers of frozen mutton and lamb with an opportunity to obtain good prices for the consignments that they succeeded in getting to the British market early in the winter. Later shipments sold at lower prices because the stocks of frozen mutton and lamb started to build up.

Fig 20.8 Freezing Room for beef at the Meat Export Works, Queensland, Australia (Leighton & Douglas, 1910).

Fig 20.9 Frozen Meat Store, Adelaide, South Australia. The low temperature was maintained by the overhead pipes carrying the brine (Leighton & Douglas, 1910).

The bulk of frozen mutton and lamb imported from Australia and New Zealand was landed at the London Docks whereas that from Argentina was mostly brought in through Liverpool, with only about 10% entering the London Docks. A major reason for this was that the heavier, better quality, well-finished but not over fat carcases from New Zealand were in good demand in the London market where they commanded best prices. On the other hand, the lighter mutton carcases from Argentina were in much better demand in the north of the country and distribution from Liverpool to the North was easier and cheaper. Quantities of New Zealand mutton and lamb were sent on from London to the provinces and attempts were made by exporters to widen their distribution network by landing meat at other ports; a few small consignments from New Zealand went to Liverpool in 1892, 1893 and 1894. Australia was landing up to 5% of its mutton and lamb at Liverpool and Manchester in the latter half of the 1890s. Although it was cheaper to land cargoes at other ports it usually took less time for the voyage from New Zealand to London as the faster ships were allocated to this run. As the later arrivals usually obtained lower prices for the meat, time of arrival was important. The provincial markets had much less sales potential than London and were therefore more easily overstocked, with a consequent fall in prices. London was to continue to be the main focus of the Australian and New Zealand mutton and lamb trade well into the 20th century.

It was not many years after the Australian and New Zealand frozen meat trade had started that there was forward selling of consignments. The first transaction was probably the sale of 2,000 sheep carcases to Messrs W. & R. Fletcher Ltd. in 1888, sold by A.S.Paterson & Co. of Dunedin through its London agents W.Weddel & Co. The system for forward trading soon became established in the 1890s as c.i.f. (cost, insurance and freight). This covered the cost of the meat and all charges including insurance up to the discharge of the meat onto the quay at the destination port. For the system to work it was necessary to have a reliably consistent form of specifying the meat in a consignment which, in the case of the mutton and lamb carcases and beef quarters, were the grading systems based on weight and quality assessment. Lamb for export was divided into prime and second grades and there was a series of grades for mutton. The New Zealand Refrigerating Company of Dunedin was the first to use grading as a basis for forward selling. The c.i.f. documents, which represented ownership of a consignment of meat, were soon to be traded between meat salesmen, agents and buyers. One of the problems to arise with this forward trading was the late arrivals of consignments, as this could significantly affect the price obtainable on the market. This often resulted in a dispute between exporter and importer. By 1900 frozen meat had become an available commodity on Smithfield market all the year round. In 1903 there were 6 million frozen rabbit carcases imported from Australia.

ESTABLISHMENT OF COLD STORE AND DISTRIBUTION NETWORK FOR FROZEN MEAT

When the frozen meat trade started in the 1880s, cold storage facilities in Britain were almost non existent. There was already some refrigerated storage to service the chilled meat trade and for the carcases from imported livestock that was required to be slaughtered at the port of entry. A chill meat store was built in 1874 for the storage of American chill meat imports. As the frozen meat trade started to expand, the necessity for frozen meat storage was soon realised. Companies operating in the London and Liverpool docks were the first to establish frozen meat cold stores.

Fig 20.10 Slaughterhouse Floor at the La Negra Frigorifico. It was from the La Negra site that Sansinena made their first shipment of frozen mutton to Britain (Leighton & Douglas, 1910).

The earliest frozen meat store in London was a converted warehouse owned by the London and St Catherine Docks Company opened in 1882 which could accommodate 500 x 56lb sheep carcases. By 1886, this store had been extended to hold 59,000 sheep carcases. The East and West India Docks Company followed by fitting two floating hulks for refrigerated storage with a total storage of 15,000 sheep carcases. Two companies attempted building a cold store under Smithfield Market but were unsuccessful. Nelson Bros., importers of New Zealand frozen meat, built a cold store in the arches under Cannon Street railway station in 1885. The same site had been used for a cold store by the Fresh and Preserved Meat Agency for the distribution of American chilled beef in 1878. The arches under Cannon Street station consisted of a central arch running from Thames Street to the Thames riverside with a series of smaller arches running off at right angles from this main arch. This layout was ideal in that the smaller arches were insulated and refrigerated for use as cold stores, with access via the central arch. Frozen meat was brought into the store after being unloaded from a lighter onto a landing stage situated at the end of the central arch. Meat being delivered from the store was taken by barrows out along the central arch to Thames Street. From here it was only a short distance to Smithfield Market or to one of a number of railway depots for meat that was destined for the provinces. The enterprise proved highly successful for the company due to the considerable savings compared with the cost of storing frozen meat at the docks and providing the company with a very good distribution depot. This led to Nelson Bros. building the largest cold store in Britain. It was built in Commercial Road, Lambeth in 1892 and consisted of five floors with a capacity for 250,000 x 56lb sheep carcases. The store was equipped with mechanical hoists (Critchell & Raymond, 1912).

In 1888 London had eight cold stores for frozen meat, with a total capacity of 300,000 x 56lb sheep carcases but this was inadequate to service the volume of frozen meat entering London at this time, which amounted to 1,220,727 carcases per annum. By 1899 the figure had risen to 4,679,336 carcases whereas the cold storage space had increased so much that the firms operating the stores were concerned that there was over capacity which could affect their rates. The rates charged initially for a 28-day storage period were about £7 per ton but by the 1890s had dropped to about £1 per ton.

Fig 20.11 Sansinena Frozen Meat Depot at Liverpool, 1909.

The other main centres were quick to follow. A cold store for frozen meat built in Williams Square, Liverpool, in 1883 operated as a public cold store. The first frozen meat store in Manchester was erected close to the meat market by the Manchester Corporation and it was also run as a public cold store. The Argentinian frozen meat exporting companies established their own cold stores in Liverpool to assist in the distribution of their meat (Fig 20.11) (*Ibid*). By 1912 the cold storage capacity for frozen meat at the ports and markets had increased very considerably. The massive investment in cold stores, refrigerated shipping, freezing works, slaughtering and processing facilities indicate the nature of the boom in the international meat industry.

COLD STORAGE CAPACITY

The following is the cold storage capacity for frozen meat storage in the main ports and markets in the UK, 1912:

	Capacity – Number of 56 lb Mutton carcases	*Weight Converted to Tons*
London	3,032,000	75,800
Liverpool	2,176,000	54,400
Glasgow	605,000	15,125
Southampton	562,000	14,050
Manchester	407,000	10,175
Cardiff	497,000	12,425
Barry	100,000	2,500
Newport	41,482	1,037
Swansea	25,000	625
Hull	344,000	8,600
Newcastle	211,000	5,275
Bristol	156,000	3,900
Totals	8,156,482	203,912

(*Ibid*)

Chapter 21

The Changing Nature of the Meat Trade During the 19th Century

LEVELS OF MEAT CONSUMPTION IN THE UNITED KINGDOM

Regular collection of agricultural statistics did not begin until 1867, therefore estimates of livestock production and meat consumption before this time cannot be relied on for a great deal of accuracy. M.G.Mulhall in his 'Dictionary of Statistics' puts the annual meat consumption figure for the 1830s as 980,000 tons or 86.8 lb per head. This figure must be considered in relation to the considerable disparity in the level of meat consumption between the different classes of the population. At the lowest level, the inmates of the Union Workhouse had very little meat. In the 1830s the general diet of the poor in the Dartford Union Workhouse, as ordered by the Poor Law Commissioners, consisted of three meals a day as follows:

> Bread and cheese for the men and bread and butter for the women for breakfast and supper.
> Dinner on 4 days for both men and women was bread and cheese.
> The only meat meal was Sunday dinner when the men had 16ozs of meat pudding with vegetables and the women received 10ozs of meat pudding with vegetables. For dinner on Tuesday and Friday there was a serving of suet pudding (men - 16ozs, women - 10ozs) with vegetables (Dunkin, 1844).

The families of the farm labourers would have seldom eaten meat as it was too expensive to afford from their meagre wages. Mulhall estimates that in the 1880s the per capita consumption in Ireland was only 56 lb per annum.

From the 1850s there was a considerable expansion in the meat trade in Britain due to the combination of the rise in population and an increase in the per capita consumption of meat. During the 1870s consumption of meat per head reached 110 lb and by the end of the century it was up to 120 lb. Growth in meat consumption was mainly a consequence of increasing wealth and higher standards of living but the low price of meat would also have contributed. The table overleaf shows some comparative prices for the 19th century (Collinge, Young & McDougall, 1929).

The importation of foreign livestock and meat was a major factor in causing the low market prices in the latter half of the 19th century, resulting in a series of complaints and representations to the Government by the farming community.

The total volume of meat consumed in the United Kingdom rose from an average of 980,000 tons per annum in the 1830s to an average of 2,334,000 tons per annum in the years 1895 to 1899.

Prices taken from the records of St Thomas's Hospital, Southwark, London.

Year	Beef	Mutton
1801	8½d lb	8½d lb
1810	8½d lb	8¼d lb
1820	7d lb	8d lb
1830	4¼d lb	5d lb
1840	5¼d lb	5¾d lb

From the Report of Committee on the Stabilisation of Agriculture Prices. Ministry of Agriculture.

Year	Beef	Mutton
1850	4¼d lb	5d lb
1860	5¾d lb	6½d lb
1870	6½d lb	6¾d lb
1880	6¾d lb	7½d lb
1890	5¼d lb	6½d lb
1899	5½d lb	6d lb

Up until 1842 all the meat was home produced (including meat coming from Ireland) but by the end of the century 40% of the meat was imported.

A large proportion of the industrial workers' wages was spent on food in the 19th century. In some areas the mill or factory owners also owned the local shop and instead of paying their workers in cash they gave them vouchers for exchange in these local shops (known as 'tommy shops'). Not only did the factory owners get extra profit from workers who were obliged to obtain food from their shops but the food was often poor quality and over priced. In 1844 a group of weavers in Rochdale got together and formed the Rochdale Society of Equitable Pioneers; each member pledged twopence per week to a fund. When eventually they had amassed the sum of twenty pounds they bought stock and opened a small shop in Toad Lane, which was the first co-operative society store in Britain. Soon co-operative societies were being formed throughout the country and their combined purchasing power became so considerable that the Co-operative Wholesale Society was formed in 1862 to supply the retail societies. The CWS became a large meat wholesaler with many depots, slaughterhouses and its own meat importing organisation.

LONDON AS A MAJOR MEAT MARKET

London as a centre for the meat trade has played an important part in the development of the trade. This is due to the metropolis having a large concentrated population, extensive inland port facilities and being well placed geographically to the rest of the country. London has always been an active commercial centre from Roman times, even when the capital was at Winchester under

Alfred the Great. The population of London in the 13th century has been estimated at 80,000 to 100,000 which was several times larger than Bristol and York, the next in size, but less than Paris (estimated 200,000). At this time the population of London was about 2% of the country as a whole. By 1600 the population of the metropolis had risen to 200,000, by 1700 it was 600,000 and was close to a million in 1800, when it represented almost 10% of the total population of Britain. In 1700 there were only seven towns in England with populations which were just over 10,000. The population of London in 1800 was eleven times larger than Liverpool (next in size) and twice the population of Paris (the next largest in Europe). The increase in the London inhabitants during the 17th century was not due to a high birth rate, as the records show a burial rate in excess of the baptismal rate by 2:1. Growth of the population was, as at most times, due to the influx of people from the country (Weinreb & Hibbert, 1983).

During the medieval period London received its supplies of livestock for meat from local areas or counties not too distant, but by 1600 the growth in the London market created the need to bring in animals from greater distances. With the big population increase during the 17th and 18th centuries the enlarged London market became a magnet for meat producers from all parts of Britain. Farmers in the southern counties who were supplying Smithfield were unable to get enough store stock for finishing. This made it attractive for the drovers to bring their animals to these southern counties from Scotland, Wales and from Ireland. The build-up of droving coincided with the growth of the population of the metropolis. This was a very large market for slaughter stock, in particular good quality finished animals (the London butchers were highly discerning buyers), along with the establishment of the Smithfield Club, which gave incentive and direction for livestock improvements that were taking place.

In 1851 the United Kingdom population had grown to 20,817,000, of which London's population was 2,363,341 and Greater London's 2,651,939. Within this expanding population of the metropolis there was a large number of the rising middle class whose households were good customers of the London butchers. At this time the level of demand for meat was outstripping the ability of the British farmers to produce sufficient livestock. The lifting of restrictions in 1842 opened the way for large scale importation of livestock and meat. London was an unparalleled massive concentration of meat consumers. The prospect of this very promising market, which had good access through the Port of London, was soon recognised by the livestock producers and dealers in Europe and the Americas. The establishment in the capital of a substantial trade in imported meat was a basis for the expansion of the trade to other towns. By 1901 the population of the United Kingdom had reached 37 million of which London consisted of 4,536,267 and the whole of Greater London 6,506,889. There was a continuing rise in the volume of meat needed to feed the populace which was well able to absorb the frozen meat from the southern hemisphere in the latter part of the 19th century.

REGIONAL VARIATION IN DEMAND

There were marked variations regionally with regard to prices for cuts of meat and demand for different types of meat. Until the 1850s when the railways began carrying carcase meat, there was no way of moving cuts of meat from one area where they were in poor demand to areas where demand would be greater. Before transport of meat by rail all the cuts of the carcase and

Fig 21.1 Typical carcases of Blackfaced Sheep in Yorkshire. The dressing included draping the carcase with the caul fat (Leighton & Douglas, 1910).

the offals from each animal slaughtered had to be sold locally. In London there were large numbers of wealthy households (large numbers of the aristocracy and landed gentry had their town houses in the capital) which meant a high demand for the best quality roasting joints. In 1837 good quality ox beef was selling as follows:

Rump 8d lb	Aitch Bone 5d lb
Loin 8d lb	Brisket 5d lb
Fore Rib 8d lb	Thin Flank 5d lb
Buttock 6d lb	Neck 3d lb
Thick Flank 6d lb	Leg and Shin 2d lb
Middle Rib 6d lb	

As it was mainly the poorer classes who bought the boiling and stewing quality cuts, this meat had to be cheap enough to be affordable to those people. Much of the coarser meat was used in the manufacture of pies and sausages, which found a ready sale to the working classes. By contrast, the beef prices in Glasgow and Edinburgh had much less disparity between the best roasting cuts and the coarser meat. Rump, loin, and fore rib were 6d to 7d lb with neck and brisket 5d to 5½d lb. This difference was to some extent due to the preference in Scotland for broths and stewed or boiled dishes, which tended to reduce the consumers' level of discernment between the qualities of the different cuts. The English towns, other than London, had beef prices roughly intermediate between those of London and the Scottish towns. Throughout the rural areas there was little scope to obtain higher prices for the roasting quality cuts, therefore there was very little retail price differentiation for any cuts of beef. Much the same pattern existed for mutton. Bacon was generally cheap and more commonly purchased by the working classes (Perren, 1978). This regional variation in the retail pricing structure was a major factor (apart from the anatomical structure of the animal) governing the methods of cutting employed. The London butchers would have been under economic pressure to cut carcases to maximise the proportion of roasting quality meat. This resulted in the degree of finesse and craftsmanship required of the cutters employed in the retail establishments. The emphasis on the roasting quality cuts being to varying degrees less important in the other areas, reflected in the regional methods of cutting that became established. It was probably about the mid 19th century that these methods of cutting were established that have carried through to the present day (apart from some retailers who have taken up muscle seaming in the Continental style).

The railways provided the opportunity for areas such as Scotland to send to London the best roasting quality meat to obtain the top prices and sell locally the coarser stewing meat (where there was a good demand), therefore making more money overall. As this practice became established it gave rise to the wholesale cuts 'scotch roasting' consisting of loin and fore rib and 'Scotch short side' consisting of a side less the clod, sticking, chuck, blade, leg of mutton cut and shin. Another variable in regional demand was the size of mutton carcases. The north of the country required the smaller carcases, thus attracting the small sheep carcases from Europe and the smaller frozen mutton carcases from Argentina. London was the best market for the heavier, well-finished New Zealand mutton carcases.

ESTABLISHMENT OF THE LARGE MEAT COMPANIES

The 19th century saw a very considerable change in the meat industry. At the beginning of the century the meat trade was very much in the hands of individual traders, i.e. butchers, livestock dealers, drovers, market salesmen and carcase butchers (meat wholesalers). There would have only been few of the latter as the trade of carcase butcher was just emerging at this time. Some of the meat and livestock businesses at this time were quite large employing many workers, but were still run by individuals or in some cases business families. By the end of the century the volume of the trade had almost trebled and many of the aspects of the 20th century meat trade were already established.

In the latter part of the 19th century the structure of the meat trade was changing, with the establishment of a number of large and many medium-sized companies. The companies Thomas Borthwick & Sons, Towers & Co. Ltd. and W.Weddel & Co. Ltd. took full advantage of the opportunities offered by the frozen and chilled meat trade, not only as importers, wholesalers and distributors but also by becoming very much involved in the New Zealand, Australian and Argentine end of the trade. The North American meat and livestock exports to Britain became dominated by three firms in the 1890s; Armour & Co., Morris & Co. and Swift & Co.. There was growing dissatisfaction with the returns they were getting for the meat sold on commission, including suspicion with regard to the weights of meat sold as stated by the wholesalers. As a result the American companies acquired stalls in Smithfield market and set up depots in other main centres so that they could carry out their own wholesaling function. The companies exporting meat from Argentina established their own depots and distribution networks in Britain in the 1880s soon after the first shipments of meat. The River Plate Fresh Meat Co. Ltd. and the Sansinena Co. established distribution networks covering many of the main centres throughout the country. The other main exporter of Argentine meat was the Nelson's River Plate Fresh Meat Co., later renamed Las Palmas Produce Co., which was owned by a British company, James Nelson & Sons Ltd. This was a company trading in livestock and meat able to use its organisation (which included a large number of retail shops) for the distribution of the Argentine meat consignments (Leighton & Douglas, 1910; Skaggs, 1986).

At the commencement of the New Zealand trade, consignments of frozen meat were mostly handled by finance companies or wool houses in London, as these were the British firms with whom the New Zealand farmers had been doing business. These British firms had no previous experience of the meat trade so they engaged meat brokers and commission agents to distribute these meat consignments (Perren, 1978). In 1883 Thomas Borthwick became official selling agent for the New Zealand Loan and Mercantile Company (Harrison, 1963). By 1890 the meat companies were dealing directly with the New Zealand producers. As the volume of frozen meat imports increased the market was extended to the provinces, with meat sent by rail from the ports of entry, mainly London and Liverpool. Frozen meat destined for the provinces that had formerly passed through Smithfield started to be sold ex-store going direct from the cold stores to the railway depots. This caused a reaction from the Corporation of London who claimed that they should collect tolls on the meat sold ex-store by the Smithfield salesmen even though it did not enter the market. The market, as constituted under the existing by-laws, did not encompass such trading and therefore the Corporation did not pursue this claim.

CHANGES IN THE MARKETS AND OFFICIAL REGULATION OF THE TRADE

The last decades of the 19th century saw the decline in the numbers of animals passing through the Metropolitan Cattle Market. This was mainly due to the level of foreign livestock imports which were used to supply the London market. Although foreign cattle and sheep were sold on the Metropolitan Cattle Market, Islington, most were sold through the Foreign Cattle Market at Deptford. There was further pressure on the Metropolitan Cattle Market due to the growth in chilled and frozen meat imports and the increasing amount of carcase meat from animals slaughtered in the country that was coming to London by rail. During the early period following the opening of the Metropolitan Cattle Market in 1855, the livestock numbers passing through the market were over 300,000 cattle and about 1,500,000 sheep per annum. For the last decade of the century the average was less than 100,000 cattle and about 700,000 sheep.

Through the 17th and 18th centuries and the beginning of the 19th century, trading patterns in the towns and villages had changed little since medieval times. The regulation of trading and the administration of laws were in the hands of local personages such as magistrates, the mayor, aldermen and officers of the trade guilds. In the absence of a police force, watchmen were employed to patrol towns. Towns and cities had a great deal of autonomy within the overall rule of the crown and central government. Officers of the trade guilds would form the local governing body in many towns, meeting in the Guild Halls. The guilds controlled the number of individuals who could practice the various trades in the towns and the way they conducted their business. The butchery guilds' officers, particularly the Beadles, were responsible for enforcing ordinances relating to the sale of bad or diseased meat and fair trading. Every market had a Clerk of the Market who supervised the traders, especially with regard to weights and measures. The Clerk would hold a court known as *pie poudre* to settle disputes, or to mete out fines or other punishments to miscreant traders. '*The Experienced Butcher*' (1816) refers to 'the unlawful act of forestalling, ingrossing and regrating', with penalties of a two-month prison sentence for the first offence and six months for the second offence, as well as seizure of the goods. In the latter part of the 18th century the butchers of London complained that carcase butchers and jobbers were meeting the droves of livestock on their way to Smithfield, buying large numbers of animals and so diverting them from the market. This had the effect of raising the market price and the carcase butchers would then be able to sell carcases to the retail butchers at higher prices and jobbers would usually find buyers prepared to pay their higher price. This was an act of forestalling and the complaining butchers made representations to the Butchers' Company to take action in the matter but the practice still continued (Jones, 1976).

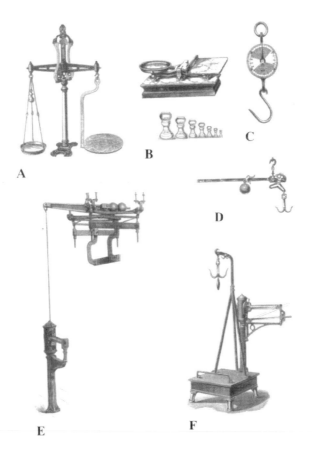

Fig 21.2 Meat Trade Scales.

A. Counter Scale; **B.** Counter Scale. Balance with columns to prevent oscillations; **C.** Salter Spring Balance; **D.** Steelyard; **E.** Slaughterhouse Weighing Machine for hanging carcases. A carcase for weighing was run along the overhead rail to a section that was part of the scale. Weight was determined by moving the counterweight along the lever bar until the bar was in balance; **F.** Bulk Meat Scale used mainly by meat wholesalers. Suitable for weighing carcases or primal meat cuts. The lever bar shows the weight gradations. On the lever bar is the counterweight. The handle below the hook was for the porter to steady and direct the hook as he dropped the carcase/quarter on to the hook.   (Douglas, 1905)

Through the 19th century trade was freed from many of the restrictions. There was the freeing of the importation of livestock and meat in 1842 followed by the final abolition of the corn laws in 1846. The laws against forestalling, ingrossing and regrating were no longer in force, although butchers and traders in the Metropolitan Cattle Market petitioned the City of London Corporation to act against jobbers who were buying animals from salesmen before official market times and selling them later at a profit through other salesmen, thereby forestalling. The committee that dealt with the matter was informed that the laws against forestalling had been repealed for being in restraint of trade and therefore nothing could be done to stop this pre-market trading. The local authorities became responsible for enforcing most of the legislation on fair trading and food safety. The trade guilds' prerogative to regulate the pursuit of the trades in the towns and cities was curtailed by Parliament in 1835 and abolished in 1846. Although there was more freedom for business people to trade and make profits there was also the beginning of the flow of legislation aimed at protecting the consumer and constraining the unscrupulous merchant. There were the Towns Improvement Clauses Act 1847, the model bylaws issued by the Local Government Board in 1877, the Weights and Measures Act 1878, Merchandise Marks Act 1887 and the Public Health Acts. The Municipal Reform Act 1835, constituted the rule of elected local councils and the Local Government Board (a government department) was instituted in 1871 to supervise local services and the administration of the Poor Law. The Local Government Acts of 1858, 1888 and 1894 established the structure and authority of local government (County, Borough, Urban District, Rural District and Parish Councils).

The system governing markets and fairs in the United Kingdom had changed very little from the time of the Anglo-Saxons. Through the centuries, the church, or individuals such as the lord of the manor, had been granted charters to hold a fair or market at a given place on a specified day or days. These charters were often granted in perpetuity and the charter would often give the holder a monopoly over the surrounding area. The charter generally gave the holder rights to levy tolls and collect fines and in some cases to set up a mint and issue coinage. The object of the crown granting charters in medieval times was that the lord of the manor or the bishop would have the power locally to ensure that trade was conducted in a lawful manner. The charter holder or his agent had the authority to determine rightful ownership of goods in the course of transactions. The Local Government Act 1858 gave local authorities the right, under certain conditions, to establish markets and to make by-laws for regulating markets. This enabled the establishment of markets to suit local needs (Collinge, Young & McDougall, 1929).

The Merchandise Marks Act, 1887 made it an offence to describe wrongly anything offered for sale, so that butchers were breaking the law by labelling imported meat as English or Scotch, or by advertising sausages made from beef as pork sausages. The Weights and Measures Act 1887, made it illegal for any trader to use any weight or measure that was not of the denomination of a Board of Trade standard. The act also laid down the system for the appointment of Weights and Measures Inspectors and made it an offence for any person to obstruct an Inspector from entering premises and examining weighing or measuring equipment (Gerrard, 1956).

It had been advocated for many years that finished cattle should be sold by weight (Lord Kaimes advocated this in the 18th century). The Markets and Fairs (Weighing of Cattle) Act 1887, required that weighing machines for weighing cattle be installed at markets and fairs where cattle were sold. Market authorities were reluctant to install these weighing facilities and many were inadequate for the purpose or badly sited in the market, resulting in very few farmers using them. The Markets and Fairs (Weighing of Cattle) Act 1891, extended the requirement of weighing equipment to auction markets with the provision that the Board of Agriculture was to approve all such weighing equipment so that the weighing facilities were improved. Nevertheless in the 1890s there were still less than 6% of farmers in England weighing their cattle before sale. In Scotland the practice of weighing cattle in the markets was much higher, reaching about 30%. The English farmers relied much more on their ability to judge their animals and estimate the weight, which in reality was poor, especially in comparison with the cattle salesmen and butchers. The 1891 Act included a requirement for the regular collection of prices of cattle on a price per stone basis for the maintenance of statistical records. Records of cattle prices by weight, prior to cattle weighing at the markets, were based on rough estimates of cattle weights (Perren, 1978).

CHANGES IN RETAIL MEAT TRADING

The retail butchers' premises changed very little until well into the 19th century. The general type of butcher's shop was a room with a low ceiling, sometimes with an open front which was closed at night by means of a shutter. Immediately behind the shop was the living accommodation and in the back yard was a slaughterhouse. This meant that there was a very large number of slaughterhouses throughout the country; Birmingham had some 300 slaughterhouses in the mid 1800s. There was also the shambles or 'butchers' row', which was usually a row of shops adjacent to, or in front of, a slaughterhouse from which the retail butchers obtained their meat. There was a shambles as part of the public slaughterhouse at Aberdeen which was used until the end of 19th century. Each of the shops in the row was about 15 ft x 15 ft (4.6m x 4.6m) with a large wooden shutter enclosing the front which was hinged at the bottom and when lowered was used as a bench to lay out the meat for sale. The meat cutting was done on blocks which were tree trunks (usually beech) sawn across. Such blocks were reputed to have lasted 20 years in daily use. It is interesting to reflect on how little these shops differed from the descriptions of the butchers' shops of Roman times (Leighton & Douglas, 1910).

Fig 21.3 Meat Market attached to the Glasgow Abattoir (Leighton & Douglas, 1910).

The analysis of the Manchester and Salford records by Roger Scola showed that the majority of retail butchery outlets in the 18th century were stalls in the markets or shambles. The total retail outlets increased from 153 in 1801 to 804 in 1871, by which time most of the outlets were in shops (Scola, 1992). What may affect the analysis is what is defined as a stall and what is defined as a shop. Many of the retail meat markets or shambles consisted of a row of permanent buildings, some including living accommodation, each used as a shop or stall for selling meat.

Fig 21.4 A Butcher's Shop in 1798. Drawing based on an engraving by S W Fores. The packhorse on the left was harnessed to carry carcases.

Fig 21.5 Butcher's Christmas Display in the early 19th Century.

Fig 21.6 Victorian Butcher's Shop. This shop with its low ceiling was built at the beginning of the 19ᵗʰ Century.

Fig 21.7 Shambles, part of the abattoir at Aberdeen which survived to the end of the 19ᵗʰ Century. The shops were shut in at the front by stall boards which were hinged so they could be lowered for the meat to be displayed.

In the latter part of the 19ᵗʰ century butchers were setting up shops in the main streets along with various other traders, moving away from the previous pattern of butchers trading collectively in one area.

Henry Mayhew in '*London Labour and the London Poor*' (1861/62) described the 'hawking butchers' and the 'game and poultry hawkers'. According to Mayhew he was assured that there were never less than 150 hawking butchers in London and sometimes there were 200 or even 250.

He described them as butchers or journeymen butchers who were unable to obtain work. They would attend one of the meat markets (Newgate, Leadenhall, Whitechapel), wait around until they judged that the market prices were at their lowest and then buy some cheap cuts of meat. Normal retail butchers would have bought their meat and left the market early to open their shops and on the late market there were few buyers to whom the meat salesmen could sell their remaining stocks. They were therefore obliged to make deals with the hawking butchers. The hawking butchers carried the meat they had bought in baskets. The most common places for them to sell their meat were the public houses, especially those establishments not too distant from the markets. Mayhew described the hawkers as being hard-drinking men of strong constitution. There were hawking butchers (or carkers) in the other large towns, especially where there was a meat market as a source for their supplies, although in many cases trading with hawking butchers by members of the butchers guild was prohibited (Dodds, 1917).

By the end of the 19th century large, elaborately appointed butchers' shops were appearing in the towns. These consisted of large, light airy shops with high ceilings and fully tiled walls; in some cases the ceilings were also tiled. Generally there were marble shelves in the shop, marble topped counters and a marble window bed for the cut meat display. The windows of these shops were fitted with rails on which to hang joints and carcases for display and outside the shops were rails on which were hung carcases and quarters of beef. Around the walls of the shop were rails for hanging carcases and a variety of joints, poultry, game, sausages, etc. The rails in the shop and the windows were not of the modern stainless steel type but were ordinary steel that required polishing using emery-cloth to get them bright and shiny. The shops had French hornbeam blocks for meat cutting. The cashier's office (usually a small compartment at the back of the shop or a kiosk constructed in the shop) was appropriately placed for the payment of all purchases. Other than in the hot weather large quantities and wide varieties of carcase meat, poultry, offals and sausages were on display. Most of these large shops had rooms at the back of the premises for quite extensive sausage making and meat pickling (salting), although a cellar was often the place for the pickling. Such shops were built and decorated in the fashion of the Victorian era and may have seemed lavish and extravagant to many in the meat trade at the time but it was soon realised that these light, airy shops with a spotlessly clean appearance were a great attraction compared with the dark and dingy shops with low ceilings that were still common. Although the scientific principles of hygiene were not well understood, there was a marked preference to buy food from bright clean shops with shiny surfaces everywhere. This led to butchers' shops, especially those purporting to be high class, being lavishly decorated with tiles and in many cases having tiled rural scenes, including cattle, sheep and pigs. The livery of the staff was regarded as important for good appearances. Many of the town butchery retailers at this time preferred to call themselves purveyors of meat, probably to create a distinction from the shambles or 'butchers' row'.

In the latter part of the 19th century most retail food businesses were family affairs with all of the family, as soon as they were old enough, taking on their share of the work. There was no great rush for retailers to open branches to start multiples. By 1875 in London there were only twelve multiples with 108 shops between them. Often the opening of new branches depended on the number of sons in the family.

John James Sainsbury opened his first shop at 173 Drury Lane in 1869. By 1891 he had opened or acquired 13 branches and established his main depot and headquarters at Blackfriars. Sainsburys expanded to 115 branches by 1914 (Boswell, 1969). The number of butchery businesses in

Fig 21.8 Open Fronted Butcher's Shop c1900.

Fig 21.9 Standard Type of Butcher's Shop c1900.

Manchester and Salford in 1871 with two outlets was 58 out of a total of 804 butchery outlets with no record of a butchery business with more than two outlets (Scola, 1992).

Apart from the high class butchers' shops catering mainly for the middle classes there were the growing working class meat consumers towards the end of the 19th century. In the first half of the

Fig 21.10 Inside View of a Pork-Purveyor's Shop at Glasgow c1900.

19th century the incomes of the working classes were low and the cost of food high which resulted in most working class families having insufficient to eat, therefore carcase meat was beyond their purse. The main content of working class meals was bread, oatmeal, potatoes, fat and tea. A dish that was common was boiled potatoes with melted lard poured over them and, for those who were lucky, it was garnished with a few pieces of fried fat bacon (Drummond & Wilbrahan, 1939).

Change was brought about by the repeal of the Corn Laws and the freeing of the import trade in the middle of the 19th century. This resulted in a dramatic reduction of food prices. Coupled with this was the general rise in the wages of the skilled and unskilled workers. The working class could then afford to buy enough food and their money would stretch to some meat.

This change could not be regarded as affluence as price of any food was still an important factor to the working class housewife. Where there were large catchment areas of working class people there would be at least one street market. The butchers with stalls in the market would obtain the cheaper cuts of meat and keep their prices low looking for a high volume of sales. With the volume importation of frozen meat towards the end of the 19th century, the market butchers took advantage of this lower priced meat.

Apart from the market stalls there were some butchers with shops in working class areas and they would work with open fronted premises. They would often have a block on the pavement and would keep up an endless sales pitch to potential customers and passers-by.

It was a normal practice to pay workers after they had completed a full week's work; therefore paying out at the end of the Saturday's working. This meant that many housewives would be shopping for their Sunday joint late on Saturday, which resulted in butchers working long and late on Saturday. Many would open again on Sunday morning.

MANUFACTURED MEAT PRODUCTS - SAUSAGES AND SMALL GOODS

During the medieval period it was the cooks who made the sausages, brawns, etc., rather than the butchers. In the towns and cities there were those whose trade it was to make and cook pies and cook meat joints to sell to the public. The home making of sausages continued well into the 19th century as a widespread practice.

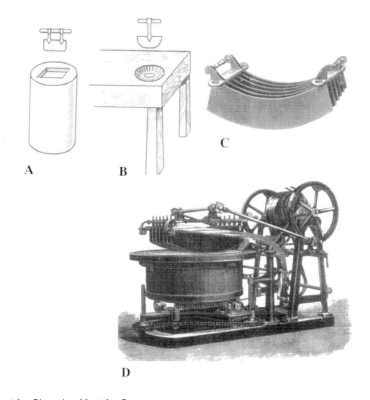

Fig 21.11 Equipment for Chopping Meat for Sausages.

A. Early Type English Block and Hand Chopper; **B.** Early Type Scottish Block and Hand Chopper; **C.** Hand Rocker Meat Cutter for preparing meat for sausages; **D.** Power Rocker Cutter. Sausage meat cutting machine. The series of curved sharp blades were rocked back and forth on a rotating block. Meat fed on to the block was chopped without the meat becoming heated. These machines were widely used in Germany in the late 19th and early 20th Centuries. (Leighton & Douglas, 1910).

According to Youatt the trade of a pork-butcher was unknown in almost all of our country towns before 1820, but by the 1840s there was on average one pork-butcher to every two or three 'meat-butchers' (Youatt, 1847). A possible reason for this could have been that the returning troops after the Napoleonic wars included large numbers of butchers serving in the army who had become acquainted with the continental pork-butcher ('le charcutier') who used their acquired knowledge to open their own pork-butchers' shops in this country. In France the first records of 'charcutier guilds' were in 1415 and 1475. The present guild, 'Confédération Nationale des Charcuteries' was founded in 1805.

The following is a recipe for sausages from a recipe book published in 1665:

> "To make good sausages"
>
> "Take the lean of a Legge of Pork, and four pound of Beef suet, or rather butter, shred them together very small, then season it with three quarters of an ounce of Pepper, and half an ounce of Cloves and Mace mixed together, as the Pepper is, a handful of sage when it is chopt small, and as much salt as you think will make them taste well of it, mingle all these with the meat, then break in ten Eggs, all but two or three of the whites, then temper it all well with your hands, and fill it into Hoggs gutts, which you must have ready for them, you must tye the ends of them like Puddings, and when you eat them you must boyle them on a soft fire, a hot will crack the skins and the goodness boile out of them."(Isitt, 1987)

Street traders selling food have been a common feature of the towns and cities through the ages, including the sausage sellers, the pie man, those selling ready cooked poultry, oyster sellers, etc. Henry Mayew's '*London Labour and the London Poor*' gives a graphic description of various street traders in the mid 19th century. It seems evident that butchers became very active in the manufacture of meat products during the 19th century, in particular those butchers who became specialist pork butchers or pork purveyors. The term pork butcher seems to have originated in the 19th century; likewise the term 'small goods'. 'Small goods' was a comprehensive term which included black puddings, saveloys, Vienna sausages, German sausages, cooked hams, roast pork, savoury ducks, sausage rolls, boiled cabbages, boiled peas, etc. (Douglas, 1905). Pork had emerged as the most popular meat for curing; it was also the most popular meat for use in many of the types of meat product.

The preparation of sausages by cooks and by butchers before the advent of meat chopping machinery was all done by hand. For chopping the meat there was usually a block with a shallow hollowed out portion into which the meat was placed. Using a hand chopper which had a handle fixed to the back of the blade, the meat was chopped finely by an up and down chopping action. The seasoning consisted of salt, pepper and spices that had been ground using a mortar and pestle, and in some cases herbs that had been chopped finely. If required, soaked bread would be used in the sausage mixture. The prepared ingredients were mixed together by hand and then filled into prepared sausage casings or skins (cleaned and scraped intestines). Filling the sausage meat into skins was usually done using a funnel which was small enough at one end for the skins to be threaded on and widening at the other end to a few inches. The sausage meat was placed in the wider end of the funnel and using a wooden plunger the meat was forced through the funnel into the casing. In Scotland, a type of sausage produced in the farmhouses and cottages was a 'saster' which after filling into skins was tied to form a circle. These 'sasters' were hung up in the kitchen to dry and would remain there until required. They would keep for several weeks but tended to get harder with time and their character would change being enjoyed mainly by those who had acquired a taste for them (*Ibid*).

The English type butchers' sausage, or fresh sausage as distinct from the dry or Continental sausage, became widely established in the 19th century. The main difference between the fresh and the dry sausage was the use of non-cured meat in the fresh sausage and the inclusion of a binder (which was mainly soaked bread). There was a wide range of recipes for fresh sausage, the difference between the recipes being the type of meat and the spices and herbs used. The following is a 19th century recipe for pork sausages:

    15lb   lean pork,
     6lb   back fat (pork),
     4lb   soaked and pressed bread,
     8oz   salt
     5oz   ground white pepper,
     ¼oz   ground nutmeg
     ¼oz   ground ginger
     ½oz   rubbed sage
     2oz   dry antiseptic as a preservative (borax – now illegal)

In the early part of the 20th century the soaked bread was replaced by soaked biscuit powder by some sausage makers. During the 1920s and 30s specially manufactured yeastless rusk became commonly used as the binder.

It was the case with some of the less scrupulous traders that the sausage was used as a means of selling meat that had deteriorated beyond being saleable as fresh meat. These traders would rely on a liberal amount of herbs and spices to mask the taint of the meat.

In the latter part of the 19th century tools and machines were developed for sausage and other meat product manufacture, leading to better organised output of these products by the butchers. The availability of these meat-manufacturing machines also led to factories being set up for the large-scale manufacture of meat products. In some cases these factories were additions to bacon factories whose owners saw meat products as an ideal opportunity for expansion of their business, especially as meat products complemented their existing production.

Many of the meat cutters, fillers, etc., produced in the late 19th century were very similar to those in use today. The 'silent meat cutters' were of French origin and the earliest types of this machine were in use in Britain in the 1850s. They were called silent meat cutters because in comparison with other machines they made much less noise. These machines consisted of a dished bowl mounted on a vertical shaft; over this bowl was a fixed horizontal shaft between the centre and the circumference of the bowl on which was fixed a number of curved knife blades that rotated within a millimetre of the surface of the bowl. The bowl was rotated by a worm gearing on the vertical shaft moving the meat under the rotating knife blades. The silent meat cutter would be easily recognised today as a bowl chopper. The other type of meat cutting machine was the 'Alexander meat cutter' which consisted of a horizontal barrel containing a spiral propeller. Meat was fed into the barrel from a hopper and was pushed forward by the spiral propeller to a four bladed knife that rotated against a plate; there were a number of holes in the plate through which the meat was pushed to be cut by the knife. The size of the holes in the plate governed the coarseness or fineness of the meat when chopped. The Alexander meat cutter would be recognised today as a mincer.

Fig 21.12 Early Bowl Choppers.

A. Hand-Operated Silent Meat Cutter (Bowl Chopper). The shaft turned by the handle was geared to turn the bowl and to rotate the curved knives under the protective cover which cut the meat. The gearing for these knives rotated them at a much higher ratio than the rate of the bowl turning. This type of machine was of French origin and designs of these machines did not appear in Britain until after 1851. The term "Silent" was given in contrast to the vertical meat chopper which was extremely noisy. The modern bowl choppers still work on the same principle as the Silent Meat Cutters. **B.** Power Driven Silent Meat Cutter (Douglas, 1905).

Sausage fillers were very similar to those of today with the machines being either the vertical or horizontal design. The basic principle of the fillers, as today, was a metal barrel into which the meat was placed and the end of the barrel was closed except for a hole leading to a nozzle. There was a plunger that was pushed into the barrel forcing the sausage meat along the barrel and out through the nozzle. Sausage skins were threaded onto the nozzle so that the sausage meat would fill into the skins as it was forced through the nozzle. The plunger was fixed to the end of a ratchet bar with which a cog wheel engaged and as the cog wheel was turned it pushed the plunger into the barrel (Douglas, 1905).

To begin with the silent meat cutters, Alexander meat cutters and sausage meat fillers were hand-operated machines. In the latter part of the 19th century, larger power driven machines were being constructed that were largely belt driven using steam engines or electric motors.

The 'rocker' meat cutter was in common use in Germany in the 19th century. This consisted of a number of curved blades (six or eight), fixed in a parallel arrangement. Meat for chopping was placed on a block and the instrument was used with a rocking action to reduce the meat to finely chopped pieces. Power driven versions of this instrument were being made in the latter part of the 19th century. These machines had a rotating block on which the meat was placed so that the meat was continuously moving under the blades which rocked back and forth fractionally above the block surface (Leighton & Douglas, 1910).

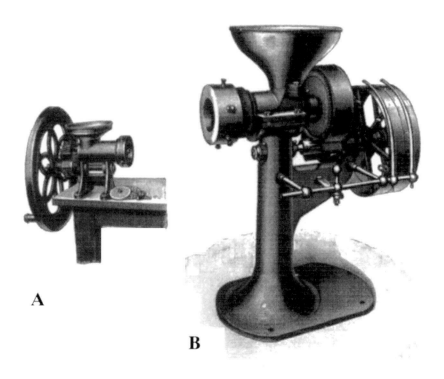

Fig 21.13 Early Mincers.

A. Hand Driven Alexander Meat Cutter (Mincer)
B. Large Alexander Meat Cutter (Mincer), power driven (Leighton & Douglas, 1910).

Many pork butchers became very successful in the urban areas during the last half of the 19th century, building reputations for high quality meat products. They sold a considerable range of sausages, pies, ham, bacon and other products such as faggots (savoury ducks) and saveloys. Some of these pork butchers expanded their production capacity beyond the needs of their shop so as to supply hotels and restaurants. It was in the last half of the 19th century that a number of large scale manufacturers of meat products became established and built factories in which they employed hundreds of workers and were producing sausages and other meat products in huge quantities. Some of these factories were very large establishments complete with engine room, meat pickling rooms, boning and cutting rooms, machine rooms (where the manufacture took place), smoking chambers, drying and chilling rooms and cold stores. These manufacturers had retail shops in the main shopping centres and also sold their products to grocers for resale. The sale by the grocer of sausages, ham and bacon brought them into competition with the butchers and pork butchers.

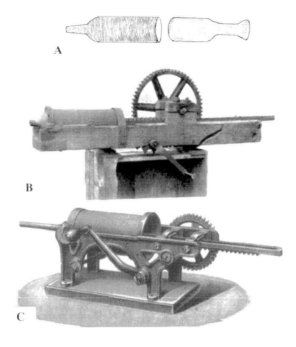

Fig 21.14 Early Sausage Fillers.

A. Hand-held Sausage Filler. Soaked sausage casings were threaded on to the nozzle and sausage meat was packed into the barrel, forced through the nozzle with the wooden plunger, filling the casings. This type of filler was frequently used by cooks for filling their sausages.
B. An early 19th Century Sausage Filler.
C. A Horizontal Hand-operated Sausage Filler. The plunger was in the form of a circular plate attached to a ratcheted bar. Turning the handle pushed the plate into the barrel, forcing the sausage meat through the nozzle. Operating this type of filler allowed one hand free to guide the sausage meat into the casing. This style of filler is still in use in butchers' shops today (Douglas, 1905).

Fig 21.15 Vans ready to start their deliveries from a sausage and meat products factory c. 1900.

Although electric motors were coming into use by the end of the 19th century, the main power for factories was steam engines (usually housed in the engine room) driving an overhead shaft which ran through openings in the partition walls to the machine rooms. Positioned along the shaft were a series of pulley wheels and from each pulley wheel would run a belt to drive a machine; namely a meat cutter, mixer, filler, etc. By varying the size of the pulley wheels the speed at which the machines ran could be altered.

CORNED BEEF AND MEAT EXTRACTS

Justus von Liebig was born in Darnstadt, Germany, in 1803 and became renown for his work in organic chemistry for which he was made a Baron. In the 1840s, von Liebig developed a concentrated meat extract which could be used as a substitute for beef tea and had various other uses in cooking (Fig 21.16). In 1847 von Liebig publicised his extract in a treatise "*Extractum Carnis*". The main drawback to this extract commercially was the high price of meat in Germany. Georges Giebert met von Liebig in 1860 and told him of the vast herds of feral cattle in Uruguay which were only utilised for their hides, tallow and strips of meat to produce the dried beef charqui. The bulk of the carcase meat was left to rot.

Justus von Liebig and Georges Giebert set up a factory for the production of meat extract in Villa Independencia which was on the River Uruguay. This gave it access to ocean going ships. Villa Independencia was later re-named Fray Bentos.

With the rapid growth of business Giebert went to London in 1865 to establish a new company "Liebig's Extract of Meat Co. Ltd". To attract investment the Liebig Company extensively advertised the meat extract, emphasising its therapeutic and body building attributes, in Britain and Europe. It

Fig 21.16 Late 19th Century Advertisement for Liebig's Beef Extract.

was advertised in women's magazines and newspapers and displays were set up at all the exhibitions. In 1899 Liebig's extract of beef became Oxo.

By the time of the death of Baron von Liebig in 1873 and Giebert in 1874, the Liebig Company was well established for continued trading. The Leibig Company extended their operations into Argentina and Paraguay and in about 1897/8 began production of canned corned beef, taking advantage of the complementary nature of meat extract and corned beef. The Boer War and later the First World War proved to be great stimuli to the production of canned corned beef. Canned corned beef became one of the most important commodities for supplying troops in the field due to its virtual unlimited shelf life.

Dr Edward Kemmerich was appointed to the Leibig Company in 1873 and in 1882 he resigned to form a company in partnership with Giebert's son Walter, "Compagnie des Produits Kemmerich, S.A." in Argentina. This Kemmerich company established two factories at Santa Elena and San Javier which were taken over in 1908 by John Lawson Johnson, founder of Bovril. He disposed of the San Javier factory and the Santa Elena factory formed the basis of his meat extract and corned beef operation.

Canned corned beef production originated in the USA. Arthur Libby founded his meat canning company in 1868 and was producing corned beef in tapered cans in the 1870s and in 1878 exported the first corned beef to Britain. Armour was another company canning meat, including corned beef, in the late 19th century.

From the 1860s, meat canning became a major industry in Australia but corned beef did not seem to feature strongly in their production. In New Zealand, Hellabys of Auckland in the 1880s were canning various meats and produced corned beef and corned mutton. This corned beef had a high fat content (25%) which was to suit the tastes of the South Sea Islanders.

The corned beef product of South America set the standard for canned corned beef. The manufacture was to cut the meat into small pieces. The meat was parboiled for 15-20 minutes and the liquor drained off to be concentrated into meat extract. The meat was then mixed with curing salts, packed into cans, sealed and sterilised; the curing and final cooking taking place in the can.

THE RANGE OF SLAUGHTERHOUSES BY THE END OF THE 19TH CENTURY

At the close of the 19th century butchers in the rural areas and many of the independent butchers in the smaller towns still maintained their small slaughterhouses. This enabled these butchers to continue their practice of buying livestock either direct from local farmers or from the local market, which they slaughtered themselves. Although it was a very small scale operation there were savings because there were no middlemen, no transport costs and no slaughtering costs, but it necessitated the butchers being able to dispose profitably of the inedible offals (hides, skins, fleeces, tallow, etc.). It meant a great deal of extra work for butchers to do their own slaughtering and required a wider range of skills i.e. the skills of the slaughterman as well as those of the retail butcher. Many rural butchers would have had some grazing land close to their premises, which gave them flexibility when buying from the livestock market. Some butchers had enough grazing land for them to make additional profit as graziers, buying in store stock to fatten.

Fig 21.17 Interior of a small Private Slaughterhouse illustrating the lack of importance given to hygiene in some of these places.

Although there still remained a very large number of small private slaughterhouses, generally one slaughterhouse serving only one retail shop, during the Victorian period many large slaughterhouses were built. The small private slaughterhouses in the towns were frequently situated in built up areas. The trouble caused by driving livestock through the streets to the slaughterhouses, as well as the noise and smells, resulted in growing pressure against these establishments. Town dwellers were becoming less tolerant of this type of nuisance. The majority of the larger slaughterhouses were public slaughterhouses or abattoirs, all of which were built to serve a reasonable size town or large conurbation. The perceived structure of a community was still such that slaughterhouses were rated as an essential service along with markets, water supplies and drains. Because of this there was a strong body of opinion in favour of public slaughterhouses owned by the local authority. The *Scotsman* newspaper of January 29, 1849 carried a piece on "The Necessity for Public Slaughterhouses". Of the many public slaughterhouses operating at the end of the 19th century, the probability is that very few of them were running at a profit. Notable among the larger private slaughterhouses were a number owned by the Co-operative Societies. The Middlesborough Co-operative Society's slaughterhouse was a good, well run establishment and in the year 1888 to 1889 had sales of £10,550, showing a gross profit of £1,137 and a net profit of £353.

Many of the small private slaughterhouses from the early part of the 19th century were still in use at the end of the century. These were dilapidated buildings, the floor generally consisting of uneven flagstones with grime filling the gaps between the stones and the brick walls covered only with limewash. The larger slaughterhouses built in the last decades of the 19th century were more

Fig 21.18 Killing a sheep in a Private Slaughterhouse (Leighton & Douglas, 1910).

like the factory type constructions that became common in the 20th century. The floors were impervious, being mainly of concrete and the walls had an impervious covering, often of ceramic tiles, to at least a height of six feet. There were overhead rail systems on which ran roller hooks for whole carcases or sides of beef to be moved around the slaughterhouse. Hoists were used to raise the carcases to the overhead rails. Scales were built into the overhead system so that carcases could be weighed on the rail. Engineering companies in Britain, USA and Europe (especially Germany) were becoming very involved in designing and producing slaughterhouse equipment, resulting in a constantly improving wide range being available.

Public slaughterhouses were constructed either in the booth system or the open system. For the booth system the slaughterhall was separated into a series of booths or compartments by partition walls. Each booth was large enough for the slaughter and dressing of a beast. Two or three butchers, generally a slaughterman and two assistants, worked as a team slaughtering and dressing one animal at the time. In the slaughterhouses with a large throughput there were a number of such teams working simultaneously in separate booths, each team killing their allocation of animals (as distinct from the line systems of today). The larger slaughterhouses constructed on the open hall system had a slaughterhall that was a large open room with none of the partition walls of the booth system. An advantage of the open system was that it was easier to clean. The booths had a ring fitted to the wall to secure the animal's head for stunning. In the open hall system rings were embedded in the floor allowing 10 feet in each direction from the ring for the slaughterers to work.

Fig 21.19 Scalding a Pig in a small Slaughterhouse. At the back can be seen a built-in boiler for heating the water and a ladle on the top for transferring the hot water to the tub (Leighton & Douglas, 1910).

Fig 21.20 A Slaughterhouse in Dumfriesshire early 1900s. This illustrates some of the standards that still existed at this time.

Fig 21.21 The Co-operative Society Abattoir at Stockton. Photographs of abattoirs often show individuals merely present for being part of the photograph (Leighton & Douglas, 1910).

Building slaughterhouses on the open hall system was favoured where animals could be slaughtered in large groups e.g. for a meat company. Public slaughterhouses constructed on the booth system were more appropriate for serving the independent butchers with small numbers of animals to be slaughtered. These butchers would either slaughter the animals themselves or pay for them to be slaughtered. In some public slaughterhouses butchers could rent a booth on an annual basis with an additional headage payment on each animal they slaughtered. Butchers not renting a booth would pay more per head for animals slaughtered. The booth system was in fact a number of small slaughterhouses built together on one site. In some places there were separate pig slaughtering sheds. Large scale pig slaughtering took place in the bacon factories. A number of bacon factories had been built in the latter part of the 19th century. The Roscrea Bacon Factory in County Tipperary, Ireland, was established by a farmers' co-operative which began in 1888.

An example of the type of public slaughterhouse established in the smaller towns was the one at Falkirk erected in 1873, which was owned and managed by the Corporation. The public killing-chamber was described as spacious and lofty and the walls were covered with a smooth cement rendering to a height of six feet. Beyond the killing-chamber there was a large spacious chamber completely lined with glazed white tiles where meat was hung after slaughter. There were two private booths let out each year to the highest bidder for their exclusive use; no sub-letting permitted. There was a separate 'sheepery' (a place for slaughtering sheep), with lairage and hanging space for carcases and separate accommodation for slaughtering pigs. A tripery in connection with the slaughterhouse was under the management of the Corporation. Gut scraping and disposing of blood was dealt with by a contractor, for which purpose special accommodation was provided. The dungstead was emptied regularly by the local authority.

Fig 21.22 Photograph of the old Leeds Slaughterhouse. Note its mainly wooden structure.

LEGISLATION TO CONTROL SLAUGHTERHOUSES

There was a growing awareness during the 19th century of the need for hygiene in regard to food. There was also an increasing number of people becoming concerned over cruelty to animals. These developments and the nuisance caused by many slaughterhouses, led to legislation aimed at controlling slaughterhouses. The Towns Improvement Clauses Act 1847 contained the following provisions:

Fig 21.23 Photograph of the Slaughterhouse built in 1899 to replace the old slaughterhouse shown in Fig 21.22.

Fig 21.24 Stunning Pen for Cattle. When the animal was stunned the floor of the pen dropped and the animal rolled out on to the slaughterhouse floor.

"The Commissioners (Urban Authority) shall, from time to time, make regulations for the licensing, registering and inspection of slaughterhouses and preventing cruelty therein, and for keeping the same in a cleanly and proper state, and for removing filth at least once in 24 hours, and requiring them to be provided with a sufficient supply of water; and they may impose pecuniary penalties on persons breaking such bylaws; providing that no such penalty exceed for one offence the sum of five pounds, and in the case of a continuing nuisance the sum of ten shillings for every day during which such nuisance shall be continued after the conviction for the first offence".

Fig 21.25 Tripery in the Glasgow Public Abattoir (Leighton & Douglas, 1910).

The next section of the Act provided that any person convicted of offences under the regulations could, additional to other penalties, have their licence suspended for not more than two months. On a second offence the person could have his licence revoked and could be refused the granting of any future licences. Slaughterhouses that continued slaughtering after their licence had been suspended or revoked would be subject to a fine not exceeding five pounds and five pounds per day for the continuing offence.

There was a section that related to the construction of a slaughterhouse which stated therein that:

> "No slaughterhouse or its lairages should be erected within 100ft of a dwelling house.
> There should be free ventilation by direct communication to the outside air on at least two sides of the building.
> The floor should be covered with asphalt or concrete sloping to a gully that must be properly trapped.
> Internal walls should be covered with impervious material to a sufficient height.
> No water closet, privy or cesspool should be built within, or directly communicate with, a slaughterhouse.
> An adequate tank for water should be provided and raised to a height of not less than six feet above the slaughterhouse floor.
> No part of the slaughterhouse should be lower than the adjoining ground.
> No room or loft should be constructed over a slaughterhouse.
> Lairages should be properly paved, drained and ventilated."

These provisions were incorporated into the Public Health Act 1875.

Fig 21.26 A Gut Room in an Irish Bacon Factory. This is the part of the slaughterhouse that has always been regarded as most unpleasant (Leighton & Douglas, 1910)

CRAFT GUILDS AND LIVERY COMPANIES

The role and importance of the craft guilds changed significantly from the Middle Ages to the 19th century. With the emergence from the Dark Ages the guilds were of major importance in the establishment of the towns, sponsoring and controlling the commercial activities and being very much involved in the administration of the town's affairs in general; as evidenced today by the presence of guild halls in many towns. Through time much of the guilds' power and influence had passed to other municipal authorities, such as the mayors and aldermen, leaving the guilds with little more than their fraternal activities.

The Enlightenment of the 18th century evoked criticism of the craft guilds in Europe. This was followed by decrees abolishing the craft guilds in France in 1791, Spain in 1840, Austria and Germany in 1859 – 60 and Italy in 1864. Craft guilds continued to flourish in India, China, Japan and the Islamic World into the 20th century but they too eventually succumbed to the impact of the western industrial organisation (Encyclopaedia Britannica 1999.)

In Britain the Municipal Reform Act of 1835 established the elected councils to take over responsibility for the administration of the urban areas. In the country areas the authority still remained under the Justices of the Peace meeting at the Quarter Sessions until the Local Government Act of 1888 which established the county councils. Most of the craft guilds throughout the country ceased to exist by the end of the 19th century but even today there are the Fleshers Guild of Glasgow, The Butchers' Guild of York and The Worshipful Company of Butchers of London, all very active. In fact the Guilds and Livery Companies of the City of London are still expanding in number with some of them representing the latest occupations such as information technology. The liverymen of the Butchers' Company are still predominantly people employed in, or associated with, the meat trade. Some of the livery companies still retain their age-old authority as with the Goldsmiths' Company carrying out the hall marking of gold and the Fishmongers' Company employing the fish inspectors for the City. The Butchers' Company continue to play an active part in the education and training in the meat trade.

NATIONAL FEDERATION OF MEAT TRADERS' ASSOCIATIONS

Towards the end of the 19th century life was becoming more complex for the butchers of Britain with increasing imports of meat from all parts of the world. There was also the growing tide of legislation relating to hygiene, the fitness of meat for sale, weights and measures and the control of animal diseases. As a result butchers began forming themselves into associations locally. In 1886 Mr Edward Darby of Leeds, along with some Yorkshire meat traders, were convinced that the establishment of a unified national body was necessary to act on behalf of the meat traders. At the annual conference of the Yorkshire Confederation of Meat Traders' Associations held on the 12th March 1888, it was resolved to form the National Federation of Meat Traders' Associations of the United Kingdom. The following are a list of demands that the federation resolved to pursue for appropriate government action:

Humane treatment of livestock in transit by sea and land.
Minimum mileage speed per hour on cattle trains.
Special rates for carriage of dead meat, offals, &c.
Special railway rates on livestock.
Free passes (as before) for men travelling in charge of cattle.
Bovine tuberculosis: compensation for butchers from imperial exchequer.
Private slaughterhouses: compensation to proprietors where premises are compulsorily closed, &c.
Meat inspection: general adoption of the butchers' jury system.
Uniformity of veterinary inspection.

Additionally, the federation decided to press for a requirement that farmers give a warranty with their cattle when sold on the open market. Throughout the associations there was a strong commitment to technical education in connection with the meat industry (Leighton & Douglas, 1910).

BUTCHERS' CHARITABLE INSTITUTION

The Butchers' Charitable Institution was founded in London on 16th October 1828, "for affording relief to decayed and distressed master butchers, master pork butchers, cattle and meat commission salesmen, and hide and skin salesmen, their widows and orphans".

Chapter 22

Meat Inspection and the Sale of Unfit Meat

It had long been an offence under common law to sell unsound meat and some statutes were enacted for this purpose, but it was the Public Health Act of 1875 and the Public Health (Scotland) Act 1897 that started effective control over the fitness of the meat offered for sale in Britain. To prevent the sale of unsound meat the onus continued to be on the meat trader. It was an offence to sell (or offer for sale) for human consumption meat that was unfit. It was many years after the Public Health Act 1875 was enacted before the operation of a total meat inspection service was to become a legal responsibility of the respective authorities (Meat Inspection Regulations 1963). (The requirement for both ante-mortem and post-mortem inspection was contained in a Bavarian regulation of 1615. This stated that animals for slaughter for human consumption should be inspected alive, as well as after slaughter, by ordained meat inspectors who were chosen from suitable persons, one to be appointed for each village by rural courts.)

AWARENESS OF THE NEED FOR MEAT INSPECTION

Although microscopes had been invented as early as the 17th century by the Dutch scientist Anthony van Leeuwenhoek (1632-1723) who also produced and published the first drawings of bacteria, it was not established until the last decades of the 19th century that these micro-organisms were a major cause of disease (Burrows, 1973). Before the late 19th century it was a common belief by many, including medical practitioners, that a major cause of disease was the miasmas or infectious and noxious vapours arising from filthy or putrescent matter. Foul smells had been associated for many centuries with the risk of infection, hence the practice of carrying nosegays of flowers by gentlewomen for protection. 'The Experienced Butcher' quotes from Tissot's Essay on the 'Diseases of Literary and Sedentary Persons' that "they should fix themselves at a distance from places which emit unwholesome exhalations, such as slaughterhouses, the shambles, tanners' yards &c." This quotation touches on another belief that the lower classes were less vulnerable to suffer disease from living and working in bad conditions than the upper classes; also the poorer classes were not in need of as good a diet as the upper classes. The attitude that connected disease with filth, putrescence and anything with an obnoxious appearance or smell, although in many aspects based on scientific inaccuracies, was the incentive for improving hygiene in meat handling. There have been many statutes making the sale of diseased or unwholesome meat an offence.

By the 1840s the death rate in the large conurbations had reached a level causing such concern that a Board of Health was established in 1848. The considered causes of the diseases taking toll of the urban populations was contained in a report in the *Journal of the Statistical Society* 1847;

"It is well known... that the excessive mortality from disease....in towns is occasioned by animal or vegetable poisons... depending on accumulated filth, crowding in dwellings and workshops, the closeness of courts, imperfect supplies of water, want of efficient sewers... The precise degree of influence to which the various agencies have in causing the high mortality in the towns, is not easily determined. Opinions differ as to what fraction of the suffering and death is to be set down to the want of water or of sewerage - crowded lodgings, narrow streets, ill ventilated workshops - the destitution of skilful medical advice - neglect of children - doses of opium and overflowings of quackery - slaughterhouses and rank churchyards."

Edwin Chadwick (later Sir Edwin Chadwick), who had been the secretary of the Royal Commission on poor law became a commissioner of the Board of Health and was a driving force for the Board in obtaining improvements in the water supply, sanitation and removal of decaying refuse in urban areas.

The empirical knowledge relating to cause of disease in humans had established that some disease was transmitted from animals, as a result of eating infected meat or drinking infected milk. The general belief was that infected meat would be in poor condition lacking the bright appearance of fresh killed meat. There was also an inherent belief that putrefaction increased the level of infection. The general attitude was that meat that was judged by its appearance as unfit for sale was therefore a danger to health, which was often not the case. '*The Experienced Butcher*' quotes from Dr Buchan's '*Domestic Medicine*':

"Animal food may be rendered unwholesome, by being kept too long. All animal substances have a constant tendency to putrefaction; and, when that has proceeded too far, they not only become offensive to the senses but harmful to health."

Putrefaction can produce toxic products called ptomaines but this would only be after extreme decomposition of the meat. The putrefactive process will destroy some disease organisms such as the anthrax bacilli and research has shown that salmonella organisms cannot compete with the putrefactive bacteria.

The unfortunate situation with regard to anthrax was the general belief that it was caused by highly nutritious or artificial feeds resulting in apoplexy. Many people retained this belief for some years after Koch established the cause being the *Bacillus anthracis*. The result was that farmers finding animals showing signs of the disease would slaughter the animal on the farm in an attempt at least to salvage the value of the skin and possibly have a carcase to sell to the butcher. The effect was that the blood of the infected animal would have contained large numbers of the bacilli and by releasing this blood, spores would have formed from the bacilli to contaminate the farm buildings, yards and surrounding area. The presence of the spores perpetuated the disease by infecting other animals, even years later. Persons slaughtering the animals and others on the farm were put at risk from anthrax; likewise persons handling the skins and meat. Anthrax bacilli need contact with air (i.e. oxygen) to form spores.

RESPONSIBILITY FOR MEAT INSPECTION

Responsibility for meat inspection had long rested with the butchers' or fleshers' guilds. In 1623, Wardens of the Butchers' Company in London declared that mutton sold by John Boon was "scarce fit for any Christian to eat". For his offence, John Boon was paraded through the market streets and then taken to Newgate prison. Some beef was seized by the Beadle of the Butchers' Company from Richard Lucus in Leadenhall Market in 1775 and when he appeared before the Court of the Company his behaviour was so contemptuous that he was ordered to be indicted at the Quarter Sessions. The Market Act of 1674 continued the right of the officers of the Butcher's Company to supervise and inspect meat and confirmed their right to prosecute offenders and seize unfit meat. The Company continued to exercise these rights up to the beginning of the 19th century but the maximum fine that they could impose was forty shillings, which proved inadequate as a deterrent and poor compensation for the Company for the cost of inspection in the markets. Pork was more commonly found to be unfit, 'measles' pork often presenting problems. In an attempt to reduce the problem of the sale of bad pork in the summer, the close season for pork had been extended to six months in 1607 but was later reduced to just over three months in 1752. Up until the beginning of the 17th century meat seized as being unfit for human consumption was then distributed to the prisons. In 1763, meat was seized from Richard Whitehead in Newgate market and ordered to be thrown in the River Thames by the Lord Mayor of London but for most other occasions unfit meat was burnt in Smithfield or Moorfields (Jones, 1976).

'*The Experienced Butcher*', 1816, quotes from Dr Buchan on the subject of inflating calves:

> "The abominable custom of filling the cellular membrane of animals with air, in order
> to make them appear fat, is every day practised. This not only spoils the meat, and
> renders it unfit for keeping, but is such a dirty trick, that the very idea of it is sufficient
> to disgust a person of any delicacy, of every thing that comes from the shambles.
> Who can bear the thought of eating meat which has been blown up with air from the
> lungs of a dirty fellow, perhaps labouring under the very worst of diseases?"

SALE OF UNFIT MEAT

Concerns voiced in the middle of the 19th century about diseased animals being slaughtered and sold as food did not distinguish between the risks to human health and the risks to animal health. Notable among the 19th century crusaders intent on obtaining government action with regard to the sale of meat from diseased animals, were John Gamgee, a veterinary surgeon, and Joseph Sampson Gamgee, who qualified as a veterinary surgeon but took up human medicine. John Gamgee published a monthly journal the '*Edinburgh Veterinary Review*' from 1858 to 1865. He included in this journal articles relating to practices in the meat trade that he considered unacceptable and consequently pressed for reform. Revelations made by John Gamgee between 1858 and 1865 disclosed a practice of slaughtering diseased animals and the sale of the meat after the removal of those parts showing signs of disease. Aberdeen was one place singled out by Gamgee as a place where this occurred. Aberdeen was an important centre for the slaughter of cattle and dispatch of carcase meat to London. The slaughtering was dispersed among many slaughterhouses spread over the district, including a significant number of animals being slaughtered on farms outside the city. This made any attempt at control very difficult, if not impossible. The city had a meat inspector, Mr D.Mellis, but he was overworked endeavouring to carry out all meat inspection and enforce hygiene within the city (Edinburgh Veterinary Review, 1858-1865).

There were problems with the sale of unfit meat in Leeds that led to the appointment of James Higgins as the corporation's meat inspector in 1858. Higgins had formerly been a butcher but he had no training in veterinary subjects so he had to rely entirely on his experience. His responsibilities were to supervise the butchers' shops and slaughterhouses in Leeds and prevent, as far as possible, the sale of unfit meat. He managed to restrict the traffic in meat from diseased animals reaching the butchers' shops in Leeds, to a large extent, because he had the power to seize such meat and have it destroyed. As there was money to be made by unscrupulous traders, they found outlets for this meat by taking it to other towns where meat inspection was non-existent. This situation was made possible due to the lack of a national policy. Glasgow was open to abuses as there was no inspection in the slaughterhouses and only an inspector of markets who, according to Gamgee, had very little knowledge of disease in animals and would only reject meat if it was in a such a state as to be patently obvious to anyone that it was unfit for food (Perren, 1978).

John Gamgee in correspondence published by the 'Scotsman' and 'Glasgow Herald' in 1857 described the circumstances relating to diseased meat that was being sold in Edinburgh. A summary of his findings is as follows:

> This meat was mainly from farms outside the city or the city dairies (a situation also occurring in other towns). When a cow died in one of the city dairies it was taken to a farm at Corstorphine, which was outside the city and therefore outside the jurisdiction of the Edinburgh inspectors. At Corstorphine the carcases were dressed and evidence of disease removed and the meat taken back into Edinburgh for sale to the general public. Some farmers, if they had a sick animal that would be doubtful for acceptance by the inspectors as fit for human consumption, slaughtered the animal on the farm and took the carcase, or those parts not showing signs of disease, to the city for sale. Carcases from livestock that had died on these farms were also sold in the city after skinning and dressing. When the Edinburgh inspectors became aware of this practice, although they did not have power to stop the activities on the farm at Corstorphine, they made it much more difficult for this meat to enter the city, with a result that the meat was taken elsewhere, in particular to Glasgow (Edinburgh Veterinary Review 1858-1865).

There were similar problems in Birmingham as detailed in the Town Clerk's report of 1863. According to this report, the inspector employed by the city had seized five tons of diseased or unsound meat in 1861 and four tons in 1862. This unfit meat had been discovered in slaughterhouses, markets and at premises where meat products were manufactured, e.g. the manufacture of sausages, saveloys and faggots. The premises used for making meat products were sometimes ordinary domestic premises with no separation between the domestic occupation and the manufacturing. Some of the unfit meat was detected in public-house yards where carriers brought their carts loaded with produce from the country. The situation in Birmingham, as with most other towns and cities, was that it had only one inspector to oversee some 300 slaughterhouses, the markets and butchers' shops and the meat arriving by carrier from outside the boundaries of the borough; this gave the unscrupulous ample opportunity to trim their meat, removing any signs of disease. A report by the Select Committee on the Adulteration of Food, Drinks and Drugs 1856 includes evidence by the officer of the Local Board of Health for the Newton Heath district of Manchester. According to the officer, R.J.Richardson, three of the sixteen slaughterhouses in the district specialised in slaughtering diseased animals and preparing the meat for sale for human consumption. These animals had suffered various diseases according to the descriptions of their condition, including some described as being 'graped' (tuberculosis) and some meat was called 'slinked meat'. Meat that was reasonable in appearance was retailed as fresh meat and the more dubious looking parts of a carcase were used for meat products, such as sausages. Successful prosecutions occurred from time to time but the level of the fines were no deterrent to the traders engaged in this business. A large proportion of the poor people of Manchester at this time were tied to a retailer by debt. When they paid their week's bill they would have no money left to buy meat for the following week and therefore relied on that butcher's further credit to feed their families. This meant that the customers could not afford to change their butcher regardless of their opinion on the quality or nature of the meat he sold.

In a letter to the Home Secretary in 1857, Joseph Gamgee relates an occasion in Newgate Market when he drew the attention of the inspector, Mr Pocklington, to some beef in a putrid state, which in Gamgee's opinion was unfit for human consumption. The meat was being offered for 1½d lb. compared with the normal price of about 6d lb. The inspector, who had previously been a trader in the market, disagreed with Gamgee and took no action in the case. The Cattle Plague Commissioners' report of 1866 includes details from Dr Letherby, Medical Officer of Health for the City of London, relating to the situation in London. The total amount of meat that was seized as unfit from the London markets from 1861 to 1865 was 418 tons but Dr Letherby considered that much more than this actually passed into the shops of the lower class butchers. A good deal of this meat would have escaped the notice of the inspectors and the absence of inspection outside the city permitted a regular trade in diseased meat immediately outside the city. According to Dr Letherby, butchers within the city justly complained that they were closely watched and liable to legal prosecution if they did what the butchers outside the city could do with impunity.

In those towns and cities where carcases were seized to be destroyed as unfit, there was a considerable representation by the local meat traders complaining that many of the seizures were unjustified. The result of such representations in Leeds led to an arrangement in 1860 that any animal suspected of having a disease condition had to be notified to the inspector who would inspect it post-mortem and judge the fitness for food of the carcase. In 1878 a system was introduced in Birmingham known as the 'Butcher's Jury' that consisted of six members or past members of the trade selected by the Markets and Fairs Committee from a list submitted by the trade. If an inspector seized a carcase or other meat and the owner of the meat disputed the reasons for the seizure, three members of the 'Butcher's Jury' would be called to give opinions on that meat. After considering the opinions of the inspector and the members of the 'Butcher's Jury', the Medical Officer of Health and the veterinary inspector would give the final decision (Leighton & Douglas, 1910).

It was estimated by John Gamgee that meat from diseased animals sold for human consumption in Britain in the middle of the 19th century was as much as 20% of the total consumed (Edinburgh Veterinary Review 1858-1865). It appears from the records that the problem of meat from diseased animals was not significant prior to 1840, which needs to be considered in relation to the change in the pattern of animal disease from the late 1830s. The first appearance in Britain of foot and mouth disease was 1839 and contagious bovine pleural-pneumonia in 1841 (Stratton, 1978). There were severe epidemics of these diseases which meant that instead of a farmer losing the occasional animal to disease, many farmers were facing substantial losses. There was a strong inducement for farmers to recoup some of their losses by sending animals for slaughter that were in the early stages of one of these diseases before the animals lost weight and condition. Town dairies suffered considerable losses from contagious bovine pleural-pneumonia and tuberculosis because the close confined space in which the cows were kept was most conducive to the spread of these diseases. According to Youatt (1834) the problem of tuberculosis did not arise until after 1830. Culling their cows at the first signs of disease and selling them to the butcher became a common practice among the town dairy keepers. A major cause of losses in sheep, especially following wet summers, was sheep rot (known today as fascioliasis, liver fluke or liver rot). It was reported that in the years 1830/1831, over two million sheep died of sheep rot (Stratton & Brown, 1978).

To put Gamgee's estimate of 20% of animals slaughtered for meat being diseased in perspective, a large proportion would have been suffering with diseases that were not transmissible to humans, such as foot and mouth disease and contagious bovine pleural-pneumonia; therefore not posing a public health hazard. The reader must bear in mind that Gamgee and his supporters were reaching their conclusions during a period when the knowledge of animal diseases and human health was still lacking in many respects.

With regard to bovine tuberculosis, the main method of transmission to humans was through infected milk. When guidelines were established for inspectors in relation to tuberculosis in cattle, it was stated that unless the disease was generalised in the animal, only the affected parts should be rejected and the remainder permitted for sale. It was (and still is) common for a number of slaughtered animals to have livers affected with liver flukes or abscesses or lungs affected with pneumonia but providing there was nothing wrong with the carcase it was to be regarded as fit for food. A major reason for rejecting meat as unfit for food has been the aesthetic consideration. Flesh of animals that had died of natural causes would not be acceptable even if it did not present a health hazard. Likewise any part of an animal affected with a pathological condition that was not infectious would still be rejected. These aversions were not as strong in the past and the consumers of the early 19th century would not have found the idea of eating meat from an animal that had died or had been afflicted with disease as repulsive as today's consumers. It was not unusual on a farm for the workers to have the benefit of the meat of an animal that had died, providing the carcase was in a reasonable condition. In parts of Scotland the flesh of a sheep that had died of braxy was considered a delicacy. *'The Experienced Butcher'* (1816) quotes from Dr Buchan's *'Domestic Medicine'*:

> "Diseased animals, and such as die of themselves, ought never be eaten. It is a common practice, however, in some grazing countries, for servants and poor people that eat such animals as die of any disease, or are killed by accident. ... Animals never die themselves, without some previous disease; but how a diseased animal should be wholesome food, is inconceivable: even those which die by accident must be hurtful, as their blood is mixed with the flesh, and soon turns putrid."

The efforts of John Gamgee in exposing the corrupt activities of some sections of the meat trade prompted some attempts at getting legislation to curb these activities. In 1864 Sir George Grey and Mr George Bruce put forward the Cattle and Meat Importation Bill and the Diseased Cattle Bill, which should have had some effect but the combination of the vociferous opposition from the trade and the disinterest of the government of the day resulted in their failure. The Nuisances Removal Act 1855 enabled local authorities to engage persons in a meat inspection role but as this was a charge on the rates which restricted the level of remuneration for these posts, the individuals recruited were often lacking in any appropriate qualifications or experience. The standards for the control of unfit meat, as with the control of slaughterhouses and slaughtering under the Towns Improvement Clauses Act 1847, were entirely dependent on the local authorities. This ranged from some authorities carrying out their responsibilities as well as they could, to those that did nothing.

CONTROL OF ANIMAL DISEASES

There are records of outbreaks of epidemic disease affecting cattle which had a high mortality rate, going back to the early Greek and Roman civilisations. From the descriptions of the diseases it is concluded that in most cases they were epidemics of cattle plague (rinderpest). Cattle plague was referred to as murrain during the medieval period, although the term was used to cover other diseases. In the 18th and 19th centuries the term murrain was more specific to cattle plague.

A severe epidemic of murrain started in Padua, Italy in 1711 and was thought to have originated from cattle brought to Italy from Dalmatia. The epidemic spread throughout the Venetian states and by 1714 had reached Piedmont where it was estimated by a professor of medicine at Turin that more than 70,000 cattle had died. From Piedmont the disease spread to France affecting all the provinces of the south of France. By the end of the year the epidemic had reached Holland and from there it passed to England. The effect on the cattle populations of Britain and much of Europe was devastating, with the loss of hundreds of thousands of animals (Youatt, 1834).

In 1743 another outbreak of murrain occurred in the north of France and the greater part of Germany. In 1745 the epidemic spread throughout Holland causing the death of an estimated 200,000 cattle. From Holland the disease again spread to England, probably brought in by imported cattle, although an alternative suggestion was that hides imported from Zeeland, Holland, were the cause. The Privy Council decided to take action to control the disease, probably due to the memory of the devastation caused by the epidemic of 1714. By order of the council, boards of health were established to control the sale and movement of cattle and to ensure the isolation of those parts of the country where the disease had occurred. An order dated March 12th, 1745 began as follows:

> "His majesty being desirous of doing all in his power to put a stop to the spreading of this distemper, has thought it fit, by and with the advice of his privy council (whom have consulted physicians and surgeons thereupon, and they have given it as their opinion that all the methods of cure, which have been put into practice both at home and abroad, have proved so unsuccessful, that they have rather contributed to propagate than stop the infection; for while means have been using to save the sick, the disease

spread amongst the sound, and is increasing more and more, in proportion to the number seized with it), ..."

The order required all cowkeepers, farmers and owners of cattle who had an animal showing signs of the disease to:

"immediately remove such cattle to some place distant to the rest, and cause the same to be shot, or otherwise killed, with as little effusion of blood as may be, and the bodies to be immediately buried, with the skin and horns on, at least four feet in depth above the body of the beast so buried, having first cut and slashed the hides thereof from head to tail, and quite round the body, so as to render them of no use.[1] ... That they do cause all the hay, which such infected cattle have breathed upon and all the hay, straw, or litter they have touched or been near, to be forthwith removed and burned; and no person who shall attend any infected cattle, shall go near the sound ones in the same clothes. ...

They do cause the houses or buildings, where such infected cattle have stood, to be cleared from all dung and filth, and wet gunpowder, pitch, tar, or brimstone, be burnt or fired in several parts of such buildings, at the same time keeping in the smoke as much as possible; and that the same be afterwards frequently washed with vinegar and warm water; and no sound cattle be put therein for two months at least. ... That no person whatsoever do buy, sell, or expose for sale, the milk, or any part or the flesh or entrails of any such infected cattle; or feed, or cause to be fed, any hog, calf, lamb, or any other animal therewith; or drive, or cause to be drove, any such infected cattle to any fair or market, either in or out of the county where the said cattle now are, or to or from any place whatsoever, out of their own respective ground while they are so distempered. ... That no person do drive or remove any of the said sorts of cattle, whether infected or not infected, from any farm or ground, where such infected cattle are, or shall have been, within the space of one month before such removal. ... That as soon as the distemper shall appear in or amongst any of the said sorts of cattle of any cowkeepers, farmers, or other persons, they do immediately give notice to the constable of the town or parish, and also to the church wardens and overseers of the parish or place where such infected cattle shall be, of the appearance of such infection, or to the inspector to be appointed by the justice of the peace of the district where such parish or place shall be, ... That whosoever shall disobey these said rules, orders, or regulations shall be strictly prosecuted for the penalties inflicted by the said act. ... And for the encouragement of the owners of such infected cattle, his Majesty doth hereby promise, that they shall be paid by the commissioners of the treasury, for every such infected beast as shall be killed according to these rules, immediately after the affection shall appear upon them, one moiety, or half the value of his such

---

[1] Note: The requirement to slash the hides was based on the fact that unscrupulous persons were known to dig up the bodies of animals that had died of cattle plague and remove their hides to sell to the tanners.

cattle, not exceeding the sum of forty shillings for each of the said sorts, excepting calves, and not exceeding ten shillings for each calf, the numbers, and values, and conformities to the said rules to be ascertained by oaths of the owners, and two of the said constables, church wardens, overseers, or inspectors, to be taken before one or two of the said justices, who shall certify under their hands, or the hand of one of them, the sums of money which such owners shall appear to their or his satisfaction to be entitled to, by virtue of this order, for infected beasts shot or killed, slashed and buried, according to the above regulations." (Youatt, 1834)

Although the above regulations were sound and well constructed, showing a surprisingly advanced understanding of the nature and spread of the disease, they failed because of ineffective supervision in the country. The enforcement and administration of these regulations was by the justices of the peace, constables, church wardens, or overseers of the poor law, which were the only form of local government structure for most of the country. (In the majority of cases the responsibility for enforcement fell to the church wardens or the overseers of the poor law.) None of these persons could have had more than a layman's knowledge of animal diseases and any inspector appointed by the justice of the peace could, at best, have been a stockman with some empirical knowledge of the disease.[2] In view of the lack of competence of the persons responsible for judging the animals suspected of having the disease, farmers were presenting them with their old worn out beasts, or animals suffering diseases other than cattle plague, to obtain the compensation. By contrast, many animals infected by the disease were not reported by their owners. The restriction of movement of animals was constantly evaded. The general effect of the lack of local enforcement was the failure of the regulations to control the epidemic (Youatt, 1834).

It was more than a century later before another catastrophic epidemic of cattle plague (rinderpest) in 1865 resulted in the government of the day taking positive action in the control of animal diseases. The epidemic caused the death of 253,000 cattle. The Cattle Diseases Prevention Act was rushed through Parliament in just two weeks in February 1866.

The Cattle Diseases Prevention Act 1866 did not differ significantly in its provisions from the order of 1745. The 1866 Act required that animals affected with cattle plague be slaughtered and:

"Every Local Authority shall cause every Animal that has died of Cattle Plague, or has been slaughtered in consequence of being affected with Cattle Plague within its district, to be buried as soon as possible in its Skin in some proper Place, and be covered with a sufficient Quantity of Quicklime or other disinfectant, and with not less than Six Feet of Earth."

There was no reference in the 1866 Act to the effusion of blood. The 1866 Act required, in much the same way as the 1745 order, that:

"... the Yard, Shed, Stable, Field, or other Premises in which an Animal affected with Cattle Plague has been kept while affected with the Disease, or has died or been

---

[2] Note: This was before the existence of veterinarians. The first veterinary school in Europe began in France at Lyons in 1761. The London Veterinary College was established in 1791.

slaughtered, to be thoroughly cleansed and disinfected and all Hay, Straw, Litter, Dung, or other Articles that have been used in or about any such Animal to be burnt or otherwise destroyed; and no fresh Animal shall be admitted into any Yard, Shed Stable, Field, or other Premises in which any Animal affected with Cattle Plague has been kept while affected by the Disease or has died or been slaughtered, until the Expiration of thirty days after the cleansing and disinfecting of such premises in pursuance of this Act; and every Local Authority shall direct the disinfecting the clothes of , and the use of due precautions by inspectors, cattle overseers, and others in contact with animals affected by the cattle plague, with a view to prevent the spreading of the contagion."

The only restriction on movement in the 1866 Act was that any cattle brought by sea, either from outside the United Kingdom or other parts of Great Britain, were not to be moved alive from the port of entry and were to be marked by clipping the hair off the end of the tail. This resulted in all imported cattle having to be slaughtered at the port of entry. For the restriction on the internal movement of cattle the reliance was on the clause in the Act that no compensation would be paid in respect of animals found affected with cattle plague in a market or on a highway or in respect of any animal that had been moved or otherwise dealt with in contravention of the Act.

Compensation under the 1866 Act in respect of any animal slaughtered because it was suffering with cattle plague was not to exceed twenty pounds (two pounds under the 1745 order) or not more than half the value of the animal before it was affected with the disease. The compensation under the 1866 Act was to be paid by the Local Authority out of the rates and not from the Treasury.

The major difference in the 1866 Act was that it provided for the establishment of effective enforcement of the main provisions of the Act which was to result in the complete eradication of cattle plague by 1871. The responsibility for enforcing the Act was placed on the Local Authorities and each Authority was required with all convenient speed to appoint such number of inspectors and other officers necessary to carry out the provisions of the Act within their districts. The Authorities were authorised to pay such salaries and allowances as they thought expedient. The Act, by the inclusion of the following clause, left no room for dispute over the diagnosis of cattle plague in an animal:

> "The Certificate of an Inspector of the Local Authority that an Animal is affected by Cattle Plague shall for the Purposes of this Act be conclusive Evidence in all Courts of Justice and elsewhere of its having so been affected."

An element of the 1866 Act was a clause giving inspectors or officers authorised under the Act, the power of entry into premises within their district at all times. The Act included penalties for any person who obstructed inspectors or officers in the execution of their duties. This was an important enforcement feature of subsequent animal disease control legislation and public health legislation.

The Cattle Diseases Prevention Act 1866 was followed by the Contagious Diseases (Animals) Acts of 1869, 1878 and 1892, with progressively firmer control measures. The Acts required the slaughter of affected animals and, in some cases, the contact animals. There was also the restriction on the movement of livestock, especially the imported animals. As well as reducing the level of disease among livestock, it also reduced the freedom of the unscrupulous traders from moving diseased animals or dubious carcases. To supervise the requirements of the Acts, a team of veterinary officers were engaged who were directly responsible to the Privy Council. This team of veterinary officers became the Veterinary Department and later the Agricultural Department of the Privy Council, until 1889, when the Board of Agriculture was established. Local authorities supplied inspectors in their areas to carry out the requirements of the Acts. This arrangement proved inefficient in many respects and the local authorities had the responsibility to pay compensation to the animal owners out of the rates; a feature of the legislation not well liked locally. The term 'contagion' was important at this time because it defined those diseases that were freely transmitted from animal to animal by contact. The understanding of the nature and aetiology of disease was still lacking in the days before Pasture, Koch, etc. Clater's '*Every Man His Own Cattle Doctor*' in reference to murrain or the pestilential fever states:

"There is every reason to suppose, that this distemper is a contagious one, and is drawn in by the breath, at the nose and mouth of the animal, from others that are infected; and if the latter were timely separated, there is no doubt but that the further progress of the infection would be prevented. This disease is of the putrid kind, and is first observed by its effects in disordering the whole animal frame for several days before it makes its outward appearance."

During the closing decades of the 19th century there were very remarkable discoveries in the field of microbiology and disease processes which had a dramatic affect on veterinary and human medicine; also on meat inspection and meat hygiene. One of the misconceptions of the past was the belief in spontaneous generation; the belief that organisms developed spontaneously on rotting material. Experimental work by the French chemist Louis Pasteur in the mid 19th century proved the relationship between yeast and fermentation and the part played by bacteria in the decomposition and spoilage of food. These discoveries led to the realisation that putrefaction of meat was due to the presence and growth of bacteria on the surface of meat. In 1867, the British surgeon Joseph Lister used the knowledge gained from studying Pasteur's work on bacteria in putrefaction, to develop antiseptic surgery with the use of carbolic acid. The German Physician, Robert Koch, developed experimental methods that established the causal relationship between specific bacteria and diseases. Although the *Bacillus anthracis* had been observed in the blood of infected animals in 1849 by Pollender, it was Koch in 1877 who conclusively connected the organism with the disease. Koch isolated the tubercle bacillus in 1882, which was followed by the isolation of many other disease causing organisms. By the end of the century, the organisms causing most of the major diseases had been identified. In spite of this enlightenment, in 1889 the Medical Officer of Health for the Central Meat Markets, London, Dr Septimus Gibbon, stated his belief that tuberculosis was the result of environmental factors and he regarded the theory that it was caused by a bacillus as nonsense.

MEAT INSPECTION

Until the middle of the 19th century, meat inspection, where it did exist, was carried out either by the officers of the butchers' or fleshers' guilds or persons employed by the market authorities. In many cases the market authority was the local authority.

An ordinance of the Butchers' Company of Newcastle in 1755 states:

> "No brother shall sell any messed pork unless the same shall be sufficiently salted after they are discharged by the stewards or constable for the time being."

It is not clear what is meant by messed pork; it could refer to measled pork. In 1787 an ordinance states:

> "Forfeit meat to be viewed and destroyed by stewards without going before a magistrate." (Dodds, 1917)

This would seem to be a form of 'voluntary surrender' which was to become a key factor in meat inspection in the 20th century.

Fig 22.1 Inspection of the Intestines. A most inappropriate way for the inspector to work (Leighton & Douglas, 1910).

The Nuisances Removal Act 1855 and the Towns Improvement Clauses Act 1847 gave the local authorities scope to engage meat inspectors and become involved in meat inspection and meat hygiene generally and not be restricted to their markets. The local authority was the elected council (after the Municipal Reform Act 1835) in the towns and cities, whereas the authorities in the rural areas were the Justices of the Peace assembled at the Quarter Sessions, until the Local Government Act 1888. As already outlined, meat inspection throughout the United Kingdom was very patchy and largely non existent in rural areas. Where inspectors were employed, they usually had an impossible task due to the extent and dispersal of the slaughtering and trading in meat. By the end of the century the number of inspectors had increased, but without a unified national policy there was still a shortfall. Scotland was better organised for meat inspection at the end of 19th century than the rest of the country. The first authority to employ a veterinary surgeon for meat inspection was Edinburgh in 1889. A number of urban authorities in other parts of the country with large public slaughterhouses followed Edinburgh's example and engaged veterinary surgeons for meat inspection duties on a full-time basis. Some authorities, in accordance with the Public health Act, engaged local veterinary practitioners on a part-time/consultancy basis as a back-up to their meat inspector and M.O.H. In a number of places the duties of the superintendent of the public slaughterhouse included responsibility for meat inspection. There was a body of opinion in the country that considered the best type of person for the job of meat inspector was an experienced butcher because he would be able to judge good meat from bad. The counter argument was that without the appropriate scientific training, butchers would lack the necessary knowledge of diseases to be fully effective as meat inspectors.

The Royal Commission on Tuberculosis, 1895, recommended that no person should be allowed to act as a meat inspector unless he had passed an examination before some authority prescribed by the Local Government Board or the Board of Agriculture, such examination to comprise of the following subjects:

(a) The law of meat inspection and such by-laws, regulations etc., as may be in force at the time he presents himself for examination.
(b) The names and situations of the organs of the animal's body.
(c) Signs of health and disease in animals destined for food, both when alive and after slaughter.
(d) The appearance and character of fresh meat, organs, fat and blood and the conditions rendering them, or preparations made from them, fit or unfit for human food.

The Royal Sanitary Institute (later to become the Royal Society of Health) began training courses for meat inspection in 1899. The first examinations for meat inspectors were held in December 1899.

The Public Health Act 1875 and The Public Health (Scotland) Act 1897 laid down the fundamentals of meat inspection that were to carry through to the 20th century. Under the Acts, Medical Officers of Health were appointed with meat inspection as one of their responsibilities. This gave the M.O.H.s full control of meat inspection and from the beginning they had, more or less, 'carte blanche' for the running of meat inspection in their districts. This resulted in a considerable diversity of levels and standards of meat inspection throughout the United Kingdom, ranging from a virtually non-existent service to a fairly high level of meat hygiene involvement. The Public Health Act still put the onus on the meat trader in that it was an offence to sell, offer for sale or have in one's possession for sale, meat not fit for human consumption. The Act provided a safeguard for the trader from prosecution in that the trader could voluntarily surrender unfit meat to the authority for disposal. But the surrender had to be done genuinely and not as a means for the guilty trader escaping prosecution, having been caught with unfit meat.

There were complaints of disparity between authorities as to the standards applied for the rejection of meat and its condemnation as unfit for human consumption. One reason given for this was that many of the inspectors had no scientific training and were therefore unable to assess properly any abnormal condition of a carcase, to arrive at a correct judgement. In Glasgow from 1875 to 1899 the meat inspector was a police constable. To overcome complaints of unfair condemnation of meat, a system was set up in Glasgow whereby a butcher could appeal to a court consisting of two butchers and the police surgeon. Although this system worked satisfactorily on the whole, the court's decision was challenged in 1889 when it upheld the inspector in the total condemnation of two beef carcases affected with tuberculosis. The objection was that only part of the carcases should be condemned, allowing the rest to be sold. There was a hearing at the Glasgow Sheriff's Court and witnesses from different parts of the country giving evidence bore out the disparity that existed in judgement of fitness for food. The Scottish witnesses from Edinburgh, Greenock and Paisley supported the total condemnation of carcases affected with tuberculosis, while the English witnesses from Birmingham, Hull, Leeds, Liverpool and London were all of the opinion that only those parts of the carcase affected by the disease should be condemned. The decision on the extent of meat condemnation for all authorities rested with the M.O.H., and butchers in many parts of the country felt they were being unjustly treated, which prompted many to band together with their grievances and form associations (Perren, 1978).

BOVINE TUBERCULOSIS

Dealing with carcases of animals affected with tuberculosis was a major problem in the last decades of the 19th century. It was estimated that 20% to 30% of all cattle in Britain were affected with tuberculosis and up to 75% culled dairy cows going for slaughter showed signs of the disease (Fig 22.2).

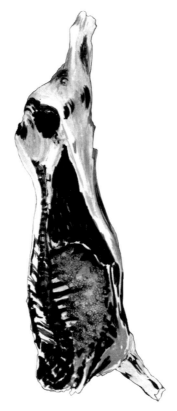

Fig 22.2 A Side of Beef badly affected with tubercular lesions covering the pleura. This is the condition known as "grapes" Leighton & Douglas, 1910).

There was a Royal Commission on Tuberculosis which reported in 1898 and gave the following recommendations for guidance of meat inspectors in respect of tuberculosis in cattle:

When there is milliary tuberculosis of both lungs. When tuberculous lesions are present on the pleura and peritoneum. When tuberculous lesions are present in the muscular system, or the lymphatic glands embedded between the muscles. When tuberculous lesions exist in any part of an emaciated carcase.	The entire carcase and all organs may be seized.
When the lesions are confined to the lungs and the thoracic lymphatic glands. When the lesions are confined to the liver. When the lesions are confined to the pharyngeal lymphatic glands. When the lesions are confined to any combination of the foregoing, but are collectively small in extent.	The carcase, if other wise healthy, shall not be condemned, but every part of it containing tuberculous lesions shall be seized.

(Leighton & Douglas, 1910)

In some European countries there was a system called 'Freibank', still operating at the beginning of the 20th century, which enabled the sale of meat that was rejected as unfit for human consumption after it had been appropriately treated. In some cases all such meat had to be cooked and therefore sterilised. There were some cases where part of the carcase was regarded as fit for human consumption uncooked. The benefit of this system was that it reduced the losses for the owners of the livestock found to be diseased and at the same time it provided the poorer people with cheaper nutritious food.

There were many problems relating to the control of the system. There were some cases where uncooked 'Freibank' meat was sold by butchers at full price. There were complaints by butchers that 'Freibank' meat affected the price they could get for their normal meat. There were 'Freibanks' in some German towns in the Middle Ages such as Hamburg and Danzig in 1375 and Lubeck, Stade and Zwickau in 1348 (Schwatz, 1901).

By the end of the 19th century, sheep pox, rinderpest (cattle plague) and contagious bovine pleural-pneumonia had been eradicated from the United Kingdom. There were still frequent outbreaks of swine fever and foot and mouth disease and a very large proportion of the cattle population was affected with bovine tuberculosis. Anthrax was still occurring from time to time, usually affecting single animals or small numbers of animals, the presence of the disease being a risk to humans.

IN CONCLUSION

An object of this book is to outline the interrelationship of the progress of society and technology with the development of meat trading and the meat industry. From the earliest period of human history consideration of the methods of butchering carcases and the use of stone tools has been a salient factor in Palaeolithic archaeology. This use of stone tools, along with the development of implements for hunting, relates to the importance of meat and animal products to the prehistoric communities.

The importance of animals for their meat and other products became essential for the emergence of the early civilisations. The value of domestic animals was borne out by their appearance in wall paintings, friezes and statuary. In some cases they were venerated, as in the statues of the Apis Bull in ancient Egypt.

The nature of meat trading during the period of the Roman Empire was very much like the meat trading of the Middle Ages, with the retail butcher of the town being involved in a major part of the trade.

The rate of the technological and commercial development of the meat trade followed a rising curve towards the beginning of the 20th century. Changes took thousands of years to begin with and had a gradual acceleration as time progressed. Some changes initiated further developments; an example being the domestication of animals and the beginning of Neolithic farming, which was a prelude to the first civilisations.

The massive changes that occurred in meat trading in the last decades of the 19th century continued unabated right through the 20th century.

Glossary

abattoir
In the 19th century the term 'abattoir' was coming into use in Britain in place of 'slaughterhouse'. Initially it was mostly applied to public slaughterhouses, as the term 'abattoir' was imported from France along with the concept of public slaughterhouses. Napoleon, by imperial decree in 1807, established five public abattoirs in Paris. He was so pleased with the first of these abattoirs that he ordained that public abattoirs be erected in every large and medium sized town in France. Public slaughterhouses established in the United Kingdom in the 19th century were modelled on the Paris abattoirs, hence the adoption of the French term. The term 'abattoir' simply means slaughterhouse in French and is derived from 'abattage' (to knock down). 'Abatteur' is French for slaughterer. The extension of the term abattoir to all slaughterhouses in the UK is more recent.

acater
Medieval for caterer. Person responsible for provisioning in the large houses. Later the term became caterer.

agora
Ancient Greek market place.

amber
Anglo-Saxon liquid measure (Whitelock 1979).

bailie
A Scottish magistrate.

barrow
Male pig castrated young. Also hog or shott.

bi-sulphite of lime
Used as a preservative in meat products, the active ingredient being sulphurous acid.

brawner
An old boar no longer used for breeding that was castrated to fatten for slaughter.

broach
Pierce or prick (Markham, 1615).

broiling
Grilling. Usually in the past grilling on a gridiron (Markham, 1615; Smith, 1758).

burh
Anglo-Saxon market town.

carker
A hawking butcher (Dodds, 1917).

cattle
In the past the term was used for all domestic livestock, i.e. cattle sheep, goats, pigs and horses. The word *cattle* comes from the Medieval *catel* which relates to the old French word *chatel* (likewise *chattel* – moveable possessions). Some old books and documents use the term neat cattle or neats to distinguish bovines.

cattle market	A market for all domestic livestock; cattle sheep, goats, pigs and horses.
ceap	Anglo-Saxon for market. Hrypera ceap – cattle market.
chine	Loin.
collegia	A Roman guild or fraternity for persons belonging to the same trade or craft.
collops	Slices of meat or rashers of bacon (Chaucer, 14th century; Markham, 1615; Smith, 1758).
cony or coney	Rabbit.
couper	Dealer (Scottish).
cur	Type of dog used for herding cattle.
demesne	Land kept in the lord's possession in the Middle Ages in Europe that was not leased out but maintained under the system of villeinage (i.e. worked by villeins to supply the lord's household).
dry antiseptic	Borax or boracic acid or a mixture of the two used as a preservative in meat products.
dug	Udder of a bovine or sheep before it is transformed into lactating tissue and consists mainly of smooth, creamy fat.
engrossing	Buying goods to hold them back for a rise in the market price; to corner the market.
escheit or escheat	Confiscate.
farmes	Scraped and cleaned intestines ready as casings or containers for sausages or puddings (Markham, 1615).
fell or woolfell	Skin of a sheep complete with fleece.
flair fat	Fat deposit inside the flanks of a pig.
flœsc-scamol	A meat-stall (Anglo-Saxon).
flesh meat	In the past the term meat was often used with reference to food in general and for reference to the meat of animals the term flesh meat was used.
forum boarium	Roman cattle market.
forestalling	Intercepting and buying goods before they reach the market with a view to making extra profit. Some butchers would have met farmers bringing their livestock to market. This would also have deprived the market authority of their tolls.
gob hook	A hook for suspending pigs during singeing. It is inserted under the pig's jaw in the angle of the mandible.
graped	Term used to describe a carcase affected with tuberculosis, having clumps of

tubercle lesions over the lining membrane (parietal pleura) of the thoracic cavity.

green sides; bacon — Unsmoked sides of bacon.

haruspex — A Roman inspector of animals slaughtered for and judged for their suitability for sacrifice.

haslet or harslet — Intestine or pig's pluck (Markham, 1615, The Experienced Butcher, 1816).

hern — Heron.

heronshaw — Young heron. Also heronshew, heronsewe and hernshaw.

hide — An area of land varying from 60 to 100 acres.

hogoo — Exudate that issues from meat that has undergone decomposition (Eliza Smith, 1758).

huckle bones — The hip bones. Tuber coxae.

huckster — Hawker.

hundred — An Anglo-Saxon division of an area said to contain a hundred households.

kernel — Lymph node.

ketmangergata — Anglo-Saxon for horsemeat butcher.

kine — Cow, usually dairy cow. Also kye (Scottish).

leaf fat — Fat lining the inside of the flanks (bellies) of pig carcases. (Smith, 1758) Also called flare fat.

lenten butchers — Butchers licensed to slaughter livestock and sell meat during lent.

lighter — Type of barge used for transferring cargo from ship to shore.

macellum — A Roman market for the sale of food.

mess — A serving of food usually for four people.

nach bone — Pin bones, part of the ischium that forms a prominence either side of the bovine's tail. Tuber ischii.

pannage — Pasturing of swine in woodlands to feed on acorns and beech masts.

petresalt — Unrefined saltpetre.

pluck — The liver, lites (lungs) and heart of an animal.

pottage — Boiled vegetables or soup which may contain oatmeal.

poulter — Medieval for poulterer.

purse — Scrotum of a bovine or sheep which becomes filled with lobulated fat in the well-fed castrated animal. Also known as the cod.

puddings	The entrails of a slaughtered animal, in particular the intestines which were scraped and cleaned and used as casings (skins) for sausages. This is why sausages were called puddings and for some types of sausages the name survives i.e. black puddings.
purtenance	The pluck; the liver, lites (lungs) and heart.
reeve	A bailiff, steward or manager of an estate or market. Port reeve – the lord's reeve of a town. Shire reeve – the King's reeve of a shire (sheriff).
regrating	Buying goods on the market to hold them back to sell later at a profit.
reiver	Scottish for robber, usually cattle stealer or rustler.
rot or liver rot	Fascioliasis or liver fluke infection. Sheep were most seriously affected, occasionally resulting in annual loss of a million sheep or more (Youatt, 1840).
runt	Modern definition a small animal, the smallest in a litter. Older definition during the droving era, small cattle, particularly the Welsh runts; also the Scottish runts.
rusty or reasty	Rancid.
sal prunella	Saltpetre is heated causing the crystals to fuse and much of the nitrates being reduced to nitrites (KNO_2 or $NaNO_2$) making it more immediately effective in the meat curing process.
saltpetre	Refined petresalt. Potassium nitrate (KNO_3) or Chile saltpetre, sodium nitrate ($NaNO_3$).
saster	Scottish farmhouse sausage.
scotch	Score, cut into a piece of meat without cutting through the meat (Markham, 1615).
seigniorage	The Lord's rights over his villeins.
sergeand	Supervisor and inspector of markets in Scotland.
shambles	A collection of butchers' stalls or shops. Because a shambles was often associated with a slaughterhouse the term became used for a slaughterhouse (archaic, from the Anglo-Saxon flaese-seamol).
sinking the offals	This term is used when the value of the offals is not taken into account in calculating the value of the carcase against the value of the live animal.
sirloin	From the French word *sur* (on or upon) plus loin, the meat on the loin.
slink veal	Term given to the flesh of a calf taken from a slaughtered cow or the flesh of a still-born or aborted calf, although in some of the earlier references slink meat is used to describe the flesh from livestock that had died on the farm or dead on arrival at the slaughterhouse. Clater's *Every Man His Cattle Doctor* (18th century publication) uses the term 'slinked' for the abortion of a calf.

stall	The primary meaning of the word stall is a board or stall-board which was set up in the marketplace or in the covered market and on the board was displayed the goods for sale. Boards set up in front of an open fronted shop were also called stalls.
stilliard	Steelyard, weighing machine. Roman scale (Named after the Hanseatic depot in London).
stoa	Ancient Greek covered colonnaded part of the market where traders set up their stalls.
sumptuary laws	Laws specifying the quality and amount of food a person should have according to their rank. Control or moderation of extravagance.
tron	Public weighing machine (Scottish).
umbles	The pluck; the liver, lites (lungs) and heart of deer.
vennel	Lane (Scottish).
villein	Originally a free villager but from the 13th century refers to a serf, one tied to his lord but free of all others. Villeins would be called upon to do labour service for their lord.
wether	Castrated male sheep.
wic	Anglo-Saxon for a trading centre i.e. Hamwic (Southampton), Lundenwic (London).
wiches	Areas where there are deposits of salt, giving rise to place names, eg. Droitwich, Nantwich and Northwich.
yoe	Ewe, adult female sheep.

Nomenclature of Livestock: G. Culley 1807

Domestic animals, at different ages, being called or known by different names, in different parts of the kingdom, it may not be amiss to note a few of the principal distinctions.

A stone-horse, or stallion, is the name by which the full-grown male of the horse kind is distinguished. Whilst sucking he is a colt foal ; then a yearling colt ; afterwards a two or three—years-old colt, until four, when they are most commonly called horses.

The female is called a mare; when sucking, a mare or filly-foal; then a year-ling filly; afterwards, a two or three-years-old filly; and at four, becomes a mare.

The general name of the male in neat-cattle is bull; during the time he sucks, he is called a bull-calf, until turned of a year old when he is called a stirk or Yearling-bull; then a two, three, or four-years-old bull, until six, when he is aged; but when castrated or gelt, he is called an ox, or stot-calf, until a year old, when he is called a stirk, stot, or yearling, then a two-years-old steer; and in some places, a twinter; at three, he is called a three-year-old steer; and at four, he first takes the name of ox or bullock:—though formerly, I believe, the castrated male was not called an ox or bullock until six years old, when he is looked upon to be at the best, though some people think an ox improves until seven, eight, or even nine years old. I apprehend the taking the name of ox or bullock at four instead of six years old, has taken place since the drawing or working of oxen has been so much disused.

The general name of the female of this kind is cow; when sucking the dam, she as called a cow-calf; then a yearling quey, or heifer, or twinter; the next year, a three-years-old quey, or heifer; and when four, she is first called a cow, which name is retained till the last. If castrated or spayed, she is called a spayed or cut heer, or spayed or cut quey, in the north parts of this island.

The general name by which the male sheep arc known, is ram or tup when lambs, they are called ram or tup-lambs, as long as they suck; from weaning, or taking from the ewes, to the shearing or clipping for the first time, they are called hogs, hoggerels, or lamb-hogs; then they take the name of shearing, shearling, shear-hog, or dinmond-tups, or rams; after that, according to the year they are clipped or shorn, they are called two-shear, three-shear, and so on, which always takes place from the time of shearing. But when gelt or castrated, they are called wether-lambs while sucking then wether-hogs, until shorn or clipped, when they take the name of shearlings, &c. until they are shorn a second time, when they are young wethers, or two-shear wethers; then three or four shear wethers, or more, according to the times they are clipped or shorn.

The general name by which the female sheep are known is ewe; while sucking, they are called ewe-lambs, or gimmer-lambs; but when weaned, or taken from the dams, they are called ewe-hogs, or gimmer-hogs, until clipped or shorn, for the first time, when they take the name of gimmer; which name continues only one year, until they loose their fleeces a second time, when they obtain the name of ewes, which they retain as long as they live ; only every time they are shorn, they add a year to their age, and are called two-shear, three-shear, or four-shear ewes, according to the times they have been clipped or shorn and this holds good of all other sheep for the age of sheep is not reckoned from the time they are lambed, but from the time of shearing; for although a sheep is generally 15 or 16 months old when first shorn, yet they are not called shearlings until once clipped, which is understood to be the same as one year old.

What we call gimmers in the North, in many of the midland parts of England are called theaves; and when twice shorn, double-theaves. There are other variations of names, in different parts, which I do not recollect.—In some places they call the male lambs heeders, and the females sheeders; and in others, hogs are called tegs, and two-years-old ewes, twinters, and three—years-old, thrunters.

Of the pig-tribe, the male is called a boar or brawn; the female, a sow; the cut or castrated female, a gilt or gaut.—In the southern parts, pigs are in general called hogs; and in the northern parts they are frequently called shots, after being weaned.

Pigs or swine are common names for the whole tribe.

Note: The modern definition of the term gilt is a female pig before her first farrowing.

Bibliography

Ainsworth-Davis, J. R., 1931, Cooking Through the Centuries. London: J. M. Dent & Sons Ltd.

Bahn, Paul & Vertut, Jean, 1997, Journey Through the Ice Age. London: Weindenfeld & Nicolson.

Bennett, H. S., 1990, The Pastons and Their England. Cambridge University Press.

Besant, Sir Walter, 1902, London in the Eighteenth Century. London, Adam & Charles Black.

Besant, Sir Walter, 1904, London in the Time of the Tudors. London, Adam & Charles Black.

Besant, Sir Walter, 1906, Mediaeval London Vols. 1 & 2. London, Adam & Charles Black.

Bicknell, Frank W., 1903, The Animal Industry of Argentina. Washington, USA.

Birley, Anthony, 1964, Life in Roman Britain. London, Book Club Associates.

Bloom, Roy, Bloom Ltd., English 18th Century Cookery.

Blumenschine, R. J. & Cavallo, J. A., 1992, Scientific American (October 1992).

Bonser, K. J., 1970, The Drovers. London, Macmillan & Co. Ltd.

Boorde, Andrew, 1542, Compendyous Regyment or Dyetary of Health. London.

Boswell, James, 1969, JS 100, The Story of Sainsburys. London.

Brears, Peter, 1985, Food & Cooking in 16th Century Britain. English Heritage.

Brion, Marcel, 1976, Pompeii & Herculaneum. London, Book Club Associates.

Burke, John, 1978, Life in the Villa in Roman Britain. London, B. T. Batsford Ltd.

Burrows, William, 1973, Textbook of Microbiology. USA, W. B. Saunders & Co.

Buxbaum, Tim, 1987, Scottish Doocots. UK, Shire Publications Ltd.

Buxbaum, Tim, 1992, Icehouses. Shire Publications Ltd.

Calger, J. E. L., 1966 & 1967, in Kent Archaeological Society Newsletter, 1994.

Canby, Courtlandt, 1980, The Past Displayed. London, Book Club Associates.

Carver, Martin O. H., 1994, Environment and Commodity in Anglo-Saxon England; in J. Rackman (Ed), Environment and Economy in Anglo-Saxon England. London, Council for British Archaeology.

Chartres, John, 1990, in Agricultural Markets and Trade 1500 – 1750. Cambridge: Cambridge University Press.

Chew, Helena M. & Kellaway, William, 1973, London Assize of Nuisance 1301 – 1431. London Record Society.

Chibnall, M., 1986, Anglo-Norman England, 1066-1166. Oxford

Clater, Francis, 18ᵗʰ Century, Every Man His Own Farrier & Cattle Doctor.

Cleland, Elizabeth, 1755, A New and Easy Method of Cookery. Ediburgh.

Close R., 1997, Planning and Building Records in Scottish Local History Journal, Ed. C. Simpson. Edinburgh.

Clutton-Brock, Juliet, 1981, Domesticated Animals From Early Times. London, British Museum (Natural History).

Clutton-Brock, Juliet, 1989, Five Thousand Years of Livestock in Britain. London, British Museum (Natural History).

Cobbett, William, 1822, Cottage Economy. London.

Coghill, N., 1949, The Vision of Piers Plowman. London.

Collinge, G. H., Young, T. D., & McDougall, A. P., 1929, The Retail Meat Trade.

Collins, Desmond, 1975, The Origins of Europe. London, George Allen & Unwin Ltd.

Collins, Desmond, 1976, The Human Revolution. London, Book Club Associates.

Collins, Marie, 1988, Caxton, The Description of Britain. New York, Weidenfeld & Nicolson.

Combes, Helen, 1997, Piety and Belief in 15ᵗʰ Century London: in LAMAS Transactions Vol. 48, 1997. London, Museum of London (144).

Context No. 12, City of London Archaeological Society.

Crabtree, Pam J., 1994, Animal Exploitation in East Anglian Villages; in Environment and Economy in Anglo-Saxon England; in J. Rackman (Ed), London, Council for British Archaeology.

Critchell, J. T. & Raymond, J., 1912, A History of the Frozen Meat Trade. London.

Culley, George, 1807, Observations on Livestock. London: Paternoster Row.

Cunliffe, Barry, 1974, Iron Age Communities in Britain. London, Book Club Associates.

Curtis-Bennett, Sir Noel, 1949, Food of the People. London, Faber and Faber Ltd.

Darby, H. C., 1976 a, Anglo-Scandinavian Foundations; in H. C. Darby (Ed), A new Historical Geography of England Before 1600. UK, Cambridge University Press.

Darby, H. C., 1976 b, Domesday England; in H. C. Darby (Ed), A new Historical Geography of England Before 1600. UK, Cambridge University Press.

Darby, H. C., 1976 c, The Age of the Improver; in H. C. Darby (Ed), A new Historical Geography of England After 1600. UK, Cambridge University Press.

Davis, Simon J. M., 1987, The Archaeology of Animals. London, B. T. Batsford Ltd.

Dodd, George, 1856, The Food of London. London.

Dodds, Madaleine Hope, 1917, The Butchers' Company of Newcastle-upon-Tyne. Newcastle-upon-Tyne.

Donkin, R. A., 1976, Changes in the Early Middle Ages, in H. C. Darby (Ed), A new Historical Geography of England Before 1600. UK, Cambridge University Press.

Douglas, W., 1905, Douglas's Encyclopaedia. London.

Drummond, Sir J.C. & Wilbrahan, Anne, 1939, The Englishman's Food.

Dunkin, 1844, The History & Antiquities of Dartford.

Dyce, K. M., Sack, W. O. & Wensing, C. J. 1987, Textbook of Veterinary Anatomy. Philadelphia, W. B. Saunders Co.

Emmison, F. G., 1964, Tudor Food and Pastimes. London: Ernest Benn Ltd.

Encyclopaedia Britannica CD 1999.

Evans, John G., 1975, The Environment of Early Man in the British Isles. London, Book Club Associates.

Evelyn, Hugh, 1972, Patriotism with Profit. London, Hugh Evelyn Ltd.

Everitt, Alan, 1990, in Agricultural Markets and Trade 1500 – 1750. Cambridge: Cambridge University Press.

Ewan, Elizabeth, 1990, Townlife in Fourteenth-Century Scotland. Edinburgh, Edinburgh University Press.

Experienced Butcher, The, 1816. London.

Fisher, D.J.V. 1973, The Anglo-Saxon Age. London, Longman Group Ltd.

Forman, Martin, 1992, Objects of Bone Antler and Shell; in Excavations at 33-35 Eastgate, Beverley, D. H. Evans & D. G. Tomlinson. UK, Sheffield Excavation Reports.

Frayn, Joan, 1995, The Roman Meat Trade: in J. Wilkins, D. Harvey & M. Dobson, 1995, Food in Antiquity. UK, University of Exeter Press.

Frere, Sheppard, 1972, Verulamium Excavations. London, The Society of Antiquaries.

Geddes, Olive M., 1994, The Laird's Kitchen. Edinburgh, HMSO.

Gerrard, Frank, 1956, Meat Technology. London: Leonard Hill.

Glasscock, R. E., 1976, England *c.* 1334, in H. C. Darby (Ed), A new Historical Geography of England Before 1600. UK, Cambridge University Press.

Glasse, Hannah, 1747, The Art of Cookery Made Plain and Easy (reprinted 1983).

Grant, Michael, 1978, History of Rome. London, Book Club Associates.

Grant, Michael, Ed., 1986, Greece and Rome. London, Thames & Hudson Ltd.

Grantley-Smith, Martin, 1998, Crisis in the Fifth Quarter, in The Worshipful Company of Butchers' Guild Bulletin Vol. 5 No. 1. London.

Greep, S. J., 1987, Use of Bone, Antler and Ivory in the Roman and Medieval Periods; in Archaeological Bone Antler and Ivory. The UK Institute for Conservation.

Gras, N.S.B., 1918, The Early English Customs System. USA, Harvard Economic Studies.

Hagan, Ann, 1992, Anglo-Saxon Food, Processing and Consumption. UK, Anglo-Saxon Books, Pinner, Middlesex.

Hagan, Ann, 1995, Anglo-Saxon Food & Drink. UK, Anglo-Saxon Books, Norfolk.

Haldane, A. R. B., 1968, The Drove Roads of Scotland. Edinbugh, Edinburgh University Press.

Hammett, R. C. & Nevell, W. H., 1929, Hand Book on Meat. London: Meat Trades' Journal.

Hammond, P. W., 1993, Food and Feast in Medieval England. UK, Alan Sutton Publishing Ltd.

Hansell, Peter and Jean, 1988, Dovecotes. UK, Shire Publications Ltd.

Hardyment, Christina, 1997, Behind the Scenes. UK, The National Trust.

Harrap, G. T. & Douglas, L. M., 1901, Public Abattoirs & Cattle Markets. London.

Harrison, Godfrey, 1963, Borthwicks - A Century in the Meat Trade, 1863 - 1963. London.

Henderson, Robert, 1814, A Treatise on the Breeding of Swine and Curing of Bacon. Edinburgh and London.

Hetherington, Jill, 1987, Dairy Farming in Islington in the early 19th Century, in London & Middlesex Archaeological Society, Vol. 38.

Hindley, Charles, 1885, History of the Cries of London. London.

Hinman, R. B. & Harris, R. B., 1939, The Story of Meat. Chicago.

Hodder, Ian, 1990, The Domestication of Europe. Oxford, UK, Blackwell Publishers.

Hodges, Henry, 1970, Technology in the Ancient World. London, Michael O'Mara Books Ltd.

Hogan, William, 1978, The Complete Book of Bacon. London.

Horne, Thomas, 1810, Treatise on Live Stock. Paternoster Row, London.

Hoskins, W. G., 1950, Essays in Leicestershire History. Liverpool at the University Press.

Houpt, T. Richard, 1970, In 'Duke's Physiology of Domestic Animals' Ed. Melvin Swenson. USA, Cornell University Press.

Ingram, M. & Simonsen, B., 1980, Meat and Meat Products; in Microbial Ecology of Foods Vol. 2. International Commission on Microbiological Specifications for Foods.

Isaac, Glynn, 1978, Scientific American (April 1978).

Isitt, Verity, 1987, Take a Buttock of Beef. Southampton, UK: Ashford Press Publishing.

James, T. G. H., 1985, Egyptian Paintings. London, British Museum Press.

James, T. G. H., 1988, Ancient Egypt and its Legacy. London, British Museum Publications Ltd.

Jensen, L. B., 1954, Microbiology of Meats. USA, The Garrard Press, Illinois.

Johnson, Paul, 1978, The Civilisation of Ancient Egypt. London, Book Club Associates.

Jones, P. E., 1976, The Butchers of London. London: Martin Secker & Waburg Ltd.

King, Anthony, Villas and Animal Bones: in The Economies of Romano-British Villas. UK, University of Sheffield.

Langland, William, 1332-1400, The World of Piers Plowman. Edited and translated by J. Krochalis & E. Peters, 1975, University of Pennsylvania Press, USA.

Larousse Encyclopaedia of Animal Life, 1974. London, Hamlyn.

Lawrie, R. A., 1998, Lawrie's Meat Science, 6th Ed. Cambridge, Woodhead Publishing Ltd.

Leakey, Meave & Walker, Alan, June 1997, Scientific American.

Leakey, Richard, 1981, The Making of Mankind. London, Book Club Associates.

Leakey, Richard & Lewin, Roger, 1992, Origins Reconsidered. Little Brown & Co.

Leeson, T. S. & Leeson, C. R., 1970, Histology. London, W. B. Saunders Co.

Leighton G. & Douglas, L. M., 1910, The Meat Industry & Meat Inspection Vols. 1 – 5. London.

Lipson, E., 1959, Economic History of England Vol. 1. London: A. & C. Black Ltd.

Lipson, E., 1956, Economic History of England Vols. 2 & 3. London: A. & C. Black Ltd.

Lister, D., Gregory, N. G. & Warris, P. D., 1981, Stress in Meat Animals, Developments in Meat Science – 2. UK, Applied Science Publishers Ltd.

Liversidge, Joan, 1976, Everyday Life in the Roman Empire. London, B. T. Batsford Ltd.

Maisels, Charles K. 1993, The Near East: Archaeology in the Cradle of Civilisation. London, Routledge.

Markham, Gervase, 1615, The English Huswife, in Michael R. Best (Ed), 1986. Canada, McGill University Press.

Marsden, Peter, 1987, The Roman Forum Site in London. London, Museum of London.

Mayer, Edward, 1968, History of the Worshipful Company of Curriers. London.

McDougall, A. P., 1929, in The Retail Meat Trade. London, The Gresham Publishing Co. Ltd.

Merriman, Nick, 1990, Prehistoric London, HMSO.

Microsoft Encarta 1998 Encyclopedia.

Miller, Edward & Hatcher, John, 1995, Medieval England: Towns Commerce and Crafts, 1086 – 1348. London, Longman Group Ltd.

Miller, Harry, 1985, Halls of Dartford. London.

Murphy, Peter, 1994, Anglo-Saxon Landscape and Rural Economy; in J. Rackman (Ed), Environment and Economy in Anglo-Saxon England. London, Council for British Archaeology.

Noddle, Barbara, 1989, Flesh on the Bones, Circaea Vol. 7-1, UK, Association of Environmental Archaeology.

Noddle, Barbara, 1997, 'Animal Bone' in Simon Buteux 'Settlements at Skaill, Deerness, Orkney'. University of Birmingham.

O'Connor, T. P., 1983, Feeding Lincoln in the 11th Century; in M.K. Jones (Ed), Integrating the Subsistence Economy. UK, British Archaeological Report, Oxford.

O'Connor, Sonia, 1987, The Identification of Osseous and Keratinaceous Materials at York; in Archaeological Bone Antler and Ivory. The UK Institute for Conservation.

O'Donovan. J., 1940, The Economic History of Livestock in Ireland.

Owen, R., 1846, A History of British Fossil Mammals and Birds. London, John Van Voorst.

Pearce, A., 1929, The History of the Butchers' Company. London: Meat Trades' Journal.

Percival, John, 1986, The Villa Economy: Problems and Perspectives: in The Economies of Romano-British Villas. UK, University of Sheffield.

Perren, Richard, 1978, The Meat Trade in Britain 1840 - 1914. London: Routledge & Kegan Paul Ltd.

Plimsoll, Samuel, 1890, Cattle Ships. London.

Power, Eileen, 1941, Mediaeval English Wool Trade. London.

Pullar, Phillippa, 1970, Consuming Passions. London: Hamish Hamilton.

Quennell, M & C. H. B., 1959, Every Day Life in Roman and Anglo-Saxon Times. London, B. T. Batsford Ltd.

Rankin, Capt. Sir Hugh Rhys, Bart., FSA.(Scot.). Cattle Droving from Wales to England. London, In Agriculture, Vol LXII – No. 5, August 1955. Published by MAFF.

Reynolds, Peter J., 1979, Iron Age Farm – The Butser Experiment. London, British Museum Publications Ltd.

Riddler, Ian, 1990, Saxon Handled Combs from London; LAMAS Transactions Vol. 41. Museum of London.

Riley, H. T., 1861, *Liber Albus*. The White Book of the City of London. Originally compiled by John Carpenter, Common Clerk and Richard Whitington, Mayor, 1419. London, Richard Griffin & Co. Stationers Hall Court.

Robertson, A. J., 1956, Anglo-Saxon Charters. Cambridge University Press.

Rogers, Thorold, 1866 – 1902, A History of Agriculture and Prices in England from 1259 to 1793. Oxford, Clarendon Press.

Rose, Giles, 1682, A Perfect School of Instructions for Officers of the Mouth.

Rouse, W. H. D., Translation of Homer's Iliad. London, Thomas Nelson & Sons, Ltd.

Rye, W. B., 1965, England As Seen by Foreigners in the Days of Elizabeth and James I; Reprint of 1865 Edition. New York.

Sabine, Ernest L., 1933, Butchering in Mediaeval London in Speculum – Journal of Mediaeval Studies. USA, Cambridge, Massachusetts.

Saggs, H. W. F., 1989 Civilisation before Greece and Rome. London, B. T. Batsford Ltd.

Saltzman, L. F., 1926, English Life in the Middle Ages. London, Oxford University Press.

Schwatz, Oscar, 1901, Public Abattoirs and Cattle Markets, Eds. G. T. Harrap & L. M. Douglas. London.

Scola, Roger, 1992, Feeding the Victorian City. Manchester University Press.

Scotsman, The, 1902, Edinburgh.

Sim, Alison, 1997, Food and Feast in Tudor England. Gloucestershire, UK: Sutton Publishing Ltd.

Sisson, S., & Grossman, J. D., 1953, The Anatomy of the Domestic Animals. USA, W. B. Saunders Co.

Skaggs, Jimmy M, 1986, Prime Cut, Livestock Raising and Meatpacking in the USA, 1607-1983. Texas, USA.

Smith, Adam, 1776, An Inquiry into the Nature and Causes of the Wealth of Nations.

Smith, Bruce D., 1994, The Emergence Of Agriculture. New York, USA, W. H. Freeman & Co.

Smith, Eliza, 1758, The Compleat Housewife, (Studio Editions Ltd. 1994). London.

Smith, H. A., Jones, T. C. & Hunt, R. T., 1972, Philadelphia, Veterinary Pathology, Lea & Febiger.

Stead, Jennifer, 1991, Necessities and Luxuries, in Ed. Wilson Anne, Waste not Want Not. Edinburgh University Press.

Steele, Jess, 1993, Turning the Tide, History of Everyday Deptford. London.

Stenton, Doris Mary, 1951, English Society in the Early Middle Ages. UK, Penguin Books Ltd.

Stobart, J. C., 1964, The Glory that was Greece, Revised R.J. Hopper, London, Sedgwick & Jackson.

Stow, John, 1598, A Survey of London, Edited by Henry Morley 1994. UK, Alan Sutton Publishing Ltd. Gloucestershire.

Stratton J. M. & Brown J. H., 1978, Agricultural Records A. D. 220 – 1977. Ed. Ralph Whitlock. London.

Strouhal, Eugen, 1992, Life in Ancient Egypt. London, Opus Publishing Ltd.

Strype, John, 1720, Strype's Edition of Stow.

Swanton, M. J., 1996, The Anglo-Saxon Chronicle. London, J. M. Dent.

Swatland, H. J., 1994, Structure and Development of Meat Animals and Poultry. USA Technomic Publishing Co. Inc.

Swatland, H. J., 1998, Beef and Liberty, Worshipful Company of Butchers' Guild Bulletin. London.

Taplin, William, 1796, Modern System of Farriery. London.

Tattersall, Ian, 1997, Scientific American (April 1997).

Thornbury, Walter, 1987, Old London – Shorditch and Smithfield. London, The Alderman Press.

Trevelyan, G. M., 1949, Vol. 1, Illustrated English Social History. London, Longmans, Green & Co.

Trevelyan, G. M., 1960, Vol. 2, Illustrated English Social History. London, Longmans, Green & Co.

Trow-Smith, Robert, 1957, A History of Livestock Husbandry to 1700. London, Routledge & Kegan Paul Ltd.

Trow-Smith, Robert, 1959, A History of Livestock Husbandry 1700 – 1900. London, Routledge & Kegan Paul Ltd.

Trow-Smith, Robert, 1980, History of the Royal Smithfield Club. Bath, UK.

Vehling, J. D., 1977, Apicius - Cookery and Dining in Imperial Rome.

Vince, Alan, 1990, Saxon London: an Archaeological Investigation. London, B. A. Seaby Ltd.

Vince, Alan, 1994, Saxon Urban Economies, in J. Rackman (Ed), Environment and Economy in Anglo-Saxon England. London, Council for British Archaeology.

Wacher, John, 1974, Towns of Roman Britain, London, Book Club Associates.

Wallace-Hadrill, Andrew, 1994, Houses and Society in Pompeii and Herculaneum. USA, Princeton University Press, New Jersey.

Watson, J.S., 1963, History of the Salters Company. London.

Webster, T.B.L., 1969, Life in Classical Athens. London, B. T. Batsford Ltd.

Wedgwood, C. V., 1984, Spoils of Time. London, Guild Publishing.

Weinreb, B. & Hibbert, C., (Editors) 1983, The London Encyclopaedia. London, Book Club Associates.

Weinstein, R., 1994, Tudor London. London, HMSO.

West, Barbara, 1988, Birds and Mammals in Excavations at Jubilee Hall and 21 – 22 Maiden Lane, Ed. Robert Cowie. Transactions of London & Middlesex Archaeological Society, Volume 39. London.

Whitehouse, Ruth, 1977, The First Cities. Oxford, UK, Phaidon Press Ltd.

Whitelock, Dorothy, 1979, English Historical Documents, Vol. 1, 500 – 1042. London, Eyre Methren.

Whyte, I. D., 1995, Scotland Before the Industrial Revolution. London: Longman.

Wilkins, J., Harvey, D. & Dobson, M., 1995, Food in Antiquity. UK, University of Exeter Press.

Wilkins, John & Hill, Shaun, 1994, Life of Luxury: Translation of Archestratus, *c.* 330 BC. Totnes, Devon, UK, Prospect Books.

Wilson, C. Anne, 1973, Food and Drink in Britain. London, Constable & Co. Ltd.

Wilson, C. Anne, 1991, Waste Not Want Not. Edinburgh, Edinburgh University Press.

Winlock, H. E., 1955, Models of Daily Life in Ancient Egypt. Cambridge, Massachusetts, Harvard University Press.

Wright, Lawrence, 1964, Home Fires Burning. London, Routledge & Kegan Paul.

Wrightson, John, 1905, Sheep, Breeds and Management. London.

Wymer, J. J., 1991, LAMAS Vol. 42.

Youatt, William, 1834, Cattle; Their Breeds, Management, and Diseases. London.

Youatt, William, 1840, Sheep; Their Breeds, Management, and Diseases. London.

Youatt, William, 1847, The Pig; A Treatise on the Breeds, Management, and Medical Treatment, of Swine. London.

Young, T. Dunlop, 1929, In - The Retail Meat Trade. London, The Gresham Publishing Co. Ltd.

Index